Library of Congress Control Number: 2011904553
ISBN: 978-0-9835820-9-0

Copyright 2011 Hadeland Lag of America, Inc.
www.hadelandlag.org
All Rights Reserved

Copies of this book are available on Amazon.com

THEY CAME FROM HADELAND

A Centennial History of the
Hadeland Lag of America
1910 - 2010

Editors
Anne Sladky
John Oien
Verlyn D. Anderson

Dedicated to

"Our Founding Fathers"
Thomas Walby, B.L. Elken, Mikal H. Froslee, John Ballangrud Holm, H. H. Rasaasen, E. S. Gunderson, H. P. Rekstad, H. H. Heen, Hans Larson Hole, Erling Jacobson, and John Lee

"Architect of the Hadeland Lag's Renewal" for his vision and determination
Morgan Olson

"All Members, Past and Present, of the Hadeland Lag of America"
for their commitment to preserving our shared Hadeland heritage

Table of Contents

Dedication i
Table of Contents ii
Acknowledgements v
Introduction vii

About the Lag 1
    The Guiding Lights of the Hadeland Lag 1
        Thomas Walby
        Morgan Olson
    Historical Overview of the Hadeland Lag 9
        The 'Rebirth' of the Hadeland Lag in 1976
    Historical Highlights 1990-2010 22
        Tom Skattum wins the "Hadeland Prize"
        The *Mindegaven* Fund is Dissolved
        Peder H. Nelson Collection
        Dr. Verlyn Anderson awarded the St. Olav Medal
        Norwegian Statehood Pioneer Project – MN Sesquicentennial
    "Home to Hadeland" Tours 31
        1921 Tour
        1978 Tour
            Archie Gubbrud's Trip to His Roots
        1990 Tour
        2000 Tour
        2005 Tour
        2010 Centennial Tour
    Hadeland Lag Stevner and Member Meetings 1989-2010 52
        The Hadeland Lag Centennial Year
    Hadeland Lag Heritage Collection 85
        The Lag Banner
    Kontaktforum Hadeland-Amerika 97
        Historical Societies of Hadeland
    Officers of the Hadeland Lag 1990-2010 103
        Biographies
    Emeritus Advisory Council 126

Membership List 1990-2010 134

About the Immigrants **146**
    Hadeland Immigrants in North America 146
    Recollections of Pioneer Times 153
        Traveling by Covered Wagon
        The Drama at St. Helen
        Hadeland Settlement at Northwood, North Dakota
        Early Settlers on the Goose River (Mayville, Dakota Territory)
        The Rekstad Family
        Emigration, Women's Rights and the Writing of History
        Pioneer Life

About Hadeland **168**
    History 169
        The Norwegian Judicial System of the 1700s in Action
        The Call of the Lur
        The Dvergsten Farm: Legend and Lore
        Poet Aamund Olavsson Vinje and Gran
        Farm Names in the 1801 Census
    Churches of Hadeland 183
        The Sister Churches
        Lunner Church
        Grinaker Stave Church
        Tingelstad Old Church (St. Petri)
        Tingelstad New Church
        Sørum Church
        Jevnaker Church
        Grymyr Church
        Nes Church
        Moen Church
        Ål Church
        Recent Reforms in Church and State Relations in Norway
        The Norwegian Church and the process towards
        loosening the ties with the Norwegian State, 2003-2006
    Hadeland *Folkemuseum* 201
        Hadeland *Glassverk*, 1891

  Vann i Arbied (Water in Work) Exhibition
  Log Driving in Bjoneelva
  Hadeland *Bergverksmuseum* is now part of *Randsfjordmuseene*
Folkdress in Hadeland 212
  Vestoppland Bunad
  Excerpt from *"*Hadeland *Folkemuseum*: A beautiful woman's gown
    from Hadeland"
  Hadeland *Folkemuseum*: The *Busserull* of Hadeland
Hadelanders Visit America 218
  1977
  1980
  1986
  2001
Hadeland Today 230
  February 2002
  May 2005
  August 2003
  November 2004

Appendix **239**
  1910 Constitution 240
  1984 Constitution 242
  2004 Corporate By-Laws 244
  2007 Articles of Incorporation 254
  2010 Terms of Use (Internet Policy) 257
  Cooperative Agreement between *Kontaktforum Hadeland-Amerika* and the
    Hadeland Lag of America 261

Index 263

Acknowledgements

Contributors

Content was written, edited, translated, and/or provided by Paul Anderson, Kari Mette Avtjern, Sturla Bandlie, Rune Alexander Fredriksen, Ole P. Gamme, Mary Margaret Rekstad Gibson, David Gunderson, Adolph Hansen, Harald Hvattum, Grethe Johnsrud, George Krenos, Kjell H. Myhre, Gunhild, Kåre and Geir Arne Myrstuen, Peder H. Nelson, Dr. Larry Opsahl, Betty Rockswold, E. Palmer Rockswold, Florence Dvergsten Rognlie, Barb Schmitt, Kari-Mette Stavhaug, Torun Sørli, Dean and Carol Sorum, Marit Tingelstad, Mari Wøien, and editors John Oien, Dr. Verlyn Anderson, and Anne Sladky.

Special Thanks

The editors wish to express their gratitude to

- Marit Tingelstad for writing and Mari Wøien for translating the article on the changes in the relationship between church and state in Norway;

- Kjell Henrik Myhre for researching and revising the list of "Farm Names in the 1801 Census;"

- Torun Sørli and Kari Mette Avtjern of the *Hadeland Folkemuseum* for the time and effort each of them contributed to providing text and finding or taking specific pictures to help illustrate this book;

- Harald Hvattum of *Kontaktforum Hadeland-Amerika* for providing authoritative information on any subject we asked; and

- Ole P. Gamme, not only for the articles he authored, but also for the hours he spent tracking down pictures and information, answering questions, making suggestions, and providing enthusiastic support.

Their willingness to help make this history the best that it could be is testament to the valuable relationship the lag has with its partners in Hadeland.

Thanks to the following Hadeland Lag members for their contributions:

- Dean and Carol Sorum, for their collection of lag event photos dating back to the 1970s;

- Dave Gunderson, for tracking down biographical information and the ancestry of many of our retired and deceased lag officers;

- Barb Schmitt, for photos from the 2010 Centennial Year;

- Paul Anderson, for news articles and information about the 1976 stevne;

- The Board of Directors who proofed the book, offered suggestions, and made the final product that much better by their efforts; and

- All of the members who have over the years contributed photos and stories about their Hadeland ancestors and their own experiences in Hadeland. When choosing content for this book, we were impressed by the rich history documented by our members. It would make our ancestors proud!

About the Cover

A literal translation of Hadeland is "Land of the Warriors." "Hade" – the outline of a warrior in his battle helmet - is a logo used by many organizations in Hadeland.

Information about the coats-of-arms for (left to right) Gran, Jevnaker, and Lunner can be found on pages 172-173.

The ***History of the Hadeland Lag 1910-1990*** covered the lag's first eighty years in detail. Copies are still available on CD on the lag's website.

Introduction

As much as they were proud to be Americans or Canadians, our immigrant ancestors' identities were closely tied to the place they left behind in Norway. The Hadeland Lag was founded to help members remember and celebrate the unique Norwegian community where they were born. The organization preserved a dialect, traditions, friendships and a sense of extended family that the original immigrants cherished. For those who held their heritage so close to their hearts, it would have been a foregone conclusion that the Hadeland Lag would celebrate its centennial.

Those who lived to see the lag fade in the years after World War II might find our centennial celebration a more unlikely occurrence. The end of World War II had given birth to the Modern Age. All eyes were now on the future, not the past. The immigrant experience was a dusty piece of history. The Hadeland Lag seemed a relic of immigrant days, quaint but largely irrelevant.

By the 1970s, membership in the old social society had dwindled to less than twenty, and the newsletter and yearly gatherings had been abandoned. A new generation of Hadeland descendants was developing an interest in their family history, and a growing number seemed enthusiastic about tracing their roots and learning more about Hadeland. In 1975, Morgan Olson gathered like-minded descendants of Hadeland immigrants to reconstitute the organization. He led efforts to retool the lag's message and purpose.

Building on Morgan Olson's vision, the Hadeland Lag has evolved from its beginnings as an immigrant social society to become a non-profit corporation with over 500 member families in 45 states, Canada, and Norway. Its modern mission is to "promote education in the cultural heritage and history of the descendants of immigrants in North America from the districts (*kommuner*) of Gran, Jevnaker and Lunner in Norway; to provide assistance in support of genealogical research by descendants of emigrants from that area; to collect and preserve historical and genealogical information about this area; and to promote contact and communication among those who share these interests."

Our Hadeland ancestors had a deep and abiding love for their homeland. As the generations pass, that love is rekindled in the hearts of descendants who, with the help of the Hadeland Lag, uncover their family stories and rediscover that special part of Norway called Hadeland.

Anne Sladky, Editor

Chapter One
The Guiding Lights of the Hadeland Lag

Thomas Walby was the driving force behind the creation of the Hadeland Lag in 1910, and Morgan Olson was the architect of its rebirth in 1975. It is fitting that we begin by acknowledging these pathfinders, whose leadership and vision have allowed the Lag to move forward into its second century.

Thomas Walby

Thomas Walby's name in Norway was Torger Andersen. His father was a cotter named Anders Larson Skapalen and his mother was Sesselina Pedersdatter Framstadgjerdingen. Thomas had three sisters and two brothers. His older brother, Christ Andersen Walby immigrated to America in 1877 and sent Thomas a ship ticket to follow. Thomas used this ticket and immigrated to America aboard the ship *Angelo*. He joined his brother in Deer Park, Wisconsin, arriving on June 2, 1880.

While in Deer Park he learned the trade of blacksmithing. He used this skill during two winters in the lumber camps of Northern Wisconsin, receiving a wage of $40 a month. In 1885 he was employed as a blacksmith by Williams Wagon shop in Hudson, Wisconsin. He continued to blacksmith in the 1880s in Pleasant Valley, Cylon Township and then set up his own business in Deer Park.

On January 24, 1885 he married Olive Arnesdatter Kongsvinger who was born about 1861 on Aabogen, Kongsvinger, Norway. She had immigrated in 1880.

Thomas had an interest in politics and it was for that reason that at the age of 30 he was elected to his first political position as a township supervisor in 1891. He later became Cylon Township chairman and was elected an administrator of the public poor farm from 1894 to 1898.

At the close of the 1890s the family moved to Hudson, Wisconsin. Here Walby took a sales position with Champion Harvest Company of Albert Lea, Minnesota, and continued in that position after the company merged with McCormick Harvester. As reported in the *Hudson Star-Observer* in its sesquicentennial edition "He must have been a good salesman for he accomplished a record for the company when he sold 98 binders and mowers in the little community of Cokato, Minnesota." In 1904 he started a furniture business in Hudson with Anton Arnson under the name of Walby and Arnson. The move to Hudson had given Thomas many business and political opportunities. It also gave his children an opportunity to attend high school.

In 1905 Thomas was appointed sheriff of St. Croix County by Governor Robert M. LaFollette to fill out the term of murdered Sheriff Harold O. Harris. After finishing this term as sheriff, Governor LaFollette appointed him a Wisconsin state factory inspector responsible for food processing facilities. He worked in this job for about 6 years before resigning and taking an offer from International Harvester Company to become the company's head agent for the state of Wisconsin.

It was while he was an agent of International Harvester Company that he organized the Hadeland Lag with 12 members in 1910. He was elected as the lag's first president, a position he held for 31 years. He continued to work for International Harvester Company until 1923 when he again was named to a political position as postmaster in Hudson. He held this position until 1934. He served one year as president of the Postmaster's Organization.

Walby was a lifelong member of the Republican Party. He was a friend of Wisconsin Governor and Senator Robert LaFollette, who was well known among Norwegian-Americans. In 1924 Robert LaFollette broke from the Republican Party and formed the more liberal Progressive Party. As the leader of this party he became a presidential candidate. As his friend, Thomas took an eager part in his election campaign, although he returned to the Republican Party after the election.

Thomas was an organization man and loyal to his ethnicity. He was active in the Hadeland Lag serving as President for 31 years, the *Bygdelagenes Fellesraad* serving as president for a couple of years, and the Norwegian Peace Committee serving as president in 1921. He served as treasurer of the Committee for the Norwegian Centennial in Minneapolis in 1914. Walby was the first treasurer of the Valkyrien Sons of Norway Lodge No. 53, founded on August 23, 1905, in Hudson.

When 300 Norwegian-Americans returned to Norway in 1921, he was appointed as the group's leader. He represented the Hadeland Lag at the Norsk Festival in Winnipeg, Canada in 1928, and in 1930 was elected by the National Council of Bygdelags as alternate representative to the celebration of the completion of the restoration of Nidaros Cathedral in Trondheim. At the festival, he and five other delegates presented a large silver crucifix to the cathedral as a gift from Norwegian-Americans.

Thomas Walby died at the age of 81 on Friday June 12, 1942 at his home in Hudson, Wisconsin after an illness of several months. He was laid to rest in Hudson Cemetery.

Thomas and Olive Walby had six children, four of whom survived to adulthood. Pearl died at birth and Arthur Sigvald was born in 1889 and died at the age of fifteen; Elmer Kenneth was born October 5, 1891; Ella Mathilde was born on Christmas Day, 1893 and died on July 6, 1992; and Herbert Merian who was born in 1900 and died in 1979. Their son

Orville Perry was born in 1895 and served in WWI. He was killed by a bandit in his grocery store in 1923.

The Obituary of Thomas A. Walby
Published in the June 18, 1942 Hudson Star Observer, Hudson, Wisconsin

T. A. Walby Dies Friday; Former Postmaster Here – Funeral Held Monday; Active in Politics and Fraternal Societies for years

Thomas A. Walby, former postmaster and former sheriff of St. Croix County, died at 11:00 A.M. last Friday morning, June 12, at his home, 820 Fifth Street, after an illness of several months. He was 81 years old. In addition to being active in state and county politics for many years at and after the turn of the century, Mr. Walby was a prominent leader in Scandinavian fraternal organizations and at the time of his death he was president of the Hadelands Laget, having been re-elected to this office for the thirtieth year at Hadelands Laget's annual convention at Fertile, Minnesota last summer.

Mr. Walby was born at Hadeland, Norway, on October 18, 1861. He immigrated to America in 1880, coming direct to Hudson and then to Deer Park where he learned the trade of blacksmith, living there for about five years.

He was married to Olive Arneson at Hudson on January 24, 1885, and after a short residence here, Mr. and Mrs. Walby moved to Cylon where he operated a blacksmith shop for about two and a half years. After he sold his shop at Cylon, he moved to Deer Park where he purchased another blacksmith shop which he operated for seven years.

Mr Walby was then appointed overseer of the county poor farm which was located in the Town of Pleasant Valley. After having charge of the poor farm for four years, Mr. and Mrs. Walby returned to Hudson and in 1899 he took a position as field representative for the old Champion Harvester Company, which was later consolidated with the International Harvester Company. His first contact with the harvester company was made with J. B. Jones, who was then manager of the Eau Claire sales district.

It was during these years that Mr. Walby launched his active interest in political affairs. With his work he found frequent opportunity to participate in various political campaigns. Always identified with the Republican Party, Mr. Walby was a close friend of many of the prominent political figures of the earlier days including Senator LaFollette and Congressman James A. Frear.

As the result of his political activity, Mr. Walby was appointed sheriff of St. Croix County in 1905 to fill the unexpired term of Sheriff Harris, who was killed in the line of duty.

After serving as sheriff, he was appointed a factory inspector for the state of Wisconsin, leaving this position to again become associated with the International Harvester Company as a sales representative in this area.

His strong political affiliation with the Republican Party resulted in his appointment by President Harding to the position of Postmaster for the city of Hudson, assuming this office on May 1, 1923. He was twice reappointed, serving more than eleven years as postmaster and retiring on June 1, 1934, when President Roosevelt appointed the late Ernest Ross to the position.

After retiring from his long period of service in the postal department Mr. Walby entered the insurance business here and also served as city relief director for a time.

In addition to his personal and political interest, Mr. Walby, during his long residence in St. Croix County, devoted much time to organization work among the Scandinavian Fraternal organizations. He was one of a group of former residents of the Hadeland section of Norway to form the Hadeland Lag in the Northwest states so thickly populated by those of Norwegian birth. He was elected president of the Hadeland Lag thirty years ago and was re-elected to this office at every annual convention, including the most recent convention held at Fertile, Minnesota last summer. For many years the annual convention of the Hadeland Lag had been the vacation time for Mr. Walby and his close friend, Louis Blegan, who has served as secretary of the organization for more than 15 years.

Mr. Walby's wide acquaintance among those of Norwegian descent in this country resulted in his appointment as secretary-treasurer of the Norwegian Centennial celebration held in this country in 1925. For many years he was the local representative of the Cunard Steamship Company and in 1921 he was in charge of a large group of former Norwegian residents who returned to their homeland for a visit.

Mr. Walby also took an active roll in the promotion of local Scandinavian fraternal organizations. He was a charter member of the Sons of Norway and for some years was also prominent in the affairs of Vinji Lodge of the Scandinavian fraternity and the Aid Society Norden. At various times he served as president of these various organizations. So devoted was he to his fraternal organizations that he frequently made numerous personal sacrifices of time and money toward their welfare. This was also true of his political interests, and he seldom missed an opportunity to do some personal campaigning for the friend or neighbor who solicited his support.

Mr. Walby was a faithful member of the Ebenezer Lutheran Church, from the time it was founded some forty years ago until it was disbanded a few years ago.

Six children were born to Mr. and Mrs. Walby, three of whom preceded him in death. A son, Arthur, died at the age of fifteen; another son, Orville, died in Minneapolis at the age of 28, and a daughter, Pearl, died in infancy.

Besides his widow, he is survived by two sons, Elmer of Chicago and Herbert of Hudson; one daughter Mrs. James Carroll of Minneapolis; one brother, Chris, 86 years old, of Black Brook, Polk County; three sisters and one brother in Norway; five grandchildren and one great grandchild.

Funeral services were held at the Bethel Lutheran Church at 2:30 o'clock Monday afternoon, Rev. Oscar Thomuson, pastor of the church officiating. Rev. Coughlin of Black Brook assisted. Interment was made in Willow River cemetery. Pall bearers were Frank Calvin, Melvin Swanson, Nels Jensen, Ole Anderson, Andrew Sangslund and Louis Blegan.

In tribute to Mr. Walby's long years of service as Hudson postmaster, the local post office was closed Monday afternoon during the hours of the funeral service.

Walby Tombstone in Willow River Cemetery, Hudson WI

Morgan Olson

Morgan Olson was born February 11, 1910 in Glen Ullin, North Dakota to Obed Henry Olson and Martha Amalia Johnson.

Obed was born in 1882 in Green County, Wisconsin. His father Morgan Peter Olson was born on June 17, 1859 in Iowa County, Wisconsin. Morgan Peter's father was Rollin Olson (Ole Olesen) who was born in 1831 and emigrated in 1849 from the Gunstad farm in Jevnaker. Obed's mother Pernille Hansdatter Haug was born in 1850 at the west Hole farm in Tingelstad and came to America in 1870.

Morgan's mother Martha was born in Green County, Wisconsin. Her parents were Andrew Johnson who was born at Raaseiet in Brandbu and Petrine Mathea Pettersdatter, who was born at Smerud on the west side of the Randsfjorden.

Morgan graduated from Concordia College in 1931. After spending 5 years as a teacher, he began a career with Midland Cooperative in 1936. After serving in WWII, Morgan resumed his career with Midland and retired as vice president of advertising in 1975.

Morgan married Grace Livdahl in 1933. They had two children.

After his retirement Morgan focused his attention on revitalizing the Hadeland Lag. He served as president from 1976 until shortly before his death. During that tenure, membership grew from seventeen to more than 200. As president of the National Council of Norwegian-American Bygdelag, Olson helped seven other dormant lags reactivate.

In his book *"Civil War Letters,"* Morgan translated and published more than 100 letters written by his great-grandfather to his wife while serving in the Civil War.

The members of the Hadeland Lag owe Morgan Olson an enormous debt of gratitude for his leadership in revitalizing the organization and nurturing its growth for the next eleven years. The Hadeland Lag and the Norwegian-American community at large suffered a great loss at his passing on December 3, 1986 in Robbinsdale, Minnesota.

Grace Livdahl Olson

Grace Livdahl Olson actively supported her husband Morgan's activities in the Hadeland Lag and made valuable contributions in her own right. Not least of these was her dedicated and positive presence at the *stevne* registration desk each year.

Grace Livdahl was born on September 6, 1911 at Velva, North Dakota. Her parents were Norwegian-Americans, although not Hadelanders. Her father was born at Spring Grove, Minnesota but in 1879, when he was 2 years old, his parents moved by covered wagon to the Red River Valley. There they lived in the wagon until their house was built on land near Hickson, North Dakota.

The family moved to Bismarck when Grace was three. There she would attend school and was crowned the first "Miss Bismarck." She met Morgan while attending Concordia College in Moorhead. When they married on December 28, 1933, Morgan was already teaching in the high school at Bagley, Minnesota. In 1936 they moved to Minneapolis. After Morgan's death in 1986, Grace moved to a retirement cooperative in Golden Valley.

Morgan and Grace had a daughter, Martha Wold (Olson) Ward, and a son, James Olson, of Morris, Minnesota. Martha was born November 11, 1934, in Bagley, Minnesota and died on November 17, 1992 in Minneapolis, Minnesota. Grace outlived her husband by seventeen years. She died on April 2, 2003, in New Hope.

The Obituary of Morgan A. Olson
Published December 6th 1986 in the Minneapolis (MN) Star & Tribune

M.A. Olson dies; led Norwegian heritage groups

Morgan A. Olson, 76, a leader of Norwegian heritage groups in the Twin Cities, died of cancer Wednesday at his Robbinsdale home.

Olson was president of the National Council of Norwegian-American *Bygdelags*. The organization flourished in the early 1900s, but become dormant during World War II. Olson helped revitalize eight of the current 24 Lags – organizations of people from the same areas of Norway and who have traveled extensively in Scandinavia. He was past president of the Hadeland Lag, which he activated about 12 years ago.

Olson helped organize the Scandinavian Center in Minneapolis and was on the Board of Directors of Vesterheim, a Norwegian museum in Decorah, Iowa. He was a member of Nordkapp Men's Chorus and the National Association of Norwegian-American Singers and was elected executive vice president of the association in July.

"He's been a tremendous leader," said Orville Prestholdt, vice president of the *Bygdelags* Council. "He was very devoted to the cause of Norwegian heritage and was a terrific leader in that respect. The *Bydgelags* were falling apart and he was the one that built them up again."

Olson was born February 11, 1910 in Glen Ullen, North Dakota; the grandson of Norwegian immigrants. He graduated from Concordia College in Moorhead, Minnesota in 1931 and taught history at Bagley (Minnesota) High School for five years.

In 1936 he became a field representative for Midland Cooperatives and retired from that Minneapolis company in 1975 as vice president of advertising.

After his retirement, Olson collected more than 100 letters his great-grandfather had written to his wife while he served with a Wisconsin regiment during the Civil War. He translated the letters from Norwegian and published them in a book that is now in the Minnesota Historical Society archives.

Olson was a former trustee of Concordia College, an Army Signal Corps veteran of World War II and was active in the Boy Scouts of America. He was a member of Central Lutheran Church and twice was chairman of the stewardship drive.

He is survived by his wife, Grace Livdahl Olson; a daughter, Martha Ward of Pine City, Minnesota; a son, James of Morris, Minnesota; a sister, Lenore Sollom of Gualala, California and three grandchildren.

Services will be held at 1:30 p.m. today at Central Lutheran Church, 333 E. Grant Street. Memorials to the Church, Concordia College or Vesterheim in Decorah, Iowa, are suggested. Arrangements are being handled by the Washburn McReavy-Welander Quist DuSchane Chapel in Robbinsdale.

Chapter Two
Historical Overview of the Hadeland Lag

Hadeland Lag picnic held August 31, 1913 at Huntington, Wisconsin

    The 1910 Minnesota State Fair was held at the same location on Snelling Avenue in St. Paul, Minnesota as it is today. That year both former president Teddy Roosevelt and current president William H. Taft visited the fair – it was an election year, and they were "on the stump." Farmers gravitated toward Machinery Hill where International Harvester had its display of farm machinery. There they found its congenial salesman, Thomas Walby, who lived across the Mississippi River east of St. Paul in Hudson, Wisconsin. Thomas Walby urged American *Hadelendinger* to return on Sunday to discuss the possibility of organizing a *bygdelag* for Hadeland. The men who joined Mr. Walby at the International Harvester display the last Sunday afternoon of the fair recorded in the minutes of their meeting that here *"blev afhold et mode den 7 de Sept 1910 i International Harvester Company locale ved Minnesota udstilling"*... the meeting that gave birth to the Hadeland Lag.
    Immigrants and descendants from several Norway districts (*bygder*) had already set in motion the *bygdelag* movement. These groups, organized around specific Norwegian communities, are unique among ethnic societies in North America. Immigrants from the

Valdres district were the first to organize, founding the Valdres Samband in 1899. In 1907 the Telemark and Hallingdal *bygdelag* were organized, followed in 1908 by Numedal, Trondheim, and Sogn. Five more lags were organized in 1909: Nordland, Voss, Setesdal, Nordfjord and Gudbrandsdal. In 1910 immigrants from the Land district of Norway organized in June; Toten Lag organized in July; and the Solør Lag was organized on the same day as Hadeland: Sunday, September 7.

Thomas Walby was elected as the first president of the Hadeland Lag and a fellow townsman, Per Jacobson, secretary-treasurer. Other men present who paid dues were: B.L. Elken, Mayville, North Dakota; Mikal H. Froslee, Vining, Minnesota; John Ballangrud Holm, Hudson, Wisconsin; H. H. Rasaasen and E. S. Gunderson, Sacred Heart, Minnesota; H. P. Rekstad and H. H. Heen, Adams, North Dakota; Hans Larson Hole, Lakeville, Minnesota; and Erling Jacobson and John Lee, Hudson, Wisconsin. These 12 men constituted the Hadeland Lag pioneer organization and were our founding fathers.

After its establishment at the 1910 Minnesota State Fair the Hadeland Lag grew in its first year to include 105 members: 92 men and 13 women. Dues were $1.00 for men and $.50 for women. In June of 1911, 161 Hadelendings registered and additional visitors attended the second *stevne* in Como Park, St. Paul, Minnesota. The fourth *stevne*, held in Blanchardville, Wisconsin, saw attendance soar to 1,500, with 352 members registered. During these early years the Hadeland Lag *stevne* served not only as a time to catch up on news about friends and family still in Hadeland; it was an opportunity for extended families to come together in reunion. The American-born generations were introduced to the unique culture and traditions of Hadeland and could listen to and speak its distinctive dialect.

The 1914 *stevne* was scheduled to coincide with *Sytennde Mai* and the 100th anniversary of Norway's separation from Denmark. A cablegram was sent to the *sogneprest* in Gran, Hadeland: "Hearty greetings to all *Hadelendinger* from the Hadeland Lag meeting at the 100 years anniversary festival in Minneapolis." It was also at this *stevne* that the *Mindegaven* Memorial Fund was established with pledges totaling over 10,000 Norwegian *kroner*. The interest from the fund, deposited at the Gran Sparebank in Norway, was to be distributed to the needy in Gran, Brandbu, Tingelstad, Jevnaker, and Lunner annually on December 15th. A five person committee was established to manage the fund.

The 1918 *stevne* was held at the Court House in Minneapolis, Minnesota and recognized 147 American *Hadelendinger* who served in World War I. A U.S. service flag was purchased in honor of those who served.

The 1920s

The tenth anniversary, "*10th Jubileum Stevne,*" of the Hadeland Lag was celebrated in June of 1920 at the fairgrounds auditorium in Fergus Falls, Minnesota. The Lag asked for and received pledges equal to one thousand Norwegian *kroner* to be donated to the Nikolai Church in Gran for the purpose of installing electricity in the church. A yearbook committee was established and 140 pre-publication copies sold. There was great interest in arranging a lag trip to Hadeland. Thomas Walby and two others were assigned the task of making the arrangements.

The *Yearbook* was completed by Secretary Louis Blegan and Historian O. M. Steen and published in 1921. It included biographies and photos of many lag members.

The Hadeland Lag sponsored its first tour of Hadeland in the summer of 1921.

At the *stevne* held in September of 1921, the Hadeland tour hosts were made honorary members of the lag. It was decided that the *Brua* should be published quarterly.

In 1924 attendance reached 2,000 American *Hadelendinger* at the fairgrounds in Northwood, North Dakota. The 1925 *stevne* was held in conjunction with the Norse Centennial Celebration in Minneapolis/St. Paul, Minnesota. It marked the 100th anniversary of the sailing of the first Norwegian immigrant ship, the *Restauration*, from Stavanger, Norway to New York. Two commemorative postage stamps were issued acknowledging this landmark event. President Calvin Coolidge gave the keynote address to the impressive group of Norwegian and American dignitaries and thousands of average Norwegian-Americans who attended the festivities held at the Minnesota State Fairgrounds.

Arrival of President Cleveland and other dignitaries at the 1925 Centennial

Thomas Walby continued as president of the Hadeland Lag through the 1920s and *stevner* were well attended. At the twentieth *stevne* in June 1929, held at Luther College in Decorah, Iowa, the Vesterheim Norwegian-American Museum thanked members of the Hadeland Lag for the many antiques they had donated. It was noted that Hadeland was the first district to send objects directly from Norway to the museum.

The 1930s

The 1930 *stevne* was held in Minneapolis, Minnesota to coincide with the June 10-12 Norwegian festival commemorating the 900th anniversary of the Battle of Stiklestad and the death of Norway's Christianizing king, St. Olaf. It was noted that if it hadn't been for *bygdelag* members attending, the festival would have been a failure. It was also reported that the *Mindegaven* Memorial Fund, now 15 years old, had distributed a total of 9,500 Norwegian *kroner* (approximately $21,000 in today's currency) to the needy in Hadeland.

The early years of the Depression were difficult ones for the Hadeland Lag. The *Brua* had financial difficulties and contributions to the Memorial Fund diminished. Attendance at the annual *stevner* also showed a marked decline. In 1934 the Lag unanimously passed a resolution in protest of the possibility of removing the word "Norwegian" from the name of the Norwegian Lutheran Church in America. The protest was registered in a telegram sent to the annual church convention being held in Minneapolis, Minnesota.

During the summer of 1939, Norway's Crown Prince Olav and Crown Princess Martha were touring the United States. The attendance at the annual *stevne* which was scheduled to be held at Pelican Rapids, Minnesota was very low. The Crown Prince and Princess were at that time visiting Fargo, North Dakota, and President Walby suggested that the whole group forego the lag meeting and instead travel to Fargo to see them.

The 1940s

On June 20-22, 1940 the Hadeland Lag met at the Knights of Columbus Hall in Minot, North Dakota. Only 86 people were registered for the *stevne*. The Lag members were deeply concerned about their families, other relatives and friends in Norway after the April 9th invasion of Norway by Nazi Germany. Norway's King Haakon VII and his son Crown Prince Olav had led the fight against the German invaders, but just two weeks before the *stevne*, on June 7, 1940, the king and the prince had made a harrowing escape from Norway and were now living in exile in England.

In those very early days of the occupation, there was a virtual black-out of communication to and from Norway, so very little was known of the plight of the Norwegians. People at the *stevne* were encouraged to support Norway during the coming days of occupation.

No *stevne* was held in 1942. It would have been the last for Thomas Walby as president of the Hadeland Lag. When the Hadeland Lag met in Rothsay, Minnesota in 1943, Joseph Melaas took charge as presiding officer. In 1947, C. M. Sorum took the reins as president of the lag. *Stevne* attendance dropped to less than 100.

The 1950s

Olaf Drovdahl was elected president in 1950. In 1951 the last of the *Brua* yearbooks was published. Not surprisingly, the Lag had suffered declining participation during WW II, but membership did not rebound thereafter. The members of the Hadeland Lag were beginning to move to other parts of the country, especially the West Coast. In 1952, when

STATEMENT

Detroit Lakes, Minn. 6-20 195 3

M Hadelands Lage
June 18, 19, 20.

Room No. ....

— In Account With —

GRAYSTONE HOTEL

All bills rendered the 1st of the month, due and payable before the 10th.

	To Balance		
	To Room		
	To Laundry		
	To Dry Cleaning		
	To Telephone		
	To Dining Room		
80 adults Banquet @ 2.00		162	00
3 Childs Portion @ 1.00		3	00
		165	00

Paid June 20, 1953
John A. Krier

John Braaten presided at the forty-third *stevne* held in Minot, North Dakota, members from California, Idaho, Canada, Chicago, and one from Norway joined those from Wisconsin, Minnesota, North and South Dakota and Iowa in the assembly. John Braaten was succeeded by John Eastvold who presided over the *stevner* from 1954-1964.

The 1960s

John Eastvold declined to stand for re-election in 1965 and Chris Sherva was elected to replace him.

During the 1950s there was some talk of bringing the *Mindegaven* Memorial Fund back to America and discontinuing the Christmas distribution to Hadeland's poor, but it did not go beyond discussion until 1966. At that time it was publicly announced that no more money would be placed in the fund. Further, the money in the Gran Sparebank was to be divided equally between the Hadeland Folk Museum and Per Hvamstad for the cost of publishing his book *Gamalt fra Hadeland*. The distribution did not occur, and the fund was not mentioned in the minutes of the Hadeland Lag meetings for another decade.

In 1968, only 13 members attended the fifty-ninth *stevne*, although total attendance was between 35 and 40. President Ellef C. Erlien presided over a serious discussion about the continuation of the Lag. The old pioneer members were either too old to attend or had passed away. It was decided that the secretary would contact Landingslag about meeting jointly. Mr. Erlien declined to seek a second term, and Karl B. Stensrud was elected to replace him.

In 1969 thirty-three members registered from five states. It was decided that contact would be made with the Toten Lag about joint *stevner*, because that group had not met since World War II. It is not known if those discussions occurred or if the outreach was unsuccessful, but the Hadeland Lag continued to meet on its own.

The 1970s

Mrs. Lars Hammer, a devoted Lag member who served as secretary from 1947-1965, sent this message in 1970:

> It sounds like they had a good meeting. <u>And the Lag will carry on.</u> Lars, my husband, was quite ill for a while, and I am in very poor health. Someone reads the newspaper clippings to me because I am almost blind. So now we have to stay home, but we are along in our thoughts for every convention. So this is probably the last report from me. I can't keep up like I used to. So greetings to all I have met in the Hadeland Lag.
>
> Mrs. Lars (Marie) Hammer, Scobey, MT

By 1971 lag membership had dwindled to just 17 members. Annual *stevner* were discontinued. The Hadeland Lag was not alone. A number of *bygdelag* became dormant or disbanded in the early 1970's. There was talk about combining the lags and holding one large *stevne*, but there was a strong feeling among the dwindling membership of the individual lags that maintaining their identity was important, and in the end no record of formal talks can be found and no action was taken.

1975: The Rebirth of the Hadeland Lag

In 1974 Morgan Olson began an effort to revive the dormant Hadeland Lag. Morgan was not a member of the Hadeland Lag but he had heard about the organization from an elderly couple. On October 30, 1974 he wrote a letter to the former editor of the *Brua* Peder H. Nelson, asking for information about the organization. In a letter dated the next day, October 31, 1974, Peder replied:

> Yes, I was the editor of the Hadelandslag publication *Brua* that was published twice a year, containing news about the old pioneers from Hadeland, but I resigned from same in the late 1940s and the magazine was soon discontinued…Hadelandslaget has not had any convention for the last three years and is dissolved….I would be very glad if you could come to Northwood to see me on November 15th and probably we could do some reorganizing of the lag. There used to be a large Hadelands settlement here around Northwood-Hatton and Mayville in pioneer times. The old ones are of course gone but there are lots of American born *Hadelendings* here that will be interested in organizing over again.

Morgan then began collecting the old records from Peder, Mrs. Lars Hammer and her son Magne Hammer. Morgan wrote to Peder and Magne on January 6th, 1975:

> Main purpose of this brief note is to tell you fellows that I have all the Hadeland records and related materials in safe keeping. After Magne sent me the records which his mother had kept I had very little time to study them. My first reaction is to your suggestion, Peder, that they be given to the Norwegian American Historical Assn. at Northfield. Magne mentioned in his letter that his mother thought they could be sent to Norway – but who would it be sent to, or who would want the old Hadeland records…The possibility of having a meeting next summer would be difficult. In the short time I spent studying the old membership lists, it would be almost impossible to come up with a very good mailing list. The few long distance phone calls I made to old members indicated that they were unable to participate because of age and infirmities. I hope to see you Peder, in the spring. Perhaps we can come up with something – as the saying goes.

After several more letters a meeting was organized and held in Northwood, North Dakota on September 19, 1975. Morgan Olson presided over this meeting and Harriet Foss of Northwood served as recording secretary. Those attending decided to reorganize with Morgan as president, Peder as vice president, Harris Bakken as treasurer and Harriet as secretary. One significant concern was the status of the *Mindegaven* Memorial Fund.

Finally, after five years when there were no *stevner*, Hadeland Lag and Landingslag met at Mayville College, Mayville, North Dakota on July 9-10, 1976. 43 American *Hadelendinger* and 28 *Landinger* attended. Everyone was enthusiastically in favor of reviving both the Hadeland Lag and Landingslag, and it was agreed that a joint *stevne* should be held again the following year at Concordia College, Moorhead, Minnesota.

Officers were elected: Morgan A. Olson, president; Verlyn D. Anderson, vice president; Thomas Skattum, treasurer; Harriet Foss, Secretary; and Olaf Nelson, director. Morgan appointed Harris Bakken as caretaker of the flag and the Hadeland Lag banner. Morgan announced that the Hadeland newspaper and the *Mannskor K.K.* were coordinating plans for a possible visit in 1977. It was decided to send them a formal invitation to attend the next *stevne*.

> **From the Mayville Tribune**
>
> **Hadelands Lag-Landings Lag plan combined convention**
>
> At a meeting in Finley earlier this month plans were made to hold a combined convention of the Hadelands Lag and the Landings Lag on the Mayville State College Campus in June of 1976.
>
> Following a Concordia College Board of Regents meeting recently Mr. and Mrs. Morgan Olson of Minneapolis, Minn., visited Peder Nelson of Northwood to discuss the Hadelands Lag.
>
> The Olsons, Peder Nelson and Harris Bakken, also of Northwood, went to Finley to meet with officers of the Landings Lag in the home of Mrs. Helen Vinje.
>
> They made plans to hold their conventions jointly next June at MSC.
>
> The Hadelands Lag has been dormant for several years and the current officers are attempting to revive it.
>
> Officers for the Hadelands Lag, whm will serve until the convention are: Morgan Olson, president; Peder Nelson, vice president; Harris Bakken, treasurer; and Mrs. Percy Foss of Northwood, secretary.
>
> Officers of the Landings Lag are: Mrs. Helen Vinje, Finley, president; Oliver Stadsvold, Starbuck, Minn., 2nd vice president; Sylvia Elton, Hillsboro, secretary-treasurer; and Mrs. Agnes Larson, Fisher, Minn., and Olga Haug, Shevlin, Minn., directors.
>
> The purpose of the various "lags," which are composed of descendants from a particular area of Norway, is to preserve, and promote the best in Norwegian culture and heritage.

Gudbrandsdal Lag joined the "Three Lag *Stevne*" that met at Concordia College, Moorhead, Minnesota on June 10-12, 1977. A month later, on July 17th, the *Mannskor K.K.* arrived in Fargo, North Dakota by charter flight. Other Hadelanders made the trip with the choir, for a total of 254 visitors. After five days in the Fargo-Moorhead area, the men's choir embarked on a 10-day concert tour of the Upper Midwest.

In 1978, Hadeland Lag crossed the ocean and held its *stevne* in Hadeland, with 84 members attending. This was followed by a tour of western Norway, led by Morgan Olson.

The 1980s

The 70th anniversary of the Hadeland Lag was celebrated at its annual *stevne* on July 11-12, 1980 in Marshall, Minnesota. Hadeland's *Mannskor K.K.* performed in concert. The

Gudbrandsdal Lag had decided to withdraw from the "Three Lag *Stevne*," but the newly reorganized Toten Lag joined the "Three Lag *Stevne*" at that time.

In 1981 the *stevne* grew to include four Lags: the three Oppland *fylke* (county) lags of Hadeland, Landing, and Toten plus Telelaget (Telemark *fylke*). Again in 1982 and 1983 these four lags held a combined *stevne*. In 1984, the *stevne* grew to include five lags with the addition of Sigdalslag, representing a large portion of Buskerud *fylke*. The Hadeland Lag adopted a new constitution at the 1984 annual meeting.

In 1985, Morgan Olson contacted the Gran Sparebank and learned that the *Mindegaven* Memorial Fund had a balance of 39,995.45 Norwegian *kroner* (about $4,500) and that the bank had faithfully administered the distribution of approximately $300 in interest to the welfare committees of Gran, Lunner and Jevnaker each year as specified in their decades-old instructions. It was decided that the annual income would continue to be used to assist the handicapped in Hadeland.

The 75th anniversary of the Hadeland Lag was celebrated in June 1985 during the "Six Lag *Stevne*" at Concordia College in Moorhead, Minnesota. Lags representing Hadeland, Land, Toten, Telemark, Sigdal and Numedal participated. Morgan Olson, who had led the Hadeland Lag back from near extinction in the mid-1970s, chose to end his 10 years of service as president. Olaf Nelson was elected to succeed him.

In 1986 the *stevne* reached its current form. The 7-Lag *Stevne* included Hadeland, Land, Toten, Telelaget, Sigdal, Numedal and Ringerike-Drammen. E. Palmer Rockswold took over the helm as president of the Hadeland Lag.

On September 29, 1986 Peder Nelson, the *Brua* editor from 1931 to 1941 and a well-known Norwegian-American writer died. Morgan Olson, who had been the key to the lag's revitalization, passed away on December 3, 1986.

It was decided that, along with the joint summer *stevne*, a fall meeting of the Hadeland Lag should also be held. The first of these fall meetings was held in October 1987 at the Hjemkomst Center in Moorhead, Minnesota. It was described by President Rockswold as "A Real Winner!"

In 1988 Leslie Rogne accepted the role of genealogist. Over the next decade, the lag purchased a substantial collection of microfilmed Hadeland church and census records and other resources so that he could do more detailed research for Hadeland Lag members.

The 1990s

During the 1990s membership in the Hadeland Lag stabilized at about 300 members. Lag visits to Hadeland were sponsored in the summers of 1990 and 2000. The fall meeting continued to provide an additional opportunity for discussion, planning, and fellowship.

Ellef Erlien was editor in chief of *The History of the Hadeland Lag 1910-1990*.

In 1993 the seven lags involved created a non-profit entity, Norwegian *Stevne*r, Inc. (NSI) for the purpose of planning and managing each year's 7-Lag *Stevne*.

Margaret Wilson was elected president of the Lag in 1993 but declined to serve. In 1995, Robert Rosendahl took over as president of the Hadeland Lag.

At the fall meeting in 1998 a resolution was unanimously passed to send a request to the Gran Sparebank directing that the balance in the *Mindegaven* Memorial Fund be transferred to the Hadeland *Folkemuseum*. This was a most welcome gift for the museum which was at the time in a difficult financial situation.

13 years after his death, the *Peder H. Nelson Book Collection* was formally opened to the public at the Gran Public Library in 1999. The collection included more than 3,400 books and periodicals documenting the Norwegian-American experience that had been published during the previous century.

An all-*bygdelag stevne* was held in 1999 to celebrate the Norwegian-American *Bygdelag* Centennial. More than 1,020 Norwegian-Americans gathered at Luther College in Decorah, Iowa, for the celebration.

The 2000s

Sixty-seven members participated in the fourth Hadeland Lag trip to Hadeland in the summer of 2000. This sparked a tour of the American Midwest by 50 Hadelanders in 2001.

The Hadeland Lag created a website in 2002. It now receives more than 3,000 visitors each month, and has played an important role in recruiting new members.

Delores Cleveland was elected president of the lag in 2002.

Also in 2002 *Kontaktforum Hadeland-Amerika*, a cooperative effort among the historical societies in Hadeland and the Hadeland *Folkemuseum* was organized. One of its primary missions was the Emigrant Identification Project. This research project has led to the identification of over 11,000 Hadeland immigrants to the U.S. and Canada during the nineteenth and early twentieth centuries. The Hadeland Lag and *Kontaktforum* now coordinate their genealogical efforts and the Hadeland Lag's Limited Access Archive includes the *Kontaktforum Hadeland-Amerika* emigrant database.

Combined with the *Digitalarkivet* and other websites, Internet resources allow lag members to do most of their own family research. Lag genealogists continue to provide expert assistance to member researchers, but much of their effort is now focused on locating and tracing Hadeland descendants in America for the Emigrant Identification Project.

In 2004, the Hadeland Lag adopted a set of by-laws and was incorporated as a Minnesota non-profit in 2007. The United States Internal Revenue Service granted tax exempt status under section 501(c)3 of the Internal Revenue Code in 2008. In 2010, a formal policy for use of the genealogical information in the Limited Access Archive was developed and all members desiring access to the archive are now required to agree to these "Terms of Use."

Janice Heusinkveld was elected president of the Hadeland Lag in 2006.

In 2010, the Hadeland Lag sponsored a Centennial visit to Hadeland. At the 7-Lag *Stevne* a special Centennial Banquet was held for the three lags celebrating their centennials – Hadeland Lag, Toten Lag, and Landingslaget. At the Fall Meeting, the Hadeland Lag closed out its year-long celebration with a brunch cruise on the St. Croix followed by a meeting in Hudson, Wisconsin, the hometown of the Hadeland Lag's founder and long-time president, Thomas Walby.

The Hadeland Lag Enters Its Second Century

With membership exceeding 500 families in both North America and Europe, the Hadeland Lag moves into its second century as a strong and vital body. The organization will no doubt continue to evolve to meet its goals of assisting Hadeland descendants in their research into their immigrant ancestors and providing a modern connection to that special part of Norway called Hadeland.

The 'Rebirth' of the Hadeland Lag in 1976
"Recollections of Pioneer Times"
Brua, November 2008
By Verlyn Anderson

As we look forward to celebrating the centennial of our Hadeland Lag in 2010, it is also appropriate to look back at some of the milestones in our Lag's history. One of those is the 'rebirth' or reorganization of the Hadeland Lag on July 9-10, 1976 in Mayville, North Dakota at Mayville State College. By the 1970s the lag's membership had become so small that no annual *stevner* were held in 1972, 1973, 1974 or 1975. Then a man appeared on the scene that is certainly credited for our having a Hadeland Lag today. This man was Morgan A. Olson of Minneapolis, Minnesota who took the initiative to rescue the nearly dead lag and who breathed new life into the struggling lag. The meeting in Mayville was the first public meeting that the Hadeland Lag had held in more than five years – since June 11-12, 1971, when it met a Plaza, North Dakota under the leadership of President Karl B. Stensrud.

That meeting in Mayville was the first Hadeland Lag *stevne* I had ever attended. This month's "Recollections..." column is not about life during the pioneer times of our ancestors, but rather about that extremely important meeting that saw the rebirth of the Hadeland Lag.

Since a very young age, I had been interested in learning more about my Norwegian ancestors and where they had come from in Norway. My parents and their siblings knew virtually nothing about that history when I talked to them. Through a letter that I had found in the immigrant trunk of my grand-aunt after she had died, I was able to find my father's ancestors in Norway. But, I knew nothing about my mother's ancestors. After my wife and I had visited Norway in 1971 and visited my paternal ancestors, my maternal grandfather recalled that all of his grandparents had come from a place in Norway that he called Hadeland. That was all I needed to know! I wrote to the State Archives in Hamar, Norway with my inquiry. They suggested that I contact Hadeland genealogist Randi Bjørkvik. It was through her excellent information that I finally found where my maternal ancestors had lived in Norway – they came from all three of the Hadeland parishes, Gran, Jevnaker, and Lunner!

That Hadeland genealogy information was tucked away in a file for the next few years. Then in April 1976 Evonne and I attended a seminar in Duluth, Minnesota entitled "Norwegians in Northeastern Minnesota." Another of the attendees was Morgan A. Olson who made an announcement at one of the sessions that he was attempting to revive the Hadeland Lag of America and wondered if there were any people with Hadeland roots at the seminar. During the following intermission, I talked to him about my Hadeland ancestors and he encouraged me to attend a meeting that he and some former members of the Lag were planning for later that summer. I told him I was very interested and would make every effort to attend. During my conversation with Morgan, we discovered that my wife and I were acquainted with his and his wife Grace's two children. Their daughter, Martha, was in my graduation class at Concordia and their son James was in Evonne's graduation class!

The next time we visited my parents, Arthur and Cora Anderson, we told them of our learning about the existence of the Hadeland Lag of America and that there was going to be a meeting later that summer. They became interested and said that they would like to attend that meeting with us. Soon we received an invitation to the upcoming joint Hadeland Lag-Landingslag meeting that was scheduled to be held at Mayville State College (ND) on July 9-10, 1976. My parents had just purchased a brand new 1976 Buick, in a model that commemorated the Bicentennial of our nation's history. Dad said that we would be driving in their new car to the meeting! By the way, we still own that now-old Buick and drive it occasionally each summer!

That was my first Hadeland Lag *stevne*. Seventy-one enthusiastic people attended that meeting – 43 *Hadelendinger* and 28 *Landings*. Morgan A. Olson was the "cheer leader" of the meeting. The interest level among the attendees was very high, everyone was in favor of reviving these lags and we decided to meet at Concordia College for our *stevne* in 1977. Officers for the revived Hadeland Lag were elected: Morgan A. Olson, president; Verlyn D. Anderson, vice president; Peder H. Nelson, second vice president; Thomas Skattum, treasurer; Harriet Foss, secretary; Olaf Nelson, director; and Morgan appointed Harris Bakken as caretaker of the flag and Hadeland Lag banner. The complete minutes of that meeting are recorded in our Lag's 1990 history book. We spent much of our time the first day of that *stevne* becoming acquainted with one another because most of us were strangers and were acquainted with very few of the other people in attendance. But, we were strangers for only a very short time because that first afternoon and evening were primarily social, interesting get-acquainted events.

At the business meeting the next day, we discussed the possibility of our Lag sponsoring a tour to Hadeland in 1977. Morgan then announced that perhaps we would be having guests from Hadeland at our next year's meeting, - the *Mannskor K.K.* and the Hadeland newspaper were already coordinating plans for a possible visit in 1977, but the dates had not yet been set. Carl Lindstad, a very enthusiastic attendee from Niles, Illinois said it best – "Morgan Olson has accomplished more in just one year since he began working on reviving the Hadeland Lag than some people do in a lifetime." I remember that we all agreed! Some of us "old-timers" remember that our Lag's invitation to the *Mannskor K.K.* was accepted and yes, they came – about 250 of them from Hadeland in a charter flight to Fargo on July 19, 1977! I remember, too, that the temperature when they landed that late afternoon was 102 Fahrenheit or almost 40 degrees Centigrade!

Now back to the meeting in Mayville - that July afternoon we all drove out to the Gran Church which is located some seven miles southeast of Mayville. We met in that House of God that Hadeland emigrant pioneers had built on the Dakota prairie and named for the parish from which they had come in Norway. The Gran members presented the "Centennial Pageant" that they had written and presented during the centennial celebrations of their congregation in 1973. Many of us visited that Gran cemetery and read the familiar Hadeland names on the gravestones of the pioneers. I remember well, too, the delicious church lunch of open-faced sandwiches and cakes and cookies that the Women of the Church served us after the program.

That evening, we enjoyed a banquet in the college dining room. It was during that program that I gave a little talk about the 5-week seminar for Concordia College students and friends that I had coordinated and led to Scandinavia in May and early June of that year. I especially talked about my impressions of modern Norway and how that country had changed so remarkably since our emigrant ancestors left for America more than a hundred years before. The evening and that first *stevne* in five years closed with a patriotic musical presentation by the Finley-Sharon and Aneta (ND) Community Chorus, entitled, "I Love America."

It was late that evening before most of us went to bed, reluctant to end that highly successful meeting, which was the first Hadeland Lag *stevne* for the majority of us. The next morning we enjoyed breakfast together in the college cafeteria and then headed home, eagerly looking forward to our next Hadeland Lag *stevne*. We were all thankful for the excellent leadership of Morgan A. Olson and for the opportunity to meet so many new friends who also had family roots from Hadeland, Norway.

Chapter Three
Historical Highlights 1990-2010

Lag Member Tom Skattum receives the *Hadelandspris* (Hadeland Prize)
April 20, 1993

Tom Skattum was elected vice president at the 1976 *stevne* in Mayville, North Dakota. He was a leading member of the lag and his enthusiasm for Hadeland was infectious.

Tom's maternal great-grandparents, Torsten Rolvsen and Kari Larsdtr emigrated in 1852 from the Sogn farm in Jevnaker with their daughters, Anne, Randi and Mari. Randi married Ole Gulbrandson (Gilbertson) in Wisconsin. Randi and Ole's daughter Tilda Caroline married Anders Skattum.

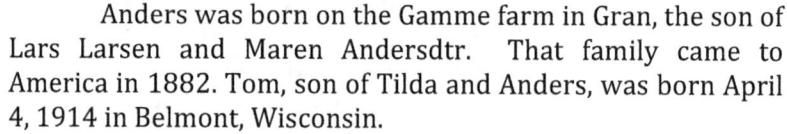

Anders was born on the Gamme farm in Gran, the son of Lars Larsen and Maren Andersdtr. That family came to America in 1882. Tom, son of Tilda and Anders, was born April 4, 1914 in Belmont, Wisconsin.

In 1993 Tom was delighted and surprised to learn that he had won the Hadeland Prize, and he quickly made plans to be at the ceremony. With no time to renew it, he returned from the trip just one day before his passport expired!

From "Hadeland" (newspaper) April 21, 1993

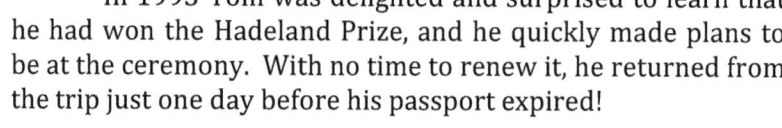

Tom Skattum was last night awarded this year's Hadeland prize. He received the award for his work as an unofficial ambassador of Hadeland in the U.S. and for guiding Norwegian-Americans visiting the 'Old Country.' The Hadeland prize was awarded for the eighteenth time.

The award ceremony took place in connection with the newspaper's general meeting in Bergslia. Per Sønsteby and editor Marit Aschehoug made the presentation to this year's laureate, who for the occasion was congratulated in both Norwegian and English.

This year's recipient of the prize, which is a replica of the Dynna Stone, was born in Wisconsin and is 80 years old. He is a third generation Norwegian-American and a farmer by profession. Skattum's grandparents emigrated from Hadeland to the USA in 1852. His grandfather was a farmer on Gamkinn, Skirstad and Gamme. On his mother's side the prize winner traces his roots to Sogn in Jevnaker.

Skattum was proposed for this year's prize by both groups and individuals. He came to Norway for the first time in June 1945 and stood on the pier with his battalion on June 7, when the King came back to Norway after World War II. Since then he has visited Norway and Hadeland several times.

Skattum accepted the prize speaking in the Hadeland dialect he learned from his grandmother when he was a boy. "I was at first surprised and then delighted," said Skattum who traveled all the way from the USA to Hadeland to accept the award.

Skattum also wanted to send a special greeting to the family of Anders Sogn and all his friends for the kindnesses shown him during his visit.

The *Mindegaven* Memorial Fund is Dissolved and Donated to the Hadeland *Folkemuseum*

One of the first official acts of the Hadeland Lag was establishment of the *Mindegaven* Memorial Fund. Feeling blessed with prosperity in their new home, Hadeland-Americans created the fund to assist the poor in their old home in Norway. The fund was maintained and administered by the Gran *Sparebank* in Hadeland. Each December it dutifully distributed funds to the needy in Gran, Lunner and Jevnaker long after the Hadeland Lag ceased to offer oversight. Occasional conversations were held about dissolving the *Mindegaven* fund, but no definitive action was taken until the late 1990s. The following letter, dated October 17, 1998, was sent to the Gran *Sparebank* in Jaren, Norway:

The Hadeland Lag in America at its annual meeting on July 11, 1998, discussed the *Mindegaven* Memorial Fund. In 1914 the Hadeland Lag in America gave the fund to the people of Hadeland at a time of very difficult economic circumstances in Norway. Since the needs of the people are now adequately provided and the annual earnings of the fund are so meager the following resolution was proposed:

"Be it resolved that the Mindegaven Fund now residing in the Gran Sparebank, Account Number 6132000, be closed and that the entire remaining amount be given to the Hadeland Folkemuseum. The trustees of the museum may use the funds for whatever purpose they choose."

The resolution was approved by a unanimous vote of the 41 members present. Please arrange for the transfer of the fund to the museum. Thank You.

Sincerely,
Hadeland Lag in America
Norma Gilbertson, Recording Secretary

Memorial Funds Transferred to the Hadeland Folkemuseum

The November 5, 1998 issue of *Hadeland* newspaper contained an interesting article detailing the *Mindegaven* Memorial Fund transfer by Gro E. Hammerstad entitled "A Gift to the Needy."

In 1914 immigrant *Hadelendingers* in America celebrated the Centennial Jubilee of the signing of the Norwegian Constitution by gathering a special fund. The interest from this fund was designed to be given to "needy persons" in Hadeland. Now the fund is closed and it has been given to the Hadeland *Folkemuseum*. This is a most welcome gift for the museum which now must be characterized as "needy" considering its current economic situation.

When viewed from today's economic perspective, the 40,208 *kroner* that was now held in the account in the Gran *Sparebank* is not a large amount in the eyes of the world. But when the Hadeland Lag in the United States established this fund in 1914, it was 12,000 *kroner*. That was a great deal of money in those days.

"It was indeed unique that they thought of those who lived in the "Old Country" in this way and then managed to gather in so much money," said Ole P. Gamme. It was he who brought his thoughts and ideas (about this fund) to Roy Stensrud and Egil Børmarken in the Hadelandslag in Oslo and then on to the Hadelandslag on the other side of the Atlantic.

But the history of the fund is long and complicated, and the museum administrator Åse A. Lange has not been able to get a reasonable summary of either what the money has been used for through the years, or how large the fund was throughout the years since 1914.

What one knows is that money from the fund has been used for the purpose it was established, namely given to the needy persons in Hadeland as a small Christmas gift and greeting from the immigrants of the district.

"By 1946 the fund had increased to 19,000 *kroner*, and as late as 1959 the interest from the fund was distributed in accordance with the original statutes. At that time the interest income was equally divided among the parishes of Gran, Brandbu, Tingelstad, Lunner and Jevnaker," said Åse A. Lange.

In the years 1982-1984, the Memorial Fund income was divided and given to the Social Welfare Boards in the three Hadeland municipalities.

"The Memorial Fund has been discussed by the Hadeland Lag in America many times throughout the years," said Egil Børmarken from the Hadelandslag in Oslo. He first became aware of the fund through Morgan Olson, a well-known person among immigrant Hadeland descendants in America.

"Together with Olson I attempted to change the use of the interest money to a Flower Fund that the Hadelandslag in Oslo could administer. Our thoughts were to give greetings with the flowers to the elderly in the home district," explained Bormarken.

This proposal was not approved by the Justice Department because it was not in agreement with the original purpose of the fund. About this time Roy Stensrud also started to think about the Memorial Fund. "It was after a meeting of the Historical Society in Lunner at which we had received an inquiry of whether we wanted to participate when the Hadeland Lag in the U.S.A. was planning to visit Hadeland during the summer of 2000. I then contacted Ole P. Gamme who I knew had contacts there to ascertain if the fund could be contributed to the museum in connection with the upcoming visit. The museum will most certainly be a central point of interest for the visitors in 2000," said Stensrud.

Gamme then contacted Verlyn Anderson, editor of the Norwegian-American publication, *Brua*. Gamme got a positive response from him in return.

Finally, in this way the *Mindegaven* Memorial Fund was closed and the money transferred to the museum to be used according to their wishes. In investigating the history of the fund it was found that the museum had already in 1964 received information that they would get the interest money from this fund. But time goes on and (Hadeland Lag) officers change. It certainly is not an easy matter to keep track and control of an account that is located in a savings bank in the "Old Country."

"The Gran Savings Bank, which has had this money for so long, ought to give the museum an equal amount of money now when the account is closed," challenged Ole Gamme and got an agreeing nod from both Stensrud and Børmarken, who are all very satisfied that the museum at last received the money.

The museum administration has some ideas of how the money will be used, but they will first discuss them with the museum's board of directors.

Hadeland Folkemuseum commissions a replica of the Dynnastein

The *Folkemuseum* used the *Mindegaven* donation to purchase a computer and subscriptions to Ancestry.com and other genealogical services, and to fund acquisition of a replica of the Dynna Stone, which dates to about 1040 AD. The replica was dedicated during the Lag's 2000 visit to Hadeland.

The monument reflects an early Christian tradition in Northern Europe and is similar to examples found in the British Isles. "Bridge stones" were believed to offer a bridge that would ease the journey of the departed from this world to the next.

The *Dynnastein*'s red sandstone slab is approximately 10 feet tall and was originally located on the north Dynna farm. Scenes from the nativity

Carvings on Replica *Dynnastein*

including the Baby Jesus, the Star of Bethlehem, and the Three Wise men are carved on its face. It bears the runic inscription

> Tyrik's daughter Gunn or made the bridge in memory of her daughter Astrid. She was the handiest maiden in Hadeland.

The Dynna stone is valued as one of the earliest examples of Christian art in all of Norway. It was being used as a salt lick for livestock in 1879 when it was moved to the Norwegian Museum of Cultural History at the University of Oslo, where it remains on display.

Opening of Peder H. Nelson's Book Collection
Gran Public Library, Gran, Norway on March 18, 1999

Peder Hilmar Nelson was born at Løvseth in Gran May 21, 1900. His mother, Marte Helene Pedersdatter, born 1873, was a servant. His father, Niels Hansen, born 1877, was a tailor apprentice in Oslo. He was raised by his mother in a log cottage in poor conditions that included a dirt floor.

Peder Nelson and his mother immigrated to North Dakota in 1914. His intention was to return to Hadeland after five years, but he stayed in Northwood, North Dakota for over seven decades. Peder passed away there on September 29, 1986.

Nelson worked as editor or contributor to Norwegian-American publications including the *Brua*, *Hallingen* and *Decorah Posten*. He also contributed emigration information for *Gamalt fra Hadeland* and articles for Hadeland's yearbooks. Over the years he collected books, articles, newspapers, and brochures chronicling the Norwegian-American experience.

When Peder died, he willed his collection to Harriet Foss. She spent some years contemplating where it could find a good home, and concluded that the *Gran Historielag* would be the best steward for this treasure. Harriet made arrangements to have it shipped to Hadeland.

© Randsfjordmuseene

The *Peder H. Nelson Book Collection* was formally opened at the Gran Library on Thursday, March 18, 1999. Representing the Hadeland Lag of America were Harriet Foss of Northwood, North Dakota and Verlyn and Evonne Anderson of Moorhead, Minnesota.

Members of *Gran Historielag* gathered at the library at 6 p.m. Harriet was given the honor of cutting the ribbon to officially open the collection. Anne Lise Jorstad, librarian for the collection, said the following about Harriet in her speech, "In all the 25 years that she has been secretary for the Hadeland Lag in America she has also been unofficial 'ambassador' for Norwegian-Americans of Hadeland ancestry, both in the Midwest and over the entire area. Harriet, whose ancestors came from Gran, has for years welcomed visitors from Hadeland into her home – reporters, writers, people searching for their relatives, tourists and musicians. She is primarily responsible for the fact that Peder Nelson's book collection is here today."

After the ribbon-cutting ceremony the crowd moved to Granvang for a program celebrating the event. The *Manskorr K.K.* opened the program. The keynote performer was Erik Bye, the well-known Norwegian entertainer and television producer. Some years ago he was in America gathering material for a television production about descendants of Norwegian emigrants. While there, he met Harriet and they have been good friends ever since. As a youth, Erik lived in Brandbu and attended elementary school there so Hadeland claims him as a citizen. Erik summed up his acquaintance with Harriet by saying, "Harriet Foss is truly the most Norwegian of all those who are sitting in this room." No one disagreed!

When the library scheduled a move to a smaller building in October of 2008, the *Historielag* asked the Hadeland *Folkemuseum* if it had room to store the collection. The *Folkemuseum* was pleased to add this valuable collection, which had been carefully indexed by Gran *Historielag*, to its Hadeland-America Collection.

Dr. Verlyn Anderson Receives the St. Olaf Medal
Nikolai Church, Gran, Hadeland, Norway, June 25, 2008

The St. Olav Medal was instituted by King Haakon VII of Norway on March 17, 1939. It is awarded in recognition of services in advancing knowledge of Norway abroad and for strengthening the bonds between expatriate Norwegians and their descendants and their country of residence. The St. Olav Medal is currently awarded by the reigning monarch, His Royal Highness Harald V of Norway. Such an occasion is not an everyday event!

In the council meeting of the Royal Norwegian Order of Merit number 67 on December 7, 2007 and confirmed by His Majesty the King on January 23, 2008, a resolution was adopted bestowing on Professor Verlyn D. Anderson the St. Olav's Medal for his promotions of the connection and solidarity between expatriate Norwegians and their country of residence. The official certificate reads in part:

Kansellisjef Egil Vindorum & Dr. Verlyn Anderson

Vi Harald Norges Konge gjør vitterlig at Vi under 15. februar 2008 har tildelt Professor Verlyn Anderson St Olavsmedaljen.
Harald R

In English: We Harald, the King of Norway makes known that we on 15 February 2008 have bestowed upon Professor Verlyn Anderson the St Olav's Medal.
Harald R

The presentation ceremony took place on June 25, 2008 in Nikolai Church, one of the Sister Churches in Gran, where Verlyn's great-grandfather was baptized in 1854. Verlyn and Evonne, their children and grandchildren, Norwegian relatives, colleagues, local *Hadelendinger*, and members of the *Kontaktforum Hadeland-Amerika* attended the presentation. Official Hadeland was represented by the mayors of Gran, Lunner and Jevnaker. The United States was officially represented by Vice-Ambassador Kevin Johnson.

Rev. Ragnar Granasen, the Dean of the Lutheran parishes in the districts of Hadeland and Land, welcomed everyone and introduced *Kansellisjef* Egil Vindorum, the head of the Chancery of the Royal Palace in Oslo who gave a short speech and then presented the St. Olav Medal to Verlyn. Verlyn then gave a short speech of thanks and appreciation and introduced the members of his family. Kevin Johnson from the American Embassy also gave an official greeting and congratulation. The official ceremony concluded with singing by the *Mannskor K.K.*

Following the ceremony, the Andersons and special guests adjourned to the Granavolden *Gjæstgiveri* where a roast reindeer dinner was served and the honors continued. Ole P. Gamme acted as master of ceremonies. Congratulations were extended from Western Norway Emigration Center at Sletta and colleagues from the Hedmark College in Hamar. Run Meier, mayor of Gran, presented Verlyn with a Gran table banner on which is pictured the Gran municipality's official shield. The festive evening concluded with the singing of the national anthems of both the United States and Norway.

Historical Highlights 1990-2010

Norwegian Statehood Pioneer Project
Minnesota Sesquicentennial, 1858-2008

As the 150th anniversary of Minnesota statehood approached, the Hadeland Lag took the lead in planning for the recognition of the state's Norwegian pioneers. The initiative, dubbed the "Norwegian Statehood Pioneer Project," was organized by the Hadeland Lag with Anne Sladky as coordinator. Eleven other *bygdelag* joined this officially sanctioned Minnesota Sesquicentennial observance. In addition, the Norwegian-American Genealogical Center-Naeseth Library in Madison, Wisconsin joined the project and agreed to provide permanent archival storage of pioneer applications and other project materials.

The project was divided into three parts:

Recognition: A plaque was designed to honor those Norwegians who were in Minnesota when it became a state in 1858. A process was developed by which their direct descendants could apply for recognition. Some parts of the state weren't settled until decades after statehood; in response to requests from descendants of these pioneers a "Century Certificate" program was developed to honor Norwegians who settled in Minnesota between 1858 and 1908.

NSPP's Statehood Pioneer Plaque

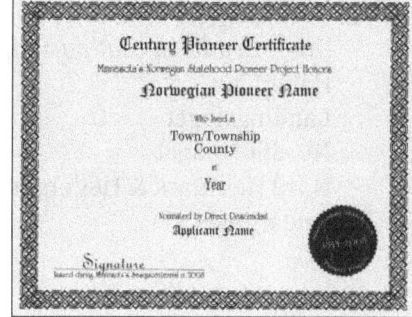

Century Pioneer Certificate

Over 450 applications were received for these programs. David Gunderson, Hadeland Lag genealogist, handled verification of applications. David Pfeffer, Hadeland Lag treasurer, managed payments and receipts. Jan Heusinkveld, Hadeland Lag president, took charge of ordering and mailing recognition plaques, while Anne Sladky handled Century Certificate preparation and mailing.

Celebration: The project sponsored a program and banquet on October 18, 2008 at the Marriott Hotel in Rochester, Minnesota. A variety of vendors offered their wares in a "Minnesota Marketplace." The afternoon program was hosted by Gary Olson. It began with a color guard of military veteran descendants of Norwegian Statehood Pioneers who trooped the colors. Dr. Odd Lovoll gave the keynote speech, "They're All Bound For Minnesota." John Berquist entertained on the button accordion. Ole and Helga Gamme from Gran, Norway led the singing of the Norwegian National Anthem.

A highlight of the afternoon program was "the Call of the Roll," during which the names of Statehood Pioneers were read by Jim Skree of Telelaget and Georgia Rosendahl of the Hadeland Lag. Pastor Per Inge Vik from Mindekirken in Minneapolis led the Memorial Service. "Those Lutheran Ladies," humorists Janet Letnes Martin and Suzann Nelson, brought the afternoon to a close as they recalled growing up in Norwegian-American communities after WWII.

During the cash bar reception, the Rochester Accordion Band provided entertainment. After the evening banquet, mistress of ceremonies Sandra Hendrickson introduced LeRoy Larson and the Minnesota Scandinavian Ensemble. A good time was had by all! Anne Sladky, Anne Janda, David Pfeffer, DeLos Olson, and Jan Heusinkveld were involved in celebration planning.

Remembrance: The book *Celebrating Our Norwegian-Minnesotan Heritage 1858-2008* includes biographies and photos of Statehood Pioneers, a list of Century Pioneers, stories from the pioneer era, and a recap of the October celebration. It was edited by Anne Sladky, with a foreword by Verlyn Anderson. Over 500 copies have been sold to date.

Applications are still being accepted for "Minnesota Norwegian Pioneer Certificates" and books are still available for purchase at http://www.mn-nspp.org/

Other Bygdelag that participated in the Norwegian Statehood Pioneer Project:

Hallinglag	Romerikslaget
Landingslaget	Telelaget
Nordfjordlaget	Toten Lag
Nord Hedmark & Hedemarken	Trønderlag
Opdalslaget	

Chapter Four
Home to Hadeland

Visiting ancestral farms is just one of the special features of a Hadeland Lag tour

The unique itinerary of the lag's visits to Hadeland has made them one of the lag's most successful programs. The opportunity to visit the farms and churches that immigrant ancestors left behind in Gran, Jevnaker, and Lunner makes these tours much more meaningful than ordinary tourist fare.

Since 2000, the visits have been choreographed by *Kontaktforum Hadeland-Amerika*. The efforts of the local historical societies and the Hadeland *Folkemuseum*, coupled with the expert planning and guidance of Dr. Verlyn Anderson and his wife Evonne, have allowed the Hadeland Lag to create unforgettable memories for members who make the journey. The Lag has also sponsored extended tours to other parts of Norway immediately prior to or following the Hadeland visit.

The first lag-sponsored return to Norway occurred in 1921. It would be 57 years before the Lag again brought its members 'home to Hadeland' in 1978. The third tour took place in 1990. After the visit in 2000, a commitment was made to schedule tours every 5 years. Lag members returned to Hadeland in 2005, and were delighted to celebrate the lag's centennial in Hadeland in 2010. There is already interest in the 2015 visit.

The Hadeland Lag's First Visit to Hadeland
Da Hadelandslaget kom til Norge (The Hadeland Lag Comes to Norway)
The original article appeared in the first issue of the Brua in the fall of 1921. It was translated and republished in the August 2010 Brua.

220 visiting Americans arrived on the Wilson Line steamship *Rollo* at 6:00 a.m. on Saturday, May 14, 1921. At 9:00 *Nordsmanns Forbundet* president F. G. Gade officially welcomed them to Oslo and to Norway. Thomas A. Walby responded with thanks. They then sang three songs: *"Ja, vi elsker dette landet," "Gud Signe Norigs Land,"* and "My country, 'tis of thee." Each of the visitors was given a map of Oslo, together with a printed program of the planned activities for later that day. Then they were transported to their various hotels.

At 12:30 p.m. the Americans assembled at the Historical Museum at the University of Oslo where Conservator Gjessing welcomed them and showed them the Oseberg Viking Burial Ship and the rich contents of that 1904 historic find. He reviewed Norway's cultural history from the Viking Age to their present time. The large group traveled to the Akershus Fortress where Chief Architect Sinding-Larsen spoke to them about the long history of the Fortress. They then toured the fortress and concluded their visit there with a short organ recital in the fortress' chapel.

At 5:00 p.m. they were given a tour of the then western suburb of Majorstuen on their way to the Holmenkollen Ski Jump and Museum where they enjoyed an interesting tour. At the conclusion of the day, Pastor Kolstø from Plummer, Minnesota thanked the *Nordmanns Forbundet* for the hearty welcome that the visiting *bygdelag* members had experienced. Dr. Gade closed the day's visit with the wish that all the visitors would have a wonderful time during their visits in Norway. That evening some of the Americans continued on their way to the various districts from which they had emigrated many years earlier. Others decided to remain in Oslo to celebrate the 17th of May the following Tuesday. Thomas A. Walby traveled on to Hadeland that evening.

June 23, 1921 – Norwegian-American Day in Hadeland
2,000 people gathered on Halvdanshaugen at the *Hadeland Folkemuseum*

Norwegian-American Day in Hadeland was a special day that happens very infrequently and that will not be forgotten for a long time by both the Hadelanders from America and the people from the home community. It was a wonderful day from the beginning to the end. The community was bathed in the wonder of St. Hans' sunny splendor and the flags waved over everyone in the light breeze. The day seemed to be created for a celebration and the celebration was both in nature and in the minds of the people.

The day began with a worship service in the Gran Church, which was beautifully decorated for the occasion with Norwegian and American flags, leaves and flowers in the high summer season's most attractive colors. The Women's Committee who had been in charge of decorating the old beautiful church had transformed it in a very deserving manner. One became in tune with the festive church holiday immediately as one stepped through the door and heard Pastor Olssen's moving sermon, the beautiful organ music, the melodious singing under the church's high arch, together with the wonderful combination of the sun's rays, the colorful leaves and flowers – all created a very moving effect.

The church filled to overflowing with people and many had to remain outside when they couldn't come in. The church service was festive from first to last and gave much honor to Gran's remarkable parish pastor. After the church service the Americans visited the *Steinhus* located next to the Gran Parsonage while the Hadeland Glassworks Band played outdoors, where the remaining people were gathered.

By 1:30 p.m. the Hadelanders from America gathered with some local people, about 60 in all, for lunch at *Gregersstuen* at Granavolden. To the tune of "*Ja, vi elsker*" they were welcomed to the tables and to Chef Schou's remarkable menu which awaited the attention of the guests.

Sheriff Hvamstad wished everyone welcome and told about how happy the Gran community was to have the Hadelanders from America as their guests. Chairman of the Hadeland Lag, T. A. Walby thanked them. Pastor Olssen introduced *Nordmanns Forbundet* President Medical Dr. Gade, who acknowledged with a lively talk everything that was being done by all to give the Norwegian-Americans a hearty welcome.

Chairman of the welcoming committee Attorney Gulden spoke to the Hadelanders in America and asked Mr. Walby to bring greetings to the Hadeland Lag from the home community. Mr. Walby thanked Gulden for his hearty greetings and said that the well wishes that he and the other Norwegian-Americans were met with here in Hadeland would always remain with them as rich, delightful, and beautiful memories. Teacher Hjemsø recited a poetic welcome greeting written by the festivity's hostess:

> "We wish a hearty welcome to the Norwegian American Hadeland Lag that has come to Gran today! It is a magnificent time of the year – St. Hans' Day – when the fields and meadows and all of nature display themselves in full splendor. It was a long time ago that you journeyed across the ocean in order to set your feet under your own table. We know that you have toiled and struggled, yes even more than we have realized. But now, all that is to your great credit. You love the land of your birth, your father and mother. And there, now old, they have worried and prayed so fervently for their young girls and their young boys whom they once set out into the world. But now they have their reward again, now their children have returned as brave women and brave men. Now it is time for a toast! Reach for your glass and take a drink!"

On behalf of the host committee Editor Lie answered with a hearty welcome and a toast for the women's committee who had made the arrangements for the delicious lunch.

Acting as representative for the Sognelag in America, Mr. Underdal gave a wonderful talk in his clear Sogning dialect to the Hadeland community for what they had done for the visiting Norwegian-Americans. Such a celebration would never be forgotten!

About 4:00 p.m. the dinner group made its way to *Halvdanshaugen* where the Tingelstad Brass Ensemble welcomed them with rousing musical numbers. There were people on all the roads leading to the festival – old and young, all the locals who were free that afternoon were heading to *Halvdanshaugen* to celebrate with the Hadelanders from America. There were an estimated 2,500 people in attendance so it was very crowded on that beautiful hill that is surrounded by so many reminders of our ancestors' lives and work.

Committee Chairman Gulden wished everyone welcome. This was followed by several beautiful musical selections by the *Mannskor K.K.* and the Hadeland Glassworks Band. Parish Pastor Olssen then gave an outstanding address about the historical monuments and the old buildings in the outdoor museum and their connection with the district's history from the ancient times to the time of Gregers Granavolden. Following another musical number, Mayor Egge delivered a hearty greeting on behalf of the home community. In it he said that the emigrated sons and daughters would always be remembered in Hadeland. He went on to describe the growth and developments in Hadeland that had taken place during the past generation since the emigants had left Norway. He ended his speech with the wish "Long Live the Hadelanders in America!"

Then came the most formal part of the program. On behalf of the Hadeland municipalities, Chairman Attorney Gulden presented a beautiful silk Norwegian flag to Mr. Walby and asked the Hadeland Lag Chairman to take it back to the Lag members in America. At the same time he expressed the wish that the Hadelanders in America would always hold Norway's colors high with both respect and honor. Mr. Walby accepted the flag while the musicians played "*Ja vi elsker*." During that music, it was as quiet on *Halvdanshaugen* as in a church! In a most touching manner, Mr. Walby thanked for both the flag and the honor that had been shown all the visitors from America. He further stated that he was certain that the bonds between the Home District and the Hadelanders in America would for all time be strong and never broken. His response was met with strong applause.

The more formal or solemn part of the Festival was ended and then began the lighter part of the evening's program. Actor Harald Stormoen from the National Theatre in Kristiania was greeted with much applause when he appeared at the speaker's platform. He told his best stories with infectious wit and good humor. The people laughed until tears were running down their cheeks. Then the music began again. The Committee's Dancemaster Teacher Volla led the dancing, the *Mannskor K.K.* sang, the Hadeland Glassworks Band and the Tingelstad Brass Ensemble continued to perform. Dancing and splendid fireworks were the finale to the day's long program. And the dancing continued on the 'green' far into the summer-lit St. Hans' night.

Unfortunately, although we know that seventeen Hadeland Lag members accompanied President Walby to Norway, their names were never recorded in the Lag's records.

June 23 - June 25, 1978

The Hadeland Lag held its annual *stevne* at Concordia College, Moorhead, Minnesota on June 10-12, 1977. At that meeting, a possible tour to Hadeland in 1978 was discussed and unanimously supported by the attending Lag members. The *Mannskor K.K.* arrived in Fargo on July 19, 1977 and had a highly successful concert tour during the following two weeks. At each concert, the anticipated tour to Hadeland was announced. Interest continued to increase as the Hadeland Lag membership grew and many of the new members indicated a strong interest in visiting Hadeland in 1978. Plans continued for the lag visit to Hadeland and by May 1, 1978, eighty-eight Hadeland Lag members had registered for the tour!

On Wednesday, June 21st most of those eighty-eight travelers boarded a Brekke Travel (Grand Forks ND) sponsored charter flight in Fargo that flew overnight to the Gardermoen Airport, north of Oslo. The majority of the people who went on this second tour were able to understand and speak Norwegian. The Norwegians decided to open their homes for those American guests who wanted to experience the Norwegian culture first-hand. However, a few of the Americans preferred to stay at the Sanner Hotel. Upon arrival in Hadeland, the busses drove to the Sanner Hotel where the visiting Americans were met by their host families, while others checked into the hotel.

"Meet and Greet" at the Sanner Hotel

The official 3-day visit to Hadeland began the next day, **Friday, June 23.** Busses transported the Americans and local planning committee members to Jevnaker for a tour of the Hadeland Glassworks. The tour was followed by a short visit to the near-by Kvelsrud dairy farm where Dag C. Weberg, owner and a member of the *Storting*, the Norwegian Parliament, was their host. Lunch was served at the *Bøndernes Hus* where the *Jevnaker Bondeungdomslag Dansegruppe* (Jevnaker Youth Folk Dance Group) performed. Randi Bjørkvik, well-known Hadeland genealogist, gave an interesting and informative lecture about emigration from Hadeland. The planned afternoon boat trip on the Randsfjorden was cancelled because of very strong winds. That evening, the Americans and their hosts met at the Sanner Hotel for an evening of food, conversation and music.

Saturday, June 24th began with the Hadeland Lag business meeting at the Sanner Hotel at 11 a.m. At 12:00 noon, busses transported the visiting Americans to *Bislingen Fjellstue* in Lunner where they were served a delicious trout dinner, with entertainment by the Lunner Dancers. After the dinner, the busses took the visitors on a tour of Hadeland. During some of the tour, the busses traveled on the historic *Kongeveyen,* the "Old King's Highway" that crossed Hadeland on its way from Oslo to Trondheim during Medieval times. The afternoon bus tour ended at Røykenvik Bay on the Randsfjorden, near Brandbu. A boat trip scheduled to the King's Island was cancelled because of high winds and rough water. Instead a picnic was held and the group was served waffles, sour cream and fresh strawberries.

Sunday, June 25th began with worship services at the Nikolai Church, one of the Sister Churches on Granavolden. In addition to the regular sermon, Rev. Casper Nervig, a Hadeland Lag member, brought a greeting in both Norwegian and English. The *Mannskor K.K.* also sang several songs during the service. At 1:00 p.m. the American visitors, their hosts and hundreds of local people enjoyed a special program at the Hadeland *Folkemuseum,* an outstanding 80-acre museum area around and on the historic *Halvdanshaugen. Rømmegrøt* and *spekemat* were served that afternoon and a musical program by the Hadeland Band, some local folk-dancers and musical ensembles added to the enjoyment of the visiting American's final day in Hadeland.

Entertainment by *Mannskor K.K.*

On Monday morning, June 26th, Morgan Olson's escorted tour into western Norway left from the Roa train station with some of the Americans. Others left for further travel in Norway, Sweden or Denmark or for visits to relatives in other parts of Norway. Thus ended a very successful Lag visit to Hadeland.

Participants in the 1978 Visit

Albert & Alma Anderson, Rothsay MN
Arthur & Cora Anderson, Rothsay MN
Mr. & Mrs. David Anderson, Moorhead MN
Dr. Verlyn Anderson, Moorhead MN
Anna Graven Aws, Madison MN
Etta Berge, Marshall MN
Mr. & Mrs. Harold Braaten, Mayville ND

Robert Bredeson, Belmont WI
Gardes Dahle, Twin Valley MN
Nora Dahle, Twin Valley MN
Mr. & Mrs. Iver Eide, Milan MN
Alice Edwards, Seattle WA
Ellef & Alfield Erlien, Twin Valley MN
Judy Fogdall, Cedar Falls IA

Hans Froslie, Vining MN
Vernon & Carol Grinaker, Moorhead MN
Mr. & Mrs. Grant Grinna, Waukon IA
Archie & Florence Gubbrud, Alcester SD
Harlick & Alice Gunderson, New Auburn WI
Mathilde Haga, Velva ND
Adolph & Mildred Hanson, Mayville ND
Ansgar & Adeline Hanson, Kloten ND
Ed Haugen, Gully MN
Anna Lynne Jacobson, Binford ND
Julia Krohn, Mt. Horeb WI
Helen Larsen, Hudson SD
Orice & Vivian Larson, Montevideo MN
Carl Lindstad, Niles IL
Palmer Lynne, Montevideo MN
Mr. & Mrs. Tom Mason, Kalamazoo MI
Lt. Donald & Judy Mau,
    Wesley and Melissa, APO, Germany
Richard & Janet Mau,
    Kaari & Krista, Youngstown OH
Mr. & Mrs. Paul Monson, Gratiot WI

Abner & Luella Nelson, Montevideo MN
Olaf & Rhoda Nelson, Montevideo MN
Mr. & Mrs. Walter Nelson, Hatton ND
Dr. & Mrs. Casper Nervig, Williston ND
Louise Nervig, Minneapolis MN
Mr. & Mrs. Duane Nysveen, Hillsboro ND
Borghild Olson, LaCrosse WI
Morgan Olson, Minneapolis MN
Mr. & Mrs. Glen Rabenberg, Britton SD
Adeline Rudh, Rothsay MN
Mr. & Mrs. Sherman Sandven, Milan MN
Thorvall Septon, Montevideo MN
Thomas Skattum, Belmont WI
Marvin Skogrand, Montevideo MN
Lynn Snelling, Billings MT
Arne Solend, Minneapolis MT
Doris Sorum, Moorhead MN
H. Dean & Carol Sorum, Moorhead MN
Kristen Stormoe, Fargo ND
Lyla Vinje, Hollandale, WI
Mr. and Mrs. Iver Western, High River, AB CAN

Archie Gubbrud's Trip to His Roots
Brua, November 1993
By Verlyn Anderson

    The former governor of South Dakota Archie Gubbrud and his wife Florence went to the *stevne* which met in Hadeland, Norway in 1978. One of the things that Archie wished to do on that trip was to visit the farm from which his ancestors had emigrated. Gudbrand Skjaker knew where the farm was and offered to take Archie and Florence to visit the farm.
    There was one problem – Archie and Florence spoke very little Norwegian and Gudbrand did not speak English, so Verlyn Anderson volunteered to go along as translator. They drove north from Gran through the scenic countryside to Brandbu and on to the small farm, located halfway up the long hillside overlooking the town below. It was a Sunday afternoon, irrigation pumps were watering the nearby potato fields and lush strawberry patch, but no one seemed to be at home. The Gubbruds had come a long way so they wanted to take a few pictures before leaving.
    They wandered among the buildings, taking photographs and wondering which buildings might have been there when Archie's ancestors lived there. Suddenly from out of one of the small storage buildings appeared a short disheveled man, certainly over 80 years

old and looking like he had just awakened from an afternoon nap. He immediately asked what the strangers were doing on his farm. Gudbrand explained to the little man that he had nothing to fear, that these people were the Gubbruds from South Dakota who were visiting Norway and wished to see this farm which had been owned by the visitor's grandfather before he had emigrated to America. Thereupon, the man became much more hospitable and told that it was his father who had bought the farm from those Gubbruds.

Florence & Archie Gubbrud

Without waiting a moment for anyone to ask questions, the man started excitedly telling what he remembered about the Gubbrud farm and the former owners who had moved to America. "Yes," he said, "that's an interesting tale," and smiled broadly as he eagerly started telling what he knew. Verlyn was kept very busy translating as the storyteller kept talking, almost without stopping for a breath.

In the mid-1920s a son of the emigrant had visited the farm. He was from South Dakota and he drove a big American car – a Cadillac! "Yes," said Archie, "that was my father." The man seemed especially to delight in telling that the Cadillac had gotten stuck in the muddy roads that summer and he and a couple of his Norwegian friends had had to pull the car out of the mud with their horses! "That was fun!" he commented.

Then after World War II, probably in the early 50s, two well-dressed women from the Gubbrud family came to Hadeland to visit the farm. "Yes," said Archie, "they were my aunts." The man went on to tell that his sister and some other people in the area continued to correspond with the South Dakota Gubbruds. From what he had heard, the family in America was quite prosperous. The Norwegians had heard that in South Dakota the Gubbruds farmed thousands of acres and that they owned hundreds of beef cattle! Clearly, the man was very skeptical of these claims. "Thousands of acres! Hundreds of cattle! Unbelievable!" "Those Americans have a habit of adding to the truth, you know," he said, " Maybe they had a lot of land and maybe, too, they had many, many head of cattle!" This seemed to him hard to believe. "But now they have gone too far!" he continued with firm doubt in his voice, "Now they say there is a governor in the family!" Clearly he did *not* believe this latest claim.

Gudbrand spoke directly to the man, "Take off your hat, little man, look up and put out your hand! Shake hands with this gentleman, for here stands that governor before you."

The man's mouth fell open, his eyes widened and after a moment, he yanked his hat from his head and began to bow and bow and bow! Like Doubting Thomas of New Testament times, the old Norwegian farmer believed! After many handshakes and many more bows, he looked proudly up at the tall, six-foot governor and smiled. But that smile was the smile of belief, not of doubt. That afternoon the old man who now owned the Gubbrud farm in Hadeland had another chapter to add to those stories he could tell of the South Dakota Gubbruds and the governor he had met.

June 22-June 24, 1990

The Hadeland Lag celebrated its 80th anniversary by sponsoring another trip to Hadeland. On this visit the majority of the fifty-five Americans made their own flight arrangements. The headquarters for the 1990 Hadeland visit was the Tourist Hotel in Gran. E. Palmer Rockswold coordinated with the *Mannskor K.K.* and the *Jevnaker Bygdeungdomslag Leikarring* (the Jevnaker Youth Folk Dance Group) who planned activities in Hadeland and were the hosts for this visit. The touring schedule while the group was in Hadeland was very similar to that followed during the 1978 visit.

The visit began on **Friday, June 22** with an annual meeting of the Hadeland Lag attended by the visiting Americans and their Norwegian guests. According to the information in the Hadeland Lag newsletter, *Brua*, there was a "Welcome to Hadeland" program by the Host Committee that afternoon after which a delicious *smørbrød* luncheon was served. There must have been an evening program, but there is no evidence of it in the Hadeland Lag records.

Saturday, June 23 was *St. Hans Day* (Mid-Summer Day) in Norway. There was a bus tour of Hadeland that included a guided tour of the Hadeland Glassworks and visits to selected sites in Hadeland. A delicious buffet banquet and program were held that evening at the Tourist Hotel. A traditional Mid-summer celebration bonfire was planned for later that evening, but because of the extremely dry conditions, no outdoor fires were allowed in Hadeland that June.

Sunday, June 24 worship services were again held at the Nikolai Church with special music by the *Mannskor K.K.* The afternoon was spent at the Hadeland *Folkemuseum* where the visiting Americans and hundreds of Norwegians enjoyed a program by the *Jevnaker Bygdeungdomslag Leikarring* (the Jevnaker Youth Folk Dance Group). Special presentations to the Hadeland *Folkemuseum* were made by two of the visiting Hadeland Lag members. Robert Means, Edina, Minnesota, presented the museum with a World Craft Show Gold Medal which was awarded to his grandfather, Hadeland immigrant Lars Grinager, for the violin he crafted and which was exhibited at

Grinager's Gold Medal   © Randsfjordmuseene

the World Craft Show in Paris in 1886. At the same ceremony, Paul Grinager, Sacramento, California, presented his exact and very intricate model of the old Grinager Stave Church. Åse A. Lange, director of the *Folkemuseum,* accepted the gifts. Both of these items are on permanent display at the Hadeland *Folkemuseum.*

Three extended tours for visiting lag members were offered. Each had a different length and traveled through different parts of Norway. Tom Skattum's 14-day tour of western and central Norway departed Oslo on June 7 and ended in Hadeland on June 21. Verlyn and Evonne Anderson's 7-day tour into western Norway left Hadeland on June 27 and returned to Oslo on July 1. Priscilla Sorkness Grefsrud's 14-day tour began at Alta in northern Norway on June 27 and visited scenic north Norway, including North Cape, *Sami* (Lapp) villages, Tromsø and the Lofoten area before heading into the western fjord country where the tour ended in Bergen on July 10th.

Participants in the 1990 Visit

Verlyn & Evonne Anderson, Moorhead MN
Arlene Bockoven, Renton WA
Norman & Mae Brynsaas, Decorah IA
Ruth Edick, Portland OR
Leland & Esther Embrey, Novato CA
Carl & Wanda Erickson, Hitterdal MN
Ellef & Alfield Erlien, Twin Valley MN
Percy & Harriet Foss, Northwood ND
Earl & Priscilla Grefsrud, Minneapolis MN
Patricia Grinager, Palo Alto CA
Paul & Eunice Grinager, Sacramento CA
Annette Jelen, Green Bay WI
Alphina Mahle & Daniel Gunter, Mentor MN
Robert & Margaret Means, Edina MN
Charlotte Miron, Green Bay WI
Thelma Moline, Tacoma WA
Harry & Irene Navarre, Albuquerque NM
Luella Nelson, Montevideo MN

Olaf & Rhoda Nelson, Montevideo MN
Paul Paulson, Minneapolis MN
James Peterson, Stillwater MN
Sidney & Lois Rand, Northfield MN
Palmer & Betty Rockswold, Eagan MN
Elaine Roder, Marshall MN
Elsie Roder, Montevideo MN
Leslie Rogne, Kindred ND
Robert & Leona Rosendahl, Decorah IA
Leslie & Ruth Rud, Montevideo MN
Marian Sarles, Portland, OR
Marvin Skogrand, Montevideo MN
Vernon & Ruth Solien, Fargo ND
Dean & Carol Sorum, Moorhead MN
Floie Vane, Cliffside Park NJ
Betty Volney, Long Lake MN
Margaret & Wilfred Wilson, Red Wing MN

June 19-June 25, 2000

To celebrate the 90th anniversary of the Hadeland Lag of America, the lag again sponsored a group tour to Hadeland. The Hadeland *Amerikabesøk* Committee that year included Harald Hvattum, Kjell Myhre and Hans M. Næss from the Gran Historical Society, Ester Haga from the Lunner Historical Society, Ole Roen from the Jevnaker Historical Society and Ole P. Gamme from the *Mannskor K.K.* They prepared a busy 7-day schedule for the Lag

A souvenir from the Hadeland Lag in America's 90th Anniversary celebration in Hadeland on June 19-25, 2000 – "The Hadeland Lag builds a bridge between the immigrants and the Old Country." This printed placard, created by artist Kari Ruud Flem, features her line-drawings of the nine churches in Hadeland, together with the dates that each church was built. Also pictured are Hadeland's Bronze Bucks from about 500 B.C. and the Dynna Runestone from 1050 A.D., both rediscovered centuries after their creation.

visitors who arrived on Monday, June 19 at the Gardermoen Airport. They were met there by members of the host committee who had arranged for busses to transport the 66 visiting Americans to the Hadeland Hotel, the headquarters for the week-long visit.

At 8:30 on the morning of **Tuesday, June 20**, the group left the hotel in tour busses for their visit to Oslo. The first stop was a very special visit to the *Storting,* Norway's National Parliament at 10:00 o'clock. Two representatives in the *Storting* from Hadeland, Berit Brørby *need* add mine from Jevnaker and Marit Tingelstad from Brandbu were the guides who escorted the visitors through that beautiful public building. The next stop was the *Hjemmefrontmuseet* – the World War II Resistance Museum at Akershus Fortress. After the tour of that interesting and educational museum, lunch was served on the Fortress grounds. The group visited the Viking Ship and Kon-Tiki Museums that afternoon after which they made a stop at the Holmenkollen Ski Jump en route back to Hadeland.

Wednesday, June 21 was spent touring the Gran-Brandbu area, hosted by members of the Gran Historical Society. The day-long tour included visits to the *Steinhus*; the *Klokkerlaven,* some of which was constructed of salvaged material from the Grinager Stave Church which had been torn down in 1866; the site of the old Grinager Stave Church; the Stone Ring at Bilden; the Tingelstad and Næs churches; the Grinaker Weavery; and the Peder Nelson Book Collection in Gran *Sentrum.* The tour also included a visit to the Hadeland Manufacturing Company where lunch was served. That evening ther was a beautiful concert by the *Mannskor K.K.* in the Nikolai Church.

Thursday, June 22 was the Lunner touring day, hosted by members of the Lunner Historical Society. This included a visit to the administrative center for Lunner, a tour of the *Bergverksmuseum* (Mining Museum) plus a visit and short concert at the Lunner Church.

Gathering before the Saturday Banquet

Friday, June 23 was the Jevnaker touring day, hosted by members of the Jevnaker Historical Society. The day included a tour and shopping stop at the world famous Hadeland Glassworks, and visits to the Kistefos Museum, *Nesbakken* and downtown Jevnaker. Dinner that evening was at the Torbjørnsrud Seminar and Conference Center.

Saturday, June 24 was an "open date" where the visiting Americans could visit their relatives or ancestral farms, do some private sight-seeing or spend some time with local genealogists researching their Hadeland roots. That evening there was a wonderful banquet at the Hadeland Hotel with lots of food, music and stories of by-gone days!

Sunday, June 25 began with a morning worship service at the Nikolai Church. The afternoon was spent at the Hadeland *Folkemuseum* where a special Mid-summer Day celebration and program were presented. All of the historic museum buildings were open and staffed by local people who were acquainted with the history of their buildings. A highlight of the afternoon was the dedication of the replica *Dynnastein,* acquired by the *Folkemuseum* with the *Mindegaven* Memorial Fund donated by the Hadeland Lag.

Churches in the United States named in honor of parish churches in Hadeland were contacted prior to the trip. Gran churches near Mayville, North Dakota and in rural Hawley, Minnesota and the Jevnaker churches in rural Montevideo and Borup, Minnesota donated congregational histories and membership books, anniversary mementos and pictures of their churches. These were presented to the Hadeland *Folkemuseum* during their cultural program.

Wonderful gifts were received by the lag from our hosts as well. Jevnaker *Kommune* presented a covered glass goblet with Jevnaker's coat-of-arms etched on its face. The Lag received two beautiful framed pictures of the Sister Churches, a summer scene and a winter scene, from Gran *Kommune.* During the visit to Lunner *Radhus* (city hall) each Lag member received a centennial history of the community entitled *Lunner Kommune, 1898-1998*.

In addition each visiting Lag member received a specially designed drawing by Kari Ruud Flem that included pen and ink sketches of the 10 churches of Hadeland and the 11th Century *Dynnastein*.

It was a wonderful week in Hadeland, a "once-in-a-lifetime" event for the visiting Americans.

"Discover Norway" extended tours to other parts of Norway were available: June 11-19, before the Hadeland visit and June 26-July 4, immediately thereafter.

Unveiling of the *Dynnastein* replica

Participants in the 2000 Visit

Jeanne Anderson, Hallock MN
Verlyn & Evonne Anderson, Moorhead MN
Darrell & Sharon Babcock, Eagan MN
Owen, Bodil & Amy Bratvold, Coeur d'Alene ID
Harris Brown, Albert Lea MN
Norman Brynsaas, Decorah IA
Robert Brynsaas, Mesa AZ

Rodney & Sara Buxrude, Burnsville MN
Delores Cleveland, Sioux Falls SD
Janice Danielson, Rothsay MN
Betty Forsburg, Sioux Falls SD
Norma Gilbertson, Brooklyn Center MN
Robert & Donna Hadland, Bayfield WI
Ronald Hammer, Petaluma CA

Steve & Jean Hessler, Lake Oswego OR
Janice Heusinkveld, Rochester MN
Manfred & Leona Hill, Canton SD
Bob Holmen, Red Lodge MT
Myron Hovland, Kent WA
Lois Kalmoe, Minneapolis MN
Karen Kruse, Kindred ND
Rose Mack, Fountain Hills AZ
Judy Malacek, Sacred Heart MN
Colleen Martineau, Champlin MN
Maureen Moses, State College PA
Irene Navarre, Albuquerque NM
Harriet Ohe, Minnetonka MN
Larry Ohe, Rothsay MN
Harvey & Gloria Radtke, Pelican Rapids MN
Duane Rogne, Fargo ND
Leslie Rogne, Kindred ND
Robert & Leona Rosendahl, Decorah IA

Wilbur & Marilyn Sayles, Austin MN
Glenda Sharples, Seattle WA
Theo Sherman, Peyton CO
Dean & Carol Sorum, Moorhead MN
Jon & Ann Sorum, Harmony MN
Gail Staxrud, Minneapolis MN
Kris Staxrud, Minneapolis MN
Bonita Stock, Fergus Falls MN
Judy Tabbut, Rothsay MN
Don & Carol Thompson, Albuquerque NM
Beverly Toelle, Coeur d'Alene ID
Denny & Maxine Tunell, Sioux Falls SD
Ronald & Deanna Ulven, Hawley MN
Betty Volney, Long Lake MN
Diane Wagner, Westminster CO
Keith & Beverly Webster, Willmar MN
Janice Wheeler, Marion NC

2005
June 19-June 25, 2000

The Storting

The travelers who were in Hadeland June 20-26 had exciting, interesting days meeting relatives, exploring their roots and getting a sense of the countryside. The members of the *Kontaktforum Hadeland-Amerika* were the planning committee in Hadeland for the Lag-sponsored tour. The members of the *Kontaktforum* at that time were Ole P. Gamme, Chairman, Harald Hvattum, Kjell H. Myhre, Geir Arne Myhrstuen, Hans M. Næss and Ester Haga. The "home base" for the 2005 visit was the Sanner Hotel. The touring and visiting in Oslo and Hadeland in 2005 followed a similar schedule to the one for the visit to Hadeland in 2000.

The visiting American lag members arrived at the Sanner Hotel on **Monday, June 20**. There was an informational orientation meeting for the Hadeland Lag members that evening.

During the day-tour to Oslo on **Tuesday, June 21** a "walk through" of Frogner Park was added to the 2000 itinerary.

The **Wednesday, June 22** tour of the Gran municipality included the following sites: the new Grymyr Church, constructed in 2003 after a fire destroyed the original church in 1999; the Grinaker Weavery; the Næs Church and the Raukr Viking Museum. Lunch was served at the Sangnes apple farm. On the return trip to the hotel the group toured through the countryside of Gran and Brandbu. Following the dinner at the Sanner Hotel, there was a concert by the *Mannskor K.K.* in the Nikolai Church.

Thursday, June 23 was Lunner municipality touring day which included a visit to the Lunner Church, built during the Middle Ages and the Grua Church,

Touring Grinaker Weavery

built much later in the 18th century for the Grua mining district. Lunch was served at *Bislingen*, a boarding house up in the hills, filled with a large private collection of antiques. Before returning to the Sanner Hotel, there was an interesting stop at the scientific observatory, *Solobservatoriet* (Solar Observatory). A cultural program by local musicians was presented that midsummer evening at the hotel.

Friday, June 24 was Jevnaker municipality touring day. The morning was spent touring the Hadeland Glassworks, observing the artisans at work producing many types of glass products. The group also toured the Norema Manufacturing Company and after the tour, lunch was served in the company dining room. The early afternoon was spent enjoying the Kistefos Museum, a former wood pulp mill which is today an industrial museum, sculpture park and art gallery. Before heading back to the hotel, the group received a guided tour of the Jevnaker Church.

Saturday, June 25 was an open day for the participants

Visiting Lunner Church

to do genealogical research, visit their immigrant ancestors' farms or visit other sites not included earlier in the week. Local residents provided transportation to the various farms. Anne Lise Jorstad gave a special guided tour of the Granavollen area, including visits to the Sister Churches, the Stone House and to the current exhibition entitled "Granavollen in 1905" which was on display at one of the local historic buildings. Dinner was served at the *Granavollen Gjæstgiveri* because there was a wedding at the Sanner Hotel.

An 11:00 a.m. worship service at the Nikolai Church began the **Sunday, June 26** festivities. A fascinating afternoon was spent at the Hadeland *Folkemuseum* where the museum staff hosted a special "Hand-work" Day. The historic buildings in the outdoor museum were all open with local artisans demonstrating traditional handwork and skills. The afternoon at the *Folkemuseum* marked the official end of the 2005 Hadeland Lag visit to Hadeland. It was a very fitting conclusion to a memorable week!

After the unforgettable week in Hadeland, Evonne and Verlyn Anderson escorted an 8-day "Exploring Norway" tour which traveled through the western fjord country to Bergen and returned to Oslo through Hallingdal, arriving in Norway's capitol city on July 4th.

Participants in the 2005 Visit

Verlyn & Evonne Anderson, Moorhead MN
Carol Firth Baxter & Jonathan C Baxter, Sacramento CA
Elizabeth Botti, Red Hill, Pennsylvania
Owen & Bodil Bratvold, Kelsy Bratvold, Coeur d'Alene ID
Jean Broshius, Ocean View DE
Jean Brown, Osseo WI
Brian Christensen, Floyds Knob IN
Delores Cleveland, Sioux Falls SD
Dave Gunderson, Fergus Falls MN
Jean Hackman, Rudd IA
Jon Halvorson, Lacey WA
Steven & Josephine Hessler, Lake Oswego OR
Manfred Hill, Canton SD
Verlyn Hill, Aurora SD
Joseph & Martha Juel, Keswick VA
Jeanne Keith, Las Vegas NV
Lauren Kollecas, Ocean View DE
Doris Kornfeld, Williams IA
Lacy Kornfeld, Greenville SC
Linda Lee Larson, Muncie IN
Odelle Leonard, Greenfield WI
DeLos Olson, Rochester MN
Don Olson, Rochester MN
Bruce & Julia Plomasen, Ocean View DE
Donna Robinson, Arvada CO
Pete & Barb Schmitt, Burnsville MN
Glenda Sharples, Normandy Park WA
Marlene Sommers, Minnetonka MN
Dean & Carol Sorum, Moorhead MN
Pauline Stowman, Rothsay MN
Andy Tweito, Pickens SC
Daniel Tweito, Irmo SC
Ted Tweito, Spring Grove MN
Ronald & Deanna Ulven, Hawley MN
Karl Vigen, Madison WI
Larry & Mary Ann Vigen, Moorhead MN
Ellen (Bratvold), Robb, Ryan & Ashley Webb, Folsom CA
Keith & Beverly Lanning Webster, Willmar MN
Delmar & Joyce Wevik, Chamberlain SD
Wendy Winkelman, Coon Rapids MN
Gerald Ziesemer, Fergus Falls MN

2005 Hadeland Tour Participants

2005 "Exploring Norway" extended tour participants

Hadeland Lag Centennial Year

June 22 to June 27, 2010

33333332The members of the *Kontaktforum Hadeland-Amerika* were again the planning group in Hadeland for the Lag-sponsored 2010 Centennial tour. They planned a similar daily schedule as the visiting Americans had enjoyed in 2005. Therefore only the additional sites that were visited or toured will be included in this historical account of our Centennial visit to Norway. The majority of the 58 Americans arrived at the Gardermoen Airport – Oslo on Tuesday, June 22. They were met by Ole P. Gamme and Verlyn D. Anderson. As soon as the first bus was filled, Ole accompanied them to the Sanner Hotel while Verlyn stayed at the airport and met and gathered the rest of the incoming Americans. By 6:00 p.m. the final visitors had arrived and everyone was safely transported to the Sanner where dinner was served. A "Welcome to Hadeland" orientation meeting was held that evening.

On **Wednesday, June 23**, the group toured Gran and Bjoneroa. They were special guests of the mayor of Gran, Inger Staxrud at the Gran *Rådhus*. There President Jan Heusinkveld presented the mayor with a Native American Peace Pipe,

President Heusinkveld and Mayor Staxrud

made in Pipestone, Minnesota. The Americans then visited the Tingelstad Church and afterwards drove to the ferry which took the lag members across the Randsfjorden to Bjoneroa. After a visit to the local Sørum church, they were luncheon guests at the **Bjoneroa** *Kulturbygg*, **followed by a bus tour to Søråsen**. After touring Bjoneroa, the travelers headed back to the ferry and across the Randsfjorden to the east side of the lake. Dinner was served at the Sanner. The genealogy room was staffed and open that evening as it was during each of the "open" non-programmed evenings that week.

Thursday, June 24, the lag members toured Lunner and Jevnaker. The first stop was at the Lunner Church, one of the four medieval churches in Hadeland. They then drove on to Jevnaker where they toured the Hadeland Glassworks and also did some shopping in both the "seconds shops" of both the Hadeland Glassworks and Porsgrund Porcelain. The touring Americans were luncheon guests of the Glassworks at which time President Heusinkveld presented a Peace Pipe to Jevnaker's mayor, Hilde Brørby Fivelsdal. There was a short visit at the Kistefos Museum after which the group toured the Jevnaker Church on their way back to the Sanner Hotel. After dinner at the hotel, the *Mannskor K.K.* presented a beautiful concert at the Nikolai Church.

On the morning of **Friday, June 25**, two touring busses picked up the visiting Americans and headed for Oslo. They visited the same tourist sites as were visited in 2000 and in 2005. In addition, they also visited Oslo's new Opera House and the newly renovated Oslo Cathedral. It was a long touring day; the group returned to the Sanner after 6:30 p.m. and enjoyed another delectable meal that evening.

Saturday, June 26 was an "open day" as it had been during the lag's previous two visits to Hadeland. Anne Lise Jorstad again guided tours in the Granavollen area – to the Sister Churches and the Stone House. Some people also made a shopping visit to the Grinaker Weavery (*Grinakervev*) to buy some of their popular *busserull* shirts.

Hans Gudmund Lunder and Ole Gamme

The festive evening included a banquet and program, celebrating the centennial of the Hadeland Lag. It began with an outdoor concert by the Moen *Musikforening*, followed by a buffet dinner. President Jan Heusinkveld presented engraved desk sets to the members of the *Kontaktforum Hadeland Amerika* and a Native American Peace Pipe to Anders Larmerud, mayor of Lunner. Gifts were presented to President Jan and Verlyn Anderson by the Hadeland *Folkemuseum* staff. Everyone then adjourned to the hotel lounge where they were entertained by Kristine Bjerkrude, a well-known singer at the Norwegian Opera. This was followed by an uproarious rendition of some Swedish student drinking songs by Hans Gudmund Lunder and Ole Gamme. Their physical agility and strong singing voices were enjoyed by everyone. Ole Gamme and Karl Hanson, from Kenner, Louisiana sang "Old Man River." Afterwards everyone enjoyed Centennial birthday cake and coffee.

Sunday, June 27 began with a worship service at the Nikolai Church, led by Pastor Kari Lette Pollestad Høghaug. Scripture readings were read in Norwegian by Helga Gamme and in English

`Pastor Kari Lette Pollestad Høghaug

by Evonne Anderson. Kari Lette preached and sang in both Norwegian and English, which was much appreciated by the Americans. After the service, busses brought the group to the Hadeland *Folkemuseum*, where they were lunch guests of the museum. It was the annual "Family Day" at the museum. All the outdoor buildings were open with demonstrations of traditional crafts. Folk dancers performed on the outdoor stage. Later in the afternoon the visiting lag members toured the Tingelstad Old Church which is also located on the museum grounds. The afternoon at the Hadeland *Folkemuseum* was a very special conclusion to the week-long visit to the land of lag members' ancestors.

The next morning, **Monday, June 28**, the members of the *Kontaktforum Hadeland Amerika* and some Norwegian relatives of the visiting Americans gathered at the Sanner Hotel to bid farewell to their departing guests. Some of the Americans were flying home later that day while others were touring in Norway or visiting Norwegian relatives or friends. 43 people departed on the tour of southern and southwestern Norway, escorted by Verlyn and Evonne Anderson. The week in Hadeland had created memories for all of them - memories that would last for a lifetime!

Dancers at the Hadeland *Folkemuseum*

Centennial Visit to Hadeland Participants

Allison Aamodt, Newburyport MA
Jason Aamodt, Pataskala OH
John Aamodt, Laporte MN
Verlyn & Evonne Anderson, Moorhead MN
Loren & Marlene Balkan, Faribault MN
Carol Baxter, John Hull, Jenna Baxter, Jack Hull, Sacramento CA
Eric Beastrom, Hudson WI
Gary & Barb Beastrom, Athens WI
Elizabeth Botti, Harleysville PA
Owen Bratvold, Coeur D'Alene ID
Thomas & Erik Bratvold, Richland WA
Allan & Kathy Carlson, Farwell MN
Darrold & Linda Dean, Sioux Falls SD
Susan Guttormson, Moorhead MN
Karl & Kelsey Hanson, Kenner LA
Jan Heusinkveld, Rochester MN
Bob Holman, Red Lodge MT
Larry Hovland, Pelican Rapids MN
Sonja Jensen, Fargo ND
Wilbur & Barbara Lider, Sun City West AZ
Michael Miller, Montrose MN
Carl Max Morstad & Jerie Torbeck, Louisville KY
Noel & Mary Morstad, Littleton CO
DeLos Olson, Rochester MN
Norman Olson, Dayton OH
LeRoy & Sharon Petersen, Rock Springs WI
David Pfeffer, Maple Plain MN
James & Mary Rolf, Brandon MN
Pete & Barb Schmitt, Burnsville MN
Karen Schulz, Stillwater MN
Karen Shoemaker, Hobart WA
Dennis & LouAnn Skattum, Livingston MT
Dean & Carol Sorum, Moorhead MN
Beverly Stadum, Øyer, Norway
Ron & Deanna Ulven, Hawley MN
Carol Vind, Hackensack MN
Faith Waldoch, Rothsay MN
Laura Waldoch, Forest Lake MN
Cynthia Young, Tustin CA

Chapter Five
*Stevne*r and Member Meetings 1989-2010

A sampling of meeting logos

Each summer since 1986, Hadeland Lag has joined Landingslaget, Numedalslag, Ringerike-Drammen Districts Lag, Sigdalslag, Telelaget, and Toten Lag in hosting the 7-Lag *Stevne*. This 3-4 day event is held on college campuses or hotel/conference centers in various locations in the Upper Midwest. The lags take turns assuming responsibility for planning and coordinating the *stevne*, so each lag takes the helm once every seven years. The *stevne* offers members open access to each lag's genealogical resources and the expertise of lag genealogists to further their family research. Classes and demonstrations educate members on a wide variety of topics. Vendors offer books, clothing, and a broad array of gift items. Entertainment celebrates our Norwegian-American heritage. Tours of local points of interest have become a popular part of each *stevne*'s agenda. A good time is had by all!

In the fall, the Hadeland Lag sponsors a Saturday event that includes a business meeting, lunch, and an afternoon activity. It is not unusual for more Hadeland Lag members to attend the fall meeting than attend the lag meeting held at the *stevne*. For that reason, beginning in 2011, although the lag will continue to hold a meeting during the *stevne*, the fall meeting of the Hadeland Lag will be designated as the organization's annual meeting.

The *History of the Hadeland Lag 1910-1990* included a synopsis of each Hadeland Lag *stevne* through 1988. A prospective look at the plans for the 1989 *stevne* was also included. This valuable chronological account continues here with information about *stevner* and meetings from 1989 through 2010.

7-Lag Stevne July 6 - 8, 1989
St. John's Abbey & University, Collegeville, Minnesota

Members and guests of the seven lags began arriving at St. John's Abbey on Thursday July 6, 1989. On Friday genealogy continued along with displays of crafts and books for sale, and a visiting area where coffee was provided.

On Friday afternoon the 7-Lag meeting was held in the Humphrey Theatre with coordinator, Eunice Helgeson as mistress of ceremonies. Earl Grefsrud and Lois Rand led the group singing. Father Timish, president of St. John's, welcomed the group to the university. Each of the seven lag presidents offered a welcome. Marilyn Sorenson, genealogy coordinator, introduced each of the genealogists. A moment of silence was observed in memory of Glen Nelson, past coordinator of the 7-Lag *Stevne*. Don Rasmussen gave an interesting talk on Norwegian fjord horses, illustrated by slides.

The Friday evening program was held in the Humphrey Theatre with Palmer Rockswold as master of ceremonies. Earl Grefsrud led the singing of the national anthems. Sidney Rand, former ambassador to Norway, and his wife Lois spoke about Norway and the phrase "*Enig og Tro*" found on the Hadeland Lag banner. It dates back to the framing of the Norwegian Constitution at Eidsvoll in 1814. The highlight of the evening was the 6-projector slide show "Images of Norway" presented by Hadeland Lag members Bob and Andrea Holman from Red Lodge, Montana.

1989 7-Lag Stevne Banquet

Saturday night the menu for the buffet banquet included baked torsk and meatballs with the usual trimmings plus lefse and rømmegrot. Earl Grefsrud served as master of ceremonies for the evening program. *Dalagutta,* a musical group from Norway, played several numbers. This was followed by comedienne Marilyn Belgum, who kept the audience in stitches during her entire performance. The evening came to a close with a traditional bunad parade.

Hadeland Lag Annual Meeting
On Saturday morning, the Hadeland Lag business meeting took place in the basement

of the library at St. John's University.
- Lois Rand spoke on "Mass, Glass, and Class."
- Ellef Erlien, primary editor of the *History of the Hadeland Lag 1910-1990*, reported on its positive reception and sales of the book.
- Paul Grinager spoke briefly about his model of the Grinager stave church, which had once stood on the Grinager farm in Hadeland and was torn down in 1866. (The model he created was presented to the Hadeland *Folkemuseum* in 1990.)
- Earl Grefsrud led a sing-along during a break in the program. Later he spoke on the State Church in Norway and its influence on the immigrants who came to America.

Fall Meeting October 7, 1989
Montevideo VFW, Montevideo, Minnesota

Thanks to Olaf and Rhoda Nelson, 53 Hadelanders had a great time at the Montevideo VFW on October 7, 1989. Highlights included a greeting from the mayor; group, duet and solo singing by the Grefsruds; a few words by Grace (Mrs. Morgan) Olson, who was presented with a copy of the *History of the Hadeland Lag;* accordion music by Ellef Erlien; and remarks by Palmer Rockswold on his impressions of the Soviet Union. Vernon Lund, a one man band, entertained as well.

The program ended with the singing of *Kan Du Glemme Gamle Norge* and *America* just in time for Olaf to bring out his 75th birthday cake with ice cream and coffee.

Hadeland Lag Annual Meeting
June 22, 1990
Turisthotel, Gran, Norway

The 1990 annual meeting was held during the visit to Hadeland. Topics related to the visit were discussed, and Olaf Nelson and Ellef Erlien were re-elected to the board of directors.

1990 Annual Meeting

7-Lag Stevne July 12 - 14, 1990
Theme: *"Trolls at Wahpeton"*
North Dakota State College of Science, Wahpeton, North Dakota

Members of the Hadeland Lag gathered for the 7-Lag *Stevne* at North Dakota State School of Science, beginning on Thursday July 12 with registration and genealogy.

Numedalslag served as coordinator for this event. On Friday, the first session of the 7-Lag *Stevne* began with a procession to the Cultural Center was led by the banners of the 7 lags. This was followed by group singing led by Larry Opsahl. Dignitaries from Wahpeton and visitors from Norway were introduced. Next was a skit written by Carol Nelson, "*Going to the Stevne.*" The session ended with a film, "*Letters from America,*" based on the work of Ole Rolvaag.

1990 Bunad Parade

The Friday evening program began with Ron Anderson who entertained as a one-man band and with humor. Chuck Suchy, the North Dakota Singing Cowboy, was next. He received a standing ovation from the audience. The Detroit Lakes *Leikarring* (dance group) ended their performance with audience participation and dance lessons.

Of the many classes and presentations offered, rosemaling, a bentwood box demonstration and a presentation on *stabbur* building were particular favorites.

On Saturday a Norwegian bunad parade preceded the traditional banquet. This was followed by visiting musicians. At 8 PM *stevne*-goers gathered at the Cultural Center for the evening program. "*Kringen Klub Kor*" (choir) from the Sons of Norway lodge in Fargo entertained with familiar songs in both English and Norwegian. Humorist Leonard Johnson rounded out the program and left the audience laughing.

Fall Meeting October 6, 1990
Sons of Norway Hall, Rochester, Minnesota

On a pleasant autumn day 40 Hadelanders found their way to the Sons of Norway hall in Rochester for the fall meeting. The program opened with songs and audience introductions. Willard C. Johnson presented "Songs of Faith." This was followed by a delightful meal.

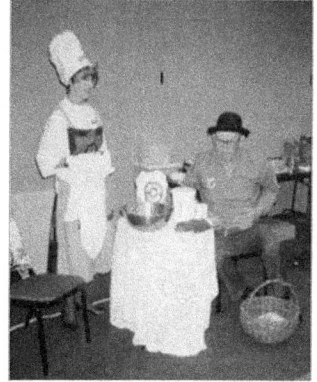
Rhoda and Olaf Nelson

In the afternoon, Ellef Erlien led a sing-along of old songs. DeLos Olson showed slides of an area near Oslo seldom seen by tourists because it includes sites for military defenses. Palmer spoke briefly about the summer's trip to Norway and Harriet read her poem about her experiences in Gran. Genealogist Les Rogne spoke of his work and willingness to help anyone discover their Hadeland roots. Dean Sorum finished the program with an excellent slide show of pictures from the trip to Norway. Olaf and Rhoda Nelson presented a humorous skit. The afternoon came to a close with ice cream and coffee.

1991

7-Lag Stevne *July 11 - 13, 1991*
Theme: "Call of the Lur"
University of Wisconsin, River Falls, Wisconsin

The largest group to attend in several years gathered for registration and genealogy sessions on the beautiful University of Wisconsin campus at River Falls. Friday morning included special demonstrations and presentations. Chet Habberstad showed a video taken in Norway recently, Russell Wangen gave a demonstration on bentwood boxes, and Norman Brynsaas explained the detailed process of moving an 1860 immigrant barn from the Decorah, Iowa area to the museum at Hamar, Norway.

Paul Rockswold provides the 'Call of the Lur'

On Friday afternoon the 7-Lags were called together by the sound of the lur played by Paul Rockswold, Palmer Rockswold's grandson. The call of the lur, so rich in Norwegian history and legend was, of course, the theme of the *stevne*. Greetings were brought to the group from the *Bygdelagenes Fellesraad*; Lars Løberg, the Norwegian Vice Consul; and the presidents of the 7-Lags. Dick Rees, professional accordionist, offered a variety of Norwegian music followed by a video and commentary on Norwegian Stave Churches by Jim Rupert of the University of Wisconsin, River Falls.

The evening program was again begun with the call of the lur by Paul. Palmer Rockswold provided some history and shared the legend of the lur. Dr. Larry Opsahl led the group in a sing-along of Norwegian songs. *Narrona Leikarring* demonstrated several Old Norwegian dances; Torre, a hardanger fiddler, played several solos; and *Spelmanslag*, a violin ensemble group, played several enjoyable numbers.

On Saturday evening the program that followed the 7-Lag banquet opened with songs and humor by the *Norsk Sangere*. *Narrona Leikarring* and *Spelmanslag* performed again, Olaf Nelson told *banqskrønner*, violinist Torleif Braaten played some tunes, Verlyn Anderson spoke about King Olav V's death, and Earl Grefsrud led a sing-along.

Hadeland Lag Annual Meeting

The Hadeland Lag Annual meeting was held in the Fine Arts Building with about 60 members present.

- Membership and attendance at the *stevne* have increased. Credit was given to the *Brua* and the "Are Your Roots in Norway?" brochures.
- The performances of the Hadeland Dancers, Sverre Sørum and Anne Synove Sørum, were the highlight of the day. They demonstrated dancing in the old Hadeland tradition. Ellef Erlien played his accordion for group singing, including *Nidelven* and other Norwegian songs.
- Norman Brynsaas shared his personal experiences during the transfer of the immigrant barn from Iowa to Hamar, Norway.

Fall Meeting October 5, 1991
Montevideo, Minnesota

Despite adverse weather, a group of about 50 Hadeland Lag members plus a number of guests found their way to the Fall Meeting. They were greeted as usual with good coffee and special *småkake* made by Rhoda Nelson.

The Monte Trio, a genuine old time band, furnished music for the day, including the accompaniment for the sing-along led by Olaf Nelson.

Coffee and Conversation

Brian and Martha Ward interpreted some Civil War period letters, Olaf and Rhoda teamed up to present a funny skit, and an appetizing *smørgåsbord* featuring roast beef and turkey was served for lunch. After lunch, members toured Fort Renville, the trading post and mission at Lac qui Parle State Park; and the Arv Hus museum in Milan.

7-Lag Stevne July 9 – 11, 1992
Theme: "Amerika Feber"
North Dakota State College of Science, Wahpeton, North Dakota

The first day of the *stevne* included registration and genealogy with Leslie Rogne as the genealogist. He shared a newly prepared "List of Emigrants from Hadeland" which he had extracted from the Emigrant Protocol of Kristiania (1867 to 1900) and an index of the 1875 census.

Entertainment was provided by the Urdal Folk Dancers & Musicians from Numedal, Norway; Elvind Lundby Orchestra from Toten, Norway; and "Fiddlers Three" from Fergus Falls, Minnesota. Charles Sorum and friends from Pelican Rapids performed Act I of the play, "Per," by E. Palmer Rockswold. Saturday evening the traditional banquet with a bunad show and parade was followed by a dance.

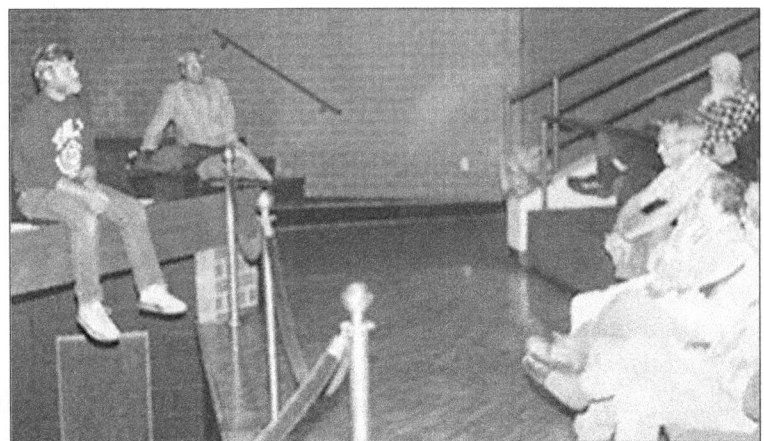
Charles Sorum explains the play "Per" by Palmer Rockswold

Hadeland Lag Annual Meeting

The meeting was held on Saturday, July 11.
- The constitution was amended to give voice and vote on the board to the immediate past president, with previous past presidents playing an advisory role.
- Sigmund and Randi Wøien from Gran attended the *stevne* and spoke at the meeting.
- Lag membership of 366 families was reported.

The Hadeland Lag's picnic was at Fort Abercrombie, the old Indian fort dating back to 1858 that was under siege for about six weeks in 1862 during the Sioux uprising.

Fall Meeting September 26, 1992
Nybo's Landing, Red Wing, Minnesota

Vice President Olaf Nelson called the meeting to order. The audience sang "*America*," and "*Ja vi Elsker*" followed by the Pledge of Allegiance. This was followed by recognition of visitors from Norway: Hans Braastad, his wife Aase Braastad, and daughter Vigdis from Lunner and Gulbrand Egge from Brandbu.

Next Palmer Rockswold reported on his trip to Norway and Hans Braastad offered some interesting observations on life in Hadeland and Norway today. Fred Johnson, a local resident of Red Wing, Minnesota, gave a talk about the history of the area. The meeting was adjourned and the group proceeded to the buffet line for a chicken dinner. Following dinner the group visited the newly renovated Sheldon Theater and later took a historical tour of Red Wing. Forty members and four guests were present.

Introduction of Norwegian Visitors

1993

7-Lag Stevne July 8 – 10, 1993
Theme: "Passage to the Prairie"
North Dakota State College of Science, Wahpeton, North Dakota

The opening session was held on Friday afternoon. It included greetings by the college and city officials and lag presidents followed by a sing-along, an historical lecture entitled "Immigration, When, Who and Why?" by Verlyn Anderson and remarks by Tom Skattum and Olaf Nelson.

Entertainment was provided in the evening by Jadde Johnson, a young violinist, and by the Buskerud Old Time Orchestra. This was followed by a dance with music by Harold and Vonnie Anderson of Fargo, North Dakota.

1993 7-Lag Banquet

Saturday evening after the *stevne* banquet, those in attendance were entertained by a performance of Act II of "Per, Immigrant and Pioneer." This play was based on the book of the same name by Palmer Rockswold. The play was followed by piano selections by Paul Sorum and a bunad parade.

Hadeland Lag Annual Meeting

Hadeland had its annual meeting Saturday morning, July 10. Vice President Olaf Nelson presided.

- Officers were elected: Margaret Wilson, President; Bob Rosendahl, Vice President; Alfie Erlien, Secretary; and Dean Sorum, Treasurer.
  Margaret declined to serve as president, and the office was left vacant.
- Tom Skattum spoke about the *Hadeland Pris* (Hadeland Prize), an award he received for his work as "ambassador" for Hadeland in the United States and for guiding Norwegian-Americans in the old country.

A catered lunch at Chahinkapa Park was followed by a tour of the Bagg Farm, one of the original bonanza farms in the area.

Fall Meeting October 2, 1993
VFW Hall, Montevideo, Minnesota

The day began with coffee and goodies. A moment of silence was held for Percy Foss, Harriet's husband, who died in September. After a sing-along, Verlyn Anderson spoke about

General Store in the Pioneer Village

Governor Archie Gubbrud's visit to his ancestral farm during the lag's 1978 visit to Hadeland. Dean Sorum reported that the 7-Lags involved in the 7-Lag *Stevne* had been incorporated as Norwegian *Stevne*r Incorporated (NSI).

Olaf Nelson and Frances Gilsrud entertained with a skit and Vernon Lund, as a one man band, played the Hawaiian guitar, a harmonica, drums and cymbals. The meeting adjourned and a hearty noon meal was provided at "Ja Mom's" restaurant. The afternoon was spent on a bus tour to Chippewa City Pioneer Village.

1994

***7-Lag Stevne** July 14 – 16, 1994*
Theme: "Land of Milk and Honey"
University of Wisconsin, La Crosse, Wisconsin

The *stevne* began as usual on Thursday with registration and genealogy sessions in the Cartwright Center at the University of Wisconsin. The opening session was on Friday afternoon with welcomes from the mayor of La Crosse, an official from the University of Wisconsin and the 7-Lag presidents. This was followed by a presentation on Norskedalen and the Koshkonong settlement, the largest Norwegian settlement in Wisconsin.

After the opening session, entertainment was provided by LeRoy Larson and the Minnesota Scandinavian Ensemble Band.

LeRoy Larson and the Minnesota Scandinavian Ensemble Band

During the Saturday evening banquet entertainment was provided by the Norskedalen Trio. The program also featured special music by violinist Pat LaRue and pianist Ellen Bronson, the Wergeland Dancers directed by Sandra Kawatski. During their visit, Ole and Lena (Don and Phyllis Jacobson) sang some very interesting World War II songs and told Ole and Lena stories.

Hadeland Lag Annual Meeting

On Saturday the Hadeland Lag had its annual meeting at Norskedalen, a 400 acre ethnic, educational and research area.
- Paul Grinager reported on "Civil War Letters," a book by Morgan Olson. It was based on letters written by Morgan's grandfather Rollin Olson of the 15th Wisconsin (Scandinavian Regiment) during the Civil War.
- Tom Skattum reported on his visit to Hadeland and shared some Hadeland newspapers with those present.

A tour of the Bekkum Homestead, located on the Norskedalen campus, was held in the afternoon.

Fall Meeting September 17, 1994
American Legion Club, Fergus Falls, Minnesota

The meeting was called to order by Verlyn Anderson. Vice President Robert Rosendahl and member Harriet Foss were unable to attend, but sent greetings. After the meeting adjourned, an enjoyable lunch was served by the American Legion. Members spent the early afternoon at the Otter Tail County Museum. The day ended with birthday and anniversary cake and coffee back at the American Legion Club.

Leslie Rogne explains the custom of *bar*

7-Lag Stevne July 13 – 15, 1995
Theme: "Ever the Land"
North Dakota State College of Science, Wahpeton, North Dakota

This was the tenth anniversary of the 7-Lag *Stevne*. It began on Thursday, July 13, with registration and genealogy sessions. On Friday afternoon the opening program began with the call of the lur and a lag banner parade. Banners from all 7-Lags were carried in and lag songs were sung or played. A musical variety show performed by Bill and Susan Goodman was the afternoon's entertainment.

The program on Friday evening was hosted by Verlyn Anderson. It included music by "The Wanderers," a four-piece orchestra from Hamar and Oslo, Norway. This was followed by a dance with the music of Marlin Westby from

Pelican Rapids, Minnesota.

Following the banquet on Saturday evening, "Per, The Dakota Pioneer" was performed, based on Palmer Rockswold's book. The evening ended with a bunad parade.

Hadeland Lag Annual Meeting

Saturday morning Hadeland Lag had its individual lag meeting in the Campus Connection Room of the Student Union, with vice president Bob Rosendahl presiding.

- Paul Grinager announced that there were copies of Morgan Olson's book, *Civil War Letters* available.
- Harriet Foss told a little about the banner she made for the Hadeland Lag in 1977. It was made in honor of the visit of the *Mannskor K.K..* She painted the Sister Churches from Gran on one side and a woman wearing a Hadeland bunad on the other side.
- Following the meeting, a catered lunch was shared with Landingslag at Chahinkapa Park.

Fall Meeting October 14, 1995
Bethania Lutheran Church, Decorah, Iowa

The meeting started with coffee, cookies and conversation at the Bethania Lutheran Church. Now a part of the Vesterheim Museum, it was originally located in rural Northwood, North Dakota. It was proposed and approved that we purchase a microfilm reader for our genealogy work and that this be kept at Leslie Rogne's home. Tom Skattum brought greetings from relatives and friends in Hadeland, Norway and a wedding picture of Ole and Helga Gamme's son, Paul, and his wife Birgithe. A tasty buffet lunch included Norwegian delicacies. During the afternoon members visited Vesterheim Museum or drove to rural Glenwood Church. The day concluded back at Bethania Church for birthday and anniversary cake, coffee and conversation.

7-Lag Stevne July 11 – 13, 1996
Theme: "Treasures from the Trunk"
Waldorf College, Forest City, Iowa

The *stevne* began on Thursday, July 11 with registration and genealogy sessions. Program chairman Norma Gilbertson hosted the opening session on Friday afternoon. Welcomes were offered by Forest City by Mayor Paul Jefsen; Dr. William Hamm, president of Waldorf College; and the 7-Lag presidents. Entertainment was provided by an instrumental group from Volda, Norway and the "Skandinavian Hottshots," Dick Rees and Art Bjorngjeld.

The Friday evening program included a presentation entitled "Treasures *not* from the Trunk" by Lois and Sidney Rand (former U.S. Ambassador to Norway and president of St. Olaf

College from 1963 to 1980).

The Saturday evening banquet was held in the Campus Center followed by a program in the Atrium. Kris Meyer, a story teller from Forest City, was followed by more music from the "Skandinavian Hottshots." The evening ended with the traditional bunad parade.

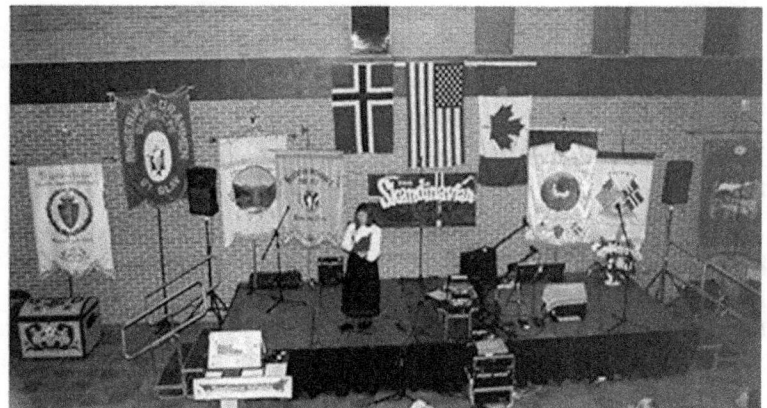
Storyteller Kris Meyer

Hadeland Lag Annual Meeting

The Hadeland Lag annual meeting was held on Saturday morning.
- Tom Skattum thanked Leslie Rogne, the Hadeland Lag genealogist, for all of his good work with the genealogical portion of the *stevne*.
- Verlyn Anderson spoke about his experience teaching at the Teachers College in Hamar, Norway over the winter.
- Lunch was held at Winnebago Church in rural Forest City with the Landingslag.

The afternoon was spent with a visit to the new "Promise of America" immigrant sculpture at Lake Mills and the very interesting museum at the farm home of Stanford and Ruth Holtan.

Fall Meeting September 28, 1996
Montevideo, Minnesota

The meeting included greetings by Montevideo's mayor, Joyce Hagberg. There was an animated discussion of the planned trip to Hadeland in 2000. Attendees were entertained by the toe-tapping music by Vernon Lund, the One-Man Band. There were laughs at a few Ole and Lena jokes, and all of this was followed by a good lunch.

During the afternoon, members enjoyed a tour of the Montevideo-Milan area. The ladies saw a presentation on the altar hanging at Kviteseid Lutheran Church while the men visited the *stabbur* built by Halvard Pettersen from Vinstra, Norway, on the Don Nelson farm.

Vernon Lund, the One Man Band

1997

7-Lag Stevne *July 10 – 12, 1997*
Theme: "Keeping the Old Traditions"
North Dakota State College of Science, Wahpeton, North Dakota

The 1997 Seven-Lag *Stevne* began Thursday, July 10 with registration, members getting together to renew friendships, and in genealogy sessions. The opening program began on Friday afternoon with the call of the lur, played by Bob Gustafson. There was a banner parade of the 7-Lags and greetings were brought by the presidents of each lag. Jack Discher presented "Norway – A Photographic Adventure."

The Friday evening program was hosted by Verlyn Anderson and featured the *Jutullaget* band from Vagamo, Gudbrandsdal, Norway.

On Saturday evening the banquet was followed by a program at the Sterns Cultural Center which featured the delightfully warm-hearted humor and harmony of Tina and Lena and the traditional bunad parade.

Picnic at Chahinkapa Park

Hadeland Lag Annual Meeting

The meeting was called to order Saturday morning, July 12, 1997 by President Robert Rosendahl.

- A motion was made and approved to authorize the board to proceed with application for tax exempt status. (This application under 501c10 of the tax code was unsuccessful.)
- Verlyn Anderson announced that 1,000 new "Are Your Roots in Hadeland" brochures were printed.

The meeting was adjourned and Hadeland and Landingslag members proceeded to Chahinkapa Park for a picnic.

Fall Meeting *October 12, 1997*
Bethania Lutheran Church, Decorah, Iowa

A small but enthusiastic group met at the Bethania Lutheran Church in Decorah, Iowa. Verlyn Anderson read letters of greeting from Tom Skattum and Ole Gamme. Lunch served by members of the church was followed by a trip to Spillville, Iowa and the Bily Clock Museum. The afternoon concluded with coffee and Norwegian pastries back at Bethania.

1998

7-Lag Stevne July 9 – 11, 1998
Theme: "We All Have a History"
North Dakota State College of Science, Wahpeton, North Dakota

The *stevne* started on Thursday with registration and genealogy. Friday afternoon's opening session included entertainment by the "Kjell Habbestad Family" from Oslo, Norway. Kjell is a composer of music and professor in theoretical disciplines at the Norwegian State Academy of Music. He played the piano and his children joined him on the flute, violin and cello, and his wife sang.

Friday evening's program in the Stern Cultural Center featured story teller Dr. Stephen "Gabe" Gabrielsen. A dance followed with music by "The Scandinavian Melodies" from Elbow Lake, Minnesota.

Entertainment following the Saturday evening banquet was provided by fiddler Per Midsteigen of Flesberg, Numedal, Norway and story teller and folk tune singer Judith Simundson from Dubuque, Iowa. The evening ended with the traditional bunad parade.

Per Midsteigen and Judith Simundson

Hadeland Lag Annual Meeting
The Hadeland Lag annual meeting on Saturday, July 11 was filled with new business items.
- The proposed itinerary for the June 2000 trip to Norway was explained and many questions were answered.
- The membership agreed to direct the Gran Sparebank in Norway liquidate the *Mindegaven* Fund and donate the balance to the Hadeland *Folkemuseum*.
- The board was expanded and the new member added was Betty Volney of Long Lake, Minnesota.

Fall Meeting October 17, 1998
Hjemkomst Center, Moorhead, Minnesota

Coffee along with rosettes and *krumkake*, were enjoyed by all present, thanks to Dean and Carol Sorum. A resolution was unanimously passed to send a request letter to the Gran (Norway) Sparebank to have the *Mindegaven* Memorial Fund transferred to the Hadeland *Folkemuseum*. The current balance is 40,208.70 Norwegian *kroner* or approximately $5,435.

The lag also voted to buy full a page ad in the Centennial book for the *Bygdelagenes Fellesraad* Centennial celebration to be held in Decorah, Iowa in July 1999. Another subject was the Hadeland 2000 trip and suggestions for appropriate gifts to bring to our Hadeland friends. Karin Andreasen, a student at Oak Grove High School in Fargo, North Dakota entertained with several Norwegian folk tunes on her violin. This was followed by lunch and a video tape of Vern Solien's travels in Norway. The day ended with a tour of the Hjemkomst Center and the newly-built stave church.

Norwegian-American Bygdelag Centennial 1899-1999 July 29-31, 1999
Luther College, Decorah, Iowa

Decorah extended a warm welcome to 1,020 *bygdelag* members who met and celebrated the centennial of the organization of Bygdelagenes Fellesraad, Inc. Marilyn Sorensen and Chris Skjervold were the *Bygdelag* Centennial Co-Chairs for this celebration.

The genealogy room was open on Thursday and that evening the *stevne* was officially opened with the call of the lur by Paul Ulvilden, Decorah, and a Norwegian Folk Dance program by *Leikarring Noreg* from Drammen, Buskerud, Norway.

Many seminars and workshops were held during the day on Friday and that evening there was a Parade of *bygdelags*. The Hadeland Lag was represented by Paul Grinager, who carried the Hadeland banner; President Robert Rosendahl; and Carol Sorum, wearing her newly-sewn Hadeland bunad.

Saturday morning there were more workshops and in the afternoon individual lags held their meetings.

The *Bygdelag* Centennial Banquet was held in the evening, and featured Christian Skjervold as master of ceremonies; "The Lost Norwegians" from Northfield, Minnesota; and the Luren Singing Society directed by Dr. David Judisch from Decorah, Iowa.

Hadeland Lag Annual Meeting

The Hadeland Lag held its annual meeting at Luther College on July 31, 1999. A short joint meeting was held with members of Landingslag to discuss the 2000 extended Norway tour, being titled "Discover Norway." The two lags then parted to complete their own Lag business. Twenty-seven members were in attendance, from as far away as Arizona and Idaho.

- A thank you letter from the Hadeland *Folkemuseum* in Gran, Norway was read. The balance of the *Mindegaven* Memorial Fund was donated to the museum.
- Greetings from Tom Skattum and Harriet Foss were relayed by Robert Rosendahl. Harriet has been honored by the community of Gran for her efforts in giving them Peder Nelson's book collection.
- Gifts to bring to Hadeland were discussed.

Fall Meeting October 2, 1999
Mindekirken, Minneapolis, Minnesota

The fall meeting was at the *Mindekirken* in Minneapolis. Committee members were Don and Betsy Anderson, Mary Halbert and Betty Volney. Pastor Gunnar Kristiansen from Bodø, Norway, extended greetings and led the group singing. Kari Burke, an Augsburg College student from Willmar, Minnesota and an intern at the *Mindekirken*, presented an interesting history of the *Mindekirken*.

Members then drove to St. Stephen's Church in St. Paul for a delicious dinner, followed by the fall meeting which was opened by President Bob Rosendahl. Verlyn Anderson led a discussion of the planning for the visit to Hadeland in June of 2000. This would be followed by the Discover Norway Tour, a nine-day tour of the Norwegian mountains and fjords open to members of both Hadeland and Landingslag.

7-Lag Stevne July 13 – 15, 2000
Theme: "We All Have a History"
North Dakota State College of Science, Wahpeton, North Dakota

Members of the Hadeland Lag met in Wahpeton, North Dakota with members of the 7-Lags for genealogy, Norwegian and American entertainment, good food and lots of visiting. Musical entertainment on Friday afternoon was given by the "Uff Da Brudders" from Britton, South Dakota.

Style Show

The Friday evening program featured a style show presentation by Dorothy Durkee of Morris, Minnesota, featuring men's and women's clothing dating from the Civil War to recent times. Models were members of the 7-Lags. Musical entertainment was presented by Paul Wilson and Mary Abendroth of Brainerd, Minnesota; later participants danced to the music of Tilford Kroshus and his band from Wahpeton, North Dakota.

Saturday evening included a banquet followed by a cultural program that included "Sing for Joy," a women's group from Benson, Minnesota; and the "Troll Boys" from Aurskog, Norway.

Hadeland Lag Annual Meeting

The Hadeland Lag annual business meeting was held on Saturday with vice-president Manfred Hill presiding.

- Dean Sorum announced that, because of a favorable turn in the exchange rate, the two *Discover Norway* tours sponsored by the Hadeland Lag and Landingslag netted a larger surplus than expected. He suggested, and membership approved, the donation of 50,000 Norwegian *kroner* to the Hadeland *Folkemuseum*.

After lunch in the campus center, members spent the afternoon looking at slides of the visit in Hadeland and the tour of Norway.

Fall Meeting September 23, 2000
Hiawatha Golf Club, Canton, South Dakota

Kennedy House

President Rosendahl brought the business meeting to order. Gifts received during the June trip to Norway were displayed. Murray Rowe and Harlan Hoff of Canton presented a program about Bid-Well Concrete Pavers.

A tour of Canton followed lunch served at the Golf Club. The first stop was the historic Kennedy house, followed by a visit to the Gubbrud Room in the public library to view memorabilia from Archie Gubbrud, former governor of South Dakota and a member of Hadeland Lag. The tour continued to the Canton Lutheran Church, built in 1909. The meeting ended with birthday cake and coffee at the Golf Club.

7-Lag Stevne July 12 – 14, 2001
Theme: "Discovering Norwegian Heritage in the Old West"
South Dakota School of Mines, Rapid City, South Dakota

Over 50 visitors from Hadeland concluded their tour of the Midwest at the *stevne*. Thursday evening's opening ceremony included the parade of flags, welcome speeches, and entertainment provided by the *Leikkaring Dancers* from Borgund Lodge in Rapid City and the *Skalmusikk Group* from Brainerd, Minnesota.

On Friday the genealogy room was open and a full schedule of classes were available, along with an all-day tour of the Black Hills that concluded at Mount Rushmore.

The banquet and bunad parade were followed by a performance by the *Skalmusikk Group* and Chuck Suchy, a folksinger, farmer, songwriter and storyteller from Mandan, North Dakota.

Sunday morning church services were held in the stave church at Chapel in the Hills.

Leikkaring Dancers

Hadeland Lag Annual Meeting

President Bob Rosendahl offered a special welcome to the 50 plus Norwegian visitors.
- Hans Næss led the singing of the U.S. and Norwegian national anthems.
- Lois Rand spoke about the Norwegian-American Historical Association and encouraged membership in the organization.
- Ole P. Gamme, Hadeland, told of his visit 24 years ago with the *Mannskor K.K.*
- Kåre Lyngstad, director of the Hadeland *Folkemuseum*, read a message from the mayors of Hadeland.
- Kjell Myhre and Don Thompson presented research on whether or not Calamity Jane had Hadeland ancestry.
- Norma Gilbertson suggested that a web page be prepared for the Hadeland Lag.

After lunch at the Surbeck Center, members visited Mt. Moriah Cemetery where Calamity Jane and Wild Bill Hickok are buried. The day was made a little more exciting by a hailstorm just as the tour group arrived in Deadwood.

Fall Meeting October 20, 2001
Kandi Entertainment Center, Willmar, Minnesota

After 14 years of service Leslie Rogne announced it was time for him to retire as genealogist. Development of a lag website was approved. Don Miller of the Kandiyohi County Historical Society gave a speech entitled "The Sioux Uprising and Norwegian Connection." A gift of 10,000 *kroner* to the Hadeland *Folkemuseum* was approved in honor of the Centennial of the *Mannskoret K.K.* After lunch, members toured the Kandiyohi County Historical

Museum, the Schwanke Museum of old cars, or the Mikkelson Collection (classic and antique boats). After the tours coffee and cake were served at the Kandi Center.

2002

7-Lag Stevne July 11 – 13, 2002
Theme: "Join Hands and Dance"
St Olaf College, Northfield, Minnesota

Registration, genealogy room and vendors were open on Thursday, July 11, 2002. The Junior *Spelemannslag*, Bø Telemark, Norway entertained on both Friday and Saturday evenings.

Saturday afternoon busses took *stevne* goers on two tours to southeastern Minnesota where visits were made to the two oldest Norwegian Lutheran congregations in Minnesota, Highland Prairie Lutheran Church in Fillmore County, and the Stone Church in Houston County.

Genealogy Room

The banquet was held Saturday evening at the Northfield American Legion Ballroom.

Hadeland Lag Annual Meeting

35 members attended the Saturday morning annual meeting.
- *Kontakforum Hadeland-Amerika* was formed with members from the Hadeland *Folkemuseum* and the three historical societies in Hadeland.
- A newly revised version of the *Han Ola og Han Per* video was shown.
- Chad Muller spoke about his recently published book, *Spring Grove: Minnesota's First Norwegian Settlement*.
- Two additional board positions were created and filled by Jan Heusinkveld and Anne Sladky.

After lunch members took an automobile trip to historic Valley Grove Lutheran Church.

Fall Meeting October 19, 2002
Fargo, North Dakota-Moorhead, Minnesota

The Saturday meeting was well attended. A motion was approved to make our next Lag visit to Hadeland in 2005. Verlyn Anderson showed his summer slides of Hadeland that brought back memories of the 2000 trip to Hadeland. A buffet lunch followed the meeting, after which members toured the Hjemkomst Center, home of the Viking ship "Hjemkomst" and the full-sized replica of the Hopperstad Stave Church.

Lag Members toured the Stave Church at the Hjemkomst Center

7-Lag Stevne July 9 – 12, 2003
Theme: "Rivers, Rails and Trails"
Winona State University, Winona, Minnesota

The genealogy library was open Wednesday evening, all day Thursday and in the morning on Friday. Genealogy lectures and a computer lab were available for participants. Two videos, *Kristin Lavransdatter* and *Cool and Crazy*, were also on the schedule.

The program began on Friday afternoon in Somsen Hall. Christine Midelfort, St. Paul, Minnesota presented her story of early Norwegian – American doctors who were part of her family. Pastor Ron Nowland presented a slide show entitled "Vikings in Istanbul."

Wergeland Dancers

Friday evening, entertainment was provided by the Winona Fiddlers, the Wergeland Dancers and humorist and author Janet Martin.

Saturday afternoon Hadeland Lag members joined in two *stevne*-sponsored tours of landmarks in southeastern Minnesota.

The evening banquet was followed by a bunad parade, "Sound Traditions," a barbershop quartet and singing comediennes Tina and Lena.

Hadeland Lag Annual Meeting

30 members gathered for the annual meeting on Saturday.
- Our membership has grown by a net of 80 members since last year.
- Leslie Rogne gave his last genealogy report. When it was completed, Delores Cleveland surprised him with gifts and a life membership for his faithful years of work as the lag's genealogist.
- Planning has begun on the 2005 trip to Hadeland.

Fall Meeting October 18, 2003
Holiday Inn, Rochester, Minnesota

Marvin & Ardis Witte

Thirty-four Hadeland Lag members attended, including Helga and Ole P. Gamme from Gran, Norway. There was a discussion of the 2005 trip to Norway. The continued surge in membership was credited to the website and excellent quality of the *Brua*. A committee was formed to investigate re-applying for tax exempt status with the IRS. Ole P. Gamme gave an enthusiastic report from the *Kontaktforum Hadeland-Amerika* on the progress of the "Hadeland Immigrant Identification Project." Marvin and Ardis Witte of Rochester presented an enjoyable musical program, "Music and Memories of Edvard Grieg." The business meeting adjourned and we toured the Franciscan monastery located at Assisi Heights, a hill overlooking Rochester.

7-Lag Stevne July 7 – 10, 2004
Theme: "Amber Waves of Grain"
Willmar Convention Center, Willmar, Minnesota

The *stevne* had a full schedule of 19 lectures on history and genealogy. Thursday included an informal workshop on Hardanger embroidery. Entertainment included Eric Bergeson, a singer/story teller/author from Fertile, Minnesota; the *Malm Basselurskan* Harmonica Orchestra from Trøndelag, Norway and "Ole and Sven" (Dave Nelson and Phil Dybdal) from Wisconsin. *Stevne*-goers could choose to take a pontoon dinner cruise on Green Lake, and tours of local points of interest, including the Endresen cabin.

The *stevne* ended with a banquet on Saturday evening, hosted by Calvary Lutheran Church, complete with lefse and rømmegrøt. This was followed by the traditional bunad parade and entertainment from *Ole* and *Sven.*

Hadeland Lag Annual Meeting

Twenty three Lag members attended the annual meeting on Saturday, July 10th.

Endresen cabin

- The membership approved increasing dues as follows: U.S. at $15 per year or $25 for two years and Canada at $20 per year or $30 for two years. Norway dues will be set by *Kontaktforum* members based on the U.S. dues/exchange rate.
- The lag will file articles of incorporation in Minnesota and continue to pursue a tax exemption from the IRS. A new set of by-laws will have to be adopted, and this process was discussed.

Following the meeting, a picnic was held at Robin's Island.

Fall Meeting October 16, 2004
Minnesota History Center, St. Paul, Minnesota

29 members registered and 27 members attended the fall meeting. Wendy Winkelman introduced herself to the membership as the new lag genealogist and spoke about her efforts and the challenges of getting acquainted with the lag's genealogical materials. The new by-laws were discussed and approved. Delores Cleveland presented Dean Sorum with a certificate and gifts in recognition of his work as treasurer, director and his work on the tax exemption issue. Verlyn Anderson presented the tentative schedule for the Hadeland visit.

The meeting adjourned and lunch was shared at the History Center's Café Minnesota. Members then viewed the exhibits and used the research libraries.

Delores Cleveland & Dean Sorum

7-Lag Stevne July 13 – 16, 2005
Theme: "A Century of Norwegian Independence"
University of Wisconsin-Whitewater, Whitewater, Wisconsin

This year's theme was chosen because 100 years ago Norway became an independent nation. The *Storting* (Norwegian Parliament) offered Denmark's Prince Carl the throne on

November 18 and he accepted, announcing that he would be known as Haakon the VII. He was crowned on November 27, 1905.

East Koshkonong Church

On Wednesday afternoon a bus tour of the Koshkonong Prairie included the 1840 Anderson Farm where Pastor Dietrichson held the first Norwegian church service in 1844, East Koshkonong Church and West Koshkonong Church where dinner was served. The bus then passed through Cambridge and Rockdale on its way back to Whitewater.

All day Thursday and Friday morning the genealogy room was open for research. A number of interesting classes were offered and many unique items were available in the vendor area. Friday afternoon's opening program included a performance by humorous folk singers, 'The Corner of G & S.' After the Friday evening banquet, the Grieg Men's Choir of Madison performed.

Hadeland Lag Annual Meeting

Twenty four members were present at the annual meeting on July 16, 2005.
- The main topic of discussion was on-going work on the lag's incorporation and application for tax exempt status.
- There was high praise for the experience by those who had participated in June's visit to Hadeland and extended tour of Norway.

The members shared a picnic lunch with Landingslag at Cravath Park.

Ole Gamme explains the work of *Kontaktforum Hadeland-Amerika*

Fall Meeting October 15, 2005
Sons of Norway Kringen Lodge #25, Fargo, North Dakota

The meeting was called to order by president, Delores Cleveland. Forty-eight people were in attendance. The new by-laws assign board members specific areas of responsibility and this was explained and discussed.

Lunch was served, followed by a presentation by Ole Gamme about the *Kontaktforum* work in Hadeland.

Displays of some of the lag's artifacts and newly available *busserull* lunch plates and mugs were of great interest to those in attendance. The afternoon came to an end with coffee and cake honoring all members with October birthdays.

2006

West Coast Gathering May 6, 2006
Clackamas, Oregon

Twenty five members from California, Oregon, and Washington gathered at the home of member Susan Baird for a picnic. Those who attended shared research stories, sources and resources, and enjoyed the opportunity to get to know their fellow West Coast lag members.

West Coast Hadelanders enjoyed good food and good company

7-Lag Stevne July 12 – 15, 2006
Theme: "From the Fjords to the Falls"
Holiday Inn Convention Centre, Sioux Falls, South Dakota

Hadeland Lag took its turn planning and managing the *stevne*, with Delores Cleveland as *stevne* coordinator. On Wednesday, a tour of Sioux Falls included the Butterfly House, pioneer buildings at Augustana College, East Nidaros Church and Renner Lutheran Church, where supper was served. It was a *stevne* to remember, because *stevne* goers enjoyed a great schedule of events in air conditioned comfort indoors…and temperatures outside soared above 100 degrees!

On Thursday morning the opening session began with the call of the lur, by the *stevne*'s special guest from Hadeland, Kari Lette Pollestad Høghaug.

Three Voices: Speaking from the Past

It included a presentation of "Three Voices: Speaking from the Past." The genealogy room opened and classes began after lunch. An afternoon tour of the EROS Data Center was also offered.

On Thursday evening a special showing of "Vikings: Journeys to New Worlds" was presented at the Washington Pavilion Cinedome. On Friday classes and presentations continued.

Friday evening's banquet was followed by the traditional bunad parade, and a performance by Minnehaha *Mannskor*, featuring solos by Kari Lette Pollestad Høghaug.

Hadeland Lag Annual Meeting

Members gathered for the annual meeting on Saturday morning.
- A memorial service was held for members who are no longer in our midst and have joined our ancestors.
- Out-going president Delores Cleveland was presented with a gift certificate for her service, with special thanks for her efforts as *stevne* coordinator from newly elected president Jan Heusinkveld.

A catered picnic lunch was held at Falls Park.

Fall Meeting October 21, 2006
Saron Lutheran Church, Big Lake, Minnesota

After enjoying coffee and goodies the fall meeting was called to order by Jan Heusinkveld. DeLos Olson reported that the Hadeland gifts have all been photographed by Gerald Ziesemer and the photos assembled into a notebook. The photos were also added to the lag's website.

Touring the Kelly Farm

Focus has shifted to pursuing tax exempt status as a 501-C3 non-profit corporation.

Ole and Helga Gamme once again journeyed from Hadeland for the meeting. Ole reported that the *Hadeland Emigration Identification Project* is going well.

Ralph and Mary Halbert of St. Paul, Minnesota presented a gift of two wooden plaques with the Coat of Arms of Norway and Lunner, Norway.

The meeting was adjourned for lunch at the Victory Restaurant and a tour of the historic Kelly Farm.

7-Lag Stevne July 12 – 15, 2007
Theme: "Let's Rally in the Valley"
North Dakota State College of Science, Wahpeton, North Dakota

The twentieth 7-Lag *Stevne* began with classes and genealogical research on Thursday morning. Thursday afternoon, an area tour included the Otter Tail County Museum and Phelps Mill near Underwood, Minnesota, with coffee served at Tingvold Church.

The accordion band from the Kringen Klub - Sons of Norway Lodge in Fargo provided entertainment at the opening session on Friday.

Friday evening, "Plain Hearts," a series of vignettes, explored the life of prairie women from the 1850s through the 1920s.

The banquet and bunad parade on Saturday evening were followed by jokes and music by Tennessee Ernie Fjord & Company.

Genealogy Room

Hadeland Lag Annual Meeting

The meeting was called to order by President Jan Heusinkveld. 46 Hadeland Lag members registered at the *stevne*. Hans Næss attended as the invited guest of the lag.
- Verlyn Anderson reported that he and Evonne had been in Norway recently and attended the May 28 *stevne* of the Hadeland Lag in Norway.
- The lag reached the 500-member milestone with 507 member units.
- Work has begun on the centennial history book.
- Hadeland Lag of America, Inc. was officially incorporated as a non-profit organization in Minnesota.

After lunch, Hans Næss presented "Recollections of My Experiences during World War II."

Fall Meeting October 20, 2007
Norskedalen Nature and Heritage Center, Coon Valley, Wisconsin

During the meeting there was a lively discussion regarding the proposed closure of the Norwegian Consulate in Minneapolis, and the members voted to direct President Heusinkveld to send a letter to the Consul General opposing this action.

The regular business meeting was followed by a presentation by Ole Gamme. Following a buffet lunch, Blaine Hedberg from the Norwegian-American Genealogical Center-Naeseth Library in Madison provided an overview of this organization. Saturday evening members gathered for dinner at the Days Inn in La Crosse.

Blaine Hedberg of NAGC-NL

7-Lag Stevne July 16 – 19, 2008
Theme: "Land, Logging, Legends"
Ramada Stevens Point Hotel & Conference Center, Stevens Point, Wisconsin

The *stevne* began after lunch on Wednesday with a tour of Portage County that included stops at the Nelsonville Mill, Reflections Antiques, a century farm, and South New Hope Lutheran Church. The tour concluded with a Norwegian meatball supper at the Nelsonville Lutheran Church. That evening at the conference center the movie "Sweet Land" was screened.

The *stevne* opening session was Thursday morning. It included a presentation on "Logging: A Visit to the 1870s Pineries of Central Wisconsin with Lumberjack Louie" and the traditional welcomes by lag presidents and local elected officials. It also featured music and comedy by *"Aslak og Engebret."* This was followed by a full schedule of classes. The genealogy room was open all day. The vendor area offered an enticing collection of books, clothing, and gift items. Thursday evening the 1945 film classic "Our Vines Have Tender Grapes" starring Edward G. Robinson was shown.

On Friday evening, banquet entertainment included dancing by *Landingsleiken* from Søndre Land, Norway, and three members of the Twin Cities *Hardingfelalag* who offered wonderful hardanger fiddle music.

One of many classes

Hadeland Lag Annual Meeting
The Saturday morning meeting was attended by 30 Hadeland Lag members.
- Hadeland Lag of America, Inc. has been granted 501(c)3 status by the IRS.
- In June, Verlyn Anderson's work in the Norwegian-American community was recognized by King Harald with the St. Olav's Medal

Following the meeting, a picnic was held in a local park with Landingslag.

Fall Meeting
Norwegian-Minnesotan Sesquicentennial Celebration October 18, 2008
Rochester City Library and the Marriott Hotel, Rochester, Minnesota

A brief meeting was held at the Rochester Public Library on Saturday morning at the

Rochester Public Library on Saturday morning. The 2010 Norway trip was discussed.

In the afternoon members joined the gathering at the Marriott Hotel for the recognition of Minnesota's Statehood Pioneers. The Hadeland Lag took the lead in organizing and underwriting this event.

The festivities included interesting educational displays, vendors, music, and remarks that made the past come alive. A memorial service recognized Norwegian pioneers who lived in Minnesota before it became a state in 1858. A cash bar reception preceded the evening banquet and musical entertainment,

Saluting the Colors

7-Lag Stevne July 25 – 28, 2009
Theme: "Bridging the Generations"
University Center, University of Wisconsin-River Falls, River Falls, Wisconsin

The *stevne* began on Thursday afternoon with registration, an open house in the genealogy room and a tour of the New Richmond Heritage Center. In the evening *stevne*-goers were treated to a showing of the 1965 movie "Heroes of Telemark."

The opening *stevne* session was Friday morning with greetings by the mayor of River Falls, a UW-RF official, the president of the *Bygdelagenes Fellesraad* and each lag president. This was followed by music from Telemark by Hardanger fiddler Torgeir Straand and folksinger Tone Jorunn Tveito. After a mid morning break the individual lag meetings were held.

On Friday afternoon the genealogy room was open and a variety of classes were scheduled. The Friday evening program featured Jeff Mueller, president of the Midwest Norwegian-American Chamber of Commerce. Music was provided by LeRoy Larson and the Minnesota Scandinavian Ensemble Show Band.

On Saturday there was a full schedule of classes and demonstrations, and the genealogy room was open. A banquet of roast duck and cod was enjoyed on Saturday evening along with the

Lefse Making Demonstration

traditional bunad parade and more music by Torgeir Straand and Tone Tveito. The *stevne* closed Sunday morning with a tour to the *Mindekirken* in Minneapolis, where lag members joined in worship, and the Old Muskego Church on the campus of Luther Seminary in St. Paul.

Hadeland Lag Annual Meeting

41 Hadeland Lag members registered at the *stevne*. The meeting was held on Friday morning.

- A moment of silence was held for Emeritus Advisory Council members Harriet Foss and Leslie Rogne. Harriet passed away on February 26, 2009, and Leslie followed, just weeks before the *stevne*, on June 14, 2009.

Fall Meeting October 17, 2009
Mount Carmel Conference Center, Alexandria MN

29 members attended the meeting. The board announced it was seeking a replacement for Genealogist Dave Gunderson, who had tendered his resignation. In order to protect the valuable genealogical data supplied by *Kontaktforum Hadeland-Amerika* for the website, the lag hired an intellectual property attorney to craft a "Terms of Use" policy. Plans for the centennial in Norway and at the 7-Lag *Stevne* were discussed.

Fall Business Meeting

2010 Hadeland Lag Centennial Year

7-Lag Stevne *July 14 – 17, 2010*
Theme: "Rooted in Norway, Branches Grow"
Winona State University, Winona, Minnesota

Toten Lag, Landingslag, and the Hadeland Lag all celebrated their centennials at the 2010 7-Lag *Stevne*. Presidents Helen Buche, Sandra Hendrickson, and Jan Heusinkveld are shown with their lag banners.

The *stevne* began on Wednesday evening with a time to greet old friends and make new ones with a program by the "Nor Win Singers" in the East Hall.

The opening session included a welcome from Narv Somdahl, NSI chairperson and *stevne* coordinator, singing of the national anthems, and greetings from Winona State University, the *Bygdelagenes Fellesraad*, and each of the seven lag presidents. The session was followed by classes, open genealogy room and a tour to Historic Lanesboro that included attending the play "Enchanted April".

On Friday a tour of Trempealeau County in Wisconsin drew some attendees, while others went to a full schedule of classes and researched genealogy. In the afternoon a tour of the city of Winona was offered.

Friday evening the banquet, bunad parade, and program took place in East Hall. Marilyn Somdahl, president of the *Bygdelagenes Fellesraad*, presented plates to the presidents of each of the centennial lags. The program was put on by "Scandium," a musical group with fiddle & vocal artists.

Hadeland Lag Annual Meeting

Twenty-five lag members attended the annual meeting on Saturday morning.
- A number of changes to the by-laws were approved by membership. Included was designation of the fall meeting as the annual meeting beginning in 2011.
- Norma Gilbertson was elected to the Emeritus Advisory Council.
- Pictures from the 2010 Centennial visit to Hadeland and extended tour were shown.

Following the meeting, Hadeland Lag, Landingslag, and Toten Lag held a joint **centennial picnic**.

A few of the lag members who attended the Centennial Picnic

Lag Members who attended the 2010 Centennial *Stevne*

Evonne Anderson	Norma Gilbertson	Anne Janda
Verlyn Anderson	Dave Gunderson	James Jones
Delores Cleveland	Jan Heusinkveld	Richard Jones
Susan Cooper	Manfred Hill	Karen Kruse
Elaine Dalager	Dale Hovland	Irene Navarre

Gene Nelson	Donald Olson	Anne Sladky
Lavonne Norby	LaRee Opdahl	Carol Sorum
Jennifer Oien	Loren Opdahl	Dean Sorum
John Oien	David Pfeffer	Beverly Spande
DeLos Olson	Barb Schmitt	Helen Thompson

Centennial Banquet July 17, 2010

On Saturday evening, Hadeland Lag, Landingslag, and Toten Lag came together for a joint centennial banquet. The keynote speaker for the event was Verlyn Anderson, "Discovering Your Heritage through Active Lag Participation." The comedy duo of Dave Olson and Dave Fischer kept banquet-goers laughing, and the evening ended with musical selections by singer Nancy Bollingberg.

Centennial Banquet-Goers

Evonne Anderson	Manfred Hill	Jennifer Oien
Verlyn Anderson	Dale Hovland	John Oien
Delores Cleveland	Irene Navarre	DeLos Olson
Susan Cooper	Anne Janda	Donald Olson
Elaine Dalager	James Jones	David Pfeffer
Norma Gilbertson	Richard Jones	Barb Schmitt
Jan Heusinkveld	Karen Kruse	Anne Sladky

Carol Sorum
Dean Sorum

Beverly Spande
Helen Thompson

Fall Meeting *October 16, 2010*
Afton House Inn, Afton, Minnesota and Super 8 Motel, Hudson, Wisconsin

On a sunny fall day the Centennial Celebration came to an end. 30 lag members enjoyed a brunch cruise on the St. Croix.

After the cruise, activity moved to the Super 8 in Hudson, Wisconsin (the hometown of the lag's first president Thomas Walby) for the business meeting. The *Kontaktforum* database now includes over 10,000 emigrants. New board member Sharon Peterson was elected to the board of directors. The meeting adjourned at 3:30 p.m.

The plate presented by the *Bygdelagenes Fellesraad* and other centennial gifts from Hadeland were on display. Coffee and conversation followed the meeting.

Members enjoyed the brunch cruise on the St. Croix

Business was conducted in Hudson WI

Lag Members and guests who attended the 2010 Fall Meeting

John & Joanna Aamodt
Verlyn & Evonne Anderson
Loren & Marlene Balkan
Eric Beastrom
Lee & Marie Brown
Delores Cleveland
Norma Gilbertson

Ralph & Mary Halbert
Jan Heusinkveld
Dale Hovland
DeLos Olson
Loren & Laree Opdahl
LeRoy & Sharon Peterson
Kristen Rusten

Øystein Rusten
Barb Schmitt
Dean & Carol Sorum
Tom & Carol Vind
Betty Volney
Jean Woog

Chapter Six
The Hadeland Lag Heritage Collection

The Hadeland Lag has been presented with lovely gifts commemorating visits to Hadeland and lag anniversaries from our friends in Hadeland. Over the years, the lag has also received gifts from its members and the *Bygdelagenes Fellesraad*. A few of these items are usually displayed at each fall meeting.

Heritage Collection

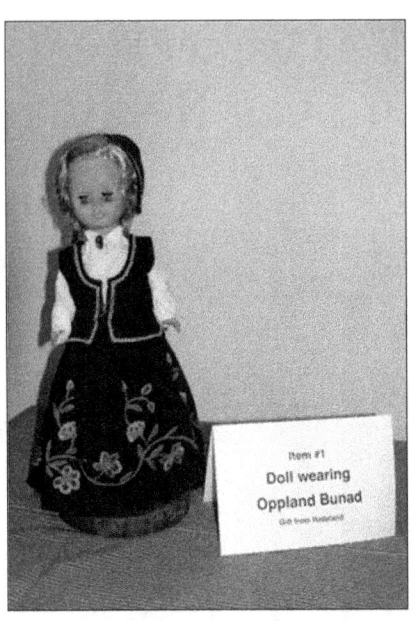

Heritage Collection

Item #3
Glass Vase
Hadeland Lag, 1910-1980
Gift from Hadeland

Item #4
Glass Bell
Hadeland Lag 75th Anniversary, Sept. 7, 1910-1985
Gift from Gran, Jevnaker and Lunner Kommuner

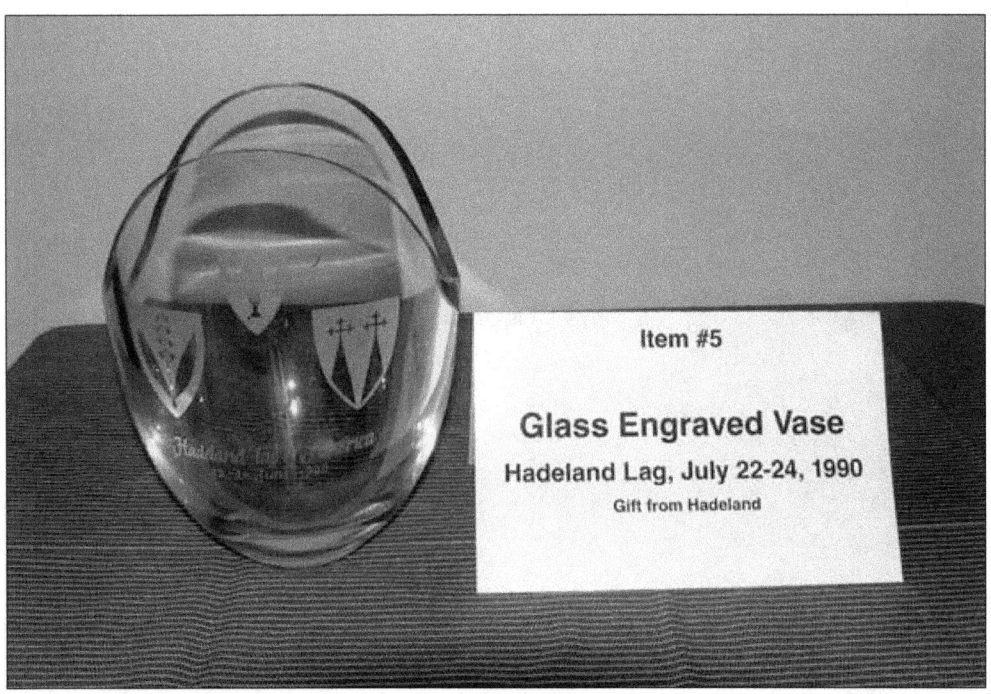

Item #5

Glass Engraved Vase

Hadeland Lag, July 22-24, 1990

Gift from Hadeland

Item #6

Covered Glass Goblet

Hadeland Lag, 2000

Gift from Hadeland

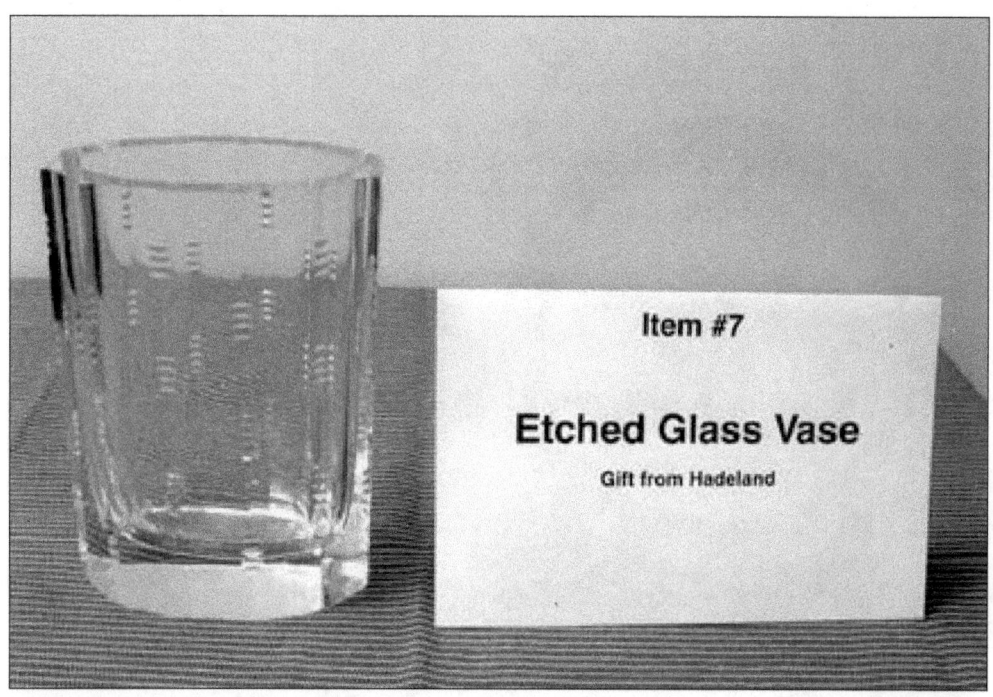

Heritage Collection

Item #9
Hilsen fra Hadelandslaget
in Norge Plate
Organized April 14, 1926
Gift to Hadelandslaget, U.S.A., 1976
from Hadelandslaget in Oslo

Item #10
USA-Norge Plate
1982
Gift from Hadeland

Heritage Collection

Item #11

Sister Churches Plate

Gift to Morgan Olson from Lunner Music Association, 1982

Item #12

Sister Churches Plate

Gift from Hadeland

Heritage Collection

Heritage Collection

Plaques bearing the Royal Norwegian Coat of Arms and the Coat of Arms of Oppland County were given to the lag by members Ralph and Mary Halbert

Plate given in recognition of the Hadeland Lag centennial in 2010 by the *Bygdelagenes Fellesraad*

The Hadeland Lag Banner

1957 Banner

The original Hadeland Lag banner (or *fane* in Norwegian) was unveiled at the 1957 stevne and reported in the local newspaper as follows:

From the *Madison (SD) Daily,* Friday, June 14, 1957
As reprinted in the *Brua,* May 1987

Hard work and a longstanding dream were fulfilled Thursday afternoon when the Hadelands Laget banner was unveiled at the annual convention in the Park Hotel. The assembly in the Hotel Park dining room burst into applause as the veil was pulled aside.

Hand painted on a dark blue background was the Norwegian national emblem, a shield bearing a lion rampart backed by the Norwegian flag. Arched over the emblem was 'Hadelandslaget' and the date of its founding, 1910. Below was the motto 'Enig og Tro' which means 'united and faithful.'

The reverse side of the banner was cream-colored silk and centered with the Lutheran symbol *(rose)* and motto "God is our heritage." Both sides of the banner were decorated with rosemaling, a type of Norwegian art painting. Handwork on the flag was done by Laura Hjelle Hoeg, Decorah, Iowa.

The gilt flagpole was topped by a hand carved Norse battle ax and the cross bars were tipped with spearheads, also hand-carved. A case had been made for the flag by Mrs. Hans Aschim. It was also decorated in rosemaling by Mrs. Hoeg.

Mrs. Alfred Sivesin, Mabel Minn., who was in charge of having the banner made, explained the symbols to the group. She was dressed in a Norwegian costume which she had made herself and was detailed with beadwork, crochet, and embroidery.

The Hadelands Laget was started in Minneapolis in 1910 by immigrants from the Hadeland district of Norway, a farming district about 40 English miles north of Oslo, the capital. The principle crops are rye and potatoes.

Rev. Ernest Nelson, main speaker for the afternoon, spoke on contributions of the Norwegian heritage to the American way of life. He concluded his talk in Norwegian.

The Hadelands Laget banquet will be held at 6 p.m. today. O. H. Olseth is scheduled to be main speaker. Melvin Juel, Canton, will sing a solo. The Norse Glee Club of Sioux Falls is to give a concert. The glee club is directed by Mr. Adolph Tideman.

In 1977, Harriet Foss made a "Welcome Banner" to honor the arrival of the *Mannskor K.K.* from Hadeland. This banner featured the Sister Churches on one side and a woman wearing a Hadeland bunad on the other. The whereabouts of the 1977 banner is unknown.

In 2006, Jan Heusinkveld created a new banner for the lag based on the original design. Beneath rosemaling and gold fringe, "Hadelandslaget" and "1910" hark back to the beginning of the lag. The Norwegian national emblem again forms the centerpiece of the banner, with the motto "*Enig og Tro*" beneath it.

Added to the bottom of the cream-colored banner are the coats of arms of the three *kommuner* that comprise the Hadeland region: Gran, Jevnaker, and Lunner.

The Meaning of *"Enig og Tro"*

"Enig og Tro" means, literally, "united and true (faithful/loyal)." That is certainly a fitting motto for an organization that dedicates itself to uniting people from the U.S., Canada, and Norway with a common interest in their shared heritage, and is committed to helping its members learn about – and keep faith with – the immigrant ancestors who had called Hadeland home.

Over the years, many lag members have wondered about the origin of the motto. The following is based on an article written by E. Palmer Rockswold and published in the February 1989 *Brua*.

Although Denmark had attempted to maintain official neutrality during the Napoleonic Wars, it had repeatedly demonstrated that its sympathies lay with France. On the other hand, Sweden had joined Russia, Prussia, and Austria in defeating Napoleon at the Battle of Liepzig. "To the winners go the spoils" - the Treaty of Kiel, signed in January of 1814, transferred control of Norway from Denmark to Sweden.

2006 Banner

As it became clear what the end result of the treaty negotiations would be, the Danish prince who ruled Norway made a last ditch attempt to maintain his position. He called a Constitutional Assembly at Eidsvoll. On the 25th of February in 1814, each church parish elected delegates who took an oath to risk "life and blood" to defend Norway's independence.

On Easter Sunday, April 10, 1814, 112 men gathered at Eidsvoll and created a Norwegian Constitution. Since Norway had no native royal family, the Danish prince, Christian Frederik, was (as he had hoped) elected king. On the last day of the assembly, May 20, 1814, the delegates formed a large circle, clasped hands and swore allegiance to the Constitution in the name of the mighty Dovre mountains, pledging in unison, *"Enig og tro til Dovre Faller!"* In English, "United and True until Dovre Falls!"

Unfortunately, outnumbered by vastly superior Swedish military forces, the Norwegians had to give up on complete independence. Swedish Prince Carl Johan became the new monarch of Norway, but the political union with Sweden retained the fundamental ideas contained in the Eidsvoll constitution signed on May 17, 1814. That is why *Syttende Mai* is celebrated by Norwegians and their descendants everywhere – including the U.S.A. and Canada – and explains the significance of the motto found on the Lag's banner.

Chapter Seven
Kontaktforum Hadeland-Amerika
by Ole P. Gamme and Harald Hvattum

Members of *Kontaktforum* L to R: Ole P. Gamme, Hans M. Næss, Kjell Henrik Myhre, Kirsten Heier Western, Geir Arne Myhrstuen, Harald Hvattum

The *Kontaktforum Hadeland-Amerika* was organized February 4, 2002, as a cooperative project among the Gran Historical Society, Lunner Historical Society, Jevnaker Historical Society and the Hadeland *Folkemuseum*. The *Folkemuseum* has left the project, but it has expanded to include the Vestoppland Genealogical Society and the Hadeland Lag of America.

Purpose
The purpose of the *Kontaktforum Hadeland-Amerika*:

    1) Responsible for managing the Hadeland Lag memberships in Norway and distributing to those members the Hadeland Lag of America's periodical *Brua*;

    2) Responsible for the distribution of the *Årbok for Hadeland*, the *Hadeland Kalendar* and related Hadeland publications to American and Canadian Hadeland members;

3) Responsible for acting as the central agency for genealogical questions, etc. from America to Hadeland and from Hadeland about immigrants and their descendants in America.

4) To collect immigrant letters, periodical articles, books and personal genealogical studies about Hadelanders in America. All collected materials are added to the Hadeland-America Collection in the Hadeland *Folkemuseum*.

Background of the Organization

The Hadeland Lag of America celebrated its 90th anniversary in the year 2000 The Lag wished to celebrate the anniversary in Hadeland and contacted the *Mannskor K.K.*, who together with the *Jevnaker Bygdeungdomslag* (Jevnaker Community Youth Organization) had been the hosts when the Hadeland Lag celebrated its 80th anniversary in Hadeland in 1990. Acting on behalf of *Mannskor K.K.,* Ole P. Gamme contacted the three historical societies in Hadeland, plus the Hadeland Folk Museum, to seek their assistance in planning for the visit of the Americans.

The following committee was formed to plan a week-long program for the Hadeland Lag: Ole P. Gamme, *Mannskor K.K.*; Ole Roen, Jevnaker Historical Society; Hans M. Næss, Kjell H. Myhre and Harald Hvattum, Gran Historical Society; Ester Haga, Lunner Historical Society; and the administrator of the Hadeland Folk Museum. Ole P. Gamme was elected as chair and Harald Hvattum was chosen secretary/treasurer of the planning group.

During this 2000 Lag visit an invitation was made to all Hadelanders to attend the 7-Lag *Stevne* in Rapid City, South Dakota the following year as part of a 14-day tour of America. The planning committee for the American tour in 2000, with the exception of the museum's representative, became the arrangement committee for the American tour in 2001. Ole P. Gamme continued as chair and Harald Hvattum, secretary/treasurer for the tour.

The Hadeland Lag visit in 2000 and the American tour in 2001 created many new contacts. In the local communities of Hadeland as well as in the Hadeland Lag of America, there was a desire to continue this cooperation. Upon the initiative of Ole P. Gamme a project was begun to create a permanent committee who would work with emigration history from Hadeland. After some preliminary meetings the *Kontaktforum Hadeland-Amerika* was organized in February 4, 2002. In the first year it was decided that the Vestoppland Genealogical Society, Hadeland section, should also be represented in the committee. Hans M. Næss has represented that group since 2002.

Reorganization in 2006

The Hadeland Folk Museum unfortunately left the *Kontaktforum* in 2006. The Hadeland Lag of America then became a full cooperative partner.

Working Projects

Recording information about Hadeland emigrants into the Hadeland Emigrant Database

The recording of information on personal data forms about emigrating Hadelanders has been one of the primary tasks of the *Kontaktforum*. The data forms are placed on the Hadeland Lag's website, www.hadelandlag.org, and are available to lag members, using their personal password. An effort has been made to combine the information on the data forms in order to get the most information about each emigrant family assembled onto one family data form. As of April 1, 2010, over 1,440 data forms contain information about almost 10,200 Hadeland emigrants. Ole P. Gamme has, since its inception, been the director of this important project.

The *Rowberg Biographical File* has been an excellent source of information about Hadeland emigrants. An American newspaper man, Andrew A. Rowberg, gathered more than 200,000 clippings of biographical articles about Norwegian-Americans from Norwegian-American newspapers, English language country weeklies, church publications and lodge periodicals during the period from 1914 to 1978. The original file is in the collection of the Norwegian-American Historical Association at St. Olaf College, Northfield, Minnesota. Hans M. Næss has searched through a microfilm copy of the entire collection and has retrieved the information about emigrants from Hadeland. This valuable information has been recorded on the data forms in the Hadeland Emigrant Database.

Many Hadeland Lag members from the United States, Canada and Norway have submitted information about their families and also about other families who emigrated from Hadeland. *Tusen takk* to all of you! Without your participation this project would not have been so successful.

Answering genealogical questions and other service tasks

In connection with visits to Hadeland by descendants of emigrant Hadelanders, the members of the *Kontaktforum* have been helpful through the years in assisting visiting Americans and Canadians with their family research, recommending Hadeland hotels for their stay, helping to locate distant relatives who live in Hadeland and taking them to places where their ancestors lived before they left for America.

The periodical Brua: the membership newspaper of the Hadeland Lag of America

The *Kontaktforum* has assumed responsibility for recording memberships, collecting subscriptions and distributing the *Brua* to Norwegian members. At the end of 2010 the Hadeland Lag had 97 members in Norway. Harald Hvattum is responsible for recording memberships.

The America visits in 2005 and 2010

The *Kontaktforum* has had the pleasure of being the host for the visits of the members of the Hadeland Lag to Hadeland in 2005 and 2010.

The Committee in 2010

The *Kontaktforum Hadeland-Amerika* committee members in 2010 were Ole P. Gamme (Hadeland Lag of America), chair; Kjell Henrik Myhre (Gran Historical Society); Kirsten Heier Western (Lunner Historical Society), Geir Arne Myhrstuen (Jevnaker Historical Society) and Hans M. Næss (Vestoppland Genealogical Society, Hadeland section). Secretary/treasurer is Harald Hvattum.

Ole P. Gamme has been the chair since the beginning. Myhre, Næss and Hvattum have also been members since the beginning. Kåre Myhrstuen became a committee member in 2002; however, his son, Geir Arne, is currently the Jevnaker Historical Society's representative.

Kontaktforum Hadeland-Amerika

The Historical Societies of Hadeland

By Harald Hvattum

The Hadeland Lag is delighted to have developed a close working relationship with the historical societies of Hadeland, and believes that these associations strengthen the lag's ability to serve its members.

Lunner Historical Society

Lunner Historielag was founded in 1975 by a small group of people who wanted to give the past a future. The purpose of the society has been to collect and preserve oral and written accounts about life and work in Lunner, traditions and habits of times past, and everything else that could be of historical interest. The society also hopes to register and preserve all historical and cultural memorials and monuments to the extent possible, and in this way support museums, collections and scientific research. The society now has about 100 members.

For a few years a lot of work has been done to register old places of habitation in Lunner. The plan is to display information, pictures, and GPS map coordinates of these places. Many of these old places of habitation and tenant farms belonged to families that emigrated to America in the 1800s.

The Lunner Historical Society also arranges numerous meetings and tours throughout the year. Good speakers pay visits, and the society take trips to places of historical or cultural interests.

We extend a welcome to everybody to visit its website: www.lunnerhistorielag.net

Gran Historical Society

Gran Historielag was founded in 1976. The aim of the association is to promote interest in our community's history and traditional culture. This is done by collecting, preserving and underwriting the publication of works based on written as well as oral sources that describe traditions of daily and working life, common practice and usage of previous times, plus anything which may be considered to be of historical interest.

The organization has established the practice of arranging several guided excursions, and lectures by significant speakers.

The Gran Historical Society is particularly pleased and proud of its key role in bringing the legendary Peder Nelson's precious collection of books from Northwood, North

Dakota, to Gran in 1999. The unique collection of more than 3.000 titles is of national value. It was donated to Gran *Historielag* by Peder Nelson's good friend, Mrs. Harriet Foss.

The Gran Historical Society assisted in the creation of, and plays an active role in the work of *Kontaktforum Hadeland-Amerika*. In an amazingly short time, this project has become the most comprehensive effort our organization has ever undertaken. It also has great historical significance!

For further information on Gran *Historielag*, please visit our website www.gran.historielag.org

Jevnaker Historical Society

Jevnaker Historielag was founded in 1971 and has grown from 65 members in 1972 to over 200 today. The society works actively in the preservation of cultural history and places of historical interest.

One of the historical society's most notable projects has been the restoration and preservation of *Drengestua*" (the farmworkers' house) at Jevnaker parsonage. It was formally opened 29 November 1985 and has been the location for meetings since that time. It has become a useful and important center for the activities of the Historical Society.

We also want to mention the restoration of the Roen Bridge in Sløvika, the purchase of airplane pictures, rephotographing of old photographs, identifying and preserving places of cultural and historical interest, recording homestead names, registering cemetery memorials and monuments, and restoring and rebuilding the tenant farm Tosobråtan for Toso school's outdoor activities. Website: www.jevnaker.kommune.no

Chapter Eight
Officers of the Hadeland Lag 1990-2010

Election of officers is an important agenda item at each annual meeting. Prior to 2005, the membership elected the board of directors and the board elected its executive officers (president, vice president, secretary, and treasurer). The webmaster, genealogist, and *Brua* editor were also elected board members. Past presidents served on the board, but only the immediate past president had voting privileges.

Beginning in 2005, direct election of the executive committee by the membership was mandated in the new corporate by-laws. Board-appointed officers (genealogist, webmaster, and editor of the *Brua*) were also given voice and vote. Four elected directors and the immediate past president now round out the voting membership of the board.

Historically, attendance at the fall meeting is higher than it is at the lag meeting at the stevne. In 2010, the membership voted to designate the fall meeting as the organization's annual meeting. As a result, beginning in 2011, election of officers will no longer take place during the *stevne*.

"The History of the Hadeland Lag 1910-1990" lists all of the officers who served the Hadeland Lag during its first 80 years. That list continues here with officers who served between 1990 and 2010.

President		Vice-President	
E. Palmer Rockswold	1986-1992	Olaf Nelson	1987-1993
Vacant	1992-1995	Robert Rosendahl	1993-1995
Robert Rosendahl	1995-2002	Manfred Hill	1995-2004
Delores Cleveland	2002-2006	Janice Heusinkveld	2004-2006
Janice Heusinkveld	2006-	Anne Sladky	2006-

Secretary – Recording Secretary – Corresponding Secretary			
Harriet Foss*	1975-2001	Anne Sladky	2002-2005
Alfie Erlien	1992-1993	Norma Gilbertson	2005-2010
Norma Gilbertson	1993-2002	Anne Janda	2010-

*Harriet Foss served as a "corresponding secretary" during the last years of her involvement, with Alfie Erlien and Norma Gilbertson serving as "recording secretaries" during that time.

Treasurer		Genealogist	
Dean Sorum	1990-2002	Leslie Rogne	1987-2004
Ron Ulven	2002-2007	Wendy Winkelman	2004-2006
David Pfeffer	2007-	David Gunderson	2006-2009

Officers of the Hadeland Lag

Editor of the *Brua*		Webmaster	
E. Palmer Rockswold	1986-1992	Anne Sladky	2002-
Verlyn Anderson	1992-		

Directors

Margaret Wilson	1989-1992	Byron Schmid	2005-2007
Michael Miller	1989-1992	Gloria Cooper	2005-2008
Paul Grinager	1984-2001	DeLos Olson	2005-
Betty Volney	1998-2004	Anne Janda	2007-2010
Janice Heusinkveld	2002-2004	Barb Schmitt	2008-
Carol Sorum	2004-	Sharon Peterson	2010-

1992 Board of Directors

Margaret Wilson, Olaf Nelson, Verlyn Anderson, Harriet Foss, E. Palmer Rockswold   Seated: Ellef Erlien

Board Meeting – Fall 2005

Clockwise from left: Verlyn Anderson, Gloria Cooper, Anne Sladky, Delores Cleveland, DeLos Olson, Carol Sorum, Jan Heusinkveld, Norma Gilbertson, Ron Ulven, Wendy Winkelman, Byron Schmid

Biographies

Janice Ann Heusinkveld
President since 2006

Janice Ann (Hawley) Heusinkveld was born on December 27, 1936 in Delavan, Minnesota. She was confirmed at Our Savior's Lutheran Church in Spring Valley, Minnesota in 1951, and graduated from Spring Valley High School in 1954. She was married in 1954 and has four daughters: Dawn, Sherry, Laurie and Lisa. In 1971 she was divorced, and went back to school to study accounting and computer programming. She graduated in 1974 with a degree from ICS. In 1975 she moved to Rochester, Minnesota and went to work at the Mayo Clinic in Rochester, Minnesota. On May 17, 2003 she retired from the Information Services Department there.

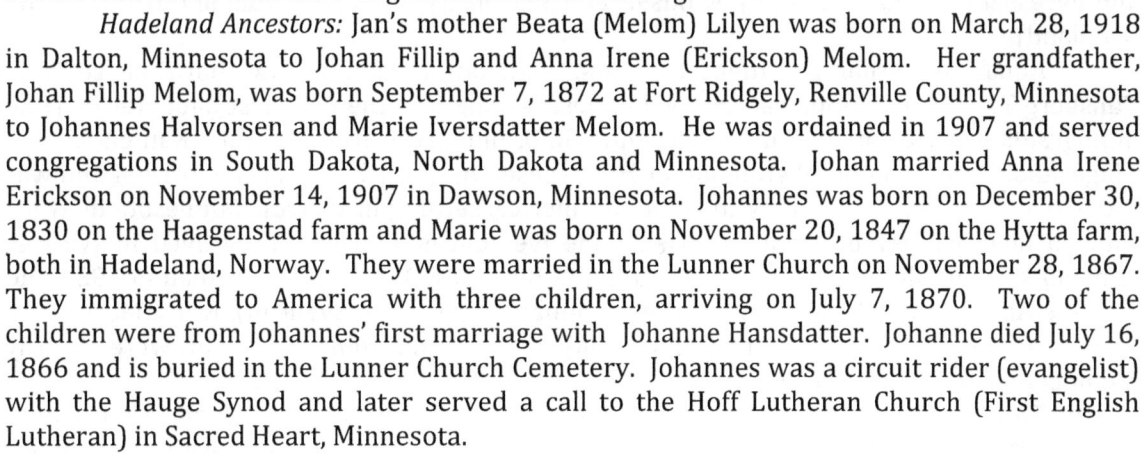

She is active in Hadeland Lag, Sons of Norway, and Toastmasters. Jan enjoys sewing, bowling and traveling.

Along with the wide-ranging responsibilities of lag president, her contributions to the lag include helping develop the corporate by-laws and acting as the lag's incorporator, designing and crafting the lag's current banner, and planning and coordinating the centennial events associated with the 7-Lag *Stevne* and fall meeting.

Hadeland Ancestors: Jan's mother Beata (Melom) Lilyen was born on March 28, 1918 in Dalton, Minnesota to Johan Fillip and Anna Irene (Erickson) Melom. Her grandfather, Johan Fillip Melom, was born September 7, 1872 at Fort Ridgely, Renville County, Minnesota to Johannes Halvorsen and Marie Iversdatter Melom. He was ordained in 1907 and served congregations in South Dakota, North Dakota and Minnesota. Johan married Anna Irene Erickson on November 14, 1907 in Dawson, Minnesota. Johannes was born on December 30, 1830 on the Haagenstad farm and Marie was born on November 20, 1847 on the Hytta farm, both in Hadeland, Norway. They were married in the Lunner Church on November 28, 1867. They immigrated to America with three children, arriving on July 7, 1870. Two of the children were from Johannes' first marriage with Johanne Hansdatter. Johanne died July 16, 1866 and is buried in the Lunner Church Cemetery. Johannes was a circuit rider (evangelist) with the Hauge Synod and later served a call to the Hoff Lutheran Church (First English Lutheran) in Sacred Heart, Minnesota.

Anne Sladky
Webmaster since 2002; Vice President since 2006

Anne Sladky was born November 1, 1951 to parents Gerald Grover and Ruby (Alm) Grover. She grew up on a farm outside Moorhead, Minnesota. Anne attended college for two years before joining the Navy in 1971. In the Navy, Anne was sent to data processing school and programming classes. After her discharge she stayed in Washington DC and worked in telecommunications and computer operating system support. She and her first husband,

William Taylor, returned to Minnesota after their marriage in 1977. Their daughter Arielle was born in 1979 and son Graham in 1980. Anne and William were divorced in 1984.

Anne and her children moved to the Twin Cities in the late 1980s, where she worked as a systems analyst and consultant. She eventually joined the Minnesota Dept. of Human Services as a senior analyst and team leader. Along the way Anne has been a church organist and piano teacher and completed her college degree. In 2000 she remarried and retired to Walker, Minnesota with her second husband, Steven Sladky. Since that time, she has become a volunteer webmaster for a number of non-profit organizations - first and foremost, the Hadeland Lag.

Anne's contributions to the lag include developing and maintaining the lag website, helping to develop and implement the corporate by-laws, and implementing the website's Terms of Use. She also was the primary editor of this centennial history.

Hadeland Ancestors: John Anderson Kroshus left the Molstad farm in Gran with his wife Marie and daughter Oleanna in 1850. Kari Pedersdtr was born on Gudmundshagen in Tingelstad and emigrated from Dvergsten with her husband Hans Pedersen and daughter Randi in 1851. John and Kari married in Wisconsin in 1852 after the deaths of Maria, Hans and Randi. John and Kari's daughter Pauline is Anne's paternal great-grandmother. The rest of Anne's paternal ancestors came from Skafså, Vinje and Fyresdal (Telemark County), Krodsherad (Buskerud), and Sør Aurdal and Nordre Land (Oppland).

Anne's maternal grandmother, Anne Iversdatter Kanten, was born in 1872 in Tunsberg Township, Chippewa County, Minnesota. She was the youngest daughter of 1864 immigrants Iver Halvorson Kanten and Anne Gulbrandsdatter from the Hole-Kanten farm in Tingelstad. Anne's maternal grandfather Hans Olesen Alm was born in Gran in 1864 and was the first in his immediate family to come to America, settling in Watson, Minnesota in 1885. Hans, a housepainter by trade, married Anne Iversdatter in 1890. They lived in Watson, Ashland WI, and McHenry ND before settling in Binford ND in 1905. Hans died in 1931 and his wife Anne died in 1957. Hans and his siblings Randi (Evan Svenrud), Erick, Mary (John Moe), Martia (Erik Rekstad), Oline (John Olson), and Johanna (Henry Paulsrud) were all early members of the Hadeland Lag.

Through her Telemark ancestry, Anne is an 8th cousin of Queen Sonja. That distant connection isn't likely to get her an invitation to the palace, but it is an interesting twig in her family tree.

Anne Janda
Secretary since 2010

Anne Louise Peterson is the daughter of Maurice Alton Peterson and Agnes Louise Olin. She grew up in Burnett County, Wisconsin and attended Normandale Community College and the University of Wisconsin-Eau Claire. Anne married Mark Janda in 1981. They have two children: Elizabeth and Andrew. She is the Campus Director for the Village Shores

Senior Campus, which provides both independent and assisted living units to those age 55 and over. Her interests include family stories (anyone's story!) weaving, writing and the creative arts.

Anne joined the board in 2007, and accepted the secretary's position in 2010. She played a key role in planning and presenting the Norwegian Statehood Pioneer Project's Sesquicentennial celebration.

Hadeland Ancestors: Anne Olsdatter was born February 10, 1846, at Næseiet, Brandbu. She and Andreas Monson, who was born in Oslo, had three children in Norway before Andreas came to America in 1881. Anne, her mother Kari Pedersdatter, and her children Ole, Albert, and Johan Martin immigrated from Røkeneiet to Minneapolis in 1882. A daughter, Kari, was born in Minneapolis in 1883 and died in 1885, as did Johan Martin. Anne and Andreas had two more children in America. Kari (Karen) was born in Minneapolis in 1885 and John was born in West Marshland, Burnett County, Wisconsin in 1888.

Andreas and Anne's daughter Karen married John Cheney Olin in Grantsburg, Wisconsin in 1919. Karen and John had two daughters: Anne Janda's mother Agnes Louise, who was born in 1923 and Josephine Harriet (1925-2004).

David Pfeffer
Treasurer since 2007

Joe and Alma Pfeffer had five children. Their son **David Pfeffer** was born in rural Bertha, Minnesota in 1935. He would graduate from Bertha High School and attend St. John's University and the University of Texas, El Paso, graduating from the University of Minnesota in 1961. His military days were with the U.S. Army in Arkansas and Texas. During his working years he worked for Tonka Toys, became a CPA and had a career as a college and school business administrator.

David lives in the Twin City metro area near Maple Plain and is the father of three children. Dan, Nicole, their spouses and children live a short distance from his home. His daughter Rebecca passed away in 2008.

David joined the Hadeland Lag in 2005, and was appointed to complete treasurer Ron Ulven's term in 2007. He was elected to the position by the membership in 2008. David worked with the law firm Nikolai and Mersereau to develop the Terms of Use Agreement for the lag's website.

Hadeland Ancestors: Some ninety plus years ago Alma Kittelson began teaching in School District 255 in Woodside Township which is located in southeastern Otter Tail County, Minnesota. During her two years at this country school she met Joe Pfeffer, a son of local farmer George and his wife Thresia. Joe and Alma would marry in 1920. Alma's parents Anton and Sophie were children of Norwegian emigrants from Norway. Anton's parents Hans and Bertha (Stenbek) Bustul were from the

Numedal Valley in Buskerud. Sophie's parents Ole O. and Anne (Teslo) Hovland were from Hadeland. The Hovlands had come to America in 1867 and the Bustuls had come in 1870. Joe's parents left Bohemia in 1891.

Carol Christine (Orser) Sorum
Membership Secretary since 1990, Director since 2004

Carol Christine (Orser) Sorum was born in Garske, North Dakota on January 5, 1932. She is a Hadelander by marriage. Carol's maternal grandfather was born in Surnadal and her mother's grandparents immigrated from Telemark. Carol's paternal ancestors were from Holland.

When Carol was less than a year old she moved with her family to Colgate, North Dakota where she grew up, attended school and graduated from high school. She attended the University of North Dakota in Grand Forks, North Dakota, where she met and married Harold Dean Sorum in August 1953. She graduated in June of 1954 with a Bachelor of Science degree in Professional Chemistry. While attending the University she became a member of several honor societies including Phi Beta Kappa and Sigma Zi.

In 1957 the Sorum family moved to Moorhead, Minnesota where Carol continued her education attending Moorhead State University where she received a Bachelor of Science and a Bachelor of Arts degree in Science and Math Education. She began her teaching career in 1958. Carol taught for one year before retiring when her third and then a fourth child were born. In 1963 she returned to college at North Dakota State University and earned a Masters of Science in Mathematics. Carol joined the staff of South High School in Fargo where she taught chemistry, mathematics and computer programming for the next 28 years, retiring in 1993. After her retirement from teaching she did accounting work at Communication Consultants, Inc. (the firm of which Dean was part owner and president) and also for Allegiance Software (a firm owned by Sorum's oldest daughter and husband).

Carol has been a member of Sweet Adelines, Church Choir, Retired Teachers, Delta Kappa Gamma, and Minnesota Mensa. She is a charter member of the Lutheran Church of Christ the King in Moorhead. Her hobbies are reading, Hardanger embroidery, and computer work.

When her husband Dean took on the Hadeland Lag treasurer's job in 1993 she began keeping the Hadeland Lag membership list. Carol created a digital database for that purpose and has continued as Membership Secretary since Dean's retirement. She was elected to the Board of Directors in her own right in 2004.

DeLos Olson
Director since 2005

DeLos Olson was born on November 3, 1935 on a farm in Chippewa County, Minnesota, one of eight siblings. He was raised in Chippewa and Swift Counties, Minnesota, where he attended several one room rural schools and worked on his parents' farm until 1951. When the farm work was done he worked as a carpenter in Montevideo, Minnesota. In 1956 DeLos moved to Rochester, Minnesota where he received a GED from John Marshall High School in 1960. He then attended Rochester Junior College and worked as a carpenter. He graduated from Rochester Junior College in 1963 with an Associate of Arts in Business Administration degree.

After working as a carpenter in Rochester for 10 years, DeLos went to work for the City of Rochester in 1966. In 1967 he married Frances Karen McCutcheon in Rochester. They have one son, Byron, and a daughter, Kirstin.

DeLos was a member of the Minnesota Army National Guard. He joined "A" Battery of the 175th Field Artillery Battalion in Montevideo in 1953. In 1958 he transferred to an infantry unit and then in 1977 to a medical unit. He attended an Academy of Health Sciences sponsored by the U.S. Army in Fort Sam Houston, Texas and graduated from the U.S. Army Command and General Staff College at Fort Leavenworth, Kansas. DeLos retired as a major after 26 years of service. In 1996 he retired from the Public Works Department of the City of Rochester as Collection System Supervisor.

DeLos lost his battle with cancer as this book was prepared for publication, on December 28, 2011 in Rochester.

He was a member of Bethel Lutheran Church, where he has served on the council; Sons of Norway Kristiania Lodge, where he is a past president; Boy Scouts, where he has served in many areas including Scout Master; Hadeland Lag; Nordlandslaget; American Legion; Vesterheim Norwegian-American Museum; Rochester Senior Citizen Services; Rochester Civil War Round Table; and Rochester Woodcarvers Club.

DeLos served as chairman of the history and heritage committee, and was responsible for managing the vendor area at the 7-Lag *Stevne* from 2006 - 2010.

Hadeland Ancestors: Alvin and Ingeborg (Raffelson) Olson were DeLos' parents. They married on December 2, 1899 in Chippewa County, Minnesota. Alvin's mother Karen Karlson came from Lunner to Minnesota about 1909. She was the daughter of Karl Johan Andersen of Jevnaker. Ingeborg's parents were Anton Edvart Raffelson and Julia Emilia Laumb. This maternal line came from Nordland and Nanstad in Norway, respectively.

Barb Schmitt
Director since 2008

Barb (Helstedt) Schmitt has been a member of the Hadeland Lag since 2003. She was born in Minot, North Dakota and attended high school and college there, graduating in 1981 with a degree in Business Administration. After college, she was a youth director at a church in Detroit Lakes, Minnesota, and then moved to the Twin Cities where she has worked in the accounting department at Intercim, a small software company in Eagan for 24 years. She enjoys genealogy, vacationing with her husband Pete, reading and walking.

Barb and Pete went to Norway with the Hadeland Lag in 2005 where they met her relative Ester Haga who was a member of the *Kontaktforum* and was living on the Haga farm in Lunner. It was truly the trip of a lifetime. They were again able to participate in the Lag's Norway trip in 2010 and were thrilled to celebrate the lag's centennial in Hadeland. Barb was elected to the Board in 2008 and serves as a *Bygdelagenes Fellesraad* delegate.

Hadeland Ancestors: Barb's paternal grandmother, Luella Haga, was the daughter of Carl Haga (born 1871 in Lunner) and Amanda Sherva (1883). Gudmund Johnsen Haga (born 1843 in Lunner) and Eli Halvorsdtr Rya (born 1844 in Lunner) immigrated to the U.S. in 1871, settling in Northwood, North Dakota in 1879 where they raised their 10 children. Their son Carl and his wife Amanda homesteaded in Bergen ND in 1902. Amanda Sherva's parents, Anders Andersen Sherva (born 1836 in Gran) and Ingeborg Christiansdtr Sherva (born 1840 in Lunner) immigrated to the U.S. in 1870 and settled in Northwood, where they raised their family of 11 children.

Sharon Peterson
Director since 2010

All of **Sharon (Jorgenson) Peterson**'s ancestors came from Norway. She was born in Monroe, Wisconsin and grew up with two brothers on a farm near Darlington, Wisconsin. The family also lived near Wiota, Wisconsin, which was an early Norwegian settlement.

Sharon attended a one room school for eight years. After graduating from Darlington High School she attended St. Olaf College and earned a degree in Spanish Education. For the

first thirty years of her career she taught high school and middle school Spanish in New York and Wisconsin. In 2004, she changed hats when she returned to college and began to work with English Language Learners. She has been an ESL (English as a Second Language) teacher since 2004, and in 2010 she began teaching bilingual (English and Spanish) students in K, 1, 2, and 3.

She and her husband LeRoy live on a farm outside Rock Springs, Wisconsin. LeRoy is a retired wildlife biologist. They have two adult daughters. Emily, a graduate of UW-Whitewater, lives in Janesville. Sarah lives in Minneapolis and is a graduate of Augsburg College.

Sharon's favorite pastimes are reading, walking, traveling, and searching for Norwegian ancestors. In 2010 she and LeRoy went to Norway as part of the centennial tour. During the first week in Hadeland Sharon met several cousins, including Hilde Liråk and Anders Holmstykket. Next time she visits, she hopes to meet more cousins!

Hadeland Ancestors: Sharon's Hadeland connection is her mother's grandparents. Kjersti Jensdatter was born on Holmstykket in Jevnaker in 1863 and came to America in

1885. In 1887 she married Hans Iverson (Henry Everson) at Wiota, Wisconsin. He was born on Moeseiet in Jevnaker in 1848 and came to America with his parents in 1852. Kjersti died in 1896 and Hans remarried in 1899 to Berthe Ottesen, a native of Toten.

Lars Larsen Skattum (1854-1924) was born on Skirstadeiet in Gran. In 1875 he married Maren Andersdatter, who was born on Hovseiet in Tingelstad. They brought their children Anders and Berte Marie to America in 1882 and settled in Lafayette County, Wisconsin.

Dr. Verlyn Anderson
Brua Editor since 1992

Verlyn Anderson was born on October 23, 1933 to Arthur O. Anderson and Cora Orvetta (Hovland) Anderson in Fergus Falls, Minnesota. He grew up on a farm in rural Rothsay in Otter Tail County, Minnesota. He graduated from Rothsay High School in Rothsay, Minnesota in 1952. His college career includes: a Bachelor of Arts in History and English from Concordia College, Moorhead, Minnesota in 1956; a Masters of Arts in English from the University of Minnesota in 1962; Masters of Arts in Library Science from the University of Minnesota in 1965; and a Ph.D. in American Studies from the University of Minnesota in 1972.

Dr. Anderson began his teaching career as an elementary and high school teacher of English and Latin and school librarian in 1954. In 1962 he became the college librarian for Concordia College. From 1968 until his retirement in 1998 he served as director of that library. He was also Professor of Scandinavian Studies and History at Concordia from 1968 to 1998. On three occasions (1983, 1996 & 1999) he was a visiting professor of Scandinavian and American studies in Norway.

Verlyn married Evonne Oretta Beastrom on June 7, 1958. To this union three girls were born: Kristi Luann born on April 18, 1959; Karen Linnae born on August 30, 1961; and Randi Jo born on November 6, 1962.

Verlyn is a nationally recognized authority on the Norwegian-American experience. He is an engaging and sought-after speaker, has led tours for the Smithsonian Institution and served on the boards of national Norwegian-American organizations including the Vesterheim and Norwegian-American Genealogical Center. He contributes his time and talents to the Sons of Norway-Kringen Lodge in Fargo ND as well.

He has been a key member of Hadeland Lag since its revitalization and was elected vice president at the *stevne* in 1976. In 1992 he became the editor of the *Brua*, a position he has held ever since. Of his many contributions over the years, a few are most worthy of note: In 2000, 2005 and 2010 he and his wife Evonne organized and led the Hadeland Lag tours of Hadeland and Norway. He has coordinated a number of *stevner* and is a popular presenter, speaker, and master of ceremonies at these annual events. He was instrumental in developing close ties with Hadeland and the formation of the *Kontaktforum*. Verlyn was a key contributor to and editor of this centennial history.

In 2008 he received the King of Norway's St. Olav Medal for his lifetime of dedication to the strengthening of ties between Norway and Norwegian-Americans.

Hadeland Ancestors: Verlyn's mother Cora Orvetta was born on January 1, 1908 near Columbus, North Dakota and died on February 10, 1992 at Pelican Valley Nursing Home in Pelican Rapids MN. Cora's father Ole was the son of 1870 Hadeland immigrant Nils Hovland and his wife Mari Brørby. Mari, brother Jorgen and their parents Anders and Anne Brørby emigrated from Sondre Brørby, Jevnaker in 1868. Cora's mother Karen Ohe was the granddaughter of 1869 Hadeland immigrant Lars Olsen Ohe and his wife Ingeborg Torgersdtr Vaterud.

Verlyn's father Arthur was born on March 27, 1909 to Ole and Randa (Tessem) Anderson in Trondhjem Township, Otter Tail County, Minnesota. He died on August 27, 1990 and is buried at Grace Lutheran Church Cemetery in Erhard, Minnesota.

Delores Cleveland
Immediate Past President

Delores (Wevik) Cleveland was born on April 19, 1932 to Alfred and Ida (Husby) Wevik in rural Alcester, Union County, South Dakota. She grew up on a self-sufficient grain / livestock family farm in the 30s and 40s. The family had a large garden and chickens which supplied most of the family dietary needs. Delores was baptized and confirmed at Roseni Lutheran Church in rural Beresford, South Dakota.

Delores attended elementary school and her freshman year of high school in rural Alcester, Union County, South Dakota. In 1947 the family moved to Canton, South Dakota where she attended and graduated from Augustana Academy, a Lutheran High School. The summers of 1950 and 1951 she attended Augustana College and received a rural school teaching certificate. During the regular school year she taught at rural school, Sunnyside #27, in Lincoln County, South Dakota.

On April 19, 1952 Delores married Harold Cleveland at Canton Lutheran Church. He was born on October 5th, 1925 to Ingvald and Annie Cleveland. Ingvald (Kleiveland) Cleveland immigrated to America on April 15, 1915 from the island of Osterøy near Bergen, Norway. Harold was a grain and livestock farmer. On May 1, 1954 Delores began working for Agriculture Soil Conservation, US Department of Agriculture in Canton. She retired on May 1, 1987 after 33 years with the Agriculture Soil Conservation/Agriculture Soil Conservation Service, US Department of Agriculture, now called the Farm Service Agency. In 1982 Harold and Delores sold their livestock, machinery and farmland and moved to Sioux Falls, South Dakota. Harold Cleveland passed away on November 7th, 1987 and is buried along with his parents at West Prairie Lutheran Church in rural Lennox, South Dakota.

Delores is an active member of the Sons of Norway King Olav V Lodge. She served as president of her Sons of Norway lodge in 2007 and 2008. She has also been an active officer of the local rural school board and her church council.

She was first elected to the board in 1999 and served as president of the Hadeland Lag from 2002 to 2006. Delores was the coordinator of the 2006 7-Lag *Stevne* in Sioux Falls, South Dakota.

Hadeland Ancestors: Alfred Wevik was born July 24, 1887 to Ole Wevik, Sr. and Lizzie (Solem) Wevik. He was their oldest child. Lizzie was the daughter of Anders and Helena Solem. She was born on May 6th 1870 in a dug-out near Gayville, South Dakota. Anders Solem was born at Gran, Norway in December 1842. He came to America in a sailboat in 1861, a passage that took 11 weeks and 3 days. Helen Jensen (Solem) was born on April 13, 1849 in Jevnaker parish, Norway. She immigrated to America in 1866.

Ida Husby was born June 2, 1889 in Lincoln County, South Dakota to Even Husby and Johanne (Olson) Husby. Even and Johanne were married on December 10, 1885. Johanne Olson had immigrated to America in 1866 with her parents, Steffen S., and Anne (Roatterud) Olson from Jevnaker, Hadeland, Norway. Steffen was born on October 21, 1929 and Annie Roatterud on July 15, 1830 in Jevnaker. Alfred and Ida are buried at Roseni Cemetery in rural Beresford, South Dakota.

Evonne Anderson
Brua Typesetting & Design since 1992

Evonne (Beastrom) Anderson was born in Red Wing, Minnesota September 6, 1936, and grew up on a small dairy farm 13 miles from Red Wing near Ellsworth, Wisconsin. Her ancestry is 7/8 Norwegian and 1/8 Swedish, the Norwegian ancestry coming from North Odal, Eidsvoll, Stange, Stavanger, and Solvorn on the Sognefjord. After graduating from Ellsworth High School, she attended Concordia College, Moorhead, Minnesota, graduating from there in 1958.

While at Concordia Evonne and Verlyn Anderson met and married six days after she graduated. They lived in Minneapolis for a year where Verlyn was working on a master's degree and then moved to Waconia, Minnesota, in 1959 where Verlyn was teaching Latin and English. Evonne worked at the University of Minnesota 1958-59 and after moving to Waconia became a private piano teacher. Their three daughters were born from 1959 to 1962.

In 1962 Verlyn was hired by Concordia College as a librarian. Evonne continued to work as a piano teacher in Moorhead until their daughters were in school. She then began to work for Concordia College in the graphics section of the Department of Communications, where she worked for the next 26 years until she retired in 1998. Some of the skills she learned at this job she has used while working on the *Brua*. Through the years she has learned to read Norwegian and assists Verlyn with many translation jobs. She also teaches Norwegian at the local Sons of Norway lodge and at

Skogfjorden's Norwegian Adult Program, the Concordia Language Village near Bemidji, Minnesota.

Evonne and Verlyn have three married daughters, three grandsons and a granddaughter-in-law.

Evonne has been a member of the Heritage Education Commission, an organization of Minnesota State University Moorhead, which plans and conducts a one-day genealogical workshop every fall. She participates in other volunteer activities in her church and the Sons of Norway. Another of the lag's invaluable 'Hadelanders-in-law,' Evonne's contributions of time and talent go far beyond her critical role in publishing the *Brua* and helping organize and lead tours to Hadeland.

Brian Christensen
Genealogy Committee since 2005

Brian Christensen has functioned as his family's genealogist and has been a member of the Hadeland Lag since the late 1980s. He was born in March 1966 in Iowa to parents G. Wayne Christensen and Randi Hvattum. Brian's father was in agricultural sales and left Iowa in 1969 transferring to numerous locations in the Midwest, before settling in 1977 at Floyds Knob, Indiana, near Louisville, Kentucky. Brian resides there today with his wife Deanna and their three year old daughter Lia Randi. They are currently looking forward to the expansion of their family with a new daughter due in March of 2012.

Having started investigating family genealogy at age 15, Brian was able to learn a great deal about his ancestry from his grandparents and his great-grandmother, Randi Lee Hvattum (1888-1985), a 1903 immigrant from Gran, Hadeland. His great-grandmother's stories inspired him to learn more about his family history. While Brian was a student at Indiana University he traveled alone making the first of his three trips to Hadeland to research the family genealogy. He recalls one interesting moment at the State Archives in Hamar. The librarians were perplexed that an American teenager wanted hundreds of photocopies from their special collection. He recalls that they cut him off at $100 and said, "That's enough!" Thirty years later Brian still cannot get "enough" of his genealogy addiction!

Brian completed his degree in business in 1989 and followed in his father's footsteps choosing a career in sales management. He got his start selling consumer products in Kentucky and Indiana, eventually rising to district and regional management in that industry. As recently as 2000 he moved into the position of District Sales Manager in the pharmaceutical industry with sales teams promoting cardiovascular medicines from Ohio to Tennessee. He is currently a District Service Manager in Kentucky with Medtronic, a Minneapolis based manufacturer of medical devices (implantable pacemakers/defibrillators).

Hadeland Ancestors: Randi Lee, age 14, left the Skjervum farm in Gran in 1903 with Ingvald Dynna, a neighborhood friend, to live with her Uncle Andrew Lee at Forest City, Iowa. She was married in Osage, Iowa in 1909 to Thorsten "Thomas" Hovelsen Hvattum, another immigrant from Gran. Thorsten arrived in the United States in 1868, as a 6 year old boy with his parents Hovel Hvattum (1827-1892) and Rangdi (Skjervum) Hvattum (1835-1919). The Hvattums were farmers southwest of Osage, Rock Township, Mitchell Co, Iowa and are all buried at Rock Creek Cemetery, at Meroa, Iowa.

Linda Lee Larson
Genealogy Committee since 2005

Linda Lee Larson was born to Gordon Howard and Eleanora Larson in 1948 in Portland, Oregon. Gordon and Eleanora Larson, both born in North Dakota, were living in Hatton, Traill County, North Dakota until a few weeks before Linda was born. Linda grew up in a Portland, Oregon suburb and attended Oregon State University, where she earned a BS and Masters in Education in 1970. Then she moved to Richland, Washington. In the 1970's Linda went on to earn 2 accounting degrees from Washington State University in Pullman WA and passed the CPA Exam. She worked for Battelle at Hanford in accounting and internal audit for a number of years. Then she moved to Seattle where she worked as a systems auditor for several major corporations, including what is now Bank of America. While in Seattle she earned an MBA from Seattle University. She next moved to Cleveland, Ohio and earned a Doctorate of Business Administration in Accounting in 1997. She has been teaching auditing and other accounting courses at the university level ever since. She is currently teaching for Central Washington University in Lynnwood, Washington (a Seattle suburb).

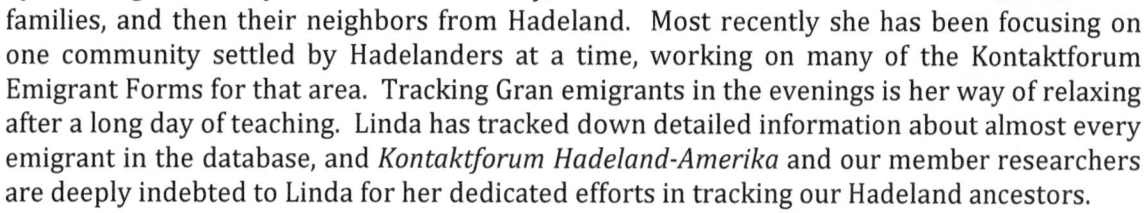

Linda loves to get on-line and do genealogy work. She started by tracking her family lines back to Norway, then worked on related families, and then their neighbors from Hadeland. Most recently she has been focusing on one community settled by Hadelanders at a time, working on many of the Kontaktforum Emigrant Forms for that area. Tracking Gran emigrants in the evenings is her way of relaxing after a long day of teaching. Linda has tracked down detailed information about almost every emigrant in the database, and *Kontaktforum Hadeland-Amerika* and our member researchers are deeply indebted to Linda for her dedicated efforts in tracking our Hadeland ancestors.

Hadeland Ancestors: Linda's father Gordon Larson was the son of Lewis Larson and Gertrude Bidne (from Opheim, near Vossestrand, Hordaland County, Norway). Gordon was born in Douglas, Ward County, ND (near Minot) in 1918. Lewis Larson was the son of Jens Larson, born at Haugtvedt, near Gran, Norway on 1 October 1851. Jens Larson was the son of Lars Larsen Myra, born at Ruden, Gran, Norway and Anne Jensdtr Knarud, also born near Gran, Norway.

In the late 1860's Jens Larson, his siblings Lars and Berthe and a very large family group of Haugtvedt aunts, uncles, and cousins left Gran and settled near Elstad in Fillmore County, Minnesota. In a few years, the family group split up and left Fillmore County. One large group, which included Jens's sister Bertha (Mrs. Stephen Hansen Furua) and the families of Jens's uncles Simon Larsen Osten, Jens Larsen Haugtvedt, and Erick Hanson

Haugtvedt all headed north to settle at or near Norwegian Grove, Otter Tail County MN. Another large family group, including Jens and his brother Lars Larson, and the families of their uncle Severt Haugtvedt Larson and their cousin Lars Torstensen Strande headed to South Dakota. The Severt Larsons and the Lars Strande family settled at North Preston in Kingsbury County SD while Jens and Lars homesteaded a few miles away just south of Brookings, SD in Moody County. Even Strande headed to Ellensburg WA, and sisters Ingeborg and Marie Strande settled at Glenwood, Iowa. In about 1878 Jens Larson married Guri Henriksdtr (from Hova, Naes, Hallingdal, Norway). They had a family of 9 children, of whom 7 survived to adulthood. Linda's grandfather Lewis Larson was their eldest son.

John William Oien
Co-Editor, Centennial History

John William Oien was born on May 27, 1943 to Paul Olaf and Kathryn Lillian (Hoffman) Oien in Long Beach, California. He is a Hadelander by marriage. His lineage is from Norway (Gubrandsdalen/Trondheim), Denmark and Germany (Elsace, France). John's grandfather Johan Pederson emigrated from Norway in 1907 through Canada to Maynard, Chippewa County, Minnesota. He homesteaded near Alexander, North Dakota. He married Matilda Anfinson and moved to her homestead in northeastern Montana.

John grew up in Southern California where his father worked as an engineer for the US Navy. He was baptized at Our Savior's Lutheran Church in Long Beach, California and confirmed at Holy Redeemer Lutheran Church in Bellflower, California.

He graduated from Paramount High School in 1961. He then attended Arizona State University and California Polytechnic (College) University, graduating in 1968 with a Bachelors of Science in Landscape Architecture.

Upon graduation he moved to Grass Valley, California where he began a career with the U.S. Forest Service in the Tahoe National Forest. His career as a Forest Landscape Architect included work on the Modoc National Forest in Alturas, California; the Toiyabe National Forest in Reno, Nevada; the Salmon and Challis National Forests in Salmon, Idaho and the Grand Mesa, Gunnison and Uncompahgre National Forests in Delta, Colorado.

In 1976 John met his wife to be, Jenifer Bjelke at his younger brother's wedding in California. They were married on June 5, 1976 in Arleta, California. To this union three children were born: Julie Kristine on February 19, 1978 in Salmon, Idaho; Janet Sue on October 20, 1980; and Jens Richard on December 21, 1983.

In 1983 he attended a 3-week, continuing education course in Recreation Management at Clemson University, Clemson, South Carolina. For this course he wrote a research paper entitled *"Recreation Opportunity Spectrum Management Applications"*. John retired in 2004 after 37 years with the U. S. Forest Service. His career was noted in the US Congressional Record proceedings and debates of the 108th Congress on May 13, 2004.

John is a member of All Saints Lutheran Church, Cory, Colorado where he has served as treasurer and president. He is a member of Vestafjell Lodge, Sons of Norway where he served four years as president. He is an editor of this centennial history.

Ole P. Gamme
Representative of the Hadeland Lag to Kontaktforum Hadeland-Amerika

Ole Paulsen Gamme was born on December 22, 1944 on the Gamme farm in Gran Norway to Paul O. Gamme and Agda Marie Brørby. Ole was educated for 10 years in school in Gran, Norway and 2 years at the Agricultural College, Oslo, Norway. Helga and Ole were dairy farmers on the old Gamme farm from 1966 to 1998. He retired in 1998 when his son took over the farm. Now they work on the farm with their son Paul.

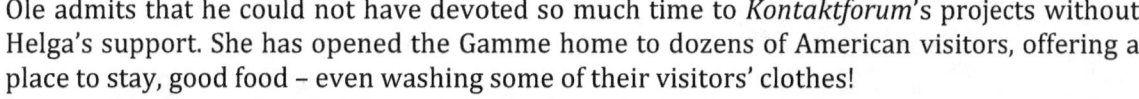

Ole served in the King's Guard in Oslo for one year (1965-1966).

His hobbies include: Leader of the *Kontaktforum Hadeland-America*; singing as a member of the *Mannskor K.K.* chorus for more than 40 years, travel and genealogical research.

Ole married **Helga Sæthre** on March 30, 1968. She was born on October 12, 1948 on the Elken farm in Tingelstad, Brandbu, Norway. They have three children. Ole admits that he could not have devoted so much time to *Kontaktforum*'s projects without Helga's support. She has opened the Gamme home to dozens of American visitors, offering a place to stay, good food – even washing some of their visitors' clothes!

Ole authors the "Hadeland Today" column in the *Brua*. He is the representative of the Hadeland Lag on the *Kontaktforum* board, where he also serves as the group's leader. He is primarily responsible for development and maintenance of the *Kontaktforum* database and has played an important role in planning the lag's visits to Hadeland beginning in 2000. He and his wife Helga frequently attend the lag's fall meetings.

Harald Hvattum
Brua Contributor and Kontaktforum Secretary

Harald Hvattum was born on April 11, 1954 on one of the Grinaker farms in Brandbu, Norway. His parents are Sigmund Hvattum and Anne Klara Dynna.

Harald was educated as an Historian and received a degree from the University of Oslo in 1982. He is the author of local historical publications and has published about 20 books on the Hadeland and Valdres regions of Norway. He has been on the editorial staff of *Årbok* of Hadeland for over 20 years and its editor since 1994.

Harald was been the director of Gran Historical Society from 2003-2006 and has been secretary of the *Kontaktforum Hadeland-Amerika* since 2002. He is a member of Hadeland Lag and a regular contributor to the *Brua* on historical subjects. Harald manages memberships for the Hadeland Lag in Norway.

Hans M. Næss
Kontaktforum Member and Researcher Extraordinaire

Hans M. Næss was born on June 25, 1925 in Gran. He graduated from the teacher's college in Elverum in 1950 and taught in Nittedal, Bamble, Kolbu, Eina and Vang before returning to Gran in 1959, where he spent the rest of his teaching career. Hans was married in 1952 and is the father of five children, although sadly he lost his wife at a relatively young age.

Hans M. Næss wearing the Gold Medal from the King and holding the Medal of Honor Proclamation and framed Congratulations from Kontaktforum

Since the 1960s Næss has worked tirelessly to preserve and share the local history of Hadeland and help Norwegian-Americans find their Hadeland roots. In 1976 he was a founding member of the Gran Historical Society and has served in many leadership positions, including chairman. Since it was founded in 1983, he has served as the representative for Hadeland on the Executive Board of the Vestoppland Genealogical Society. He has been a member of *Kontaktforum Hadeland-Amerika* since its inception.

His dedication to preserving the history and the genealogical ties to Hadeland for both Norwegians and Americans has brought him well-deserved honors. In 1999, Hans M. Næss received the Hadeland Prize and in February of 2007, King Harald V recognized his lifetime of service with the King's Medal of Honor.

His work on behalf of members of the Hadeland Lag over the past 35 years, both as a researcher and as a local guide, has been invaluable. He patiently reviewed the thousands of obituaries and other news items found in the Rowberg file for *Kontaktforum Hadeland-Amerika*, extracting information about hundreds of Hadelanders for the project. He has been a presenter at the 7-Lag *Stevne* and continues to be a source of knowledge and friendship for the members of the Hadeland Lag.

Previous Officeholders 1990-2010

Gloria Cooper
Director 2005-2008

When Gloria was asked to serve on the Hadeland Lag Board of Directors as its representative to the *Bygdelagenes Fellesraad*, she was honored but hesitant. She had never driven a car and knew it would be difficult to get to the meetings. She asked if her English husband of 59 years, Merton Cooper, could come with her. The answer was yes, and the lag got two people for the price of one!

Gloria Borgen Cooper was born February 24, 1929, the first daughter of Carl E. and Agnes (Skorud) Borgen in Red Wing, Minnesota. She grew up in "pretty Red Wing" and graduated from Central High School in June of 1947. That fall she started nurse's training at Fairview School of Nursing in Minneapolis. She graduated, passed her state boards and became a registered nurse; in those days they were called "bedside nurses." She returned to St. John's Hospital in Red Wing and worked as a night supervisor in obstetrics. She helped deliver many of the babies born in Red Wing and the surrounding area from 1950-1952.

Gloria and Merton Cooper were married July 5, 1952, in Red Wing. They were blessed with four children: Susan, Steven, Bruce and Paul. Mert's work as a food chemist took them to Wabasha MN for 17 years. The Coopers moved to Minneapolis in 1969 and now live in the suburb of New Hope.

Gloria set a record for her nursing class. She worked just THREE days as a nurse after her children were born. She has had many volunteer jobs including 27 years with Lutheran Social Services working with their "second hand stores" and 32 years working at her church's lutefisk dinners. She took classes in antiques and organized an Antiques and Collectibles Club in the western suburbs.

Genealogy and family history are a favorite pastime. She can confirm that Norwegian family history is not as easy as finding Mert's English family history. She loved to read but now uses "talking books" as she is legally blind. Because of a number of health problems, she isn't able to travel, but she reports that talking is one thing she can still do very well and keeps up on the latest news by phone, or welcoming visitors to her home. She *is* a Norwegian and the coffee pot goes on – and she and Mert can always find a cookie!

Hadeland Ancestors: Gloria's maternal grandfather Micheal (Mikel) Michelson Skorud and his young sister Gina came through Ellis Island in 1898. They were sponsored in American by Hilden relatives in the Ellsworth, Wisconsin, area. Mike worked as a farm laborer and Gina, a cleaning maid for four years, sending money to Norway so that the rest of the family could come to the United States. In 1902, Gloria's great-grandparents arrived. Christian Mickelson and Pernilla Pedersdatter immigrated with their children Kjersti, Paula

Caroline, Anna, Marie, Peter and Ole. Two months after the Mickelson family reunited, her grandfather Michael's sweetheart Mary Andersdatter Raastad came to the United States. They had been communicating by mail for four years, and were married the day Grandma Mary reached Red Wing...and the rest is history!

Alfield Erlien
1923-2010
Recording Secretary 1992-1993

Alfield Norma Erlien was born on November 8, 1923. She was the oldest daughter of Alfred and Nora Dahle and grew up on the family farm in Garfield Township, Polk County, Minnesota. All of Alfield's grandparents were born in Norway, but none had called Hadeland home. She was another of the lag's active Hadelanders-in-law.

"Alfie" married Ellef Erlien in 1946 in Fertile, Minnesota. They had two sons and two daughters. In 1959 they moved to Twin Valley, Minnesota, where the family would make their home for over fifty years. Alfield died September 12, 2010. Her funeral was held at Zion Lutheran Church in Twin Valley on Saturday, September 18.

Paul Grinager
1923-2004
Director 1984-2001

Paul Douglas Grinager was born on May 22, 1923 in Fergus Falls, Minnesota, the son of Paul Augustine and Alta M. (Isaacson) Grinager. Paul moved to Sacramento, California in 1929. During World War II he served in the 75th Infantry Division, seeing combat in France, Holland and Germany. After the war he returned to Sacramento to work for the Sacramento District Army Corps of Engineers as an Engineering Technician. He retired in 1978 after 36 years of service in the federal government.

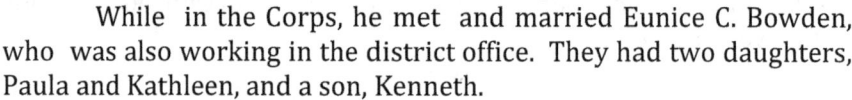

While in the Corps, he met and married Eunice C. Bowden, who was also working in the district office. They had two daughters, Paula and Kathleen, and a son, Kenneth.

Paul first joined Hadeland Lag in 1983 and was elected to the Board of Directors in 1984.

Grinager made a model of the *"gamle Grinaker Stavkirke"* and presented it to the Hadeland Folk Museum on June 24, 1990 during the Hadeland Lag's 1990 visit. It has remained on public display since that time.

Paul died on March 20, 2004 at Lake Region Hospital in Fergus Falls, Minnesota. He was buried in St. Otto's Cemetery in Fergus Falls, Minnesota.

Hadeland Ancestors: Paul's grandfather was Haavel Knutsen Grinager who was born October 23, 1863 at Grinager in Tingelstad, the son of Knud Hansen Grinager and Kjersti

Pedersdatter. Haavel left Hadeland for the United States on May 9, 1882. On September 11, 1889, Haavel Grinager married Isabel A. Martin. They had 7 children.

David N. Gunderson
Genealogist 2006-2009

David Norton Gunderson was born on December 29, 1949 in Austin, Minnesota the son of Norton Albert Gunderson and Lorraine Marie Follmuth.

Dave graduated from Austin High School in 1967, Austin State Junior College in 1969, and Minnesota State University – Mankato in June 1971. He received a BS in Social Studies and a minor in chemistry. He then entered the US Army and was assigned to the 518th & 720th Military Police Battalions at Fort Hood, Texas. In April 1973, he received an honorable discharge and entered graduate school at Minnesota State University – Mankato. In July 1974, Dave received a Master of Science degree in history. His thesis was "The Nature of Litigation in American Prize Courts in the Revolutionary War."

In 1976 Dave began working for the Social Security Administration as a claims representative. In 1984, he transferred to the Collection Division of the Internal Revenue Service as a revenue officer. In 1997, he received the "Michael Dillon Memorial award" as the outstanding revenue officer in the Internal Revenue Service. He retired in December 2004 with 30 years of federal government service.

Dave has been a member of the American Legion; Zion Lutheran Church in Fergus Falls, Minnesota; Sons of Norway, Telelaget of America and Hadeland Lag. His hobbies include target shooting, gardening, and volunteer work on the railroad at the Lake Region Pioneer Threshermen's Association in Dalton, Minnesota. This group operates a 1914 French narrow gauge steam locomotive. Dave's specialty is track maintenance.

Dave continues to be a thorough and aggressive researcher whose work can be found throughout the *Kontaktforum Hadeland-Amerika* database. He continues to assist many lag members in their search for their Hadeland roots.

Hadeland Ancestors: Dave's father was the grandson of Olaus Gunderson and Elene Tokerud. Elene Olsdatter Tokerud was born at Brunstad in Bjoneroa of Hadeland in 1836. She left Hadeland for America in April 1866 with her son, Peder Ellingsen, her parents, Ole Olsen Tokerud and Kari Nielsdatter, and her sister Ingeborg.

They initially came to the Decorah, Iowa area where her brother Ole was living with his family. In 1867, they moved near Hayward, Minnesota. In 1869, Elene Tokerud married Olaus Gunderson at East Freeborn Lutheran Church. He had immigrated from Østfold, Norway. This marriage produced six children. They later moved to Mount Valley Township, Winnebago County, Iowa where they eventually owned several farms. Elene died in 1908 and her husband Olaus died in 1905.

Michael L. Miller
Director 1989-1992

Michael Lester Miller was born near Fergus Falls, Minnesota, son of Lester Joseph and Laura Mae (Tostenson) Miller. He graduated from high school in Robbinsdale, Minnesota. Mike and his wife Susan make their home in Montrose, Minnesota and have three adult children. Mike's intense interest in genealogy led him to join the Hadeland Lag.

Hadeland Ancestors: Michael's great-grandmother Birthe Pedersdtr was born February 5, 1849 at Nordengeneiet in Hadeland. Birthe was the daughter of Peder Olsen Godli who was born August 4, 1819 on Godli in Lunner. His wife Anne Larsdtr was born at Hvalseiet in Gran on April 8, 1825. Peder and Anne left Nordengeneiet for America with Birthe and her siblings Lars, Gudbjør, and Christian in the spring of 1868. Birthe died April 21, 1938 in Steele County, Minnesota. Her father Peder died August 1, 1877 in Freeborn County, Minnesota. Birthe's mother Anne died October 28, 1878, also in Freeborn County.

Olaf Nelson
1914-1998
Vice President 1987-1993

Olaf Andreas Nelson was born October 5, 1914, on a farm in Mandt Township, Chippewa County, Minnesota. He was baptized in Mandt Lutheran Church and, as an adult, held many offices in the congregation. He and Rhonda Moen were married there on June 26, 1948. He farmed and lived in Mandt Township until he and Rhoda moved to Montevideo in 1984. He was first elected a director of the Hadeland Lag at its reorganization in 1975, and played an active role in the organization for over 20 years.

He died September 21, 1998 in Montevideo, Minnesota.

Hadeland Ancestors: Olaf's mother Bertha Stenhus was born on Bjertnæs in Jevnaker in 1882, the daughter of Lars Nilsen and Ingeborg Gudbrandsdtr. She came to America in 1900. Olaf's father Hans was born in Buskerud *fylke*, Norway and immigrated in 1893.

Byron Schmid
Director 2005-2007

Byron Schmid is a fifth generation descendant on his mother's side of Hadelander immigrants to southern Wisconsin. He is a graduate of Argyle High School, Augsburg College in Minneapolis, the Lutheran Theological Seminary in Philadelphia, and has a Ph.D. in political science from Duke University. Byron has served on the staffs of the former ALC's Commission on Research and Social Action and the Lutheran Council in the USA, as well as on the faculties of Concordia College and Moorhead State University in Moorhead, MN. He also served parishes in Lincoln, NE, and in the Twin Cities of Minneapolis and St. Paul. A retired ELCA pastor, he lives with his wife in Blaine, MN. He and his wife have two children and three grandchildren.

Byron has completed seven family histories, including four on his maternal ancestry in Norway, two on his paternal Swiss ancestry, and one on his wife's Scots Irish ancestry. He has traveled extensively in both Norway and Switzerland, and has taken three family reunion groups to each of them.

Hadeland Ancestors: One of Byron's great-great-grandfathers was Nils Torstensen Paalserud, born on Hvalebyeiet in 1828. His wife, Anne Eriksdtr., was born on Rosendahlseiet also in 1828. They lived on the Paalserud *husmannsplass* on the North Framstad farm, prior to immigrating in 1853 with their first son to Green County in southern Wisconsin where they farmed and raised eight children: Erick, Ragnhild, Ingeborg, Torsten, Caroline, Edward, Andrena and Ned. After initial settlement, the family used the surname Thompson.

Another great-great-grandfather was Paul Gulbrandsen Brynsås, born in 1820 on Helgakereiet. He married Birthe Torstensdtr. (a sister of Nils), who was also born in 1820 on Helgakereiet. They immigrated in 1877 with their four youngest children, Marthe, Ragnhild, Kari and Peter, to Green County in southern Wisconsin where three older sons (Gulbrand, Johannes and Torsten) had previously immigrated in 1870, 1872 and 1876, respectively. Paul and Birthe's children used the surname Paulson, except for the youngest son who later used Alm. Two of Paul's siblings (Lars and Kari) also immigrated to Wisconsin and Minnesota. Paul's oldest sister (Birthe) remained in Hadeland, but three of her children immigrated to Minnesota and North Dakota. Three of Paul's half-siblings (Hans called Henry, John and Margrethe) also immigrated to Wisconsin.ald

Ron Ulven
Treasurer 2004-2007

Ronald Ulven is the son of Ken and Thelma (Leverson) Ulven. He married Deanna Askviken on June 18, 1961, in Northwood, North Dakota. They raised their three sons and one daughter in Hawley, Minnesota, where Ron had a successful career as a businessman and banker. They have ten grandchildren and one great-grandchild.

Hadeland Ancestors: Ron's great-grandfather Jens Andersen Ulven was born in 1820 on the Torgersrud farm in Gran. His great-grandmother Randi Hansdtr was born in 1835 on the Gautvedt farm in Gran. Jens and Randi left Norway with their children Anders, Ingeborg, Hans, Juul, Bent, and Anne Marie in 1880 and settled in Lake Park, Minnesota.

In 1896, Anders married Anne Halvorsen who came to America from Sweden in 1875. Ron's father Kenneth (1912-2002) was their youngest son and the eighth of their nine children.

Betty Volney
Director 1998 - 2004

Betty Jane Lynne was born February 6, 1933, in North Dakota. She married Vernon "Vic" Volney and they had four children: Lisbeth Anne, Eric Scott, Michael and Kirstin Noelle. Vernon was born May 28, 1931 and died May 9, 1982.

Hadeland Ancestors: Betty's great-grandparents, Anders Guttormsen Lunden and Inger Dorthea Johannesdtr were married in 1860 and came to America in 1884. Their daughter Eline stayed in Norway and married Nils Thorstensen Lynne in 1885. They came to America in 1904 and settled in Plaza, North Dakota, with their children Torsten, Ingel, Anders, Thorvald, Edvard, Otto, and Nikolai Daniel. Betty's father was Nikolai Daniel Nilsen Lynne, born June 2, 1904 at Lynnebakken in Gran. He married Minnie Fossum who was born in 1899 in Wolf Point, Montana.

Margaret Wilson
Director 1989-1992

Elise Margaret Paulson was born March 10, 1915 in Sparta Township, Chippewa County, Minnesota, the daughter of Martin Paulson and Helga Thørstensdatter Nøkleby. Her father farmed and also worked for the railroad.

She married Wilfred "Willie" R. Wilson in 1938. He was born September 16, 1916 of Danish and French-Canadian ancestry. He was a past president of the Minnesota Petroleum Association and the Red Wing Lion's Club. Willie passed away in Red Wing on November 28, 2010.

Margaret and her husband had five children: Martin, Robert, George, Michael and Carolyn.

Hadeland Ancestors: Margaret's mother Helga Thorstensdtr. was born in Jevnaker and came to America in 1910. Helga's parents were Thorsten Jakobsen and Eline Martinsdtr. Margaret's father Martin was born in 1885 and emigrated from Toten.

Wendy Winkelman
Genealogist 2004-2006

Wendy Winkelman is the daughter of Paul Winkelman and Marlys Hanson. She graduated from Richfield (MN) High School and has three children: Erin and Kelley Drew and Paul Bellesen. In 2006, she moved to Mesa, Arizona where she works for Ameriprise Financial. She is now a District 6 officer with the Sons of Norway.

Hadeland Ancestors: Wendy's paternal grandmother Frances Larson Winkelman was the granddaughter of Hadeland immigrants Erich Larson and Maren Endresdtr Lindstad. Erich was born on Askimeiet in Tingelstad in 1823. He was a tenant on Lysen when he left for America in 1848. In 1854 he married Maren Endresdatter in Wisconsin. She was born in 1835 on the Lindstad farm in Gran and came to America in 1853 with her sister Else.

Chapter Nine
Emeritus Advisory Council

The Emeritus Advisory Council was created as part of the new by-laws adopted in 2004. The Council offers the Lag the opportunity to honor members "whose knowledge and service continue to be of value to the Hadeland Lag of America's Board and Membership despite their absence from active participation in the Hadeland Lag's Boards and Committees." Membership on the Emeritus Advisory Council is granted to all past presidents. Other former board members not otherwise serving may be nominated by the board of directors and confirmed by the membership.

As past presidents, Ellef Erlien, E. Palmer Rockswold, and Robert Rosendahl were automatically elevated to the advisory council. In addition, the membership chose to recognize Harriet Foss for her years of service to the lag and her pivotal role in the lag's re-emergence in the 1970s. As the lag's first genealogist, Leslie Rogne was honored for his work in developing the genealogy library and tireless dedication to serving the lag's membership.

In 2006, the membership recognized retiring treasurer Dean Sorum not only for his years of service to the lag, but also for spearheading the incorporation of the 7-Lag *Stevne*'s umbrella group, Norwegian *Stevner*, Inc. In 2007, Manfred Hill was elevated to the council and in 2010 Norma Gilbertson was honored for her years of service both to the Hadeland Lag and, as its representative, the NSI.

Norma Gilbertson
Retired as secretary in 2010
Elected to the Emeritus Advisory Council in 2010

Norma (Kyro) Gilbertson was born September 24, 1930 in Minneapolis, Minnesota. The daughter of Otto & Maria Emelia (Koskela) Kyro who came from Lumijoki and Llmajoki, Finland, she is a Hadelander by marriage. She married Gerald Merlin Gilbertson on September 3, 1949 at the Morgan Avenue Lutheran Church in Minneapolis, Minnesota.

Gerald's grandmother, Karen Lyngstad Olson was born in Gran on the Lyngstad farm. She was baptized and confirmed at the Sister Churches. Her uncle Christopher Lyngstad came to America and settled in Star Prairie, Wisconsin area and needed a housekeeper, so Karen joined him at the age of 16. She married and had a family of 7 children. George, one of the oldest, was Gerald's father. Gerald's other grandparents came from other parts of Norway.

Norma grew up on the north side of Minneapolis, Minnesota and graduated from North High School. She then attended Fairview School of Nursing. She became an LPN and worked for 25 years at Mount Sinai Hospital and Unity Hospital in Fridley, Minnesota. Norma and Gerald had a family of 6 children. They are: Mark

David, Paul Matthew, Stephen Luke, John Philip, Rebecca Susan, and Ruth Mary. Along with the Hadeland Lag, she is a member of the Sons of Norway-Vnrekretsen Lodge, and Cross of Glory Lutheran Church.

Gerald was born in St. Paul, Minnesota on July 1, 1922. He was confirmed at Hope Lutheran Church, St. Paul and graduated from North St. Paul High School. During World War II he served in the Army Air force in India. After the war he attended St. Olaf College and then worked as an independent salesman. Gerald died on February 4, 2002.

For a Hadelander-in-law, Norma has made significant contributions to the lag. Along with a long tenure on the board and as secretary, she spent over a decade as the lag's representative to Norwegian *Stevner*, Inc., the umbrella organization that sponsors each year's 7-Lag *Stevne*. She was elected to the Emeritus Advisory Council upon her retirement in 2010.

Manfred Hill
Retired as vice president in 2006
Elected to the Emeritus Advisory Council in 2007

Manfred Hill was born on the 13th of February in 1924 to Nora and Charley Hill. Uncle Simon Schiager homesteaded a quarter of land in 1868 that Manfred's family later bought.

Manfred grew up on that farm, and graduated from high school in 1941. He married Leona Wiebe, a beautiful redhead who was born near George, Lyon County, Iowa. She was born on September 23, 1926 to William and Marie Wiebe. To this union five children were born: Paulette, Richard, Carla, Randall and Renee.

Manfred started farming in 1943 and then branched out to producing hybrid seed for 36 years. He also did custom work and trucking.

He joined the Hadeland Lag in 1976, and remains an enthusiastic member. He retired as vice president in 2006 and was elected to the Emeritus Advisory Council in 2009.

Hadeland Ancestors: Paul Gundersen Schiager was born on the Skiaker farm in Gran, the son of Gunder Gundersen Skjervum. Paul's wife Guro was the daughter of Iver Paulsen Gamme and Rangdi Paulsdtr. Paul and Guro and their two oldest daughters emigrated from the Ruud farm in Jevnaker in 1866. They came via Quebec to Claremont, Iowa where they lived for two years before settling in Canton, South Dakota in 1868. When they arrived as part of a wagon train with 80 Norwegians, the party doubled the size of the settlement that was to become known as Canton. Paul and Guro's daughter Ingeborg married Nels Roe from Renlie in Valdres. Their daughter Nora Roe was Manfred's mother.

Manfred's paternal ancestors came from other parts of Norway. The name Hill comes from his grandfather Zacharias T. Haugland who was born on the island of Stord. When he came to America, he adopted Hill as a last name. Haug means high land, so that is probably why he ended up with Hill.

E. Palmer Rockswold
President (1986-92) and Brua Editor (1986-92)
Inaugural Member of the Emeritus Advisory Council

(Edwin) Palmer Rockswold was president of Hadeland Lag of America and *Brua* editor from 1986 to 1992. He was born in 1916 in southeast North Dakota to Norwegian immigrant parents. Palmer experienced harvesting with a horse binder, shocking grain, and

threshing with a straw burning steam rig. Because he lost his parents at a very early age, it was necessary for him to work his way through high school and college. Palmer received a Bachelor of Arts degree from Valley City State College in 1941 and a Masters of Science degree from the University of North Dakota in 1953. He was employed as a high school history teacher and a band director. He retired as superintendent of schools in Madison, Minnesota in the late 1980s.

In 1938, Palmer married to Myrna C. Peterson. She was born on February 21, 1916 and died on November 8th, 1980. They had four sons: Gaylan Lee, Gordon Alvin, Grant Allen and Gary Kent. On February 11, 1984 he married Betty Lou Thistlewaite who was also involved in Scandinavian activities. Betty was born on August 12, 1922 and died on February 6, 2008 in St Paul, Minnesota.

Rockswold is the author of *Per Immigrant & Pioneer*. He is listed in *Who's Who in the Midwest* and in *Personalities of the West and Midwest*.

Hadeland Ancestors: Palmer's father, Peder E. Rockswold was born on March 8, 1863 in the Brandbu area of Hadeland and was a charter member of the Hadeland Lag in 1910. Peder immigrated to America in 1881 and married Serianna Bergethe Haarsager on June 26, 1897. She was born on September 13, 1883 in Stadsbygd, Norway. She immigrated in 1892 from Vesteralen, where she had worked in the mountain pastures during the Arctic summers. Her father was a cod fisherman from Trondhjem. Peder died on January 14, 1917 and Serianna died on March 9, 1926.

Robert Howard Rosendahl
President (1995-2002)
Inaugural Member of the Emeritus Advisory Council

Robert Howard Rosendahl was born on August 19th, 1925 to Oscar Nelius Rosendahl and Carrie Helene Olson in Frankville, Winneshiek County, Iowa. Oscar died on April 23, 1981 in Winneshiek County, Iowa. Carrie was born on April 23, 1901 died on April 1, 1988 in Winneshiek County, Iowa.

Robert attended country school for 8 years and graduated from Decorah High School.

He was a farmer, drove cattle trucks for his uncle, and served his country during the Korean War as a US Army MP in the 212 MP campout. He also worked as a livestock sales barn clerk for 44 years.

He married Leona H. Snyder on April 27, 1956. To this union 5 children were born. He has been an active member of the Glenwood Lutheran Church, many civic organizations and a volunteer tour guide at Vesterheim museum.

Robert served the lag in various capacities, including his tenure as its president from 1996 to 2002.

Hadeland Ancestors: Robert's great-grandfather Ole Anderson died in Brandbu, Norway on August 9, 1869. The following year his great-grandmother, Siri Hansdatter Dahlen, a 46-year-old widow, immigrated to America with her sons Hans Olsen Rosendahl, age 11 and Christian Olsen Rosendahl, age 9 from Møllerstuen, Rosendalseiet in Brandbu. Hans became a naturalized American citizen in 1901. Robert's father Oscar was born on June 7, 1899, the second son of Hans Rosendahl and Emma Hatterstad.

Dean Sorum
Retired as treasurer 2002
Elected to the Emeritus Advisory Council in 2005

(Harold) Dean Sorum was born in Hettinger, North Dakota on February 19, 1931. He had two siblings: a brother, Christian Merle Lowe Sorum (1915-1963), and a sister Mary Pauline (Sorum) Stowman born in 1920.

Dean's first 7 years were spent living on a ranch near Sorum, a small village in western South Dakota. In October 1938 his parents, Chris and Ida, bought a small telephone company and moved the family to Abercrombie on the eastern edge of North Dakota. Dean grew up in the telephone industry. He enrolled at the University of North Dakota in the fall of 1950 and graduated with a Bachelor of Science in Electrical Engineering in 1954. He later did graduate studies at North Dakota State University and accounting studies at Moorhead State.

While Dean was at the University of North Dakota he met Carol Christine Orser and they were married on August 30, 1953 at the Colgate, North Dakota Presbyterian Church just before their senior year.

After their graduation Dean worked at Wright Patterson Air Force Base in Dayton, Ohio. In November he was called to active duty as a US Air Force officer in the Washington, D.C. area. After separation from active duty they moved their young family to Fargo, North Dakota where Dean was employed as an engineer at Communication Consultants, Inc. He is a registered

Professional Engineer. He was the lead engineer in developing many interactive fiber optic TV networks between high schools, libraries and technical colleges in Minnesota and North Dakota. These networks allowed students to study advanced subjects not offered locally. He worked at Communication Consultants, Inc., becoming a major owner and president of the firm. In 1998 he retired.

The Sorums have four children: Jonathan Dean Sorum, Sonja Ann (Sorum) Jensen, Susan Kristine (Sorum) Guttormson, and Paul Jeffery Sorum. They have ten grandchildren and four great-grandchildren.

Dean is a charter member and former president of the Lutheran Church of Christ the King, Moorhead, Minnesota; former president of the Grover Club, Oak Grove Lutheran School, Fargo, North Dakota; life member of the Institute of Electrical and Electronic Engineers; former president of the local chapter of the North Dakota Society of Professional Engineers; and member: National Society of Professional Engineers, Scholarship committee of the North Dakota Engineers Council, Independent Telephone Pioneers Association, Fargo Lions Club, Vestlandslaget (Sognelag), and Kringen Lodge-Sons of Norway, Fargo, North Dakota.

During the 1940s Dean accompanied his parents to several Hadeland Lag *stevner* and played piano solos at one or two of the meetings. In 1977, Dean and Carol became active members of the reorganized Hadeland Lag, and their contributions to its growth and success are too numerable to mention. Dean served as vice-president from 1986 to 1987 and as treasurer from 1993 to 2002. One of his most important achievements was in researching and coordinating efforts to incorporate Norwegian *Stevne*r, Inc. This non-profit corporation provides liability protection and a legal framework for the joint efforts of the seven *bygdelag* involved in planning and staging the annual 7-Lag *Stevne*.

Hadeland Ancestors: Christian Mickelson Sorum, Dean's father, immigrated from the Sørum farm in Moen, Tingelstad in 1905. He was president of the Hadeland Lag from 1947-1950. Dean's mother was Ida Beatha (Lowe) Sorum, a native of Ransom County, North Dakota, whose parents immigrated from Lærdal and Pløm in Norway.

Prior to their passing, the following lag leaders were honored as members of the Emeritus Advisory Council:

Ellef Erlien
1917-2011
President 1967-1968
Inaugural Member of the Emeritus Advisory Council

Ellef C. Erlien was born August 24, 1917 in Benedict, North Dakota. He graduated from Grenora High School in 1936 and from Minot State Teachers College in 1942. He enlisted in the US Army in 1943 where he served for three years. In 1946 Ellef married Alfield Norma Dahle at Fertile, Minnesota. They had two sons and two daughters: Darryl Alan born on March 18, 1947 and Duane Lavern born on June 16, 1950; Sharon Elaine born on November 26, 1951; and Yvonne Norma born on December 15, 1954.

In 1948 Ellef graduated from Worsham College of Mortuary Science in Chicago. He served his apprenticeship in Blue Earth, Minnesota. In December 1959, he purchased the Wagstrom Funeral Home in Twin Valley, Minnesota which he operated until January 1984 when he retired. Post-retirement, Ellef turned his attention to his hobbies of music, wood carving, building Norwegian coffee tables, and traveling.

Ellef served as lag president for one year in 1968. He had a long and active tenure on the Board of Directors, and served as editor, researcher and photographer for the *History of the Hadeland Lag 1910-1990*.

Ellef Erlien passed away as this book was being edited, on March 2, 2011.

Hadeland Ancestors: Ellef's father, Sigurd Hanson Erlien was born in Lunner, Hadeland, Norway on February 12, 1895, and came to America in 1912 at the age of 16 years. Sigurd first came to Benedict, North Dakota where his brother Ole had settled in 1906. From there he spent time in Montana before returning to North Dakota and settling outside Grenora. In 1940 he moved to Lake of the Woods in Minnesota, and spent the rest of his life at various locations in that state.

Harriet (Thingelstad) Foss
1922-2009
Secretary 1975-2001
Inaugural member of the Emeritus Advisory Council

Harriet (Thingelstad) Foss was born on October 9, 1922 to Hassel T. Thingelstad and Bertina Asheim. She was raised on a farm near Northwood, North Dakota and attended a one room country school on the banks of the Goose River. Harriet graduated from Northwood High School.

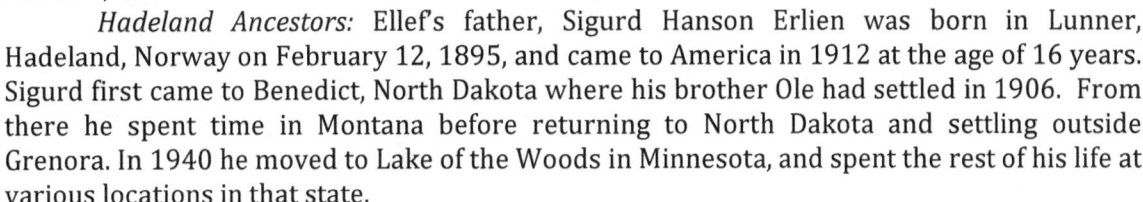

The first meeting to reorganize the Hadeland Lag in 1975 was held in the Foss's home and Harriet served as secretary, a position she held until 1990. Harriet was known in Norway as "North Dakota's Ambassador for Hadeland."

Beginning the 1970s Harriet and Percy entertained countless visitors from Norway. Erik Bye interviewed Harriet for television in 1977 while she and Percy were attending the Vesterheim Centennial. He was especially interested in her ability to speak the old Hadeland dialect. Later a crew from the Norwegian Broadcasting Company visited her home and interviewed Harriet.

Peder Nelson willed his extensive library of over 3,400 books to Harriet, and she donated them to the Gran Historical Society and attended the opening of the Peder H. Nelson collection at the Hadeland library in 1999.

Harriet married Percy Foss on February 7, 1942 in Los Angeles, California where they were employed by the defense department. Percy was born on October 19, 1920 near Buxton, North Dakota. He died on September 9, 1993 in Fargo, North Dakota.

Harriet was elevated to the Emeritus Council upon its creation, reflecting her role in the reorganization of the lag in 1975 and her vital and untiring service to the lag for over twenty-five years. She died on February 26, 2009.

Hadeland Ancestors: Harriet's great-grandparents, Ole Hansen Thingelstad (1817-1859) and Eli Olsdatter Moger came to America from the Sørumsengen farm in Tingelstad in 1849 and settled in Clayton County, Iowa. Their sons Hans and Peder were born in Iowa and arrived in Northwood ND in 1876. Eli joined her sons in Northwood, where she lived out her days.

Leslie Rogne
1915-2009
Genealogist 1987-2005
Inaugural Member of the Emeritus Advisory Council

Leslie Rogne was born on November 1, 1915, on a farm in north Richland County, North Dakota that had been his maternal grandfather's tree claim and homestead. He graduated from Pleasant Consolidated High School in 1935. After his education Leslie decided to farm with his father; however, World War II interrupted this endeavor. He served in the US Air Force as a radio operator and as a mechanic. He married Katherine Kazmark of Decatur, Illinois while in the service, on January 5, 1943. After the war, he returned to the farm with his wife and two children.

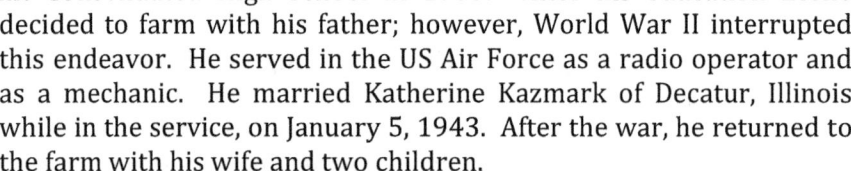

In 1961 Katherine became librarian for the Fargo City Library Bookmobile. Leslie joined her as driver and clerk. After 18 years, they retired and Leslie continued to farm, growing certified seeds, especially of native grasses. Later, their son-in-law took over the farming activities, with casual advice from Leslie. Leslie died at home on June 14, 2009.

Leslie and Katherine had three married children: Trana, retired in North Dakota; Seward, retired in Florida; and Leah, a professor at Minnesota State University, Mankato. They have five grandchildren and two great-grandchildren.

In 1987 Leslie agreed to take on the formal role of Hadeland Lag genealogist, and he devoted almost all of his time to his genealogy "hobby." Hadeland has no *bygdebøker*, so Leslie built an excellent resource library and a complete set of microfilm civil and church records from Hadeland. He couldn't count the number of family lines he researched, both in this country and in Norway. He would drive hundreds of miles to visit a county courthouse or check on records at a country church. His professional approach to research assured that the information he provided was detailed and carefully documented. Leslie took enormous pleasure in recalling the experiences he had working with the members of the Hadeland Lag, and those whose lives he touched were truly blessed by their contact with this thoughtful, soft spoken and intelligent man. In recognition of his years of untiring service to the lag and its members, Leslie was elected to the Emeritus Council at its creation.

Hadeland Ancestors: Leslie was the son of second-generation Hadeland-American Emma Trana and Brynjulf Johannesen Rogne, who was born at Rogne in Voss, Norway.

Emma's mother, Kari Ingebretson Olerud, was born in 1852 on Dahlen in Gran and came to America in 1880. Kari's mother Kari Agrimsdtr died in Norway in 1868, but her father Engebret Amundsen Olerud and two of Kari's sisters came to America in 1883.

Chapter Ten
Membership List 1990-2010

"The History of the Hadeland Lag 1910-1990" included a complete membership list for that 80 year period. Those listed here were members of the lag for at least one year from 1990-2010. Organizations in North America and Norway that pay dues or receive complimentary copies of the *Brua* are not included.

Aamodt Allison, Newburyport MA
Aamodt Jason R, Pataskala, OH
Aamodt John R, Laporte MN
Aase Donna Ballangrud, Roseville MN
Ackles Carol Formo, Huntington Beach CA
Adahl Larry E, Aberdeen SD
Aikins Margaret, Madison WI
Alexander Becky, Porterville CA
Alm Tom & Arlene, St Paul MN
Altman Sheldon & Judy, Fallon NV
Alvstad Lyle & Vernie, Ashby MN
Ambrose Nicoline Grinager, Urbana IL
Amdahl Lauren & Jane, Rochester MN
Amundsen Edward H, Kent WA
Amundson James & Elaine, Rothsay MN
Amundson Marjorie, Clermont IA
Andersen Bernt & Alice, Cottage Grove OR
Anderson Arthur & Kim, Rothsay MN
Anderson Arthur & Orris, Christine ND
Anderson Cora, Rothsay MN
Anderson Donald K & Betsy, West St Paul MN
Anderson Donald K & Barbara, Tioga ND
Anderson Donald P & Joan, LaCrosse WI
Anderson Dr Verlyn & Evonne, Moorhead MN
Anderson Elizabeth, Grand Forks ND
Anderson Gary & Elaine, Nelsonville WI
Anderson Harland, Appleton WI
Anderson Hjordis, Winnipeg MB CN
Anderson Jeanne, Hallock MN
Anderson John E, Minneapolis MN
Anderson Judith, Burnaby BC CN
Anderson Katherine, Warwick RI
Anderson Dr L E & Edna, Medicine Hat AB CN
Anderson Lucy, Myrtle Point OR
Andrson Monte, Perham MN
Anderson Norma, Arlington SD
Anderson Peter J, Columbus OH

Anderson Ronald L, Saugus CA
Anderson Stanley, Superior WI
Andvik Olive, Moorhead MN
Angermeier Sue, Annandale VA
Aschim Kurt, Marinette WI
Ashley Mark, Austin MN
Ask Elaine, Chatfield MN

Baalerud Jon, Brandbu NO
Babcock Sharon, Rosemount MN
Badker Diedre & Bernie, Janesville IA
Baird Sue, Clackamas OR
Bakken Howard, Hendersonville NC
Bakken Kåre, Brandbu NO
Bakken Orville
Bakken Richard, Buffalo MN
Balken Loren & Marlene, Faribault MN
Ballangrud Kari & Erik, Jaren NO
Bang Svein Ola, Gran NO
Bartholomew Roberta, North St Paul MN
Bates Mrs Leslie Dahlen, Concrete WA
Batts Marlene, Clinton Twp WI
Baxter Carol Firth, Sacramento CA
Beason Teresa, Santa Rosa CA
Beastrom Eric, Hudson WI
Beck Douglas & Arlene, Minot ND
Beck Stephen & Mary, Lake Stevens WA
Becker Gary M, Snohomish WA
Bednarz Barbara, Gold Canyon AZ
Behling Brian & Laura, Winona MN
Behrend Barbara, Brookings SD
Benell Jo Ann, Oslo NO
Benell Paula May, Prescott Valley AZ
Benell Tom, Verona WI
Benestuen Leif Håkon, Brandbu NO
Benson Mr & Mrs Glenn
Benson Gordon, Minneapolis MN

Berg   Odd Kjetil, Jevnaker NO
Berge   Lyle, Thornton CO
Bergrud Sigmund, Spring Grove MN
Berkvam Alethe, Clarkfield MN
Berry   Edith, Fergus Falls MN
Beto   Ruby, Madison SD
Beuter Mae, Port Townsend WA
Bilden Tilpher, Elgin IA
Bildengjerdingen Lennart, Brandbu NO
Binger Clarice, Sioux Falls SD
Bird   Betty, Bellevue WA
Bisegger Lucille, Gratiot WI
Bisgaard Ruth, Montevideo MN
Bjellum Kjell, Williston ND
Bjerke Åge, Jaren NO
Bjerke Don, Thief River Falls MN
Bjertnæs Jorun & Kåre, Jevnaker NO
Black   David, Falcon Heights MN
Blalock Marva, Salt Lake City UT
Blau   Stacy, Portage WI
Blegen Hubert A, West Fargo ND
Blegen Ralph, Brook Park MN
Bleken-Eid Stine, Brandbu NO
Bockoven Arlene Amundson, Prairie du Chien WI
Boekken Inger Marie, Grua NO
Bolken Olaf, Terrebonne OR
Bolken Paul R, Whitefish MT
Bolken Heier Liv Joran & Lars, Grinevoll NO
Boll   Marlys, Drayton ND
Bollerud Bruce, Madison WI
Borgen Agnes, Red Wing MN
Borgen Gerda C, Red Wing MN
Børmarken Eva & Egil, Gran NO
Botti   Elizabeth A, Harleysville PA
Braaten Gordon & Margaret, Calgary AB CN
Bratvold Lars, Tagish YT CN
Bratvold Owen, Richland WA
Bratvold Richard Owen, Twin Falls ID
Bratvold Thomas Erik, Richland WA
Bratvold Vicki, Jacksonville FL
Brennan Mary G, Vadnais Heights MN
Broaden Daniel & Betty, Pleasant Prairie WI
Brodin Robert & Rosalie, Windom MN
Brommel Sheila, St Paul MN
Bronson Allen W, Dakota Dunes SD
Bronson Dr Tim O, Independence MO
Brosius Jane, Tacoma WA
Brothen Edmund & Peggy, Brooklyn Park MN
Brovold Sissel Marit, Gran NO
Brown   Harris, Albert Lea MN
Brown   Jane, Osseo WI

Brown   Marie & Lee, Golden Valley MN
Brunner Todd R, Fitchburg WI
Bruns   Robert & Joyce, Fergus Falls MN
Brusveen Thomas & Crystal, Monticello WI
Brynsaas Norman & Mae, Decorah IA
Brynsaas Robert, Mesa AZ
Buchan Jeanette, Minneapolis MN
Buckentin Joselynn, Hutchinson MN
Bullock Diane, Ellensburg WA
Bultinck Bill, Mesa AZ
Burrill Alice M, Poulsbo WA
Burrill Barbara, Seattle WA
Busse   Anne Gomsrud, Oregon City OR
Busse   Linda K, Good Thunder MN
Buterin Jerome & Marcia, St Louis MO
Butler Ronald J, Roseville IL
Buxrude Rodney L, Burnsville MN
Bye   John E, Fargo ND

Cameron Patricia, San Dimas CA
Carew   Gretchen, Bemidji MN
Carinder Nelda L, Lakewood CO
Cariveau Linda, Mokena IL
Carlson Kathryn & Allan, Farwell MN
Carlson Lynn, Janesville WI
Carlson Ruth A, Ada MN
Cheadle James, Rapid City SD
Christen Cathy, Wausekesha WI
Christensen Brian, Floyds Knobs IN
Christensen Carol J, New Richmond WI
Christensen Joyce Hilden, Brush Prairie WA
Christensen Linda, Fargo ND
Christenson Aileen, Littleton CO
Christianson Everett & Margaret, Cummings ND
Clark   Joyce L, Lincoln NE
Clark   Thomas, Lennox CA
Clark   Vernon & Patricia, Milwaukee WI
Clayton Susan, South St Paul MN
Cleveland Delores, Sioux Falls SD
Condit Carol, Loveland CO
Cooper Merton & Gloria, New Hope MN
Cooper Susan E, Winona MN
Cornelius Clarence & Doris, Lake Forest CA
Cornelius Elizabeth Grinager, Rantoul IL
Cote   Jean, Coventry CT
Cross   Mrs John R, White Bear Lake MN
Cumber Jane, West Fargo ND
Curtis Shelly, Sunnyvale CA

Dahle   Anne Marie, New Brighton MN
Dahlen Jerry, New Glarus WI

Dahlen Julie, Madison WI
Dahlen Olaf & Lois, New Hope MN
Dahlen Roald, Hixton WI
Dahler Barbara, Stillwater MN
Dahlke Helen Blegen, Spokane WA
Dalager Elaine, Minnetonka MN
Danielson Myron & Janice, Rothsay MN
Davis Eloise, Madison WI
Day Valerie, Waverly NY
Dean Darrols & Linda, Sioux Falls SD
Dedrick Donald, Ann Arbor MI
Dedrick Robert L, McLean VA
Dehler Barb, Ramsey MN
Desserud Per Jacob, Alesund NO
Destrampe Ms Agnes, South Wayne WI
Dikken Laurel, Sacred Heart MN
Divette Dorothea Dahl, Minnetonka MN
Djupedal Knut, Ottestad NO
Dorsey Lizz, Decatur GA
Drovdahl Jerry, Gold Hill OR
Duis Darlene, Tucson AZ
Duklet Iris, Halstad MN
Durspek William & Mary, Marion IA
Dvergsten Cindy, Dolores CO

Eaton Eugenia M, Los Angeles CA
Eaton JoAnn Northfield MN
Edgington Dorothy R, St Paul MN
Egge Berit, Brandbu NO
Egge Bjorn, Brandbu NO
Egge Goeff & Berni, Colorado Springs CO
Egge Olaf, Kelvington SK CN
Eid Ingvald & Marit, Brandbu NO
Eide Iver & Gertrude, Milan MN
Einerson Sherry & Ray, Dodgeville WI
Ekanger Ernest, Hudson SD
Eliason Murial, Renner SD
Elken Carolyn, Pasadena CA
Elken Craig, Mandeville LA
Elken John & Colleen, Rio Verde AZ
Elken Kirk, Berwyn PA
Elken Kyle L, Berwyn PA
Elken Richard, Sun Lakes AZ
Ellefson Darlene, Moorhead MN
Eller Lillian E, Mason City IA
Ellis Carol, Hoyt Lakes MN
Embry Leland & Esther, Novato CA
Endrud Milla, Buxton ND
Enga Paul E, Port Angeles WA
Engebretson Margaret, Pelican Rapids MN
Engebretson Mark & Colleen, Breckenridge MN

Engely Egil Karlo, Jaren NO
Ensminger Rose, Walcott ND
Erickson Becky, Spicer MN
Erickson Carl & Wanda, Hawley MN
Erickson Donna, Evansville MN
Erickson E Stephen, Yokohama JP
Erickson Helen M, Decorah IA
Erickson Norman, Cedar Rapids IA
Erickson Roger D, Fitchburg WI
Erickson Sue, Eden Prairie MN
Erlien Ellef & Alfield, Twin Valley MN
Evans Cheryl, New Smyrna Beach FL
Evans Doris, Carson CA
Evans Hugh & Dorothy J, Stillwater OK
Evanson Donald K, Minneapolis MN
Evenson Frank & Gloria, St George UT
Everson John, Saratoga CA
Ewanowski Barbara & Stanley, Tampa FL

Fadness John & Lois, Chippewa Falls WI
Fallang Don, Helena MT
Fallihee, Ellen, Portland OR
Felkey, Sharon G, Peoria AZ
Fendel Marjorie, Berkeley CA
Fenno Dusty, Mountain Home ID
Fenno Jim, Chippewa Falls WI
Ferris Karen, Vermillion SD
Feulner Susan Myhre, Bloomington MN
Fieldhammer Paul A, Alexandria MN
Finhert Lila, Blanchardville WI
Firing Robert, Minneapolis MN
Fisher Rhonda, Rockwood ON CN
Flathom Daniel & Gloria, Oak Lawn IL
Flatin Daniel, Flemington NJ
Flatla Lars Fredriksen, Lunner NO
Fleck Jorun M, Des Plaines IL
Flem Kari Ruud, Jevnaker, NO
Flexhaug Richard, Calgary AB CN
Floyd Roberta J, North St Paul MN
Fonkert Barbara, St Paul MN
Formo Myrtle O'Connor, Greensboro NC
Formo Lt Col Robert, Greensboro NC
Forsberg Betty, Sioux Falls SD
Foss Beatrice, Northfield MN
Foss Erika, Remer MN
Foss Percy & Harriet, Northwood ND
Foss Sonja, Remer MN
Fosse Helen, Fergus Falls MN
Fossum Jarl, Walla Walla WA
Fossum Thore, Poulsbo WA
Fox Ronald, North Salt Lake UT

Frackman Roger P, Anchorage AK
Fried   Karen, Spring Grove MN
Froslee Bradley A, Minneapolis MN
Froslee Bruce & Susan, Clitherall MN
Froslee Ruth, Vining MN
Frøslie Arne, Drammen, NO
Funke   Karen, Sioux Falls SD

Gaffney Jan, Centralia WA
Gagnum   Gladys, Bowbells ND
Gamme   Ole & Helga, Gran NO
Gasser   Janet, Reedsburg WI
Gelbach Donna, Albany WI
Geno   Larry & Laura, Lindstrom MN
Gerde   Butch, Renville MN
Gerhardson Genevieve, Fergus Falls MN
Gesme   Dean & Ann, Cedar Rapids IA
Gibson   Lois, Regina SK CN
Gibson   Shaun, Montevideo MN
Gilbertson Allen, Hawick MN
Gilbertson Arnold, Fridley MN
Gilbertson Clifford A, North St Paul MN
Gilbertson David A, Bradenton FL
Gilbertson Elmer & Esther, Austin MN
Gilbertson Gerald & Norma, Brooklyn Center MN
Gilbertson Jon & Alice, Denver CO
Gilbertson Judith, Fargo ND
Giblertson Leroy, Montevideo MN
Gilbertson Roger, Houston TX
Gilbertson Russell & Helen, Dawson Creek BC CN
Gilbertson Stuart & Jane, Hudson WI
Gill   Gloria, Canton SD
Gillund Rodney & Sharon, Crosby ND
Gilsrud Ronald D, Longville MN
Gilstrap Kathryn, West Fargo ND
Gipp   Cyndi, Cedar Falls IA
Gjerdingen Mette, Jaren NO
Gleason Marie K, St Johns NL CN
Gnadt   Myron & Rena, Vista CA
Godfrey Anne-Lise, Hampstead NC
Golie   Jack Karston, Eagle River AK
Gomoll   Robert & Linda, Dubuque IA
Gomsrud Andrew, Walla Walla WA
Gomsrud Darrell, Milton-Freewater OR
Gomsrud Mr & Mrs Robert, Sterling IL
Goodkind Sandra, Whitefish Bay WI
Goplin   Eddie, Blue Mounds WI
Gordon   Sara, Lake Forest CA
Goulson Helge & Alice, St Cloud MN
Grady   Susan, Eden Prairie MN
Graham   Charles & Elaine, St Louis Park MN

Graham   Geraldine, Rockford MN
Graner   Judy, Minnetrista MN
Granli   Øivind, Gran NO
Gransborg Terje, Jaren NO
Granum   Tom & Doris, Athens CA
Green   JoAnn, Williston ND
Greenquist Bud & Florence, Brandon MN
Grefsrud Earl & Priscilla, Minneapolis MN
Grimes   Barbara, West Hills CA
Grina   Ragnar Arlid, Lunner NO
Grinager Gifford, Loveland CO
Grinager Lloyd & Dorothy, Sioux Falls SD
Grinager Norman, Nicholasville KY
Grinager Dr Patricia, Palo Alto CA
Grinager Paul & Eunice, Battle Lake MN
Grinna   Grant & Stella, Decorah IA
Griswold Phyllis, Springfield OR
Groff   Walter & Opal, Leeds ND
Groharing Eric C, Twin Lakes WI
Grua   Roger, Ogden UT
Gruber   Barbara M, West Hills CA
Gubbrud Florence, Alcester SD
Gubbrud John, Alcester SD
Gulbranson Kristina, Carrsville VA
Gulden   DeLos, Montevideo MN
Gunderson Alice E, New Auburn WI
Gunderson David N, Fergus Falls MN
Gunderson Marsha, Grand Forks ND
Gurney   Peggy, Magrath AB CN
Gustafson Karen, Forest City IA
Gustafson Robert, Redding CA
Guttormson Susan, Moorhead MN

Haagenstad Dale & Mary, Montrose MN
Haagenstad Gunnar, Roa NO
Hackman Jean, Rudd IA
Hadfield Marlyn, Lakeville MN
Hadland Robert & Donna, Bayfield WI
Hadland Sigurd, San Jose CA
Haga   Ester, Lunner, NO
Hagen   David L & Gerda, New Richmond WI
Hagen   Delmer, Cathay ND
Hager   Yolanda Grinager, Denver CO
Halbakken Barbara L, Plymouth MN
Halbakken Rev David & Margaret, Williston ND
Halbert Ralph & Mary, St Paul MN
Hall   Donna W, Winthrop ME
Halldorsen Elsa G, Winnipeg MB CN
Hallin   Iris & George, Sioux Falls SD
Halstad Jewel, Orangeburg SC
Halver   Bernard & Joyce, Adams MN

Halverson William H, Golden Valley MN
Halvorson Jon, Lacey WA
Halvorson Robert, Athens TN
Hammer Ronald, Petaluma CA
Hankee Karen, Viroqua WI
Hansen Phyllis M J, Webster SD
Hansen Joseph, Edgertib WI
Hansen Karen V, Watertown MA
Hansen Karl H, St Helens OR
Hanson Ansgar & Adeline, Aneta ND
Hanson Borg, Bloomington MN
Hanson Carol, Delafield WI
Hanson Geraldine, Glyndon MN
Hanson Gordon C, Hemet CA
Hanson Jerry, Waseca MN
Hanson John Alvin, Wisconsin Rapids WI
Hanson Karen, Watertown MA
Hanson Karl N, Kenner LA
Hanson Lloyd L, Hastings MN
Hanson Lorraine, Ellsworth WI
Hanson Marion, Whitewater WI
Hanson Mildred, Mayville ND
Hanson Raymond, Twin Valley MN
Hanson Robert, Highland WI
Hanson Roy V & Maxine, Breckenridge MN
Hanten Dr Carroll Egge, Pierre SD
Harfenist Jean Lippka, Santa Barbara CA
Harpestad Ona, Champaign IL
Harris Ronald W, LaCrosse WI
Harris Susan, Shelton WA
Harter Katherine R, Mayville ND
Haugen William, Laporte IN
Haugstad Edgar & Lorraine, Moorhead MN
Hayes Verlyn L, Waukon IA
Hedahl Duane C, Great Falls MT
Heier H Donald, Grand Forks ND
Hektner Mary, Yellowstone Nat'l Park, WY
Helgeson Mary, Southey SK CN
Hellum Astrid Roen, Jevnaker NO
Helm Jerry J, Lago Vista TX
Helmey Thomas P & Marie, Minneapolis MN
Helstedt Robert & Ardella, Minot ND
Henry Jackie, Northfield MN
Hermanson Sheldon & Renee, Laporte MN
Herrick Alma, Valley City ND
Herrick Dale R, Janesville WI
Hesse Jane & Bruce, Plymouth MN
Hessler Jean, Lake Oswego OR
Hessler Steven, Lake Oswego OR
Hesterly Linda, Verona WI
Heusinkveld Jan, Rochester MN

Heyen Astrid, Pelican Rapids MN
Hickey Belma M, Scandinavia WI
Hilden Arne & Gunvor, Brandbu NO
Hilden Lester B, O'Fallon IL
Hill Manfred & Leona, Canton SD
Hillier Dr & Mrs Kenneth, Portales NM
Hoff Mr & Mrs Clifford, Sioux Falls SD
Hoff Tom, Bellingham WA
Hoff Wallace J, Ellicott City MD
Hoffman Harold & Angeline, Bemidji MN
Hogan John & Lynne, Locust Grove VA
Hokenstad Al & Marion, Puyallup WA
Holliday Mr and Mrs Max, Sioux Falls SD
Holman Rick & Marilyn, Mayville ND
Holmen Bob & Andrea S, Red Lodge MT
Holtan Sanford & Ruth, Forest City IA
Holter Edvard, Jaren NO
Holter Mr & Mrs Julian, Canton SD
Honrud Viola, Moorhead MN
Houle Jeanne, Waukegan IL
Houseman Donna M, Cottage Grove MN
Hovland Ardis, Pelican Rapids MN
Hovland Dale, Bloomington MN
Hovland Jolene, Willmar MN
Hovland LaVonne, Beaverton OR
Hovland Myron, Lake Stevens WA
Howland Carolyn & Harley, Bloomington MN
Hulslander Martha Aschim, Garretson SD
Hval Marit & Gudmund, Gran NO
Hvam Judith Katherine, Beaverton OR
Hvamstad Ole, Jaren NO
Hvattum Harald, Brandbu NO
Hvinden Marlan, Petersburg ND

Igelsrud Arthur W, Parrish FL
Indset Lisa & Inge, Gran NO
Ingram Elizabeth A, Lyons MI
Isaacs Alton & Rudell, Clarkfield MN
Iverson Alvin, Spring Valley WI

Jackson Darcea Holt, Poulsbo WA
Jackson Gloria, Pocahantas IA
Jackson Terry & Sue, Monroe WA
Jacobson Norris & Selma, Fertile MN
Jacobson Tammy, Prescott WI
Janda Anne, Bloomington MN
Jeffers Stan & Fran, Decorah IA
Jelen Annette J, Wausau WI
Jensen Sonja, Fargo ND
Jensen Walter T, Poinciana FL
Jenson Richard & Nancy, Albert Lea MN

Jensrud   Oskar Petter, Harestua NO
Jeral   Julia V, Hawley MN
Jesness   Lenore, St Paul MN
Johns   Marvin & Delores, Auburn WA
Johnson   Alton & Virginia, Madison WI
Johnson   Berniece, Garretson SD
Johnson   Brian, St Paul MN
Johnson   Darrell & Bette, Brookings SD
Johnson   Dolores, Starbuck MN
Johnson   Ervin, Darlington WI
Johnson   Harvey, Wayburn SK CN
Johnson   Herbert & Mary Lou, Media PA
Johnson   Jeff L, Arden Hills MN
Johnson   Lawrence & Delphine, Puyallup WA
Johnson   Lloyd & Eleanor, New Richmond WI
Johnson   Michael, Pelican Rapids MN
Johnson   Nancy, Doylestown PA
Johnson   Nancy & Burton, Chaska MN
Johnson   Noel V & Nancy, Chewelah WA
Johnson   Robert E, Bismarck ND
Johnson   Rodney & Joanne, Yakima WA
Johnson   Ruth Ann, Dodgeville IA
Johnsrud Harlan L, Austin MN
Johnsrud Joan, Barneveld WI
Johnsrud Kirstin, New York NY
Johnsrud Reuben & Ethelyn, Dawson MN
Johnsrud Selmer J, Sioux Falls SD
Jolson   Lyle, Burnsville MN
Jones   James 1, Monticello MN
Jones   James II, Brooklyn Center MN
Jones   Jennifer, Duluth MN
Jones   Ken & Evelyn, Monticello MN
Jones   Michael & Karyn, Blaine MN
Jones   Richard & Sandy, Wyoming MN
Jordheim Verdell & Phyllis, Walcott ND
Jorstad   Anne Lise, Gran NO
Jorve   Warren R, Sioux Falls SD
Joynt   Nicole, Chanhassen MN
Juel   Joseph & Martha, Pittsboro NC
Julian   Kathleen, Portland OR
Juncker   Elaine, Canton MI

Kalmoe   Lois, Minneapolis MN
Kammerud Peter A, Star Prairie WI
Kanten   Shirley C, Montevideo MN
Kay   Burnette, Cass Lake MN
Keith   Jeanne, Tacoma WA
Kennedy   Karen, Old Hickory TN
Kerr   Jeanette, Alexandria MN
Kidder   Clark O, Milton WI
Kiefer   Penny Peterson, Portage WI

Kjørven   Christoffer, Lunner NO
Kjosmoen   Einar, Oslo NO
Klein   Janet Buraas, Miles City MT
Klemetson Justin, Ulen MN
Klinger   Linda, Madison WI
Klinkenberg Hans, Oslo NO
Klovstad   Leroy, Pelican Rapids MN
Kluetz   Michael C, Rhinelander WI
Knapp   Vera, Moorhead MN
Knudtson   Jim, Hixson ND
Knutson   Dennis D, Sioux Falls SD
Knutson   Doris, Vermillion SD
Kobe   Ervin, Grand Forks ND
Koenen   Emma, Maynard MN
Koepplin   Rosie, Bremerton WA
Kolle   Betty, Fergus Falls MN
Kooy   Roberta M, Berthoud CO
Kornfeld   Doris E, Williams IA
Kornfeld   Lacy, Greenville SC
Kramer   Karen, Valencia PA
Krantz   Carole, Minneapolis MN
Krenos   George & Nila, Marinette WI
Kristiansen Inger Buan, Lunner NO
Krohn   Julia O, Mt Horeb WI
Kroshus   Gladys, Spring Grove MN
Kroshus   Randy J, Jacksonville NC
Kroshus   Roger & Susan, Dover DE
Kruse   Karen, Kindred ND
Kuehn   Mark, Sioux Falls SD
Kupferberg Marit, Lake Tomahawk WI
Kvamme   Lois Rae, Stoughton WI
Kvenvolden Keith & Mary Ann, Palo Alto CA
Kyle   Marion, Manhattan KS

Ladd   Heidi, Hernando MS
Lamb   Linda & Kylie, Royersford PA
Lambert   Iris, Sterling CO
Langlois   Bernice, Berlin NH
Larsen   Donna, Berlin NH
Larsen   Helen, Red Lodge MT
Larson   Bernice E, Garretson SD
Larson   LeRoy, Lakeland Shores MN
Larson   Linda Lee, Lynwood WA
Larson   Orice & Vivian, Montevideo MN
Larson   Richard, Middleton WI
Larson   Robert & Joslyn, Moorhead MN
Larson   Roy & Ruby, Eagan MN
Larson   Susan, Le Sueur MN
Larson   Syver, Barnesville MN
Lavers   Thomas A, Glendale WI
Lawler   Ann, Benbrook TX

Lawson Gladys, Boone IA
Lee Bob & Chris, Jamestown ND
Lee Gordon, Aneta ND
Lee Harland E, Sheboygan WI
Lehre Astrid, Oslo NO
Lent Jean Thorson, Erie PA
Leonard Odelle M, Greenfield WI
Lidel Karen, Sioux Falls SD
Lider Wilbur & Barbara, Sun City West AZ
Lier Arne Roar, Grindvoll NO
Lier Western Ragnhild Karin, Grindvoll NO
Lindahl Glen & Ruby, Dubuque IA
Lindberg Nels W & Mildred, Yakima WA
Line Richard, Lubbock TX
Linvolden Mette, Gran NO
Liråk Hilde Gulbrandsen, Oslo NO
Lodsby Knut-Iver Molden, Gran NO
Loing Ole & Helen, Princeton MN
Lund Oscar, St Paul MN
Lund Oscar, Minneapolis MN
Lundberg Liv, Brandbu NO
Lundeen James & Beverly, Littleton CO
Lunder Jorun & Hans Gudmund, Lunner NO
Lundmark Arvid & Margaret, Hutchinson KS
Lura DeLoss & Kathryn, Paynesville MN
Lyga Julie, Vernon Rockville CT
Lyngstad Asbjørg, Gran NO
Lyngstad Kåre, Gran NO
Lynne Berit & Arve, Gran NO
Lynne Diane, Bainbridge Island WA
Lynne Palmer, Montevideo MN
Lynner James T, Clarkfield MN
Lynner Lois, Clarkfield MN
Lysakermoen Tormod, Brandbu NO
Lysgaard Robert A, Las Vegas NV
Lysgård Jaren NO

MacDonald Elizabeth Nordlie, Sioux Falls SD
Mack Kari Linstad, Harestua NO
Mack Rose, Fountain Hills AZ
Mackey Karen A, St Paul MN
Mahle Alphina, Mentor MN
Malecek Sacred Heart MN
Manson Gene & Emma Lou, Ringsted IA
Marick Charlotte, Kindred ND
Marquand Kermit W, Littleton CO
Marquette Elaine, Milnor ND
Martens Ella O, Mora MN
Marthaler Jean, St Joseph MN
Martineau Colleen, Champlin MN
Mason Douglas & Sandra, Colville WA

Mathison Zona, Moorhead MN
Maurtvedt Karin, Gran NO
Maurtvedt Nils, Olso NO
Maus Betty, Silverdale WA
McCusker Joan, Centennial CO
McKay Nels, Owen Sound ON CN
McKillip Greg, Summerville SC
Means Margaret, Edina MN
Meester Marjorie, Edina MN
Melaas Roland & Marilyn, Elbow Lake MN
Melbostad Jan Ørnulf, Ski NO
Menk Rebecca, St Peter MN
Metzger Anita, Haymarket VA
Meyer David & Jamie, Eau Claire WI
Michaelis Esther, Nampa ID
Michaelis Steve & JoAnn, Portland OR
Milestone Wayne D, Madison WI
Miller Connor James, Wyoming MN
Miller Margaret R, Apple Valley MN
Miller Merle S, Erskine MN
Miller Michael L, Montrose MN
Miller Shannon Jones, East Bethel MN
Minehart George & Betty, Marshall MN
Miron Charlotte E, Green Bay WI
Mjor Dennis, Redmond OR
Moden Doris, Fairdale ND
Moe Donald, Burnsville MN
Moe Mr and Mrs Otto, Rothsay MN
Moen Cliff & Marilyn, Erhard MN
Moen Myrtle, Waukon IA
Moger Joseph A, Edmonton AB CN
Mogerhagen Ole, Kløfta NO
Mohagen Keith, Fullerton CA
Molden Jack, Woodland Park CA
Moldstad Harald, Jaren NO
Moline Thelma, Seattle WA
Molland Doris, Williston ND
Mongoven Jan Patrick, Carlsbad CA
Monson Carol Lynn, Seattle WA
Monson John & Lillian, Castle Rock CO
Monson Paul & Bernice, Gratiot WI
Monson Theresa, Darlington WI
Morgan Lois J, Hudson WI
Mork Penelle, Moorhead MN
Morland Arden & Doris, Clarkfield MN
Morstad Carl Max, Louisville KY
Morstad Noel Leraan, Littleton CO
Mortenson Dean R, West Fargo ND
Mørtvedt Steffen A, Brandbu NO
Moses Wilson & Maureen, State College PA
Mosher Ronald D, Ruckersville VA

Munkelien Tor Kjølberg, Grindvoll NO
Murdoch Gladys, Raleigh NC
Myhre Hans, Nes pa Hedemarken NO
Myhre Kjell H, Brandbu NO
Myhre Kjellaug, Edina MN
Myhrstuen Arne, Jevnaker NO
Myhrstuen Geir, Jevnaker NO
Myhrstuen Gunhild, Jevnaker NO
Myhrstuen Kåre, Jevnaker NO

Næss Hans, Gran NO
Navarre Harry & Irene, Albuquerque NM
Nelson Alvin & Kaye, Grassy Butte ND
Nelson Bruce, Madison WI
Nelson C William, Traverse City MI
Nelson Carole, Appleton MI
Nelson Clyde & Kathryn, Appleton MN
Nelson Donald C, Glyndon MN
Nelson Gene & Marlys, Stillwater MN
Nelson Gregory, New Glarus WI
Nelson Mr & Mrs James, Blanchardville WI
Nelson John, Sioux Falls SD
Nelson Kermit & Alice, Barnesville MN
Nelson Louise, Pipestone MN
Nelson Luella, Montevideo MN
Nelson Nancy, Stillwater MN
Nelson O Davis, Boulder City NV
Nelson Olive, Blanchardville WI
Nelson Paul & Ruth, Argyle MN
Nelson R B, Madison WI
Nelson Rhoda, Montevideo MN
Nelson Russell, Madison WI
Nelson Shelby J, Sioux Falls SD
Nerby Randi, Jevnaker NO
Nerdalen Jorun, Hønefoss NO
Ness Gerald & Betty, Georgetown TX
Neugaard Edward J, Tampa FL
Newborg Gwen, Portland OR
Newman Royleen, Duluth MN
Nitz Barbara, Rothsay MN
Noack Marlene, Fergus Falls MN
Nokleby Arnold & Eileen, Montevideo MN
Nokleby Omer & Helga, Montevideo MN
Norby Lavonne J, Willmar MN
Nordahl-Hansen Unni Grethe, Oslo NO
Norland Ralph & Marilyn, Rochester MN
Norland Richard, Mankato MN
Norris Pam, Kenmare ND
Nygaard Gene, Crosby ND
Nyhus Albert & Ann, Mt Horeb WI
Nyhus Clifford & Connie, Deerfield WI

Nystrom Daniel & Emily, Waynesboro PA
Nystrom Jeffrey, Forest Lake MN
Nystrom Mary Jones, Forest Lake MN
Nystrom Steven, Hagerstown MD

O'Connor Denise, Renville MN
Oh Beverly, Coeur d'Alene ID
Ohe Donna, Fergus Falls MN
Ohe Gerald & Arlys, Moorhead MN
Ohe Harriet, Minnetonka MN
Ohe Jeff, Edina MN
Ohe Larry, Rothsay MN
Ohe Lorraine, Pelican Rapids MN
Ohe Orland, Rothsay MN
Ohe Ron, Detroit Lakes MN
Oien Jenifer & John, Delta CO
Øiom Liv Kari Sogn, Jevnaker NO
Olerud Arthur B, Fargo ND
Olerud Lesley Ann, Haines AK
Olerud Nick & Carol, Argusville ND
Oleson Ole & Marie, Elsah IL
Olimb Erik Brand, Nesbru NO
Olson Beverly, Grand Forks ND
Olson Calvin & Donna, Highland WI
Olson David & Judy, Shakopee MN
Olson DeLos & Karen, Rochester MN
Olson Donald R, Rochester MN
Olson Duane, Amherst Junction WI
Olson Ethel, Spring Grove MN
Olson Grace, Minneapolis MN
Olson James M, Battle Lake MN
Olson Keith F, Fort Collins CO
Olson Keith G, Crockett CA
Olson Laverne & Joyce, New Richmond WI
Olson Luann & Michael, Lake Elmo MN
Olson Norman V, Dayton OH
Olson Opal H, Iowa City IA
Olson Ray & Carol, Renoldsburg OH
Olson Roger, Overland Park KS
Olson Russell P, Barron WI
Olson Susan, Auburn WA
Olson Viola, Valley City ND
O'Neill Bernice, Spokane WA
Onsager Lawrence W, Berrien Springs MI
Opdahl Loren & Laree, Oakdale MN
Opjordsmoen Bjørn, Spydeberg NO
Opsahl Dr L J, Willmar MN
Ordaz Ruth Ann W, El Paso TX
Oren Keith, Sacramento CA
Oren Kent, Orangevale CA
Ostby David, Anaheim CA

Ostby Roald & Bonnie, Eden Prairie MN
Ostlie Cynthia, Brookings SD
Ouren Shirley Ann, Sun City AZ
Oveson James & Carol, Big Lake MN

Pahos Jane, Trego WI
Pahus Mary Jane, Webster WI
Palmer Vivian, Keizer OR
Parmenter James & Verna, Montrose MN
Pashby Linda Thompson, Sioux Falls SD
Patterson Linda, Portland OR
Paulson Bruce C, Mankato MN
Paulson Howard & Marlys, Moorhead MN
Paulson Keith & Lois, Auston MN
Paulson Leland, Morgantown WV
Paulson Lloyd & Evelyn, Madison WI
Paulson P E, Minneapolis MN
Paulson Robert O, Waseca MN
Pearson Jeanette, Rier Falls WI
Pearson John & Joan, Eagan MN
Pearson Rodney A, Ellsworth WI
Pedersen Trond, Høvik NO
Pederson Dave & Judy, Pelican Rapids MN
Pederson Earl & Osta, Batavia IL
Pederson Gladys C, Minot ND
Pederson Ida V M, Minot ND
Pederson Ingert J, Edina MN
Pederson James L, Stillwater MN
Pederson Joe & Lois, Hawley MN
Pederson Karen A, Blacksburg VA
Pedretti Carol A, Naples FL
Petereit Martin & Iley, Sioux Falls SD
Petersen Sharon K, Rock Springs WI
Peterson Agnes L, Richfield MN
Peterson Barry, Brush Prairie WA
Peterson Don, Milbank SD
Peterson Hans C, Portage WI
Peterson John F, Fargo ND
Peterson Kenneth, Ellsworth WI
Peterson Kenneth R, Woodstock NY
Peterson Lori, New Hope MN
Peterson Mildred, Wolverton MN
Peterson Omar, Canton SD
Peterson Peter A, Portage WI
Peterson Peter A Jr, Reedsburg WI
Peterson Russell & Alice, Amery WI
Peterson Ruth M, Emmett ID
Peterson Sally A, Edina MN
Petrich Roger, Bonlee NC
Pfeffer David, Maple Plain MN
Phelps Darrell, Wentworth SD

Pickard Arlene, Vancouver WA
Pladsen Phyllis, White Bear Lake MN
Plomasen Bruce W, Ocean View DE
Pollestad-Høghaug Sigmund & Kari Lette, Hurdal NO
Pool Dorothy, Edina MN

Quanbeck Alton H, Middleburg VA
Quickstad Donald & Alair, Milaca MN

Raaen Barbara J, Maplewood MN
Radtke Harvey & Gloria, Rothsay MN
Rækstad Per Magne, Brandbu NO
Raknerud Peter, Barnesville MN
Rand Lois, Northfield MN
Rasmus Rodney & Elaine, Forest Grove OR
Rasmussen Richard & Ragna, Chetek WI
Reek Harold & Donna, Mesa AZ
Reiersgord Thomas E, Minneapolis MN
Reiten Chester & Joy, Minot ND
Rekkestad Bill, Fergus Falls MN
Rekstad Ingvald, Sarasota FL
Rekstad Kenneth, Cocolalla ID
Rekstad Stephen, Eden Prairie MN
Resvick Diane, Chippewa Falls MN
Resvick Ethel, Chippewa Falls MN
Rinka June, West Allis WI
Risvold Pam, Austin TX
Robb Diane, Blanchardville WI
Robeck Corrine, Shoreview MN
Roberts Glen & Betty, Great Falls MT
Roberts Maxine, Sioiux Falls SD
Robinson Donna Mae, Arvada CA
Rockswold E Palmer & Betty, Edina MN
Rockswold Dr Gaylan & Mary, Minneapolis MN
Rockswold Lewis, Valley City ND
Roder Elaine, Marshall MN
Roder Elsie, Montevideo MN
Rodriguez Nancy, Fayetteville NC
Roe Laurene S, Minneapolis MN
Roe Ross N, Grants Pass OR
Roen Øistein, Jevnaker NO
Roen Ole, Hønefoss NO
Rogne Leslie & Katherine, Kindred ND
Rogneby Martin, Oslo NO
Røkenes Karl & Gerd, Flateby NO
Rolf James, Brandon MN
Ronken Virgil & Betty, Westby WI
Ronning James & Frances, Rochester MN
Rorem Betty & Harold, Brooklyn Center MN
Rose Judith S, Alexandria MN
Rosendahl Elvern & Anna, Maddock ND

Rosendahl Dr & Mrs Frederick G, Minneapolis MN
Rosendahl Georgia M, Spring Grove MN
Rosendahl Robert & Leona, Decorah IA
Røssum Reidar, Nesøya NO
Roste Jewel, Willmar MN
Rounds Eudora, Battle Lake MN
Rounseville Joann, Spokane Valley WA
Rowbury Cheri, Polson MT
Rowe Murray & Helen, Canton SD
Rud Jerome, Greencastle IN
Rud Leslie & Irene, Montevideo MN
Rude Geraldeen, Minot ND
Rude Larry & Merna, St Maries ID
Rude Leslie, Decorah IA
Rude Wendell & Diann, Bovey MN
Ruden-Kranz Randi D, University City MO
Ruehmann Melvin, Decorah IA
Ruen Howard, Lanesboro MN
Ruffcorn Marjorie, Onawa IA
Running Ronald K, Redlands CA
Rylee David & Tanya, Eden Prairie MN

Sacquitne Lyle & Lucille, Decorah IA
Saetre Roland & Janice, Vining MN
Sagengen Tommy, Bjøneroa NO
Sandbeck Olav, Gran NO
Sandsness Julian & Adeline, Minneapolis MN
Sandven Mr & Mrs Sherman, Milan MN
Sangnæs Johannes, Brandbu NO
Sansburn Meredith, Grand Forks ND
Santoro Shirley, St Paul MN
Santos Edward & Joan, Coeur d'Alene ID
Sarles Marian E, Portland OR
Sater Arnold & Hazel, Austin MN
Sather Pamela, Fargo ND
Saug Larry, Cedar Falls IA
Saugstad Peter Oskar, Gran NO
Sayles Wilbur & Marilyn, Austin MN
Schager Richard & Wendy, Shelton WA
Schau-Stein Karen, Eugene OR
Scheel Susan, West Fargo ND
Schiager Roger A, Sioux Falls SD
Schimke Janice, Bismarck ND
Schipper Mildred J, Delta PA
Schmid Byron & Leslie, Blaine MN
Schmidt Carol, Antioch CA
Schmidt Kathryn A, Rochester MN
Schmidt Norma, Harwood ND
Schmitt Pete & Barb, Burnsville MN
Schrader Joan, Oak Ridge TN
Schultz Blaine & Muriel, South Milwaukee WI

Schultz Carol J, Remer MN
Schultz Clyde & Penny, Mill Valley CA
Schultz Oriette E, Marshall MN
Schultz Robert & Ardelle, Edina MN
Schulz Karen, Stillwater MN
Schumacher Susan, Drayton ND
Schumann Jorun, Brandbu NO
Schutte Rose & Mike, Castalia IA
Schwarz Carol, New Berlin WI
Scott Sandra Haga, Vancouver BC CN
Seifert Eunice, Bismarck ND
Seigerud Eivind, Jaren NO
Seigerud Ole, Gran NO
Selden Dr Margery Stomne, Portage MI
Settles Deborah, Southgate CAS
Severson-Parkhurst Anna, Galesville WI
Sexe Ardis, Ettrick WI
Sha Rose, Pelican Rapids MN
Shadd Deborah A, Cohasset MA
Sharples Glenda, Federal Way WA
Shrake Jean, Chamberlain SD
Shreve Norma, Highland WI
Sigurdson Elin, Jevnaker NO
Simpson Deloise, Lincoln NE
Sindelar Shirley, Shakopee MN
Sjerven Melvin, Kansas City MO
Skarstad Arne Halgeir Kjos, Naples FL
Skattum Dennis, Livingston MT
Skattum Thomas A, Platteville WI
Skiaker Gunnar, Gran NO
Skiaker Gus & Susan, Racine WI
Skiaker Ragnhild & Gudbrand, Ås NO
Skinner Dorothy, Jacksonville FL
Skogrand Marvin, Montevideo MN
Skute Lars Peder, Gran NO
Sladky A Anne, Laporte MN
Sleiziz John, Middleton WI
Sletta Gudrun, Gran NO
Slocum Lillian, Monroe WI
Slotsve Wayne & Donna, Omaha NE
Smedshammer Clara, Valley City ND
Smerud Judy, Springtown TX
Smith Judy, Berkeley CA
Smith Lorraine, Los Altos CA
Smith Nancy J, Neche ND
Snelling Dorothy, Ogema SK CN
Sogn Gudbrand, Jevnaker NO
Soland Arne A, Minneapolis MN
Solberg Dale W, Soldotna AK
Solberg Glenn, Gully MN
Solberg Herb, Grand Forks ND

Solheim George & Kathleen, Drake CO
Solien Ruth, Fargo ND
Solwey Pamela, Fargo ND
Sommers Marlene, Minnetonka MN
Sommerstad Jane, Eina NO
Sonnek Delores, Carlos MN
Sørbekk Arne, Jaren NO
Sorensen Marilyn, St Paul MN
Sorenson Thomas A, Northfield MN
Sorgen Vilgard I, Moorhead MN
Sørli Torun, Gran NO
Sorlie Roger & Rosemary, Lavista NE
Sorum Charles & Mary, Pelican Rapids MN
Sorum Dean & Carol, Moorhead MN
Sørum Erik, Roa NO
Sorum Jon & Ann, Parkers Prairie MN
Sorum Troy, Minnetonka MN
Spande Beverly, Winona MN
Sponheim Beverly, Apple Valley MN
Stabo Robert, North Potomac MD
Stadum Beverly, Øyer NO
Stair Carin, Tucson AZ
Stakston Malin, Burnsville MN
Stangeland Bertha J, Moorhead MN
Staxrud Gail I, Minneapolis MN
Staxrud Lars, Brandbu NO
Steele Lillian, Seattle WA
Steen Liv Mette, Gran NO
Stenbroten Olga, Monroe WI
Stenersen Helge, Brandbu NO
Stenslie Frank, Jaren NO
Stensrud Bjørg & Roy, Roa NO
Stensrud Dianne, Salem OR
Stephenson, Raymond A & Lea, Springville IA
Sterud Knut, Brandbu NO
Stevens Allard, Granite Falls MN
Stock Bonita, Fergus Falls MN
Storlie Rolf & Janice, Houston MN
Stormo Claryce, Helendale CA
Stowitts Sonja, Madison WI
Stowman Pauline, Rothsay MN
Strand Ruth, St Paul MN
Strommen Ardith L, Muskego WI
Strømnes Anne Lise, Roa NO
Sullivan Charlotte, St Louis Park MN
Sullivan Lorna & Michael, Midland OH
Sundahl George, Beaverton OR
Sundrum Joyce, Golden Valley MN
Sunvold Darrell & Mary, Sacred Heart MN
Svendsrud Per, Brandbu NO
Swalin Gregory & Linda, Spicer MN

Swanton Milo K & Irene, Madison WI
Swenson Alf or Genevieve, St Cloud MN
Swenson Edna R, Hawley MN
Swoffer Brian, Minneapolis MN

Tabbut Judy, Pelican Rapids MN
Takeshita Sandra L, Brea CA
Taylor Arielle, St Paul MN
Taylor Sandra Kay Sandbeck, Skamokawa WA
Teigland Joy T, Excelsior MN
Thingelstad Steven, Summerset SD
Thomas John J & Christina, Gilroy CA
Thompson Dallas, Glenwood MN
Thompson David, Weston CT
Thompson Don & Carol, Albuquerque NM
Thompson Harold & Adella, McIntosh MN
Thompson Jane E, Sioux Falls SD
Thompson Jodi, Breckenridge MN
Thompson John E, Nekoosa WI
Thomsen Ernest & Anna, St Paul MN
Thon Gunnar, Oslo NO
Thon Toril, Jevnaker NO
Thoni Rev Fred & Kai, St Paul MN
Thoreson Rev Allan & Iris, Marshalltown IA
Thoreson Ardell & Lillie, Embarrass MN
Teigen Diane R, White Bear Lake MN
Tingelstad Marit, Brandbu NO
Tingelstad Merle & Kathy, Andover MN
Tisdel Mr & Mrs Thomas, Elko MN
Tollefson Dean E, Colorado Springs CO
Tollefson Helen S, Fargo ND
Tollefson Mrs Ralph, Kissimee FL
Tomren Holly, Long Beach CA
Torkelson David D, Fargo ND
Torsey Sally, Sioux Falls SD
Torvik George & Norma, Minneapolis MN
Toso John A & Joanne D, Highland CA
Trana John, San Fernando CA
Trandem Dennis, Bagley MN
Tronsrue George M, Jr, Seattle WA
Trosvig Robert A, Everett WA
Tryhus Joan & Trueman, Scottsdale AZ
Tryhus Richard O, Fargo ND
Tunell Maxine & Denny, Sioux Falls SD
Tuorila Diane, St Cloud MN
Tweeton Carla J, Fergus Falls MN
Tweeton Jackie & Daryl, Apple Valley MN
Tweito Andy, Six Mile SC
Tweito Daniel, Irmo SC
Tweito Theodore G, Lavonia GA

Membership List 1990-2010

Ulrich	Beth Benson, Aurora IL
Ulven	Chuck & Evie, Moorhead MN
Ulven	Michael S, Silverton OR
Ulven	Ron & Deanna, Hawley MN
Ulvick	Sydney, Gaithersburg MD
Urberg	Ingrid, Camrose AB CN

Vander Waerdt Lois, St Louis MO
Vane Floie M, Anacortes WA
Velohagen Kari, Jevnaker NO
Vestby Asbjørn, Hønefoss NO
Vestby Hilde, Oslo NO
Vesterli Olaug Marie Wien, Gran NO
Vesthagen Ole Arild, Oslo NO
Vick Dean, Apache Junction AZ
Vigen Larry A, Moorhead MN
Vikesland Hildred Erickson, Tacoma WA
Villars Kjerste, Minneapolis MN
Vind Carol, Hackensack MN
Vinje Lyla, New Glarus WI
Voigt Fredrick & Joan, St Louis Park MN
Volney Betty J, Minneapolis MN
Vraa Earl, Durand WI

Wade Daraleen, Salem OR
Wagner James & Dianne, Westminster CO
Wahl Allen E, Madison WI
Wahl Rev Palmer A, DeForest WI
Wahl Richard, Millersville MD
Walder Linda, Oregon WI
Waldoch Faith, Rothsay MN
Waldoch Laura, Forest Lake MN
Wallack Denise, St Paul MN
Walz Ardes, Sun City West AZ
Wamstad Ruth, Nora Springs IA
Wang Bonnie C, Argyle WI
Wanke Elizabeth M, Milan MN
Ward Martha & Brian, Rush City MN
Ward Valeria, Eilson AFB AK
Warner Barbara J, Rochester MN
Washam Ruth, Hamilton OH
Wasowicz Donna, Shoreview MN
Watkins Clayton, Argyle WI
Watson Sharon, Buxton ND
Webb Ellen Bratvold, Folsom CA
Weber Carol Harris, Wayne NJ
Webster Beverly, Willmar MN
Weckerly J W & Katherine, Albuquerque NM
Weckerly Philip & Katherine, Mt Vernon WA
Weeks Gloria Everson, West Palm Beach FL
Weigel James & Mary Anne, Carmichael CA

Welhaven Randi, Minneapolis MN
Wendt Brooke, Dawson AL
Wesloh Janelle Jones, Stacy MN
Wessling Stacey R, Sioux City IA
Westberg Arlene, Hoffman MN
Western Dale, Pelican Rapids MN
Western Eric & Linda, Oak Creek WI
Western Kirsten Heier, Grindvoll NO
Western Ragnhild Karin Lier, Grindvoll NO
Western Robert & Kay, Stanley ND
Wevik Alfreda, Sioux Falls SD
Wevik Delmar, Chamberlin SD
Wevik Ernie, Grand Island NE
Wheeler Janice, Marion NC
White Sandra Kjella, Minneapolis MN
Wicken Ken, Springfield MO
Wiedenfeld Linda, Prairie du Sac WI
Wien Hans, Roa NO
Wien Olaug Marie Vesterli, Gran NO
Wikel Patricia Eggee, Crete NE
Wilcox Kristin, Sioux Falls SD
Williams Sarah, Springfield VA
Wilson Wilfred & Margaret, Red Wing MN
Windom Larry & Kathy, Rockford MN
Windom Orlin, Elbow Lake MN
Winger Gerald D, Sterling IL
Winkelman Paul, Pequot Lakes MN
Winkelman Wendy, Mesa AZ
Winter Grace Grinager, Sioux Falls SD
Wirstad Ingrid, Lunner NO
Wirstad Ragnar, Jevnaker NO
Witt Arleen, Pollock Pines CA
Woien Amund, Gran NO
Wolander Carl, Burnsville MN
Wood Judith, South Colby WA
Woodward Avis, Madison WI
Woog Jean M, Maplewood MN
Woyen Travis, Moorhead MN
Wright Marlene J, Cedar Rapids IA
Wurden Eileen, Fisher MN

Young Cynthia, Tustin CA
Young Jane, Berthoud CO

Zablotney Helen K, Makoti ND
Zempel Arnold & Carolyn, Montevideo MN
Ziesemer Gerald, Fergus Falls MN
Zimmerman Mary Lou, Richville MN

Chapter Eleven
North American Immigrants from Hadeland

Genealogy Committee member Brian Christensen has used the *Kontaktforum* Emigrant Identification Project database to develop an interesting set of statistics about the people who left Hadeland to make their home in North America. The exact numbers change as more information about Hadeland's emigrants is collected, but with the majority identified, his model is now statistically sound. His analysis is being published in its entirety in a separate volume.

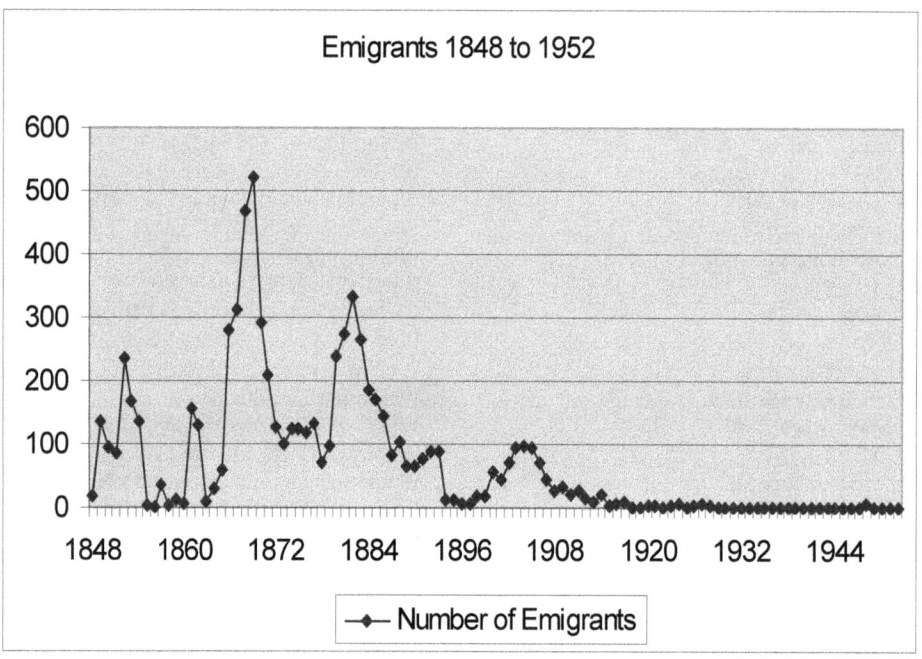

Immigration from Hadeland to North America is believed to have begun as early as the 1820s, but documented evidence about those early adventurers is sketchy. We know that in 1842 Halvor Larson Lysenstøen was the first recorded emigrant from Hadeland. Four years later in 1846 he returned to Norway and appeared unannounced one Sunday morning at a church in Brandbu. He must have engendered a strong reaction among his Norwegian relatives and neighbors, because steady emigration started a couple years later in 1848. Perhaps stories about abundant, fertile farm lands were attractive to the Norwegian relatives.

On April 1, 1848, twenty five year old Erik Larsen Myhre, a tenant farmer at Askim farm (Askimeiet) in Tingelstad, became the first in Gran parish's *udflyttede* (church register of notice of intent to move out of the parish) to list his destination as "Amerika." Sixteen more Hadeland residents also emigrated in the spring of that year. These pioneers led the waves of emigration from Hadeland that ebbed and flowed over the next 100 years.

Between 1848 and 1854, about 870 Hadelanders emigrated. The numbers dropped steadily until in 1861 when only 156 people emigrated. Another 162 followed in 1862 but then emigration almost stopped until the Civil War came to an end.

The largest group of Hadelanders came to America after the Civil War. Almost 2100 left Hadeland between 1866 and 1871. In the 1870s, emigration leveled off to about 100 per year, but migration picked up again in the 1880s, exceeding 200 emigrants a year.

The last wave of migration came at the turn of the century, from 1900 to 1905. After that only a handful migrated each year, and none came during World War I and World War II. The last emigrant listed in the *Kontaktforum* Emigrant Database is Kjell Gilbert Gulbrandsen Bjellum, who was 24 when he left Oslo in 1952.

Names of the Hadeland Emigrants

In old Norway there were very strict naming conventions, but the use of a surname as a family name wasn't one of them.

The first name was given at birth by the parents. The first son was named for the maternal grandfather, the second son for the paternal grandfather. The first daughter was named for the paternal grandmother, the second daughter for the maternal grandmother. If a spouse died, the next child of the same sex born to the surviving parent and new spouse was named for the deceased. If a child died, the next child of the same sex was named for the deceased sibling. Most first generation immigrants followed the same conventions, although it was not uncommon for the names to be Anglicized: a daughter might be named Julia in honor of grandmother Johanna; a son, Oscar, in honor of grandfather Ole.

The second name identified the individual's father. This patronym added the word "sen" (son) or "datter/dotter" (daughter) to the father's name. For example, Olav's children would all use the patronymic Olavssen or Olavsdatter. As a general rule, this name did not change over a person's lifetime. In rare instances, when a single mother married or a widow remarried, young children assumed their stepfather's patronym.

The third name was *not* a family name: it was the name of the farm on which the individual lived. If his parents were tenants on the Solberg farm when he was born, Nils Olessen would be identified as Nils Olessen Solbergeie. Perhaps he was a tenant on the Dvergsten farm when he married; church records would list him as Nils Olessen Dvergsteneie. If at the time of his immigration Nils and his family were tenants on the Alm farm, he would be listed in the *udflyttede* as "Nils Olessen Almseie." The suffixes –eie and –iet were typically used in official records to differentiate tenant farmers from the land owners, but this convention was not always strictly followed. Rather than a family name, in old Norway the third name was really more like an address. When he introduced himself, Nils Olessen Røysemeie was actually saying, "I'm Ole's son Nils, and I am a tenant on the Roysum farm."

When Norwegians arrived in America, adapting to the idea of surname as family name was a confusing transition for them. Many tried out different surnames during their first years in their new country, and this "experimentation" can make finding and following family members through land, church, and census records a real challenge. Norwegian immigrants chose their surnames in two basic ways:

- Patronym as surname. Female patronyms (e.g., Olesdatter) were not used as family names. Most quickly swapped the Norwegian "-sen" for the American "-son." The double 's' (Johansson) was usually, but not always, dropped (Johanson).
- Farm name as surname. Many immigrants chose to use a farm name as a last name. Most adopted the name of the farm from which they had emigrated, but some used the name of a farm that held other significance for them (the farm on which they were born, for example).

Brothers might both choose to use their farm name as a surname, but if they brought their families to America from different farms, each branch would have a different last name. One brother might use his patronym, the other a farm name. One immigrant's child might opt to continue to use his father's patronym while another adopted his own patronym as a surname. Add the various ways in which Norwegian patronyms and farm names might be Anglicized, and the recipe for Norwegian genealogical research disaster is complete!

With all of that in mind, here is a list of the most common patronymic names among Hadeland emigrants:

PATRONYM	Number of emigrants
Olsen/Olsdatter	961
Andersen/Andersdatter	829
Pedersen/Pedersdatter	682
Hansen/Hansdatter	651
Larsen/Larsdatter	446
Erik/Eriksdatter	391
Nilsen/Nilsdatter	313
Gudbrand/Gudbrandsdtr.	300
Halvor/Halvorsdatter	228
Iver/Iversdatter	212

Birthplaces of Emigrants

The historic parishes of Tingelstad and Brandbu are part of today's Gran *kommune*. Many Hadelanders married others from the neighboring areas of Hønefoss, Aadalen, Eidsvol, Land, Buskerud, Norderhov, and Akershus, and this is reflected among emigrant families. There were also 28 Swedes among the Hadeland emigrants – spouses of Hadeland emigrants.

BIRTH PLACE	TOTAL
Gran	1707
Lunner	1362
Tingelstad	1293
Brandbu	1194
Jevnaker	1090
Vestre Gran	327
Vestre Brandbu	211
Moen, Tingelstad	96
Hurdal, Akershus	83
Oslo (Christiania)	55

Combining the numbers from the parishes of Gran, Tingelstad, Brandbu, Vestre (West) Gran, West Brandbu, and Moen/Tingelstad brings the percentage of Hadeland immigrants from today's Gran *kommune* to over 80 percent.

TOP 20 FARMS

Alm	108	Lunder	86	Framstad	68	Hilden	46
Dæhlen	108	Kjos	78	Askim	65	Bjøralt	46
Dvergsten	100	Lynne	75	Bilden	60	Haakenstad	45
Egge	99	Molden	71	Horgen	58	Morstad	42
Næs	98	Grinager	70	Hvaleby	47	Olimb	41

Travel to North America

Emigration to North America was almost always done in the spring of the year. More than two thirds (68%) of all departures were at the beginning of spring in the months of April and May, while 86% of departures occurred in the warm months between April and August. Tenant farmer contracts typically expired in the spring, and this may help explain the spike in April and May departures. Of course, crossing the Atlantic was simply much easier during the summer months. Out of the 7,706 emigrants for whom a specific date of departure is known, none departed in January and only 24 departed in December.

The journey to America was challenging. The cramped conditions made sanitation difficult and isolation of the sick impossible. Thirty-two died during passage. Six deaths were infants under age 1, while twenty were under age 10. Older people were also among the deaths – Johannes Pedersen (Vesterneiet), age 74 and Marte Hansdatter Melaas, age 70, died during their emigration in 1869. Eli Pedersdatter Falang died at age 59 during her family's passage in 1853. Anne Olsdatter Kjos died in May 1850 a couple of months after her 51st birthday. The most tragic situation occurred with the Steen family of Jevnaker. Bernt Magnus Steen (age 42), his wife Mathilde (40), and their six children, ages 4 to 16, perished with the sinking of the steamer *Norge* when it shipwrecked at Rockall, a small rocky islet in the North Atlantic.

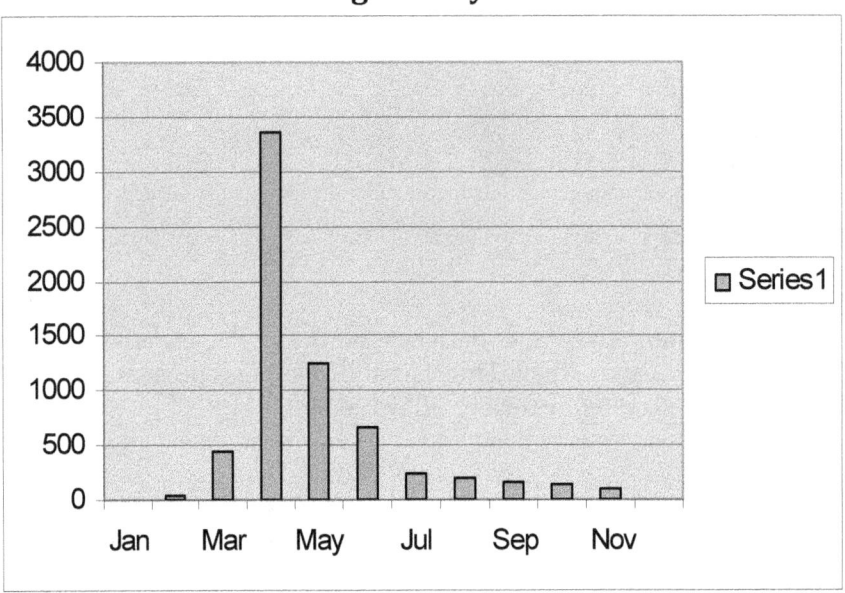

Births During Emigration

Emigration was not always tragic. Hundreds of small children made the passage to America without serious incident. There were 1,035 children 5 years and younger; 156 of these were infants under one year of age. There were 38 mothers nursing babies less than 3 months old. More surprisingly, at least seven women gave birth to children during the Atlantic Ocean crossing. A few were born aboard ships on the ocean and others were born at ports along the way. The first transatlantic birth was Randi Olsdatter, daughter of Ole Gulbrandsen Melaas, age 41 and wife Ellena Pedersdatter (from Hytta), age 36.

Name	Birthdate	Departure Date
Randi Olsdatter	18 Jun 1853	14 Apr 1853
Marthe Karine Torersdatter	29 Jun 1854	30 Apr 1854

Martin Gudbrandsen	17 May 1854	11 Apr 1854
Anne Marie Johannesdatter	9 Jun 1864	Apr 1864
Olaf Steffensen	21 Apr 1866	22 Apr 1866
Anton Refonde Gulbrandsen	Apr 1868	16 Apr 1868
Atlanta Pedersdatter	1870	10 May 1870

Age of Emigrants

The average emigrant was single and in his/her early 20s. It's not hard to picture a young person setting off for the New World to start a new life. It was not uncommon for an entire family to emigrate together, including the older generations. More than twenty of the emigrants were above age 74. The oldest was 88 year old Anne Nilsdatter Karlsrud who emigrated in 1853 with her son Engebret Syversen and wife, along with grandchildren Anne Mathea 13, Mari Elisabeth 10, Sophie 7, and Syver, 4.

Oldest Emigrants

Name	Date of Emigration	Age
Anne Nilsdtr Karlsrud	14 Apr 1853	88
Erik Johnsen Tømte	10 Jun 1875	83
Kirsti Gudbrandsdtr Wieniet	24 Apr 1871	81
Randi Eriksdtr	16 Apr 1869	79
Gudbrand Gudbrandsen	23 Apr 1869	79
Anne Olsdtr Melaas	15 May 1852	78
Ragne Eriksdtr Næs	21 Apr 1868	78
Dorthe Gudbrandsdtr Sogn	22 Apr 1880	78
Dorthe Johansdtr Sørumsiet/Hvalebyeiet	15 Apr 1868	77
Ole Carstensen Undlieseiet	21 Apr 1869	77
Ingeborg Gudbrandsdtr Berger	23 Apr 1869	77
Peder Pedersen Solum	23 Apr 1869	77
Nils Halvorsen Guldeneiet Vindorum	10 Jun 1875	77
Berthe Torstensdtr Ragnilrud	10 Jun 1875	77
Kari Gudbrandsdtr Fragot	15 Jun 1883	77
Kjersti Amundsen	26 Apr 1893	77
Iver Olsen Egge	28 Apr 1870	77
Kjersti Paulsdtr Lindstadeiet	22 Apr 1875	76
Karen Ingebretsdtr Dynna	16 Apr 1879	76
Anne Hansdtr Melbostadeiet	25 Apr 1873	75

Destination: Heartland of North America

We have been able to record a great deal of information about the destination of the Hadeland emigrants. Most were moving to the farmlands of North America to reside in Norwegian-American communities, often to be near relatives who had emigrated earlier.

Many of the Hadelanders spent a short time at their original destination before moving on to less settled areas where more land was available under the Homestead Act.

From obituaries, cemetery lists, and information provided to the Hadeland Lag genealogists, we know that the majority found a permanent home in Minnesota, followed by North Dakota, Wisconsin, Iowa, and South Dakota.

Hadeland immigration was not exclusively to the United States. Over 100 are known to have settled in the Canadian provinces - mostly in Alberta, Saskatchewan, and Manitoba. Then there was Gunder Steffensen from the Vestern farm in Lunner. He was born September 5, 1820 and immigrated to Brazil. He was the only known emigrant to South America.

Death Locations

Minnesota	1314	Canada	88	Montana	19	Idaho	12
North Dakota	645	Washington	70	Oregon	18	Illinois	12
Wisconsin	552	Norway	65	Alberta	17	Nebraska	9
Iowa	440	Saskatchewan	41	New York	13	Manitoba	7
South Dakota	229	California	30	Utah	13	Colorado	4

Chapter Twelve
Recollections of Pioneer Times

Hadeland Lag members are encouraged to submit stories about events in the lives of their pioneer ancestors for publication in the *Brua*. Since 2002 these have been published in the popular "Recollections of Pioneer Times" column. The articles paint a vivid picture of what life was like for early generations of Hadeland-Americans.

Traveling by Covered Wagon
"Recollections of Pioneer Times"
Brua, May 2003
By Verlyn Anderson

    Family stories of how our immigrant ancestors traveled to reach their places of settlement on the edge of the frontier were always fascinating for those of us growing up in the American Midwest. For Norwegian immigrants who arrived in America before the mid-1870s and who wanted to acquire a homestead, it is almost a certainty that they had to travel by covered wagon to find land available for homesteading. After about 1875, the immigrants were more apt to travel by train, at least for the majority of the distance to the frontier where this land was available.

    My paternal great-grandparents left Norway in 1868 in that great wave of emigration that followed the American Civil War. After spending two years in Fillmore County, located in the extreme southeastern corner of Minnesota, they loaded up a covered wagon and headed north to where homesteading land was available, to Trondhjem Township in Otter Tail County. They, like thousands of other Norwegian immigrants, made that journey of over 300 miles (about 500 kilometers) in a covered wagon.

What did that covered wagon look like? How fast could they travel? How long did the journey from Fillmore County to Otter Tail County take? The immigrants in the Midwest commonly used a lightweight covered wagon, sometimes called a prairie wagon. It was about nine feet (2.75 meters) long, four feet (1.25 meters) wide and had a cloth water-proof cover attached over bent wood bows. Two oxen or two horses pulled this covered wagon. Most of the immigrants used oxen because they were more hardy, stronger and less expensive than horses.

My great-grandparents did not leave any written records that told about that long journey. Nor have I been able to locate any descriptions of that trip written by any of my Hadeland immigrant ancestors. However, I have located several other accounts written by people who experienced that arduous trip. Because they traveled the same route at about the same time as my ancestors, their experiences must have been similar. These are the recollections of these pioneers.

Mathilde Berg Grevstad in her memoir entitled *Ole-Iver and Johanne Berg, Pioneers: Account of Covered Wagon Days* tells what was packed in their covered wagon for the trip from Rushford, Fillmore County to Lake Park, Becker County, Minnesota, May 23 to July 4, 1871.

> "All that we possessed of worldly goods was in the wagon. There was the kitchen stove. Two large Norwegian chests contained our clothes. There were two small trunks, a box for food, another for dishes, and many other articles such as buckets and kegs, crocks and jars, carpenter tools, a hayfork, rake, scythe, axes and smaller items that would be useful in a new settlement fifty miles or more from any village. On top of all these things was spread our bedding – feather beds, fur robes, quilts and pillows. This arrangement provided comfortable beds. Mother and father slept in the front part of the wagon. We children slept in the rear.
>
> Attached to the back of the wagon was a crate in which we kept four hens and a rooster. The rooster crowed and awakened us each morning. Our two cows walked with us as we traveled."

Mikkel A. Mellum was ten years old when he and his parents emigrated from Stange, Norway to Rushford, Minnesota in 1868. After living there two years they traveled by an oxen-drawn covered wagon into Otter Tail County and settled in Norwegian Grove, the neighboring township north of Trondhjem Township. They left Rushford on May 15th and arrived at their destination on June 6, 1870. Mikkel Mellum's granddaughter, Jeanette, was married to my mother's uncle, Theodore Ohe, whose father had immigrated from Hadeland. It was from Jeanette that I received her grandfather's memoirs that were originally published in the *Fergus Falls Journal* between November 21, 1933 and December 18, 1937. He tells about their covered wagon trip to Otter Tail County:

"On the 15th of May, 1870, we had our wagons ready to start for Otter Tail County. I and my parents in one wagon and my brother, Martin, and his wife and a two-year-old daughter in another wagon. We met two other wagons at Preston, Fillmore County. In those wagons were three Trosvik boys, John, Anders and Martin, and their mother in one wagon and Ole Granrud, Dhyre Dillerud and Ole Madsen, Jr. in another. We also had a little herd of cows that some of us drove behind the wagons.

When the road was good and the weather nice we traveled about 25 miles a day. When it rained and on Sundays we did not travel. Mother and old Mrs. Trosvik did the cooking. We had no stove but they baked bread in a kettle with a cover. It was as good bread as anyone could eat. We had plenty of milk and dried meat, so we lived well and everyone was happy.

We had the names of all of the biggest towns we should pass but sometimes we did not know what road to take. It was my job to run up to some farmhouse to ask about the right road to a certain town. We crossed the Mississippi on a long bridge for which we had to pay a toll, 25 cents for each wagon and 10 cents for each cow. They told us it was nine miles between St. Paul and Minneapolis. It was open land and plenty of grass so we camped there one night, about where the fair grounds are now.

When we got to St. Cloud that was as far as the railroad was built so we stopped and bought some provisions and we also bought our breaking plows. It was a rainy summer and the further west we got the more mud holes we had to go through. There was a long stretch of woodland on this side of Alexandria. The road was nothing but a mud hole. Once in a while we were stuck so we had to double up, but we had plenty of teams to pull us through. When we got to Evansville, we met a caravan of Indian freighters.* They were hauling furs for the Hudson Bay Company. They had two wheel carts made of wood and one pony on each cart. They said there were 300 carts, and they did not grease the axles. They squeaked and made so much noise we could hear them many miles away. They would deliver their freight to St. Cloud where they would load it on the railroad.

We got to Pomme de Terre, Grant County; our nearest post office for the settlers in Norwegian Grove. The next day I remember well is when we crossed the river in Fergus Falls. The river at that time was wide and deep. I got to admit I was scared when we crossed that river as the water went up onto the wagon box. They said there was one log house in Fergus at that time, but I did not see it. That day we got as far as Elizabeth. There was a little store there. In the evening we went out to Old Man Stetvold's place. He had settled the year before, 1869. My father was acquainted with him from Norway. The next day we started on the last leg of our journey up to Ole Madsen's place, which is now in Norwegian Grove. On the morning of June 6, 1870, my father and my brother, Martin, hauled their covered wagons onto their claims and so established their future homes. They were the first to settle on the prairie without any timber on it in Norwegian Grove."

Mikkel Mellum goes on to describe how they built their first home, about breaking up the first 15 acres of land that summer and about the many hardships that the pioneers experienced with prairie fires, grasshoppers and blizzards. He also told about many happy times. His is a most interesting memoir. I find myself returning to this primary account often to review the everyday life of our ancestors. It is very satisfying to read about these experiences, it helps me appreciate the hardships that our pioneer ancestors endured as they struggled to establish new homes and a new livelihood on the Midwestern prairies of America.

*The "Indian freighters" is a reference to the famous "Red River carts" that were driven by Meti drivers. (The Metis were Canadian persons of mixed race, the offspring of a white person, usually French, and a Native American.) For many decades they hauled freight between Winnipeg, Canada, and St. Paul prior to the arrival of the railroad. By 1870 the railroad had been completed to St. Cloud, Minnesota so the Red River carts' journeys ended there.

The Drama at St. Helen
"Recollections of Pioneer Times"
Brua, August 2004
Submitted by Gunhild, Kåre and Geir Arne Myrstuen, Jevnaker, Norway

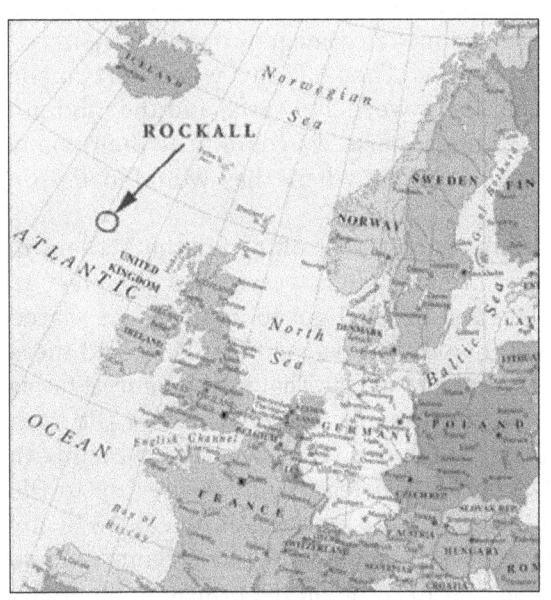

It was 7:45 Tuesday morning, June 28, 1904. The *SS Norge* had become grounded on the island of St. Helen – gashed broadside about two nautical miles east of the little cliff island Rockall in the Atlantic Ocean. Many of the 727 emigrants aboard stood in unbelief on the deck. The crew members ran in all directions. An officer who tried to make his way through the tightly-packed passengers was grabbed ahold of, "What is going on?" "What has happened?"

A gasp went through the crowd: "We are sinking!"

While the crew worked to get out the 8 lifeboats, the bow of the ship sank deeper. Soon there was water on the foredeck. Panic arose among the passengers Women and men -poor cotters from Norway, Swedish farm workers, and Russian emigrants leaving their country because of the Russo-Japanese War – all on their way to 'The Promised Land' – clumsily tried to put on life jackets. They had never seen life jackets before and didn't know how to put them on. They could not even find the life jackets for the small children.

Some found places in the lifeboats which were launched. One of the boats became so full of people that one of the tackles slipped and broke loose so the people in the boat fell into the ocean. Some boats managed to land on the water in the normal way and were pushed away from the ship.

But one of the boats had a great deal of difficulty. When it was being pushed off the upper deck, the aftmost tackle was not releasing the boat. The captain stood on the bridge and saw what was happening. Instantly he ran down to the deck, grabbed an axe, and chopped the rope in two, thus releasing the boat. The lifeboat immediately fell and upon hitting the surface, it nearly filled with water. After that no one knows what happened to that boat.

When another lifeboat had gotten a little ways away from the ship, the people on the lifeboat saw the bow of the *Norge* begin to slide into the water. Screams of terror from the 600 who stood stranded on the deck pierced the air. Instantly the people in the lifeboat became aware that a rescue boat on the back of the upper deck broke loose and began to slide down the deck. It then shot, seemingly out of nowhere, through the air and into the helpless group on the deck. By that time the stern of the ship was up in the air and the ship's propeller was exposed – high and dry! Almost immediately, the whole ship disappeared into the 40-meter (130 foot) deep ocean – while the mass of people on the deck met their fate with a "solemn stillness," as was learned from some crew members who stood with them, but who survived.

From the Records

Baker Bernt Martinsen Steen was born in 1861 at Kløvstad, South Land, confirmed in 1876 in South Land and lived at the Hadeland Glassworks, son of church singer Martin Hanvold. He married Mathilde Josefine Nilsen on January 7, 1888. She was born in 1865 at Pramhus in Eidskogen, confirmed in 1879 in Jevnaker, daughter of farmer Johannes Nilsen and Maren Olsdtr. Their children were:

1. Johan Martinius Steen, born 14 May 1888 at the Glassworks, baptized June 17 in Jevnaker. Johan Martinius Magnussen Steen was confirmed 21 Sept. 1902 in Jevnaker, lived at Nesbakken.
2. Konrad Marius Steen was born June 25, 1889 in South Land (Fluberg), baptized July 28. Konrad Marius Steen was confirmed September 27, 1903 in Jevnaker, lived at Nesbakken.
3. Borghild Steen was born June 17, 1891 at the Randsfjord Creamery, baptized July 26 in Jevnaker.
4. Osvald Steen was born May 15, 1896 at Nesbakken, baptized July 12 in Jevnaker.
5. Hjørdis Steen was born October 2, 1898 at Nesbakken, baptized October 23 in Jevnaker.
6. Hedevig Steen was born February 15, 1902 at Nesbakken, baptized May 18 in Jevnaker.

Hadeland Settlement at Northwood, North Dakota
"Recollections of Pioneer Times"
Brua, November 2007
By Peder H. Nelson, originally published in Norwegian in the 1935 *Brua*

The area around Northwood ND is one of the largest Hadeland settlements in the Northwest. The first settlers arrived 60-65 years ago and now rest in the cemetery, but their memories will live on for many generations. These old pioneers accomplished a great achievement when they settled and built their homes in this vast, lonely, and wild prairie. With many struggles and even more privation, but with untiring determination, they worked steadily forward to prosperity that can be seen in the beautiful farms where the descendants of these pioneers now live. It can be said in tribute to the descendants of these first Hadelanders that they hold their ancestors' heritage in high honor and that the Norwegian newspapers are still found in every home even though the inhabitants are second and third generation Americans. On these farms we now have people with Hadeland names such as Hagen, Tingelstad, Skerva, etc ...

In May of 1870, something was seen along the horizon. It was a prairie wagon pulled by a team of oxen. This meant that there were settlers moving into the wild prairie. There were two men in this lonesome prairie wagon, Swedish brothers named Lindstrom, the first pioneers in the Northwood settlement. During the first 4 years they lived there, their closest neighbors were 15 miles away. In 1875 they were followed by settlers from Hallingdal; Hadelanders began arriving not long after that. In 1875 Bert and Kari Tingelstad from Freeborn County, Minnesota came to join the Hallingdal settlers. On July 2 they arrived, bringing 80 head of cattle.

In 1876 Hadelanders Hans and Peder Tingelstad, Lars Haga, and Anders Sherva arrived. When they started from Clayton County, Iowa, they were part of a large caravan of about 20 canvas wagons (*segldukvogne*); during the trip many of them had left the caravan and homesteaded along the way.

Gudbrand Tandberg, Iver Tingelstad and Ole Hagen came in 1877, bringing 60 horses to the settlement. Up to that time all the pioneers had settled along the Goose River, where there were many trees which protected them from raging blizzards. But later, after all the land along the river was taken up, settlers had to go out on the prairie to find homestead land.

Hadelanders who came to the Northwood settlement in the years 1875-1880 were Ole and Anders Onsager, P. N. Watterud, Gudmund Haga, Ole and Jacob Brørby, Ole, Carl, Hans and Halvor Hovland, Fredrik and Kristian Sherva, Anders and Peter Winden, Jon and Henry Nøkleby, Paul and Jacob Bilden, Thomas Evjen, Torsten Kjos, Anders Kjørven (who is still living) and Thorvald Ruud.

Times were difficult and the settlers suffered many hardships in the early days of the settlement. Grasshoppers and droughts year after year destroyed the crops. Many tragedies occurred during the cold and lonely days of winter when the pioneers were surprised by the frigid snowstorms which could come without warning. Wives and children were stranded in sod huts, while out in the snowstorms the men struggled for their livelihood.

In 1889 a terrible diphtheria epidemic ravaged the settlement and surrounding area. Many gravestones in the cemeteries tell of this terrible tragedy. Almost all members in some families died. Ole Hilden and his wife Berthe Knotterud lost three of their children in less than a week.

In the first years the closest business center was Grand Forks, 40 miles away, and the nearest railroad was 90 miles away in Fargo. This was where they had to travel to sell their crops.

The first postal route went from Grand Forks to the Indian fort, Fort Totten on Devils Lake. In winter mailmen used dogsleds and in summer they went on horseback to deliver the mail on the 100-mile route. The mail was faithfully delivered on hot summer days and through the snowstorms of winter.

Deaconness Hospital, Northwood ND

The first Norwegian Lutheran congregation was established in Northwood in 1875. Now there are many congregations in the area where you can still hear the Norwegian language preached.

In 1884 the railroad arrived and the town of Northwood was founded. In 1885 the first drugstore was opened by Iver Tingelstad and Nils Tandberg. In 1886, they sold the business to J. Bly, who later sold it to Paul Bilden, also a Hadelander. Paul Bilden ran this business until he died. His sons Josef and Oliver Bilden continue to operate "Bilden Pharmacy" which is a business now worth $25,000 (*about $400,000 in 2010 dollars*). Paul Bilden from Tingelstad was also the veterinarian in the settlement and for many years was the *kirkesanger* (song leader) at the Lutheran Church in Northwood. His wife, also from Hadeland and daughter of Ole Nerstua Melaas, still lives in Northwood.

It was Hadeland immigrant Eli Tingelstad who gave the first support to establish a rest home and Norwegian hospital in Northwood. In 1876 Hans and Eli Tingelstad came to Northwood from Hadeland and settled on the land where Northwood is now located. When Hans died in 1902, his widow gave their large farm home to the town on the condition that it would become a hospital – something which the fast growing town needed. In 1908 the Tingelstad building was changed to a rest home when a new hospital was built in the community. When a new rest home was built in 1913, the old Tingelstad building was incorporated into that facility. In this way, Eli Tingelstad helped create the foundation for the modern rest home/hospital which is of great benefit to the community. The following Hadelanders helped organize the first rest home: Paul Bilden, S. T. Tandberg, Kari Halvorson and Mr. and Mrs. Ole O. Hagen. Other Hadelanders who served as board members were S. H. Tangen, Hans Tingelstad, P. O. Glassrud, and Albert Hagen. The first nurse at the hospital was a Hadelander, Nettie Grinager, a graduate of the deaconness school in Chicago.

Hadelanders were important in the history of the Northwood community and their memories live on. The old Hadeland settlements grew to be one of the most prosperous in North Dakota.

Early Settlers on the Goose River (Mayville, Dakota Territory)
Brua, May 1988
By Adolph Hanson

Early in the spring of 1871 a group of young Hadelandings at Kilbourn, Wisconsin, loaded up two wagons drawn by oxen with their belongings and set out for Goose River near where the town of Mayville ND is today. First they went to LaCrosse where they loaded their wagons and oxen on a boat, which took them to St. Paul. From there it was slow going, as oxen have never been known to be fast walkers. Many days later, they crossed the Red River at Georgetown MN, where the Hudson Bay Company operated a ferry. They arrived at the banks of the Goose River on June 24th, 1871, a date they often referred to as *Santhansdagen.*

Included in the group was Ingebret Larson, 31 years old; his wife, Clara; and a younger brother, Iver. The other members consisted of four persons ranging in age from 11 to 20 years. Their names were Peter Paulson, and brothers Hans, Andrew and Gulbrand Hanson (Molden). The party had all emigrated from Gran, Hadeland in the fifties and sixties to Kilbourn WI, now known as the Wisconsin Dells, along with their parents and younger brothers and sisters. Since Ingebret Larson was the oldest and had lived for many years in this country, he naturally became the leader of the expedition.

In the fall of the same year (1871) the entire families of each of the members also came to the Goose River area, where they survived the first winter in dug-outs along the river banks until log houses could be built.

In less than two years a missionary pastor visited the area and helped them organize a church, which naturally came to be called the Gran Lutheran Church. To this day it is an active congregation. In 1977, this congregation had the honor of entertaining the Hadeland Lag of America.

In June of 1987 a large number of descendants of these early pioneers who homesteaded at the Goose River Settlement in 1871, near the present Gran Church, honored their pioneer ancestors by unveiling a plaque. The first sentence is as follows:

Vi har nu reist langt nok. Lad øs nu sette øs ned her.

It means, "We have no traveled far enough. Let us set ourselves down here." These were the words spoken by Ingebret Larson as the wagons came to a stop on the river bank. The farm is now owned by Mr. and Mrs. Larry Hanson, a direct descendant of one of the Hanson brothers.

Gran Lutheran Church

The Rekstad Family
"Recollections of Pioneer Times"
Brua, November 2008
By Mary Margaret Rekstad Gibson

Erick Rekstad and his wife Martia Olesdtr Alm immigrated from Gran on the same ship in 1888. They married in Watson MN in 1890. They raised 7 children on their farm in Chippewa County, Minnesota. Mary Margaret is the daughter of their youngest son, Rudolph.

Sunday was a day of rest at the Rekstad home, but it was uncommon for the whole family to go to church. They belonged to the Jevnaker Norwegian Lutheran congregation, located in rural Montevideo, Minnesota and named in honor of the church in Hadeland where many of the local immigrants had lived in their youth. Erick would drive the buggy to church and take with him the children who were "reading for the minister" at the time. However, everyone went to the congregation's "Christmas Tree" (program) which eventually evolved into the annual children's Christmas program. Rudolph, the youngest Rekstad son, remembered being in his first program when he was five years old. Prior to the program, money was collected annually from among the church members. With this money they bought apples, oranges, and Christmas candy. Each child received a small paper bag of these goodies, together with a present after the program. Rudolph saw that each of the other children received a present, but he did not get one. All the presents were distributed and there was none for him. He remembered crying all that day and the next! The following day, his father Erick hitched up his horses and drove twenty miles to town to get a present for Rudolph. He never forgot that present – a toy with a bell on it with a hammer to make it ring.

Erick and Martia Rekstad in front of their home

Baseball was Rudolph's first love. He began playing with a rag ball and a homemade bat and ended by being one of the most sought-after players among the local teams. Nearly every township and small town had a baseball team. Each team had official uniforms and every Sunday afternoon there were games, played according to a pre-arranged schedule. The teams were allowed to 'import' players to ensure future victories. There was even a black pitcher from Minneapolis on the Milan (MN) team. Rudolph paid for his baseball uniforms, balls and gloves with money he earned trapping muskrats (32 cents a pelt), mink ($10 a pelt) and skunks ($5 a pelt).

Rudolph remembered the wild strawberries that grew in the Randall, Minnesota area in those days. There had been a forest fire one summer and the next year the strawberries were so numerous that they picked milk pails full of them.

In 1915 the whole family went to a Hadeland Lag meeting in Montevideo. Ole, Edwin, and Rudolph went in a buggy. The rest of the family rode with Lars Olson, the man who built their new house on the farm and who owned a Model T Ford. Ole and Andrew bought a new Model T Ford in 1917 for $360, but shortly afterwards they were both drafted into the army to serve in the First World War. While they were in the army, Erick learned to drive and used their car. Later, in 1919, when Ole and Andrew returned, Erick bought himself a car, but the price of cars had gone up during those past two years. His car cost nearly $700!

Both Andrew and Ole saw military action at the front lines in Argonne, France. Ole was under fire for six weeks and narrowly missed being injured when his pant leg and backpack were peppered with bullets. Andrew was in the front lines for two weeks before the cease fire came on November 11, 1918. The brothers had trained together in Fort Lewis, Washington, but they were split up when they got to France. When they got home, Andrew took off his uniform and never put it on again, but Ole wore his around the neighborhood on special occasions for some time.

Every spring the Rekstads would butcher both a steer and a pig. The pork was put in crocks and covered with salt brine. Later, it would be fried in preparation for the table. The beef was dried or made into sausage. In later years, much of it was canned. During the canning process, the meat was first browned, and then packed into glass jars and placed in a hot water bath for several hours which then hermetically sealed the food for future use. This meat was later served with a cream gravy that was "Oh, so good!" Chicken was also boiled, but never fried. Martia's garden provided almost everything else they needed for their daily table – tomatoes, beets, cabbages, onions, radishes, carrots and cucumbers. Potatoes and corn were grown out in the farm fields. Gooseberries, cranberries, apples and ground cherries were made into sauce. The first peaches were bought in 1913. They were processed into sauce, but Rudolph remembered that he stole one and rearranged the peaches so that no one ever found out about it!

Whenever the family entertained company for dinner, fruit sauce was the dessert. Pie was only served to the threshers. Martia baked bread nearly every day for her large family and for the relatives who often would come to stay, sometimes for months at a time.

From the time that Rudolph was old enough to work, Erick let him make the farm decisions – what and when to plant, what machinery to buy, when to harrow, cultivate, harvest, plow, etc. Ole, Edwin and Rudolph had a bank account together and farmed all the land as one unit. They got along very well, letting the youngest be the "boss." They farmed with a Farmall F-20 tractor and an F-12 for planting the corn, oats, wheat and occasionally flax. The corn was harvested by hand. The family owned a threshing machine, a corn sheller and a truck. These were also used when they threshed and shelled corn for their neighbors. At one time, the three brothers farmed 680 acres. Erick got all the crop from his 160 acres; Edwin got the crop from his 120 acres; Helga, whose husband Jens was accidentally killed when hunting in 1935, got the crop from her 160 acres and Rudolph and Ole split the renter's share of the remaining 240 acres.

The family was able to avoid financial tragedy during the Great Depression of the 1930s, although Erick lost $1,000 when the bank in Watson, Minnesota closed. The DeGraff Bank also closed, but he was able to get his money out of his account in the Benson, Minnesota bank. The farm was paid for, but the family took out loans to build a new barn in 1920. In 1924, a new chicken coop was built. Martia was very excited about her new chicken coop and wanted everything in that new building to be made of new lumber. Rudolph liked to tease his mother about this. One day Martia asked, "What's dad doing?" "Oh, he's in the chicken coop putting up the old nests," said Rudolph. Martia grabbed her shawl, threw it across her shoulders, and ran to the newly built chicken coop – only to find Erick was not even working there!

These recollections are mainly those that my father, Rudolph, told me. He had an accurate memory for details and of the stories his parents told him. My parents respected and revered their parents and provided for their personal needs and listened to their stories. These are some of their recollections and stories they passed on to me.

Emigration, Women's Rights and the Writing of History
By Harald Hvattum
Brua, February 2005

In this story I am going to tell you something about women's rights in the 1800s and early 1900s. This is how it was when a girl from one of the Hvattum farms in Gran wanted to marry a boy from one of the Tuff farms in the same community. Her father was against it, so the girl responded by running away to America.

[In 1935] Anne Tuff died in America, an event of which only her close family members in Hadeland were notified. Her story tells much about the situation of women in Hadeland and America in the last half of the 1800s. Anne left Norway in the fall of 1872. She had set her heart on marrying a boy named Håkon Tuff. Her father would not allow it, and he had the last word in such matters at that time. Meanwhile, Anne and Håkon took matters into their own hands and created a cunning plan.

One morning Anne was gone. This was during the time of the great wave of emigration from Hadeland to America. In the dead of night, Anne had tied some bedsheets together, lowered herself down from the girls' sleeping room which was on the second floor. Together with Håkon she left for Christiania (Oslo today), to find passage to America. It was rumored that there had been some talk about this among the women and that her mother had heard about it earlier, but this we don't know for certain.

What did the regretful father do? He took the fastest horse on the farm and rode after her as fast as the horse would go. No one asked if her mother wished to go along. Such stories have a tendency to become more and more dramatic the further it is from the actual time of the happening. It is said that the father got to the town just as the boat for America was leaving the dock. Some are of the opinion that he got there in time to give the girl money for traveling, others say that he only got there in time to wave farewell.

The young couple arrived in America, got married and, as did many other immigrant Hadelanders at that time, settled in the New Land as pioneer farmers. They bought a 'homestead right' in Martin Township in the southwest corner of Minnesota (*Rock County*). The homestead system was something that many immigrant Hadelanders encountered and participated in. To encourage settlement on the enormous prairies of the northern states, in 1862 a law was passed which gave all who registered to become American citizens the right to acquire 640 *dekar* (160 American acres) of free land. To gain full ownership they had to build a set of buildings and put into cultivation some of the land within 5 years.

In 1911 *An Illustrated History of the Counties of Rock and Pipestone, Minnesota* was published in America. It contains a series of biographical articles, among them one about Håkon Tuff, where it is told that he improved his farm and became one of the most successful farmers in the area. Anne is only mentioned as his wife and mother of their five children. She had most likely also been a major part of the success story.

Here the story could have ended, but there is more. The couple had five children. One of them was Gilbert. When he died in 1957 it became known that in his will he left a large portion of his wealth for a rest home to be built in Hills, Minnesota. As often happens in America, the rest home was named in honor of the one who had donated the money and thus it received the name "Tuff Memorial Home." This became known in Hadeland and Hadelanders do not need an invitation to visit. On one of the walls in this rest home is a memorial plaque from a concert the Gran men's choir, *Mannskor K.K.*, gave there in 1980. On one of the walls we hope there is also a memorial plaque which the rest home received from a group of Hadelanders who visited there during a tour arranged by the Hadeland Lag of America in 2001. It is a small world indeed!

Pioneer Life
Brua, November 1991
Brua editor Palmer Rockswold wrote, "I found this to be an interesting piece of history...however, I am unable to credit the source because I do not remember from whence it came..."

Grandfather Ole and his family would have a great deal to tell of the early days in Eglon Township [*Clay County MN*]. Let us reminisce a bit about those days. Many of the young men, early settlers to the area, worked on the railroad built as far as Moorhead in 1872. Some found employment on the 3,000 acre Canfield farm just south of Lake Park, or on the 2,500 acre Hawley farm just north of that village. Mr. Canfield had bought this land in early 1873, and imported Shorthorn cattle and Percheron stallions. By 1889, he had 400 head of cattle and 100 horses. His farm was surrounded by 50 miles of oak rail and barbed wire fence. To maintain such a vast operation required many hands. One young man's wages were reported as $16 a month. After 3 years, it was raised to $25, but then the worker furnished his own board.

The roads in the area were nothing but trails barely passable, but were later replaced by roads along the section lines. As overseer, Grandfather Ole could tell how the roads were built. He probably used his scraper and horses to help. The road that is now Highway 10 was built in 1916, but was not paved until 1930 or 1932.

Candles, lanterns, and kerosene lamps provided light for the home and to do chores by. The B & B Anderson Store in Audubon was selling kerosene for 80 cents a gallon in the early 1870s. Matches were 40 cents a box with 500 to a box.

Water for washing and bathing was carried from the well and heated on the wood stove in the copper boiler which sold as late as 1933 for $3.00. Grandma washed clothes by hand on the washboard or maybe used a hand powered wash machine and wringer. She made her own soap from fat and wood ashes, or maybe a commercial lye.

Straw mats served as mattresses in some of the very early homes, and feathers from the ducks, geese, or chickens provided pillows.

Very little was bought at the store. Those settlers who brought cattle with them had milk and cream to sell, or to make butter to exchange at the store for supplies needed at home whether it was coffee, sugar, yeast, flour, materials for sewing, or chewing tobacco at 25 cents a quarter pound.

Meat was smoked or cured in a brine using salt which was sold by the barrel, ½ barrel costing $3.25. Hunting and fishing provided much food for the table. Later when wheat was raised, it was taken to the mill to be ground for flour. In 1871 flour sold for $5 a sack. Beans were 7 cents a pound, and sugar, either the brown or yellowish colored sugar, was 15 to 17 cents a pound.

From 1885 to 1917 one could mail a letter for 2 cents, though one might have to pay a carrier an extra 5 cents to take the letter to the mail station.

Farming for the early settler was a real challenge. First the land had to be cleared of trees and stumps. An axe which cost $1.75, a buck saw, or a cross cut saw were his only tools. Then the land had to be plowed. Some of the early pioneers, including Ole B., used oxen, but that was slow going. With an ox drawn plow he could plow an acre in 24 hours. That same acre could be plowed with 5 horses and a 2 bottom gang plow in something over 1 ½ hours. Olaf Knutson would rather plow in the cool night air than during the heat of the day. The horse and buggy, or wagon, was the early settlers' transportation, besides being used for farm work and delivering farm products to the market.

After plowing, the soil had to be broken up. For that the early settler used a log with spikes driven into it.

At first the grain was cut with a scythe, purchased for $2; a new handle was $1.50. Grandfather Ole, no doubt, used a whetstone, for which he paid 40 cents, wagon grease at 25 cents a box, and linseed oil at 35 cents a pint.

Jules Olson, Bertina Knutson's brother, had a steam engine and threshing rig and did custom threshing. Scenes of those days can be seen in the *History of Lake Park*, a book written for the Centennial in 1981.

A Lake Park farmer, Henry Torgerson, bought the first gas tractor in that area, about 1916, paying $600 for it. Henry Ford's Model T began to make its appearance about that time, too. A Model T Touring car cost $391. The license for 3 years was $1.50, and gas was 15 cents a gallon.

The familiar blue bib overall that the men wore cost from 69 to 75 cents, and his Sunday best shoes, if bought at Sears-Roebuck, cost $3.00. Calico material for dresses cost 18 cents a yard, and unbleached sheeting 19 cents a yard.

The changes in the lifestyle, our homes, our schools, in farming, and every phase of life over the past 100 years amazes us. What would Grandfather or Great-Grandfather Ole (as the case may be) think of the paved highways, the high powered cars of today (he had never had a car), the modern farm machinery, the airplanes that fly 600 miles or more an hour at heights of 12,000 to 33, 000 feet? It's hard to believe that we can have breakfast in New York, dinner in Paris, and late supper again in New York, all within 12 to 14 hours. We can jet to Norway or Sweden in 7 hours, a bit longer via Iceland on the DC-6. And Grandmother, wouldn't she enjoy being a homemaker with all the modern gadgets and conveniences we have today?

Via radio and television, we have ... seen and been a part of many of the past 100 years' great events. We were glued to our radios in 1927 when Charles Lindbergh flew the Atlantic. We were literally spectators at the funerals of President John F. Kennedy, Senator Robert Kennedy, Martin Luther King, and of Minnesota senator Hubert H. Humphrey. We've seen the coronation of the Pope in Rome, man's trip to the moon...

It's a wonderful world we live in, and we are grateful to those early pioneers and ancestors who paved the way for us. It took a great deal of courage to leave their native land and to settle in a new land, and for many, so far from their loved ones.

To put pioneer prices in perspective, here are a few examples of what the equivalent dollar value would be today:

Year	Commodity	Price Then	2010
1871	sack of flour	$5.00	$90.00
1875	kerosene-gallon	$0.80	$15.70
1885	mail	$0.02	$0.44
1889	monthly wage	$25.00	$600.00
1916	tractor	$600.00	$11,870.00
1916	gasoline-gallon	$0.15	$3.00

Chapter Thirteen
The History of Hadeland

We from Hadeland are of a good people – broad, well-built Østlandspeople (*brede, stærkbygde, Østlandsfolk*) and we can consider ourselves related to the old Norse kings, since Halvdan *Svarte* (the Black), Harald *Hårfagre*'s father, was from Hadeland and is probably even buried there. Harald *Hårfagre*'s (Harald Fair-hair) son, Ragnvald *Retilbeine* (Ragnvald Straight-legged), was king at Hadeland and it was there he was burned (*indebrænt*) by his brother, Erik *Blodøks* (Erik Bloodaxe) as he, as the old saga tells, was a troll (*troldmand*) or giant. At that time, it would mean that he was a wiser man than all others. Those from Hadeland in our day must in fact be direct descendants of him! At Hadeland we also have the sister churches in Gran – two worthy monuments of our ancestors' time. Aasmund Olavson Vinje is buried in Gran Cemetery. He gave us some of the best of Norse poetry.

Originally published in Norwegian by Hadelandslaget in 1917
Translated by George Krenos
and re-published in the November 1990 *Brua*

A Brief History of Hadeland

Norway is made up of *fylker*, which are similar to counties in the United States. Each *fylke* is made up of *kommuner*, or municipalities, which are akin to townships. Hadeland is a district of about 500 square miles about 40 miles north of Oslo. It lies in Oppland *fylke* and is made up of the *kommuner* of Gran, Jevnaker, and Lunner. Gran includes Tingelstad, which is the name of a local *sogn* or religious parish. Another parish that may be familiar to family historians is Brandbu, also located in Gran *kommune*.

The area's soil is some of the most fertile in Norway. While Hadeland accounts for just 5 % of Norway's land area, it represents roughly 13 % of its agricultural land. Farmers raise pigs, dairy cattle and horses and harvest grains, alfalfa and potatoes.

Hadeland includes large stretches of forests. Over two thirds of Lunner and Jevnaker are covered by forest, half of which is on public land. The area is home to a host of species of birds, deer, and elk. The lakes and streams have small populations of trout, char, and bass.

During the Stone Age (10,000-1,800 BCE), it is estimated that 10,000 people lived in Norway. They arrived in the coastal areas and migrated inland. Dozens of Stone Age community sites have been discovered around the Randsfjord and hundreds of artifacts – including jewelry, tools, and weapons – have been unearthed. In the earliest times people lived by hunting, fishing, and gathering the fruits of the forests. However, by the end of the Stone Age, these ancient ancestors had been tilling the soil of Hadeland for over 1,000 years!

Three Bronze Age (1,800-500 BCE) grave mound sites have been identified. Building the mounds would have required a large and coordinated labor force to gather and haul the rocks from a wide area. This indicates that the ancient communities of Hadeland were well organized. By the end of the Bronze Age, agriculture had evolved and archeological evidence points to the division of land into family or clan-based farms.

The road between Gran and Lunner, known as "King's Highway" is lined with well-preserved burial mounds, ruins, hollows and rock engravings that testify to it having been a main trade and travel route for thousands of years. Granavollen has marked a key crossroads since ancient times.

Roman references to Hadeland can be found in documents dating from 200-400 AD. "Hade" means warrior; the literal translation of Hadeland is "Land of the Warrior." Archeologists have found a wide variety of ancient weapons in burial sites throughout Hadeland. The "Hade" logo – the outline of a warrior in his helmet – is used by the Hadeland Lag and a number of Hadeland organizations in Norway and reflects this ancient tradition. The warrior culture – existing at the same time these same warriors were tending the crops and animals on their farms – reached its zenith during the Viking Age (800-1050 CE).

Legends tell us that early Viking chieftains enjoyed hunting and entertaining their entourages in the forests and on the lakes in Hadeland. King Halvdan the Black, father of the revered King Harald *Hårfagre* who united Norway, enjoyed his visits to Hadeland. It is said that in the winter of 860 CE he and his entourage attended a banquet and, late the same night, were crossing the ice on Randsfjord en route home to Ringerike. The ice gave way and horses, men, and the 40-year-old king himself were drowned. The Hadeland *Folkemuseum* is built around a Viking burial site that tradition says contains the torso of Halvdan.

> "People respected him so much that when they heard of his death ... the strongest men came from Romerike, Vestfold and Hedmark and asked if they could bury the corpse in their county; this would give them good harvests. In the end they agreed to dismember the body ... and each took their part home with them and buried it; all the mounds were called *Halvdan's-haugen*."
> Note from *Heimskringla* by Snorre Sturlason (1179-1241).

There are some who believe that all of Halvdan was buried in Ringerike and that the other mounds were simply memorials to this beloved king. That is a debate left to others; what is important to our story is that Hadeland has been appreciated for its beauty and valued for its natural resources since Norway's earliest times.

In 1950, when the *Granavolden Gjæstgiveri* (guesthouse/inn) was being restored a slab of sandstone was unearthed. A picture of a forge had been engraved upon the stone in Viking times. The stone is now kept at the University Museum of Antiquities in Oslo.

Norway formally adopted Christianity in 1030. One of Hadeland's real treasures is now on display in the museum at Oslo. The Dynna Stone, a 10 foot tall memorial to her daughter Astrid, was commissioned in 1050 by Gunvor Tyriksdatter and is engraved with scenes from the nativity. It is one of the most beautiful monuments in all of Norway. Its existence provides evidence that local culture and society maintained their strength and vitality even as the Viking Era came to an end.

A number of Hadeland churches survive that date to the 12th and 13th centuries. Notable among them is the Tingelstad (St. Petri's) church. Built in the 12th century, it is the only church in Norway with an original interior from the Middle Ages.

The Black Death (*den svarte dod*) arrived in Norway in 1349. A wool ship left London in May of that year and a few days later the entire crew succumbed to the plague. The ship drifted until it ran aground near Bergen. The Norwegians didn't realize the nature of its deadly cargo until it was too late.

It is estimated that the Black Death wiped out two-thirds of the population of Hadeland. Farms were abandoned. According to legend, the church at Grinaker was overgrown and completely forgotten until a shepherd boy came across it decades later. It is hard to imagine how profoundly families and the entire society were affected by this plague. Knowledge of history and many valuable skills died with its victims.

At the height of the plague, in 1380, Norway and Denmark were joined by royal intermarriage. In 1536 Norway ceased to be an independent kingdom and fell under total control of the Danish court.

It was not until the early 16th century that Norwegian society began to recover from the Black Death's destructive effects. In 1540 the king ordered that anyone interested in taking over the farms abandoned during the plague could do so for taxes. Danish nobility had no interest in living on estates in Norway, so farm owners and managers (the *bonder* class) evolved as the highest echelon of Norwegian society.

Communities in most of Norway centered around a *gaard,* or farm. These farms were self-sufficient units. Farms would most often be inherited by the oldest son. Since arable land was extremely limited, the younger sons of a land owner could easily lose their upperclass status as they were forced into the tenant farmer (*husmann* or *cotter*) class. By 1814, when Norway adopted its own Constitution, land ownership was something about which most *Hadelendinger* could only dream.

Tenant farmers signed a contract with the land owner that specified the nature and amount of work they were expected to do, and what they would receive for their labors. The farm owner was responsible for providing housing for all the workers on the farm. Some tenant farmers were privileged to raise their own livestock, and some (*husmann med jord*) were given houses with a small tract of land on which to grow their own garden or cash crops. A *husmann med jord* might receive a lifetime contract, but these arrangements were usually only granted to a couple. When one or the other spouse died, the land reverted to the owner unless the deceased was survived by a married child willing to assume responsibility, or the surviving spouse remarried quickly.

Many *husmann* supplemented their incomes by learning a trade and providing services to others in the community. A boy might apprentice as a blacksmith, tailor, furniture maker, shoemaker or learn other marketable skills. All women were taught how to spin and sew, but some put those skills to use as seamstresses, bakers, etc.

Along with farming, mining played an important role in Hadeland's history. The oldest registered iron mine in Norway is located at Grua in Lunner, dating to 1538. In the course of the next four centuries, iron and lead mines operated at various times in the area around Grua. Grua's iron mine closed in the early nineteenth century, but in the late 1800s zinc was discovered and mining of that valuable ore continued into the early twentieth century. The remains of limestone, granite, and marble quarries can also be found in Lunner. There are no longer any active mining sites in Hadeland.

The world famous Hadeland Glassworks was founded in 1762, and is the oldest continuously operating company in Norway. Located in Jevnaker, it has provided employment for generations of skilled craftsmen.

Stories of the availability of rich farmland in America beckoned the first *Hadelendinger* to America in 1842. The number of emigrants steadily increased. A family might fund the cost of the trip to America for one of their sons. Once established, he was expected to pay passage for other family members to follow. In this way whole families and entire communities were transplanted from Norway to America by the first decade of the twentieth century.

As a percentage of its population, only Ireland provided more immigrants to America than Norway. It has been suggested that as many as 8 out of 10 families living in Hadeland in 1825 would eventually have immediate family members or descendants swept up in this great wave. Norwegian immigrants homesteaded more land in America than any other immigrant group.

While Norway developed into a thriving, modern nation, much of the old culture continued to be celebrated as if suspended in time in the transplanted Norse communities in America. This common history has created a bond between Norwegians and their Norwegian-American cousins, but the Hadeland Lag also seeks to introduce its members to modern Norway. The lag's goal is to explore both the old connections between Norwegian-North Americans and their immigrant homeland and new connections between the people of the United States and Canada and Norway.

Kari Ruud Flem designed the *kommunevåpen* (coats-of-arms) for all three Hadeland *kommuner*.

Against a red background, each of two yellow triangles is topped with a bottony cross on Gran's coat-of-arms. These represent the two spires of the Sister Churches.

Jevnaker's glassblowing tradition is honored by the three silver goblets that make up its coat of arms. The red background was chosen because it is the color of hot glass.

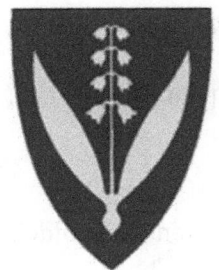

The coat-of-arms of Lunner depicts a yellow *liljekonvall* (Lily of the Valley) against a red background. The Lily of the Valley grows throughout the meadows and forests of Lunner. Its design also acknowledges the eight schools in the *kommune*.

The Norwegian Judicial System of the 1700s in Action
From a translation by Sturla Bandlie of material in *Hadeland's Bygdenes Historie, IV* with slight editing by L. Opsahl
Brua, February 1990

Gran, Hadeland, March 21, 1732   The bailiff Nernst has charged Ole Kleboe of this parish with uttering punishable words about the Holy God and about His Majesty the King. Ole Kleboe denied having spoken the words that caused his trial, but did not deny using swear words like any sinful man.
RULING: As the accused Ole Kleboe, according to five sworn witnesses, has several times while intoxicated uttered unkind words toward God and his Holy Word, and has cursed the King and his representatives, his tongue should, as an example to others, be cut from his mouth while alive, whereafter his head should be struck off and put on a pole together with his tongue.

Granavolden, November 29, 1741   The bailiff Dorph has charged Hans Christiansen with several cases of theft, and has presented sheriff Niels Rude's written specification of what has been stolen. He names Knud Eichen as defender of the accused. The summoned witnesses were cross-examined and the accused Hans Christiansen confessed the thefts.
RULING: Hans Christiansen, as confirmed by witnesses and by his own admission, has during the past year committed four minor thefts, two of which also involve breaking and entering. He will according to the law be whipped, burn-branded as a thief, and will spend the rest of his life working in irons. His property, if he has any, will be confiscated.

Bjellum, December 4, 1741   The bailiff Dorph has charged Joen Arnesen with theft. The prisoner Joen Arnesen admitted to having stolen at one place a piece of cheese, at another a piece of crispbread, at another 1 ort (one cent) and at another a pair of socks. The

summoned witnesses declared that what had been stolen was of little value and did not press for punishment.
RULING: Joen Arnesen should loose his skin in prison and have his property, if any, confiscated.
Editor's Note: To "loose the skin" means that the prisoner should be whipped.

Granavolden, November 23, 1745   The bailiff Dorph has charged Lars Olsen Korsvolden with refusing to take employment from a citizen offering him such.
RULING: As a farmhand, Lars Olsen Korsvolden, since leaving the service of Anne Myhre, has by his own admission been offered employment and has refused it. He should be brought to the penitentiary of Christiania, there to work for as long as the prison director decides.

Granavolden, November 29, 1749   The bailiff has charged Hans Kammerud who, according to the sheriff's testimony, has murdered his child with five stabs of the knife. The accused states that for a while on the day in question he was alone in the living room with the child sleeping in its crib while he himself was cutting a new knife shaft. When the child started crying, Hans Kammerud lost his temper and struck the child, but leaving the knife on the table while he dealt with the child. The child died soon after, and was found with clothing soaked in blood and five stab wounds in his body. The child's name was Ole Olsen and he was one year old. (It appears it was *not* Hans' child!)
RULING: The court finds that Hans Kammerud and no one else has murdered the child. For this cruel murder he shall be pinched with glowing tongs on the way to the place of execution, where first his hand, then his head shall be cut off. Both hand and head should subsequently be put on poles and the body on a ramp for the public to see. All his possessions are forfeited to the king.

The Call of the Lur
Based on the article in the May 1991 *Brua* by E. Palmer Rockswold

For centuries, Norwegian history and legend has been rich in tales of the lur. It developed early as a shepherd's horn used in the mountain *seters* to call the cattle or perhaps to scare away wild animals. This horn was made of wood and had a mellow tone that carried a long ways. Usually they were wrapped in birch bark so as to be airtight. It also had a mouthpiece much as a cornet. Most were 3-4 feet long and tapered and in some cases had a flared bell.

Later the lur was found in the courts and palaces of kings, often in fancy shapes and sizes and made of bronze. A few were called battle horns. These had a harsher and more military tone. Others were said to ward off evil spirits in earlier times.

The lur is said to have played an important role at the Battle of Kringen in August of 1612. A force of about 550 Scotsmen landed at Isfjorden on the coast of Romsdal and Møre and began a long march toward Sweden (Sweden was at war with Norway and Denmark at the time). The march was uneventful until they reached Gudbrandsdalen.

A beautiful local girl named Guri was placed on a mountaintop above Otta so that she could watch the advancing army as it marched along the Old King's Road. At the critical moment she alerted the farmers with a blast on her lur. The ambush began with logs and rocks crashing down from the mountainside onto the Scots and blocking the road. After an hour and a half, 2/3 of the Scots were dead while only 6 farmers had been killed.

Archeologists often unearth lurs in pairs during excavations. Denmark and Sweden also used the lur.

The Dvergsten Farm: Legend and Lore
By Anne Sladky
Loosely based on a history found in the personal papers of Florence (Dvergsten)Rognlie
Photo found in the personal papers of Ruby (Alm) Grover

The ancient Dvergsten farm sits on a hill not far from the Tingelstad Old Church. It has a commanding view of the surrounding countryside. In the middle of the lawn at Dvergsten lies a flat stone that measures about 6 ½ feet in length that is in composition very different from other stones in the area. The stone and the legends surrounding it may have given the farm its name;

Dvergsten means "dwarf stone."

There are many folktales that try to explain how the strange stone ended up on the Dvergsten farm. Most of them in some way refer to the indentations ("fingermarks") found on the face of the stone. Consider this:

A *jotul* (troll) named Sølve lived on a mountain known as *Sølvsberget* (Sølve's mountain). It had been his home for thousands of years. It was peaceful, and Sølve was happy because he could sleep most of the time. He was, after all, a very old troll.

When the old Tingelstad Church was finished about 1150, the people were delighted when the church bells rang out for the very first time. Unfortunately, the bells woke Sølve up. He did not like the sound of the bells! He ripped a big stone from the mountainside and took aim at the church. He heaved the stone as hard as he could and, although the direction was right, Sølve was too strong and the big stone sailed over the church and landed in the yard at Dvergsten.

If you doubt this story, just remember that on the top of *Sølvsberget* there is a hole in the mountain where the stone at Dvergsten would fit very well.

Some archeologists say that this is an ancient stone that was used for sacrifices in primitive times. It is known that in the earliest Christian times the farm folk gathered at the site of the stone for bonfires during Whitsuntide (the week beginning on Pentecost). By the 1800s the long, flat stone had been used as a salt lick for the farm's livestock for generations.

The Dvergsten farm likely dates back over 1,000 years. Little is known about its early history, but a diploma from 1299 mentions a man named "Haward at Duærgæstæn." From the end of the 1500s until 1649 Dvergsten was administered for the Danish crown by the diocese of Hamar. Writings around 1600 mention a small chapel dedicated to St. Catherine on the farm. The chapel was still there in the mid-1800s, but it was then being used as a storehouse.

In 1649, King Frederick III of Denmark sold Dvergsten to the mayor of Christiania, Hans Eggertsen Stockfleth. This was one of the first sales recorded from Roman Catholic Church holdings confiscated after the Reformation. When he died in 1664, Stockfleth left the farm to Niels Bentsen Tuv, and his descendants have lived on Dvergsten ever since. There are many stories about the sometimes colorful descendants who inherited Dvergsten over the centuries.

Dvergsten also served as a local military post. In 1713 one Lt. Bruse and a man named Rasmus, identified as the son of Anne Colbjørnsdatter, fought a duel on a flat piece of land on Dvergsten. That place is still referred to as "*Rasmusslette.*"

Traditionally, the workday on Dvergsten began at 5:30 AM and lasted until 8 PM, with breaks for lunch and an afternoon nap. A dozen tenant's houses could be found on the farm, with single workers housed in dormitory-like buildings. A typical week's menu might include meat and potatoes for Sunday dinner, but the rest of the week meals consisted primarily of combinations of bread, butter, cheese, and potatoes. Milk soup might be enhanced with cabbage for a special treat, and milk mush was a diet staple.

In 1783, the farm had 12-16 horses, about 50 cows, 50 sheep and an equal number of goats and some pigs. The crop harvest of 200 barrels included rye, oats, barley and peas. There were two main buildings on the farm, each with two floors. The farm had a small sawmill and other working buildings. At this time, the farm was owned by Niels Bensen Tuv's great-great-granddaughter Berte and her husband Christopher Stenersen. Descendants of the Stenersen family still own the Dvergsten farm today.

According to the *Kontaktforum* database, only the Alm and Dæhlen farms supplied more emigrants than Dvergsten. Scores of emigrants from other places in Hadeland had been born, lived, or worked for some period of time there.

Poet Aamund Olavsson Vinje and Gran
Brua, November 2005
By Harald Hvattum

Perhaps some of the Hadeland Lag visitors to Norway this summer noticed a monumental gravestone near the entrance to the Sister Churches at Granvollen. The inscription on this stone tells that it is a memorial at the grave of Aasmund Olavsson Vinje who was born in Vinje in Telemark, Norway, in 1818 and died in Gran in 1870. On the reverse side of this monument it tells that 3,000 farmers sponsored and paid for this memorial stone.

A. O. Vinje was a famous Norwegian poet and was among the first in the land to write in *Nynorsk* as the language in his poetry. That he is buried in Gran is, however, a coincidence. He had become seriously ill and was hospitalized in Christiania, which was the name of Oslo at that time. When he understood that his illness would be fatal, he wanted to make one last visit to *Jotunheimen*, the mountain range between

Vinje monument at Granvollen

Valdres and Gudbrandsdal where he had traveled so often during his healthier days. But, so far was he not able to travel that time.

On Thursday, the 28th of July 1870 in the evening when he stopped at the home of his friend, Anton Christian Bang, who at that time was an assistant pastor in the Gran parish and lived at the "Old Widow's farm" Sjo, just a short way north of the Sister Churches. Everyone who saw him realized that his travels northward to Hadeland had been extremely hard on the ailing man.

A doctor was called in to see him, but he could do little for the sick man. In the morning of Saturday, July 30, Vinje died at Sjo. One should then have thought that the poet would be buried either in his home parish in Telemark or in Christiania where he had lived for many years, but that was not what happened. For various reasons, A. O. Vinje did not want to be taken back to his

Room where Vinje died at Sjo

home community for burial, and as the sportsman he was, he also did not want to be buried in Christiania. He therefore expressed his wish to Bang that if he died in Hadeland, he wanted to be buried in the cemetery of the Sister Churches - and that is what happened. It was often the custom in Hadeland during those times to *bar*, that is, the tradition that people placed branches of pine and spruce trees on the road along the route that the casket was carried from Sjo to the Sister Churches. In front of the altar in the church there was set up a large panel which was covered with a black cloth. On this large black panel, there was mounted a facsimile of Vinje's signature. Reports of Poet Vinje's funeral service were published in numerous newspapers of the land. Many others also wrote commemorative obituaries about the poet in their newspapers.

For several years after his death, friends of Vinje worked at securing funds to place a monument over the grave of the poet. In the summer of 1873, this monument was completed and was unveiled in the presence of about 2,000 people. Among the many authors who were in attendance was Bjørnstjerne Bjørnson, who wrote the words of the Norwegian National Anthem. He was also among the speakers at the ceremony that day.

The farm Sjo was originally built as a widows' residence, that is to say, a place for the widows of Gran ministers to live after their husbands died. In 1870 there were no widows in the Gran Parish so as a result, the assistant pastor in Gran was allowed to live at

Sjo. In more recent years this farm has been sold into private ownership, but an annual memorial day for Aasmund Olavsson Vinje is maintained among the traditions of the Sjo farm, even to this day.

Farm Names in the 1801 Census
Originally compiled by Betty Rockswold; reviewed and updated by Kjell Henrik Myhre

Historically, some of the farms in Hadeland were as small as a postage stamp, and farm names changed or disappeared as ownerships transferred. A farm that existed at the time of an immigrant ancestor's departure may not have existed in 1801, and many of the farm names listed here do not appear in a current roster of Hadeland farms.

Many family names are derived from the names of the farms on which our ancestors lived. Keep in mind that specific farm names are not unique to Hadeland; many of these farm names appear in other areas of Norway as well.

Farms in Brandbu Parish (now part of Gran *kommune*)

Afkin/Avkjærn	Gullerud	Skarie
Augedal	Gulsoliden/Gulsjølia	Skarpen
Baalerud	Hond/Horn	Smedbølle
Berven	Heggen	Smedshammer
Bierke	Holmen	Solum
Bione	Jønnes	Stormyren
Blegen	Kalvskind	Svensrud
Braaum	Kielderen	Svinning
Brandhagen	Kios	Sørum
Brunstad	Lien/Avkjærnslia	Teiterud
Bukindseter/Bukjernsæter	Løvstuen	Tislo
Dyrud	Nyehus	Tislobakken
Dælen	Næs Næstegge	Tokerud
Egge	Putten	Tomt
Eid	Raae/Rå	Tømte
Eidsbraaten	Raassum	Venaasen
Enevolden/Einavolden	Retrum	Vestland
Plads	Rognlien	
Flattum	Rosendal	
Furrebraaten/Furua	Sevaldrud	
Gammlesæter	Sinnerud	

Farms in Gran Parish

Bergsrud
Biella
Biørge
Blakstad
Blekkerud
Borremarken
Brejlie
Dahl
Dihle
Dynna
Elnæs
Ensrud
Fagerholt
Fallang Forten
Framstad
Gagnum
Gamme
Gamkind
Gisleberg
Giøvig
Gougtvedt
Grans Præstegaard
Gjefsen
Grimsrud
Grinie
Grina
Grinder
Grinæker
Grymyr
Gulden
Gullixsrud
Halvorsbølle
Haslerud
Helgager
Helgum
Helmen
Heier
Hov/Hof
Hofsmarken
Hole
Holm
Horgen
Houg
Houg Hougen
Hougsbakken
Hougtvedt
Huser
Hval
Hvalbye
Hvattum
Hvinden
Joensrud
Jorstad
Kammerud
Kaste
Kiegshus
Kiegstad
Kittelsrud
Klæstad
Knarud
Koller
Lindstad
Lyngstad
Lynne
Lunde
Læhren
Løken
Melboestad
Miør
Molden
Morstad
Mouger
Mourtvedt
Myre
Oe
Onsager
Raastad
Raknerud
Ringdalen
Ruden/Rua
Rudsødegaarden
Sanne
Skaarud
Skaatterud
Skattum
Skiager
Skierven
Skio/Sjo
Skirstad
Skute
Smedsrud
Soug
Stadum
Stensrud
Strande
Sørum
Torgersrud
Tuff
Undelie
Velsand
Wien
Wienbraaten
Windorum
Wæstebraaten
Wøyen

Farms in Tingelstad Parish (now part of Gran *kommune*)

Alm
Amundrud
Andfossen
Askim
Bilden
Drøvdal
Dvergsten
Ellefsrud
Engnes
Elken
Grinager
Haug
Helgedalen
Helmey/Helmeid
Hilden
Hov/Hof
Holter
Hvamstad
Kløvstad
Knudstad
Knudstadmarken
Kolden
Lysen
Løvlien
Molstad
Olerud
Østen
Præstqværnen
Povelssæteren/
   Paalsæteren
Ragnhildrud
Rekstad
Rognstad
Røssum
Sandbakken
Skreberg
Smedrud
Stastad
Staxrud
Stubstad
Sørum
Qveen/Kværn
Tingelstad
Toverud
Velta
Wildaasen

Farms in Jevnaker Parish

Aslagsrud
Berger
Biellum
Biærtnes
Bratval
Brørby
Dahl
Enger
Faltinsrud
Felberg
Gaardsrud
Greftegrev
Gulden
Gundstad
Hadeland Glassværk
Haga
Halvorsrud
Houer
Igelsrud
Jevnaker Præstegaard
Kaarstad
Kinge
Klinkenberg
Klæggerud
Moe med Klæggerud
Norby
Nøchleby
Olimb
Qvælsrud
Roen
Rustad
Ruud
Rønnerud
Schaarud
Schiennum
Slaatbraaten
Sogn
Torbiørnrud
Opperud
Tronrud
Tømmeraas
Wang
Wasjø
Welo

Farms in Lunner Parish

Aaslund
Askelsrud
Elgstøen Plads
Ballangrud
Biøralt
Biørgesæteren
Blisten
Blyværket
Bolchen
Braæstad
Brocherud
Bækkehaldum
Dehlin
Elgstøen
Fiældet
Flatla
Fragot
Frøsli

Gagnum Sæter
Giærdingen Plads
Godli
Gromstad
Gruen
Grønbraaten
Haagenstad
Haavelsrud
Haldum
Haneknæ
Harestu Ødegaard
Harestuen
Heyer
Holt
Hovland
Huser
Hytten
Høyby
Klypen
Jorstavolda Plads
Jonsrud
Kalsiø
Kalsiømarken
Kiævlingen

Katnosa Plads
Kloppen
Klypen i Almindingen
Klæggerud
Kjørven
Korsrud
Kraggerud
Larmerud
Linstad
Liæker
Lunder
Løchen
Løvlien
Melaas
Morcha
Moncherud
Monserud
Muttabraaten i Almendingen
Mørtveten
Oppen
Opsal
Oset
Oren

Østby
Piperen
Raadstad
Rundelen
Ruud-Schiærven Saugbrug
Rødste
Schøyen
Svesbraaten i Almindingen
Solberg
Stubingen
Stumne
Stoch
Stubhytten
Svenballerud
Sørli i Almindingen
Tomasjerdet
Tveten/Tveita
Ulsrud
Ulven
Westeren
Wirstad
Wiubraaten
Wolla
Wollaløkken

Kammerud farm in Gran

Chapter Fourteen
The Churches of Hadeland

Jevnaker Church Altar – Nikolai church pulpit – baptismal font from Nes Church – Site of Grinaker Stave Church

Churches played a central role in the lives of Norway's rural communities. King Christian III declared the Lutheran faith the official state religion of Denmark and Norway when he ascended the throne in 1536. Catholic bishops were removed and the entire church structure reorganized.

As part of the reorganization, the church record-keeping of baptisms, confirmations, marriages and deaths was individualized. Previously, church record-keeping focused on reporting parish totals of baptisms, confirmations, etc. Church record-keeping now began to be focused on detailed recording of names of individuals, their sponsors and witnesses in church books. As a result, family historians can now learn much about their ancestors' church participation.

Intrepid genealogists can find a treasure trove of information by walking church and civil cemeteries in North America. In Norway, perhaps because it has always been a country in which usable land is at a premium, a different tradition has evolved. Family members purchase burial plots and lay gravestones as we do in America, but these gravesites are leased for a specific period of time. If the family does not continue to pay for the burial plot, it is reused. For that reason there are very few old graves in the cemeteries, and a visitor to a Norwegian cemetery should not expect to find the graves of the family an immigrant left behind over a hundred years ago.

Information about the churches of Hadeland has been based on articles written by Harald Hvattum and published in the *Brua* with additional information from other sources. Unless otherwise noted, photos of the churches were taken by members of the Hadeland Lag.

The Sister Churches
(Nikolai & Maria Churches)

The two church buildings, Nikolai Church and Maria Church, at Granavollen are so close together that it is natural to think of them as sisters. But the name may have originated in Catholic times when many believe the order of Cistersian Sisters had a cloister there, and the words "*søster*" and "*cistercienser*" are similar.

The churches were built during the 1100s. In the Middle Ages it was not unusual to build churches side by side that were intended to serve different purposes. It is possible to assume that the smaller Maria Church was a monastic church or perhaps the first parish church for Gran, while the larger basilica-styled Nikolai Church was intended to serve all of Hadeland.

Nikolai Church is the more imposing of the two churches, with its impressive steeple and powerful inside pillars. It was named for Archbishop Nikolaus of Bari, the protector of travelers and children. During the last restoration in 1960, the choir space was restored to

The Churches of Hadeland

what is believed to be a smaller, half-circle design. The pulpit from 1728 and altarpiece from 1625 were rebuilt and returned to their historic places. The church also received a new marble altar and stained glass in the east window.

Maria Church is much smaller and simpler in style than its sister. Distinct joints or splices in the masonry hint that the church has been altered many times. Maria Church was devastated by fire in 1813, and stood in ruins until 1865 when the roof was replaced. From then until 1978-79 the church was used as a funeral chapel. Now services are again held in Maria Church. Veslemøy Nystedt Stoltenberg is the artist who created the attractive stained glass window that pays homage to the church's namesake, the Virgin Mary.

The Sister Churches lay on "the Pilgrim's Way," an ancient path taken by kings and pilgrims from Oslo to the Nidaros Cathedral in Trondheim. The first "Pilgrim Center" on the route is at Granavollen.

The **Granavollen Runestone** is located behind Nikolai Church. It dates from the last half of the 11th century. The rune was erected in honor of a brother named Aufi and ends with a prayer for his soul.

The nearby **Stone House** is the only non-ecclesiastical building of its age left in rural Norway. Although smaller, it has much in common with other preserved urban buildings from the Middle Ages that were used by Catholic church hierarchy and the nobility.

The Stone House was built of stone reclaimed from an alteration or rebuilding of the Sister Churches near the end of the 1200s. It probably served as a residence for high-ranking visiting church officials during Catholic times.

The House has three floors: The cellar has an arched ceiling and was dug out of the building's rock foundation. The first floor, at ground level, is in the Renaissance style. A large hall occupies the entire second floor. It may well have had an arched ceiling, but the house burned in the 1500s (probably during the Seven Years War) and was likely significantly altered during the restoration.

The *Steinhuset*, which is located near the parsonage of the Sister Churches, is now used for religious, cultural, social and humanitarian purposes.

Lunner Church

The oldest part of the Lunner Church was built of stone, most likely in the 1100s. At that time it was a rectangular church. The church took on the shape of a cross when a wooden addition was added in the 1780s.

There are some remarkable figures on one of the stone walls. They were most likely carved in the 1100s, but were probably not in their current location. The figures may have been moved from another part of the building during a later remodeling, or they may have been moved to the Lunner church from another building.

The Church has gone through many restorations. In 1930 the church was badly in need of repair but there was little money to accomplish the restoration. The pastor, a resourceful fellow, placed a notice in the *Decorah Posten* hoping to attract donations from America. Jens H. Lynner in Minnesota, an emigrant from Lunner and an active member of the Hadeland Lag of America, brought the matter to the attention of the Hadeland Lag at the *stevne* in 1929. A fund-raising committee was formed, with Lynner as its chair. The fund drive collected $152 (about $2000 in 2010 dollars) that was used to purchase a new altar railing. In addition, Mr. Lynner personally donated $750 (almost $10,000 in today's dollars) for a new pulpit.

Grinaker Stave Church

The wooden Grinaker stave church was built in the 1100s. It served the Gran parish for over 700 years. Legend has it that the devastation of the Black Death caused the church to be forgotten. It wasn't until decades later that a young shepherd boy rediscovered it as he searched for lost sheep in the woods.

Population growth in the early 1800s required that church capacity be expanded. A commission decided that both Grinaker and St Petri's (Tingelstad Old Church) should be abandoned in favor of a new church. The stave church was torn down, but the old wall that surrounded the church is still visible, as is the outline of its foundation. The model shown here, photographed in its display case at the Hadeland *Folkemuseum*, was created by Lag member Paul Grinager and donated to the museum in 1990.

The wood from the stave church was used in a barn built for the church sexton on the new parish church farm. This building has been restored and it is possible to identify the panels from the stave church today.

The pulpit, bells, and baptismal font from the stave church were transferred to Tingelstad New Church. They had been added to the Grinaker church during a major renovation in the early 1700's. Many smaller items dating back to the earliest times of the church were also moved to the new building. Grinaker's altar was used in the Sørum church.

© Randsfjordmuseene

Tingelstad Old Church (St. Petri's)
Den gamle Tingelstadkirka

© Randsfjordmuseene

Immediately adjoining the Hadeland *Folkemuseum* stands Tingelstad Old Church. Prior to the Reformation it was known as *St. Petrikirka* (St. Peter's Church). It is built of stone, and was constructed during the 12th century. It is the only medieval church in Norway that retains its original interior as decorated in the 16th and 17th centuries.

The stone church is beautifully situated on a hilltop, looking out over the greater part of the parish. The north wall is decorated with a painting of King Christian IV's Danish and Norwegian royal coat-of-arms from about 1600. It has an inscription that explains that this painting was paid for by the owner of the Dvergsten farm. A model of a wooden ship hangs from the ceiling. Its inscription credits the people who lived on the Alm farm for its donation.

Archeologists believe the sparkling gold weather vane that sat atop the roof might once have been on the bow of a Viking ship. Tradition says Queen Margrethe (Margaret I who ruled Norway and Denmark from 1387-1412) donated the weathervane to St. Peter's. A replica in bronze now graces the top of the church.

This church has many original artifacts and furnishings dating as far back as the 17th century. The wall mural shown on the right has been dated to 1632.

As population increased, Tingelstad church became too small for its congregation. In 1866, it was decided that it and nearby Grinager stave church would be replaced by a larger building, known as Tingelstad New Church.

Today, St. Peter's is a popular venue for weddings. Worship services are conducted in this church three or four times a year.

Tingelstad New Church

2,000 parishioners attended the consecration of the New Tingelstad Church in 1866. This large new church replaced both Tingelstad Old Church (St Peter's) and Grinager Stave Church. Two famous Norwegian architects, von Hanno and Schirmer, designed the red stone building.

The pulpit, baptismal font, and church bells were all removed from Grinager Stave Church and installed at Tingelstad. Many other smaller objects found their way to this new parish church from both Grinager and St. Peter's.

Sørum Church

The Sørum Church is the only Hadeland church on the west side of the Randsfjord. It received its name from the farm on which it was built. Sørum, which means the southern farm, is a common farm name found throughout Norway. In the neighboring community of Gran, for example, there are Sørum farms in three completely different parts of the community. Some of the Sørum farms are in Bjoneroa where the Sørum church is located.

The Sørum Church is a white-painted wooden church. It was February 5, 1859, when Gran's parish pastor, Soren Bugge, sent out an order to all those living in the parish that they should contribute money so that a church could be built on the west side of the Randsfjord. *700 speciedollars* were raised by private contributions. In addition a *500 speciedollar* grant was received from a religious education fund, plus an additional grant of *20 speciedollars* was provided so that a well-known architect, Jacob Wilhelm Nordan, could be hired to draw the plans. The farmer on one of the Sørum farms, Anders Olsen Sørum, gave the land for the church and an owner of large forests, Lars Jacobsen Hvinden, gave the lumber. The church was dedicated on September 25, 1861.

Most of the furnishings in the church were new in 1861 but the altar was special. It was the old altar from Grinager stave church. Originally the church had only a small one-room sacristy, but in the 1930s a two room sacristy was added, along with a crypt in the basement (a place for storing caskets waiting for burial).

In the early years the hymns were sung without accompaniment, but in 1898 the church acquired its own organ. The organ served the church for 88 years before it became so worn-out that it was no longer possible to be repaired. In the 1970s a fund drive was begun to purchase a new organ for the church. The new organ was installed in 1979.

When the Gran parish was divided in 1897 the Sørum Church became part of the Brandbu parish.

Jevnaker Church

A stone church was built in Jevnaker during the Middle Ages. Records show that it was in place during the first half of the 13th century. In 1832 the original church was declared unfit for use and it was demolished. A new octagonal wooden church was erected on the same site. On October 8, 1834, the bishop from Oslo conducted the church's consecration.

From that time until 1906 Jevnaker included the present Jevnaker and Lunner parishes. Although from the Middle Ages Lunner had its own church, it was Jevnaker Church that served as the main church in the large parish. The pastor lived on and drew income from the parish farm next to the church.

Pastors had ministerial responsibilities and often did not have the practical ability to run the farm. A tenant farmer was hired to run the farm, and he was given his own home on the parish farm property. In 1959 a new dwelling was built for the tenants of the parish farm. The old building gradually fell into disrepair, but it was left standing. In time the Norwegian authorities realized the value of the old building, part of which dated from the 1600s.

The Jevnaker Historical Society has put a considerable amount of work into restoring the original farm house and uses it today for its meetings. Since 1984 the Hadeland *Folkemuseum* has owned the building.

Nes Church

The year was 1730, 46 years before the 13 English colonies in North America started their rebellion against England, and more than a hundred years before the people in Hadeland started to think about emigrating to America. On the 1st of November a small crowd gathered to dedicate a new church on the shores of the Randsfjord. The church took its name from the farm on which it was located, which in turn had gotten its name because it was situated at the *nes*, the headland of the Randsfjord.

The new wooden building replaced a stone church that had been built in the Middle Ages. A new pulpit was created for the new church, but most of the other furnishings were transferred from the old church. In the early 1700s the Norwegian government was experiencing a shortage of money. Most rural churches were supported by parish farms and, in a country where farmland was at a premium, the farms were extremely valuable. Since the church in Norway was a state church, the state actually owned the land. In 1722, the government filled its budget gap by selling a lot of churches – and their farms – to private interests. The Nes Church was sold to Christian Berg and Gregers Pedersen. They financed the building of the new church. Some years later the church was sold back to the congregation.

During a major restoration in 1863, new pews were installed and a balcony was added that spanned three interior walls of the church. In the 1930s a funeral chapel was built on the grounds of the Nes church.

This white-painted church is the head church in the Brandbu parish. During the Hadeland Lag 2000 visit to Norway the tour stopped at the Nes Church Cemetery, where family names from the middle and northern parts of Brandbu can be found. In the cemetery there is also a monument in memory of the local people who were killed during World War II.

Grymyr Church

On Friday night, October 15th 1999, the fire alarm sounded! "The Grymyr Church is burning!" Within a few hours the church was totally destroyed. The charred remains of a couple walls were all that remained standing. Only the church silver, stored in a fireproof cabinet, survived the blaze.

Members of the congregation had celebrated the centennial of the Grymyr Church less than six weeks before the fire, on September 12, 1999. The destroyed church was fully insured, and it was immediately decided that the church would be rebuilt.

A week-long celebration, from August 24 to August 29, 2003, heralded completion of Grymyr's new church building. The Hadeland Lag sent flowers to acknowledge the accomplishment.

The Grymyr Church site is located on the eastern shore of the Randsfjorden on Highway 240 about 10 miles north of Jevnaker.

Moen Church

The Moen Church is one of the youngest churches in Hadeland. It was dedicated in 1914, long after most Hadeland-Americans' ancestors left Norway. It was in the fall of 1910 when serious discussions began about building a church in Moen. Moen, which is located next to the border with Toten, is a good distance from the Tingelstad and the Sister Churches. Today it is just a short drive by car, but in a horse-drawn carriage, or for the many people who walked to church in 1910, it was a very long distance.

The land for the church was donated by Kjersti and Johan Trulserud and the lumber was given by the Tingelstad *Almenning* (communal forest lands owned by farm owners of that area). About 2,600 *kroner,* or 13% of the 20,000 *kroner* cost of the building, came from Hadeland immigrants and their descendants in America. The church was dedicated on June 18, 1914, with a large attendance, both of pastors and people from the surrounding communities. The church grounds included a stable with eight horse stalls.

Over the years, the population in the Moen area has grown and the church has been enlarged several times. In 1958 a *bårehus* was built (a mausoleum where coffins are stored between the *bisettelsen* –funeral service – and burial). Some years ago a small *kirkestue,* church social hall, was built which is connected to the church.

Ål Church

Historically Granavollen, the area around the Sister Churches, was the trading center of Gran. With the re-routing of the road to Oslo in the 1860s and the construction of the railroad station in 1900, the Sentrum moved down to the bottom of the valley around the new road and the railroad station and the population in the area grew. The people in the area wanted to have their own church. After a long career as a pastor, Johan Selmer-Anderssen in 1916 retired and moved to Eastern Gran, where he worked for 14 years to secure approval and funding for Ål church.

The church's design is reminiscent of the medieval stave churches. It was dedicated on March 2, 1930. It was a solemn occasion with participation by the bishop from Hamar, plus pastors from the entire bishopric, including Johan Selmer-Anderssen and music by *Manskor K.K.* Even a cantata was written for the opening!

Two days after the church dedication some of those who had participated in the work of the new church gathered for a meeting on one of the farms near the church. While there, Selmer-Anderssen died suddenly. So it happened that the dedicated soul who had inspired the work also became the first to have his funeral in the new church. He was buried, however, in the cemetery of the old Aker Church in Oslo.

Recent Reforms in Church and State Relations in Norway

By Marit Tingelstad, Member of the Storting (Norwegian Storting), 1993-2001; Member of the National Commission to evaluate the position of the State Church of Norway, 2003-2006. Prior to her recent retirement she was the Rektor (Chief Administrator) of the Gran Videregående Skole (Senior High School).

The coat of arms of the Church of Norway is a gold cross placed over two St. Olaf axes on a red background. It is based on the medieval coat of arms of the bishops of Nidaros.

Christianity was introduced into Norway with the death of King Olav Haraldson at Stiklestad in 1030. Olav Haraldson was later elevated to sainthood and became known as St. Olav. It was over his grave that the Nidaros Cathedral in Trondheim was built. Nidaros was an important pilgrimage destination from that time until the Reformation in 1537. At that time Norway (and Denmark, with whom we were in union) broke with the Roman Catholic Church and accepted the Lutheran teachings.

The church has always been strongly connected with the monarchy; later it was known as the State Church. At that time Norway had not developed into a proper democratic government. The king and his officials decided everything.

Norway's Constitution, written in 1814, states in paragraph 2 that the Evangelical Lutheran religion shall be the state's official religion. But the paragraph was changed later in connection with civil rights laws and is introduced with the statement, "All emigrants to the kingdom shall have full religious freedom." There is no compulsory religion in Norway; however, if a person is baptized in the Church of Norway, he/she is automatically a member of the State Church of Norway. You can withdraw your membership if you desire.

Throughout the last 100 years strong factions have risen within the church that wish to separate the Church of Norway from the State. Many reform organizations have conducted discussions both in the Church and in the *Storting* (Norwegian Parliament), but each time the result has been to retain the State Church. Many claim that it is best to maintain a broadly-based public church as is currently being done. But others, especially the most active and conservative members in the church, maintain that separation is necessary and that the church should be totally self-governing.' As mentioned above, considerable reforms have occurred in the Church of Norway in recent years; the church has been given extensive authority which previously was accorded the *Kongen i statsråd* (King in cabinet meeting) and is now delegated to the Church's various democratically elected organs such as the individual congregational church councils, joint councils of congregations in individual municipalities, the Bishopric Council, the Bishops' Council and the church-wide Synod Conference Assembly. This National Assembly, which is held annually, is the Church of Norway's highest organ or authority. Here many inter-church cases and points of view are dealt with, discussed and negotiated.

The State has continued the responsibility of naming of bishops after the church has given its advice, together with naming of *prosts* (Deans), but the placement of the pastors and lay staff in the churches are decided by the Bishopric Council and joint church councils of each community.

The Church of Norway is financed through taxes; the church income comes jointly from the State and local municipality budgets. Individual church members are not required to pay any membership fees. It is, however, necessary to have offerings taken in the churches at all worship services; additional income is commonly added through a lottery.

It is important to underscore that all registered religious denominations in Norway receive government support based on the size of their membership. In that way it is economically possible for all people to exercise their religious beliefs.

Approximately 80 percent of the population are members of the Church of Norway, which is Lutheran. Those persons who are baptized in the Church of Norway form the church's membership.

The Church was the institution that was responsible for the educational system in earlier times. However, during the last several hundred years the federal government and the municipalities have been responsible for all education. There are few private schools in our country. Public schools in Norway had until 1969 the responsibility for Christian education together with teaching dogmatics or education in (Lutheran) religion beliefs. After 1969 the schools were given the responsibility for teaching about Christianity and other religions, plus teaching ethics and a philosophy of life. But the school cannot mandate any particular religious belief or doctrine. This has been particularly underscored in later changes in the school laws.

When this change occurred, it put the responsibility for the teaching of particular faith beliefs on the Church of Norway in the same manner as other religious denominations already had been doing. It is not wrong to say that this responsibility has been neglected by the Church of Norway during the past 30 years. It is my assertion that both the State and the Church of Norway, together with many parents, have been negligent in this area.

These days the *Storting* is discussing the subject of baptism and the teaching of specific beliefs. The government proposes that the responsibility shall be given to the Church of Norway and to other religious denominations so that this work can be intensified. It is important that children and youth receive a strong foundation in their own religion and beliefs. By being confident in their own identities, they will have a greater tolerance for people with other beliefs.

The Church of Norway in 2002 dealt with a big proposal from the National Church Council called "The Same Church – A New Church Structure" with special responsibility for studying the relationship between the Church and State. The focus was on separating the Church and State. However, when that topic was discussed at open hearings, the majority of the Church members were not in favor of it, but they emphasized that reforms were needed.

In the spring of 2003 the government appointed a Commission to study and discuss the necessity for reforms that would eventually necessitate a change in the Constitution. It will also evaluate further whether the Church and State should be separated. This is a very encompassing mandate that has been given as a basis for this Commission's work. I am a member of this Commission that will begin work this summer and bring in its proposal in the fall of 2005.

This is a very serious matter for our country. We have built our culture and identity on Christian beliefs for the past thousand years, and Christianity has been the basis for the development of our society.

Today the majority of the *Storting* members are in favor of separating the Church and State such as has recently happened in Sweden. However, Denmark's national church is strongly connected with the State. It is necessary to take time to consider changing something so dramatic and fundamental as the structure of the Church of Norway. Not least the legal and economic aspects remain central to this discussion. The Church and people are strongly tied together in Norway. Likewise it will be seen that it would be desirable to have more reactions and input from Church members in many areas.

In spite of this, many say: "We know what we have, but we are not sure of what we will get." That is my starting point as I begin working on this Commission.

The Norwegian Church and the process towards loosening the ties with the Norwegian State, 2003-2006
By Marit Tingelstad. translated by Mari Wøien, August 2011

I am basing this article on the work by the Church-State Commission in the period from April 2003 through January 2006, during which time I was a member.

The Commission did a thorough and extended study of the various ties between the Norwegian Church and the State as the Ministry (Department) of Church Affairs had requested. There was a large number of mandates to consider, so large a number that it resulted in some rather demanding work for the Commission.

The culmination of the Commission's work ended with a majority in favor of recommending that the Norwegian Church loosen its ties with the State, including the church's sovereignty in matters like appointing their own bishops and other church leaders. This was the main result of the Commission's work. Until now, the State has been the main actor in the appointment of bishops after having considered the recommendations given by the Norwegian Church. The Commission also proposed that the Norwegian Church should be the only decision-making body in matters concerning the liturgy and other internal affairs within the Church. However, the Church has to this day already had the responsibility for these decisions, but only on behalf of the Ministry of Church Affairs.

The voting on the Commission ended with a minority favoring complete independence from the State. Another minority favored the continuation of the state church but with new reforms. The majority and the smaller of the minorities voted for the continuance of the financial support the Church has been receiving from the State. This would act as a reassurance that the Church will continue its position in the local communities as a Church for the people, regardless of the location of the Church. There have never been fees imposed on church members in Norway. The Church has been financed through the general tax levies and the *Storting*, the Norwegian Parliament, grants funds to the Church and other religious denominations according to the number of members in each denomination. By doing this, the right to religious freedom is ensured and highly protected. In Norway, everyone should be able to exercise their religious beliefs aided by public funds! This may sound rather alien for someone who is not accustomed to state involvement in private matters like religion, but this is how Norway has decided to deal with it.

The Commission's study was then sent out for official hearings to all church agencies as well as the numerous municipalities. The Commission members travelled throughout the country to review and clarify their recommendations to local church councils and other religious agencies who requested that they visit.

There was a tremendous amount of response to the Ministry of Church Affairs after the case study, which eventually was issued as a so-called White Paper in the Norwegian *Storting*. While the *Storting* was working on this paper, an unexpected compromise was made between all political parties: The Norwegian Church was to have looser ties with the state if a process towards democratization within the church would begin as well, i.e. the members of the Norwegian Church had to dedicate time for the election of people to the Church departments. In this way, one would ensure that the same group of members would not continually hold office, thus creating an undemocratic institution. After 2009, the election to the Church agencies and the Parliamentary elections are to be held simultaneously. This will occur during the 2011 election for the municipality and county boards, which will be held on the 12th of September. By doing this, the possible voter turnout could be quadrupled.

The articles in the Constitution dealing with the affairs regarding the Norwegian Church (Lutheran) have to be changed in order to implement the new reforms. This will be issued in the *Storting* later in 2011. It may have been a little surprising for the Norwegians that our king, King Harald V, expressed his wish to continue pledging his adherence to the Lutheran faith. Many of us appreciate this, while others found this quite strange because he is the one unifying persona in our country that we should all be able to relate to in some way. However, we can assure you that this will not change! The Monarchy's role as a rock to cling to, their compassion and appearance since the aftermath of the tragedies of July 22nd have only confirmed their position as an ever-strong Monarchy with a heart beating for each and every Norwegian citizen. The Monarchy was present at the memorials after the July 22nd tragedy in various religious denominations as well as in the Norwegian State Church.

It remains to be seen how far the *Storting* is willing to proceed in order to change the Norwegian Constitution, which then eventually will lead to amendments in Church policies. This will be crucial for the development of the relationship between the Church and the State. The implementation of the Commission's recommendations continue to be worked on – so stay tuned for further developments!

Editor's Note: The Church of Norway maintains an excellent website: www.kirken.no/english. The discussion of possible changes in the Church-State relationship was begun in 2002 with the publication of the document "The Same Church – A New Church Structure." That document is available on the website. Information about future changes in the Church-State relationship will also be posted there.

Chapter Fifteen
Hadeland *Folkemuseum*
By Torun Sørli

In the beautiful countryside of Gran you will find the Hadeland *Folkemuseum* with its Open-Air Museum, collections and genealogy centre. It is the regional museum for Hadeland (Gran, Jevnaker, and Lunner *kommuner*). Established in 1913, it is one of Norway's oldest Open-Air Museums. It is open June through August, while the collections and research center are staffed year-round.

The Open-Air Museum contains a fascinating collection of more than 30 historic buildings dating from the 17th through the 19th century. The interiors have been decorated and furnished to recreate the way the buildings were used centuries ago. The museum is set in scenic hilly countryside, and a perfect spot to take in the view is *Halvdanshaugen*. Myth says that this is the grave of the Viking king Halvdan Svarte.

During the summer months, the museum sponsors three special family events, during which the museum teems with life. There are a variety of activities and entertainment for visitors of all ages, such as folk music and dancing, demonstrations of traditional arts and crafts, and much, much more.

© Randsfjordmuseene

Tingelstad Old Church
Hadeland *Folkemuseum* is adjacent to Tingelstad Old Church, also known as St. Petri church. The stone church was built about 1220 and is renowned for its intact interior, which dates from the 16th and 17th centuries. During the summer months the museum has around 7,000 visitors from both the local area and abroad. The museum offers guided tours of Tingelstad Old Church as well as the Open-Air Museum. The guides are all committed to making sure visitors have a wonderful time.

© Randsfjordmuseene

You can take an on-line tour of the Open-Air Museum and Tingelstad Old Church on the museum's website - http://www.randsfjordmuseene.no.

Archives, collections, and genealogy

Many people contact the museum to make inquiries about the collections, local history and genealogy. The museum's genealogy centre contains a collection of local family histories covering the period from about 1700 to 1900, including photos and more. Donations of family histories and artifacts that document Hadeland's emigrants are always welcome. The centre is open on Thursdays (except in July and August) and by appointment.

© Randsfjordmuseene

The museum is committed to lifelong learning. It hosts temporary exhibits and sponsors genealogy classes for adults, along with providing speakers and other outreach activities for local organizations, schools and daycare facilities.

The Museum's gift shop is open year-round and offers a wide array of unique and educational items. You can buy souvenirs, local handicrafts, special art wares, and books, plus beverages and ice cream. The cafeteria is open Saturdays and Sundays during the summer season.

Explore the museum's collections online

Only a small part of the *Hadeland Folkemuseum*'s holdings can be displayed in the Open-Air Museum during the summer season and in its archaeology display. The museum has an inventory of some 16,000 items, 90,000 photographs and 400 films in its collections. It is now possible to explore a large part of these collections on-line. New content is added regularly as the museum works toward its goal of publishing its whole collection on the Internet.

© Randsfjordmuseene

Most of the museums in Norway participate in the "DigitaltMuseum." To see many of the *Hadeland Folkemuseum*'s holdings, visit http://www.digitaltmuseum.no

Along with such famous institutions as the British Museum and the Louvre, the *Hadeland Folkemuseum* also posts items from its collections on the European museum site, http://www.europeana.eu

Search for "Hadeland *Folkemuseum*" on either site to gain access to images and photographs from its collections from the comfort of your own home!

Hadeland Folkemuseum
Kongevegen 92, 2770 Jaren
www.randsfjordmuseene.no – e-mail: hf@randsfjordmuseene.no

Each issue of the *Brua* includes a column from the Hadeland *Folkemuseum*. The articles cover a variety of topics including the museum's current schedule of events, information about traditions and customs, and other historical subjects.

Hadeland *Folkemuseum*: Hadeland Glassverk, 1891
Brua, February 2007
By Torun Sørli

© Hadeland Glassverk

    Hadeland *Glassverk* has been in continuous operation since the first furnace was lit in 1765. The first workers came from another glassworks which had to shut down due to the lack of firewood.
    The typical glassworker lived with his family at the glassworks, as had been the custom since the first glassworks was established in Norway in 1741. Hadeland *Glassverk* was

a self-contained community with its own general store and rules of behavior. For instance, a worker could be fined for using profanity. There was a pension plan for the glassworkers and unemployment benefits when there was no work. The area's first permanent school was established at the *Glassverk* in 1771.

The glassworkers had their own terminology in regards to their tools and tasks. This came about because of the foreign glassworkers who moved from one glassworks to another and the need to be able to understand each other in any glassworks. Some words, such as "pfleger," "navel," and "shürer" are still in use today.

In the picture at the beginning of this article, the glassworkers are gathered outside the factory at Hadeland while the photographer takes their picture. The typical glassworkers in 1891 were men, along with their sons and daughters. Through the ages the art of glassmaking has been handed down from father to son.

No married women are in the photograph as they were not allowed in the factory due to this rule: *"Because there have been disputes between women in which their husbands have taken part, it will hereby be forbidden for women and young females to come to the factory except to bring food to the workers. After delivering the food they are to leave immediately."*

Every person in this photo has been identified. A number of them immigrated to America where some continued working as glassworkers. In this article I am following Anders E. Thoen and Gerhard Gulbrandsen who participated in the 1940 World's Fair in New York. Both men were employees of Gundersen Glassworks in New Bedford, Massachusetts.

An article in the 1940 *Brua* describes the World's Fair in New York as very impressive. One of its attractions was glassblowers Anders Thoen and Gerhard Gulbrandsen executing their piece of work with serenity. The objects they made were sold as souvenirs at the fair. Anders and Gerhard had by this time gained recognition as glassblowers in America and had done well in their new homeland.

Anders Thoen

Their family histories: Anders Magnus E. Thoen (#114) was born 09 March 1876 to Engebret Paulsen Thoen, a woodcutter at Hadeland Glassverk, and his wife Johanne Gulbrandsdatter Greftegrev. Anders worked at Hadeland until 1897 when he applied for work elsewhere, going first to Magnor and later to Høvik. In 1903 he left Norway emigrating to America, settling in New Bedford, Bristol County, Massachusetts. Anders continued in the glass industry working as a gaffer at Gundersens Glassworks, Inc.

Anders married Olga about 1908. She was born ca. 1882 and had immigrated from Norway in 1906. They appear in the 1910, 1920 and 1930 censuses living at 47 Jonathan, New Bedford. Anders was still living at this address in 1952 and the house is still owned by the Thoens today. Their children: Olaf born in 1909 [he was 8 months old when the census was taken in April 1910], Signa born ca. 1912, Margaret born 1919 and David C. born in 1924. The photo of Anders was taken at Magnor Glassverk between 1897 and 1900.

Hjalmar Gerhard Gulbrandsen, born 25 August 1878, was the son of glasscutter Gulbrand Johansen and his wife Karen Andreasdatter. Gerhard worked at Hadeland until 1897 when he, too, went to Magnor and then Høvik Glassworks in Norway. Like Anders Thoen, he emigrated to America in 1903, along with his brother Arnhold (Gerhard is #5 and Arnhold is #8 in the first row in the picture). After arriving in America Gerhard went to work for what became Gundersens Glassworks and was still associated with them in 1952. Gerhard visited Hadeland *Glassverk* in 1951.

Gundersens Glassworks

The Pairpoint Manufacturing Company was at first a metal works company named after Thomas J. Pairpoint. It was started in 1890 in New Bedford MA. In 1894 they merged with Mt. Washington Glassworks, a company that produced glass, silver plated pieces and lamps. Because of the Depression, some of the buildings and equipment were sold in 1938. Robert Gundersen reorganized the company in 1939 and established the Gunderson Glassworks together with Isaac Babbit. After WWII the company was reorganized and became the Gundersen-Pairpoint Glassworks. They are still in business today and it is possible to visit them in Sagamore and see experienced glassworkers at work.

Sources: *Kirkebok* for Jevnaker, *Brua* 1940 pg. 13 Nancy's Collectibles
Thanks to helpful people at Rootsweb and D. Wade.
Photo 1891 owned by Hadeland Glassverk
Photo of Anders Thoen: Photographer: H. Brinchmann, Kristiania

Editor's Note: According to the Kontaktforum emigrant database, 135 Hadelanders who were born at the Hadeland Glassworks immigrated to North America. In addition, a number of workers from Germany and elsewhere in Europe also emigrated from the Glassworks.

Hadeland *Folkemuseum: Vann i Arbeid* (Water in Work) Exhibition
Brua, August 2004
By Kari Mette-Stavehaug

Greetings from the *Hadeland Folkemuseum*,

It has been a good summer for the *Hadeland Folkemuseum*. We have had many visitors both during ordinary weekdays and also during special event days. The *Hadeland Folkemuseum* is now formally associated with the Lands Museum. This new association which is called the Randsfjord Museums now manages the *Hadeland Folkemuseum*.

Working with the Lands Museum has also resulted in an exhibition called "*Vann i Arbeid* ("Water in Work"). To give readers a glimpse into the exhibition I have selected some of the photographs and their texts. Perhaps some of your ancestors worked or had a connection to the places I have included.

Along the coastline of the Randsfjord are found many technical and industrial cultural sites, all the way from glassworks, bridges, and boats to a brewery. These are cultural sites which tell about the industrial activity and technological development in the region for the past several hundred years. The common denominator for many of these cultural sites is that they all have a connection with water. Water has been used as a power source. In the waterfalls and rapids the waterwheel and turbines gave power for production of energy, manufactured goods and food. Until the network of roads was built, the Randsfjord was the primary means of transportation. It was easier to travel by boat than to use walking paths and the rough cart roads. This brought the people along the Randsfjord together, and this was how finished goods and people were carried out and into the region...

The Industrial Revolution reached Norway about 1850. This brought about the industrial development of Norway. Work-saving machines and new methods of communication such as steam-powered machines and the railroad began to be used. Workers were bought into the newly built factories. This enabled a more effective and larger production. The emigration to America began at the same time as the industrialization of Norway.

Industrial development happened all along the coast of the Randsfjord. In the north there was good access to timber. Here relatively little industry was established. Instead the timber was floated south. There it was used by industry farther down the coastline or it was taken out of the district. In the southern part of the Randsfjord the timber was used as fuel for the Hadeland Glassworks or turned into woodpulp and cardboard at the *Kistefos Træsliberi*. Other industries were also based on raw materials from the region such as clay for the brickworks and potatoes for the brewery. Common for all was that water power was used as the power source.

Today there are only a few industrial workplaces along the coastline of the Randsfjord. The main reason is that industry is no longer dependent on water power. Cheap electricity allows businesses to be established no matter where the source of power is found. Another reason is that many industries have been closed. As a result of this, many of the early factory buildings are in disrepair. The development of highways and railroads has meant that boat transportation and smaller bridges are no longer used.

© Randsfjordmuseene

© Randsfjordmuseene

Hadeland Brewery: The Hadeland Brewery is located in Røykenvika and is the only brewery which lies along the Randsfjord. At the same place as the brewery is today, the Næs Brewery was built in 1836. The business provided work for 10 to 12 people. The brewery was closed in 1979. Today the building is used for apartments and a restaurant

Onsaker Brickworks: Brickworks were built in several locations along the Randsfjord in the 1800s. Here there was a supply of clay and transportation of the heavy stone could be done by water. The largest and best known brickworks was at Onsaker. At its peak, about 40 people were employed and 1.5 million bricks produced annually. Production stopped in 1942 and today only the chimney is standing.

Toverud Power Station: The Toverud power station in Gran opened in 1915 and was the first power station which could take care of Hadeland's use of electricity. After two years of use the electrical works had 990 subscribers. Toverud is still in use.

© Randsfjordmuseene

Hadeland *Folkemuseum:* Log Driving in Bjoneelva
Brua, November 2005
By Kari Mette-Stavehaug

In the northern part of Gran west of Randsfjorden you find Bjoneroa. Here *Østre Bjoneelvens Fellesfløtningsforening* (log driving organization) was established in October 1878. The purpose was to organize the log driving in the nine-kilometer-long waterway from Draget to Bjoneroa and Randsfjorden. The industry in the southern part of Randsfjorden – Hadeland Glasswork, brickworks, and wood pulp factories – needed timber and firewood. The forest owners would profit from a better organized log driving.

Log driving means that timber and firewood are transported on water. This was the only way to transport timber for a longer distance for several hundred years. All rivers and waterways where log driving was possible were used.

© Randsfjordmuseene

It is uncertain when log driving first appeared in Norway. We know of some log driving in the 12th century. Casual floating may have occurred earlier. By the end of the 19th century the log driving grew bigger and more organized. To an increasing extent industry was established. The industry needed timber and forewood both as raw material and fuel. The conditions for log driving in the rivers and waterways were improved. Technical arrangements like dams, stonewalls, canals, and slides were built. At the same time log driving organizations like *Ostre Bjoneelvens Fellesfløtningsforening* were established by wood owners. The organizations regulated the floating and made it more effective.

In autumn and winter several hundred lumber jacks worked in the region near the Bjonelv-waterway. Large amounts of timber were transported by horse to the waterway. Every wood owner had certain places for their piles of log. When the ice was safe on *Østre Bjonevatnet* (lake) about a half meter thick, the timbers were placed side by side on the ice. The logs were knotty and barked. This was important for the buoyancy and to avoid a log jam in the river during log driving. The timber was measured and marked by timber markers before the log driving. Every timber buyer had his own mark. The marks were necessary to be able to sort the timber when the timber came to its destination.

The log driving organization was responsible for the log driving. The board hired log drivers, repaired the technical arrangements and accepted payment for the floating. The log driving was dependent on a certain amount of water, gathered during the spring flood. The three dams had to be closed in time. This was the board leader's responsibility.

The log driving took place two to four days in the beginning of June. In the 1930s 30-35 log drivers were hired. They were local people who knew log driving both in the river and in booms on still water. There was a special technique to open the dams. The log drivers were also responsible for making booms where timber could end up in inlets or on land. The log drivers' tool was a peak pole to lead the timber and to break log jams. Along the waterway there was a log cabin where they could sleep and dry their clothes. Being a log driver could be dangerous, and was not especially well paid, but it was an often needed additional income.

© Randsfjordmuseene

The log driving in Bjoneelva ended in 1967. Then it was cheaper to transport the timber by trucks. The three dams, cabins and stonewalls along the Bjonelv-waterway remain as a memory of the log driving. This is the only surviving complete log driving installation in Hadeland.

During the last three years some of the log driving installation has been restored. The project is run by the log-driving organization *Tingelstad and Brandbu Almenning* (common land, the agriculture office in Gran municipality and Hadeland *Folkemuseum*. With money from *Fylkesmannen* (the regional commissioner) and volunteer work from former log drivers, three cabins and one of the dams have been restored. The museum has documented the history and made information boards. From 2006 the museum is responsible for further preservation of the dams and cabins. We plan arrangements and school trips to Bjoneelva. We hope the project will result in more interest and better understanding of the history of log driving in Hadeland.

Hadeland *Folkemuseum:* Hadeland *Bergverksmuseum* is now part of *Randsfjordmuseene*

Brua, February 2010
By Rune Alexander Fredriksen and Torun Sørli

The *Randsfjordmuseene* group of museums has gone through three stages of consolidation since 2004. The latest addition is the *Bergverksmuseum*, joining the group as of January 1, 2010. The amalgamation became possible as the result of allocation of resources from the Norwegian Ministry of Culture, together with financial support from the local districts and funding from Oppland County.

Hadeland *Bergverksmuseum* (Hadeland Mining Museum) is located in Grua in Lunner municipality, a rural district approximately 40 miles north of Oslo. Grua

© Randsfjordmuseene

was originally started as a small and simple mining community in the 1500s. In the last 15-20 years it has experienced an enormous growth in population…The museum is situated in the geological area known as the Oslo Rift.

Mining history of Grua

Mining activities in Grua have left a number of cultural historic sites. Throughout Grua district there are, for example, numerous closed mines and dumps, old quarries for granite, marble, and limestone, besides limestone ovens, smelters, ruins of an ore-washing plant, the remains of a cableway, and finally the remains of many houses connected to the mining activities of Grua.

The now abandoned mines at Grua surely once contributed to the development of the local area and its economy. In addition to the precious ores extracted from the mines, other interesting minerals have also been recovered. Many geologists and amateur geologists have therefore visited the old mines in recent years.

Iron Mining

Iron mining at Grua probably started in the 16th century. An iron mine from 1538 is located at Grua. It began during King Christian III's Regimental period (1836-59). It is from his Regimental Period that we have secured information about early iron mining in Norway, including the old iron mine at Grua.

In August 1538 the royal mining engineer Hans Glaser started his journey in Norway to secure the King his rights to what was worth mining. And that is how he came to

Hadelandsgruben, the iron mine at Grua. The iron ores from Grua district were transported to a smelter in Hakadal. The most recent information we have about this mining period is from a report (*Bergmannsbefaring*) dated 14 August 1799, where it states, "It is being worked in all the mines." A few years later, the iron mine at Grua was closed.

Lead Mines

The first time lead mining is mentioned in Grua is probably February 1631. At that time Mr. Christoffer Urnes wrote down an account among other things about closed lead mines in the Grua region. This means that there must have been lead mining in Grua before 1631. At Grua there are a number of mines that most certainly were lead mines.

Silver Mines

In the negotiation protocol from Kongsberg Silvermining Company, dated 26 February, 1632, it states *"Considering the continuation of silver mining in Hadeland, it is all up to the mining supervisors recommendation."* Whether or not the mining was conducted after 1632 is not certain. About 100 years later, between 1734 and 1741, lead was again mined at Grua. A third mining period started in 1790 and lasted until 1805.

Zinc Mining at Grua

In 1886 two local men, Torstein Raknerud and Ole Wien, discovered a large deposit of zinc sulfide at Nyseter, Grua. This marks the beginning of zinc mining in Grua. The rights to the finds were sold to various owners throughout the next 5-7 years. The most important mining period started in 1904 when the Belgian company *Les mines Du Hadeland* bought the rights to the mine. They engaged H. K. Borchgrevink, a mining engineer, to lead the work. They also established mines at Skjerpemyr and Mutta.

The mining at Nyster is done on four levels: It starts at ground level, and continues down. Outside the mine we find the working area where mine workers processed the ore.

© Randsfjordmuseene

For safety reasons, hardhats must be worn on the Mine Tour

Chapter Sixteen
Folk Dress in Hadeland

Bunads from all over Norway are modeled during the Bunad Parade at the 7-Lag *Stevne*. Carol Sorum and Marie Brown in their *Vestoppland* bunads are second and third from the left.

Every year at the 7-Lag *stevne*, banquet goers are treated to the "Bunad Parade." As part of the presentation, each wearer provides a detailed description and history of his or her garment that is read while the bunad is modeled.

Along with these beautifully embroidered and accessorized costumes, other types of less formal folk dress also reflect Norwegian, and specifically Hadeland, connections.

The Bunad Worn in Hadeland

A bunad is a stylized folk costume. It is worn by Norwegian men and women for important state and family ceremonies and occasions. In the late 19th century a woman named Hulda Garborg championed their development as a way to express national identity and local pride. By the time of Norwegian independence in 1905, bunads had been embraced in much of the country. Today *Husflidslag* (handcraft association) estimates that over 70 percent of Norwegian women own a bunad. A woman's bunad, complete with accessories, can represent an investment of thousands of dollars.

Verifying the authenticity of a bunad's design is serious business. The Norwegian Council for National Costumes was created after World War II and replaced previous governing groups. Its mission is to document and provide information about Norwegian folk-dress traditions.

Applications for approval of new bunad styles are scrutinized to make sure the design and detail of the basic costume and its accessories reflect the culture and tradition of the area with which it is associated. In some areas, the bunad design can be traced to "Sunday best" clothing dating back centuries. In other areas, including Hadeland, today's bunad design is based on samples of other traditional handwork from the area. Over 200 bunad styles from communities throughout Norway have received official approval.

In 1937, the Oppland County Association appointed a committee to create a bunad for *Vestoppland* (West Oppland County). The *Vestoppland* bunad was officially recognized in 1939 and has been adopted by most Hadelanders. The women's bunad was inspired by an embroidered pillow, originally used in a sleigh, found at the Augedal farm in Brandbu. The year 1762 was embroidered on it. The skirt and bodice of blue wool are decorated with embroidered roses and carnations in a rainbow of colors. A white linen shirt, embroidered at the collar and cuffs, completes the outfit. The purse of blue wool is embroidered in the same pattern as the rest of the costume. A bonnet and short cape of the same color and fabric can be added to the ensemble. Silver *solje* adorn the collar closure. Black shoes with silver buckles are the standard footwear with all bunads.

Individuals are expected to wear a bunad from an ancestral homeland or from an area for which s/he feels a strong connection. Only purses that are made for the outfit can be used. Sunglasses, common jewelry, sunhats, and other modern adornments should never be worn with a bunad. Black wool hosiery is dictated, but many women opt to wear ordinary panty hose in the summer months.

Shown here in their *Vestoppland* bunads are lag members Carol Sorum, Elizabeth Botti, and Marie Brown.

Excerpt from **Hadeland *Folkemuseum*: A beautiful woman's gown from Hadeland**
Brua, November 2008
By Grethe Johnsrud, *Randsfjordmuseene*

A folk costume from Hadeland

In 1987, Hadeland *Husflidslag* and Kjersti Prestkvern presented a reconstructed folk costume belonging to Hadeland, called *Hadelandsdrakten*. Kjersti Prestkvern had been working on the project since 1973, when she started documenting fabrics and traditional female dresses, their common features and origin. Much of the material was to be found at Hadeland *Folkemuseum* as well as from private sources. Prestkvern focused on the early and mid- 1800s and was taken by the variations and colors. She soon identified some common features. The colorful cloth was made entirely of wool, two-shaft woven with criss-crossed horizontal and vertical bands in multiple colors. The lining was of linen. A spacious skirt and bodice were sewed together presenting a narrow waist, while the skirt together with an underskirt made a wide silhouette.

Altogether, the picture of a "folk fashion" from Hadeland became visible in her studies. The design is the result of a mix among needs, resources, skills and influences from outside, such as fashion. The fabric is commonly referred to as *verken*, while the gown with long sleeves is of a type called *ermkjole*. The many different types of *verken* proved a rich and diverse home-industry in the 1800s. Around Hadeland, women were weaving beautiful multicolored cloths in tartan-like patterns, often with their own design, and always in colors that fit well with each other. This was an important part of the households' income, as many sold it to dressmakers both in Hadeland and outside. The underskirt is normally made of linsey-woolsey or in cotton, decorated with velvet ribbons. It was not unusual to wear several underskirts, just to get the right modern silhouette!

© Randsfjordmuseene

Folk Dress in Hadeland

In the 1980s, skilled members of Hadeland *Husflidslag* reconstructed the blouse, stockings, ribbons and headgear. The blouse is a slim model in fine, white cotton with handmade bobbin laces around the neckline and cuffs. Tightly knit white stockings with red ornaments are held up by woven, multicolored garters. The headgear of a married woman is of a particular type, called a *honnlue*. The name derived from the two "peaks" at the top back. The bonnet is made of black satin silk and has multicolored wide silk ribbons in the front. The backside is decorated with similar ribbons, forming a large bow. The married woman is further identified by the typical, broad needle-made lace (called *skru*). This surrounds the face, making it seem smaller, and continues to the back. Unmarried women have bright colored bonnet of silk damask with similar ribbons and a bow, although in lighter colors. Young girls could wear a white silk bonnet, also with multicolored motifs. It is said that unmarried women also would wear *skru*, however this is not costumed today. The *Hadelandsdrakt* is not completed without a large square silk shawl with variations in colors and motifs. Married women could also be distinguished by white cotton shawls, skillfully decorated with handmade tambour embroidery and bobbin laces. There is no defined silver, although some families have their own inherited brooches. Nor does the outfit come with a purse or cape.

© Randsfjordmuseene

Over the years, more people have become interested in *Hadelandsdrakten*. In 1994, the men's wear was presented. Both demand the right fabrics and skillful people to make an entire outfit, therefore they can be quite hard to get. Hadeland *Husflidslag* manufactures the dress.

In 2010 the apron with traditions back to c. 1830-50 was officially added to the costume.

The apron in this picture is from Hadeland *Folkemuseum*'s collections.

© Randsfjordmuseene

Hadeland *Folkemuseum*: The *Busserull* of Hadeland
Brua, May 2005
By Kari-Mette Stavhaug

Busserull is the Norwegian name of a short shirt worn as a jacket. Characteristic of the *busserull* is that they, like old shirts, consist of only square and rectangular pieces of fabric. In the last 130-180 years the Norwegian *busserulls* have been made of one-colored, checked or striped woolen or cotton fabric.

In Hadeland we like to think of the *busserull* as a typical Hadeland garment. But the *busserull* has traditions in several other European countries. French workers in the early 1800s wore trousers and blouses (*busserull*). During the French revolutions in 1830 and 1848 the *busserull* was used as a political symbol of the solidarity between workers and peasants.

In Norway and Sweden a garment similar to the *busserull* is known as far back as the Middle Ages. In the second half of the 1800s the ready-made clothing industry started to produce *busserulls*. New colours, fabrics, and details in the design occurred. In the same period the blue-striped *busserull* made of cotton came into common use in Hadeland. This is the same type of *busserull* used and produced in Hadeland today.

The *busserull* shirt has first and foremost been used by farmers, lumberjacks, and building workers as an everyday work garment. The *busserull* was popular because it was a loose and comfortable garment. The *busserull* has not traditionally been used by women. If the *busserull* were new with no patches or holes it was called "holiday *busserull*" and used on Sundays at home. The *busserull* was not used in church. The *busserull* wool has been available in general stores and woven at home.

The traditional *busserull* has a neck band with one button and buttonhole. In the front from the neck to the chest there is a split with a couple of buttons. Until the 1960s another design was used. This had a neck band and buttons all the way down in the front and a band in the waist. This was often used by the elderly men who had trouble pulling the *busserull* over their heads.

The Hoffsbro textile factory was established on the Hoffsbro farm in Gran in 1923 by Emil Nielsen. At first he produced woolen cloth for trousers and cotton cloth for shirts. In 1928 Emil's wife, Kari, created a new pattern for *busserull* cloth – a blue cloth with two black, four white, two black and four blue threads. The *busserull* cloth from Hoffsbro was a success. The Hoffsbro textile cloth was able to replace or take the place of most of the home-woven textiles.

Emil Nielsen's son Nils inherited Hoffsbro and the factory expanded in the 1950s. Their *busserull* cloth was known both in Hadeland and in the surrounding regions. The demand for ready-made clothes rose in the 1950s. Nils Nielsen started to sell ready-made *busserulls* in 1955. Housewives near Hoffsbro sewed *busserulls* and Nielsen offered them to general stores and dry-goods stores. In the 1960s Nielsen sold 40-50 *busserulls* a week in addition to about 150 meters of fabric.

Nielsen chose a design that the ready-made clothing industry used. The collar was turned down, there was a zipper in front from the neck and down to the chest and an elastic band on the back. The zipper and the elastic band made it easier to produce compared to the traditional *busserull*. The Nielsen *busserull* has been given the name *Hadelandsbusserull*.

Nils Nielsen produced *busserull* cloth until 1988. Since then *Grinakervev* near Brandbu has taken over the Hoffsbro pattern and is the only weaver that produces *busserull* cloth in Hadeland today.

Five handlooms and all the other items required for production purposes from Hoffsbro textile fabric were given by the Nielsen family to Hadeland *Folkemuseum* in 1997. A reconstruction of the factory can be seen on the second floor in the *Johnsrudsverksted* Building. When the weaver's widow visited the factory at the museum for the first time she said that the reconstruction was so good that it even smelled right!

For those of you who will soon visit the Hadeland *Folkemuseum* you can see the Hoffsbro textile factory. At *Grinakervev* you can also see how the *busserull* cloth is made and buy *busserull* material and other articles made of the *busserull* cloth.

References
Lange, Åse Asheim, *"Litt om busseruller på Hadeland"* in the *Årbok for Hadeland 1973*, pages 5-15.
Hadeland Folkemuseum archive Hoffsbro *veveri*

Lag Members purchased *busserull* shirts and aprons from *Grinakervev* in 2010

Chapter Seventeen
Hadelanders Visit America

Over the years, the Hadeland Lag has been privileged to host visitors from Hadeland on a number of occasions. Below, Ole Gamme shares his memories of visits by the men's choir from Hadeland, *Mannskoret K.K.*

Memories of the American Tours with *Mannskoret K.K.*
By Ole P. Gamme

Background for my interest in the emigration to America

My great-grandfather, Paul Iversen Gamme, born in 1830, had a sister, Goro, born in 1841, who was married to Paul Gundersen Skiaker. In 1866 they decided, as did so many others from Hadeland, to emigrate to America. The Ruudsbraaten farm in Jevnaker, which Goro's parents had bought for them, was sold, and together with their two little girls, Randi Maria, who was 3 years old, and Mathilde, who was a year old, left from Drammen on the ship *Peruvia* on July 10, 1866. Paul's brother Simen Skiaker also emigrated at the same time.

Letters or other contacts with the family who left were not saved, except that my father had a photograph from 1931. It was of Goro and Paul's grandchild, Kelmer N. Roe, who was on a wedding trip to Norway. They visited the farm where Goro was born, and except for that, there was no more contact between the families until many years later.

My grandmother, father's mother, came from Øvre Gamme, and married my grandfather, Ole P. from Nedre Gamme. Grandmother had a brother, Ole Iversen Gamme, born in 1875. He was the oldest son on the Øvre Gamme farm and had the right to take over the farm from his parents, but Ole I. and his father did not get along very well, so in 1897 Ole left for America, and gave the right to inherit the farm to a younger brother. This Ole I., my father's uncle, later was in contact with my father, Paul, who was born in 1910. Many letters were saved, and I read these with great interest. Father's uncle never married, he tried many different jobs, worked on the railroad, farmed, and also had a job with the city of Minneapolis. He came back to Norway many times, and he wrote that he never felt completely at home in his new homeland. In 1932 he wanted my father to come to the Midwest and take over his farm, but those were difficult times, and father decided to remain in Norway. Two years later Ole came back to Gran and built himself a little house. He said that he had now decided to stay in Norway the rest of his life. One spring day half a year later, my father found a house key and a letter in the mailbox. Father's dear uncle wrote that he could not find peace in Norway either, so he had gone back to America without saying goodbye. The house he had built was a gift for my father. Ole Iversen Gamme died alone in 1937 and is buried in a cemetery in Seattle.

A Visit from America to Gran in 1973

The *Luren Singers*, a large men's choir from Decorah, Iowa, planned a trip to Norway in 1973, and the choir also wanted to visit Hadeland. *Mannskoret K.K.* in Gran immediately said that they were willing to host the choir from America. Since I was chairman of the *K.K.* at that time, I had a lot to do with the visit. The *Luren Singers* and their wives were housed with members of the *K.K.*, and we had two couples at our house at Gamme. We maintained good contact with them, and interest in America increased after this visit. In the *K.K.* there were many who thought we should begin to plan for a return visit to the Midwest, both as an anniversary trip for the choir which soon would be 75 years old, but also to visit relatives. Many had relatives in the U.S. who had visited Hadeland, but only one of the choir members had been on a return visit. Most of them had never been outside of Norway's borders.

Planning a Trip to America

Paul G. Skiaker was the most excited about a trip to the U.S. for the *K.K.* He was very interested in family history and a big admirer of that country which had taken in so many Norwegian emigrants. Paul contacted various local people who had contacts in Norwegian America. One of these was Per Hvamstad, who had worked awhile on emigrant history of Hadeland. Per had visited Peder Nelson and Harriet Foss in Northwood, N.D., and also helped to plan the tour itinerary for the visit of the Luren Singers in 1973.

It was not long before the *K.K.* Tour Committee headed by Paul G. Skiaker could bring a presentation with ideas on how the choir could raise money for a trip to America. A lottery, with a car as the main prize, was one of the recommendations. Chartering a complete airplane and selling the seats the choir didn't need, was another recommendation. Paul was so enthusiastic and optimistic that the choir approved the committee's recommendations. In the meantime it was decided that we should wait until 1977 to travel. The *K.K.* singers wanted to bring their wives, and there was strong advice that none should be hindered from traveling because they were pregnant!

In connection with Christmas in 1976 my aunt and uncle, Ingeborg and Brynjulf Brørby, were visited by Ingeborg's nephew, Olaf Nelson and his wife Rhoda from Montevideo, Minnesota. Olaf was on the committee which worked to get the Hadeland Lag in America started again. The lag, which was organized in 1910, had not had much activity during the last few years. After Morgan Olson from Minneapolis initiated interest, a committee was formed to reorganize the lag. There was a cordial meeting with Rhoda and Olaf, and Helga and I kept good contact with them in the years that followed.

During the winter of 1976-77 there were many letters between Morgan Olson in the Hadeland Lag and the *K.K.* The Hadeland Lag wanted to host the *K.K.* and planned a great program for a round-trip in the Midwest. The lottery for the choir brought in a good amount of money, and a DC8 from Trans-International Airlines with seating for 254 passengers was chartered. The *K.K.* with spouses needed 68 seats, the rest were sold at a profit so that the singers received free airline tickets. The newspaper *Hadeland* was also a good supporter, and planned a trip for those who weren't going on the *K.K.*'s concert tour.

The *K.K.* rehearsals were very intense during the winter and spring of 1977, with up to three rehearsal evenings in a week during the final weeks before leaving. Our director, Jan Reidem, did his utmost to make certain that the choir would be the best it possibly could be. The *K.K.*'s previous director, Gudbrand Bøhmer, a violinist who now lived in Lillehammer, came along on the tour together with organist and accompanist Leif Solberg, and soprano Else Doseth, with their spouses. Brandbu's organist, Birgit Røken, the regular accompanist for the *K.K.*, also went along. New uniforms were purchased for the tour, and the *K.K.* went to Oslo and made a phonograph recording that we could take along to the U.S. both for sale and as a gift to the choir's hosts. The timing was not good for that; we did not know that the U.S. was using cassette tapes most of the time, not many had phonographs any longer, so the sale of the records was not a success.

Fourteen days before we left, the *K.K.* had a visit from Verlyn Anderson of Moorhead, Minnesota. He was librarian and teacher at Concordia College in Moorhead and was visiting the archives in Norway. Verlyn was also one of the members of the committee for reorganizing the Hadeland Lag. This visit was the beginning of a lifelong friendship between the *K.K.* and Verlyn and his wife Evonne, and especially between them and Helga and me.

The 1977 Trip to the U.S.

July 19th was the day which was remembered for a long time afterwards by many in Hadeland. 254 expectant Hadelanders went to Gardermoen where the airplane stood waiting for the trip to the U.S. Not many had been outside of Norway, indeed for some the trip to Oslo was the farthest they had been. For Helga and me, who had gotten married nine years earlier, this was the first time we would be away from the farm for more than a day since we were married. Many in the choir had small children whom they had never been away from, so there were many tears at the departure. We thought about how it must have been 130 years earlier when the first Hadelanders left for America; we were only going to be gone for three weeks.

Boarding busses at Hector Airport in Fargo

After a landing in the state of Maine on the East Coast, we flew to the airport in Fargo, arriving there about 8:00 in the evening. We were met by a large crowd of Hadeland Americans. A beautiful hand-painted banner with the wording: "*Velkommen Hadelendinger 1977*," made by Harriet Foss, brought the tears running down our cheeks for most of us. We felt very welcome and the next three weeks would only strengthen that impression. Warmth streamed toward us, not only from the outside temperature which were often over 95 degrees Fahrenheit, but also from the people who had come to meet relatives from Norway.

Concordia College in Moorhead was our base the first five days. From here there were tours to districts in the area where Hadelanders had settled. The first concert was held in the Gran Church in Mayville. Wives of the singers modeled their bunads, and everywhere we were met with the greatest hospitality. There were concerts in the Jevnaker Church in Borup and the Gran Church in Hawley. In all the places we were surprised by the great numbers of people who came to hear us. It was the middle of harvest season, but the farmers took off from their work and came to the churches. Food was served at all the churches. At the cemeteries we could read familiar Hadeland names on the gravestones, we felt almost as though we were at a church at home. We also held concerts in auditoriums in many schools in various towns around the Red River Valley. We had remarkable guides on the busses, Olaf Nelson and Verlyn Anderson were familiar people, and the Hadeland Lag's president, Morgan Olson, saw to it that the program for the days was followed with punctuality. There was a TV recording and one evening there was a big party at the Sons of Norway Lodge, Kringen Club in Fargo. Here the newly-elected board of the Hadeland Lag of America and Peder Nelson were admitted as special members of *Mannskoret K.K.*,

Manskoret K.K. performed on local television

and were given *K.K.* pins for all their work in planning and carrying out the tour in the Midwest. There at Kringen Club we met Thomas Skattum for the first time. He was the treasurer of the Hadeland Lag and his father was born on a cotter's place at Gamme in 1879.

Then the tour went south to the Montevideo area in Minnesota and a concert in the Jevnaker Lutheran Church. Here we were housed with families for three days, more concerts were given, and we were part of a huge party at the farm of Rhoda and Olaf Nelson, who had cleared out their machine shed and invited nearly 400 guests to a cook-out. A whole beef cow was barbecued and was served with everything that goes with it. There was a dance afterwards that lasted into the morning hours.

On July 27th we traveled to Minneapolis and were welcomed by the *Nordkapp Mannskor*. Together we had a concert in the Norwegian Memorial Church in a terrible thunderstorm. The next day the tour continued to Decorah, Iowa. Here we took part in the Nordic Festival for three days with concerts alone and together with the *Luren Singers*. This was a fantastic folk festival in this beautiful town. We stayed at Luther College, and

Party at the Sons of Norway in Fargo

Helga and I also stayed there until we flew home to Norway from Minneapolis on August 8th. A fantastic trip was over, all who were along had an experience which we never forgot. Memories constantly come back to us, and the trip along with the *K.K.* was the beginning of all later contact with the Hadeland Lag of America. A thousand thanks!

Another America Tour with *Mannskoret K.K.* in 1980

When the Hadeland Lag of America visited Norway in 1978, we made many new acquaintances, and for the first time I met descendants of Goro Gamme who emigrated in 1866. Along on the tour to Norway was Goro's great-granddaughter, Florence Gubbrud, and her husband Archie, former governor of South Dakota. They were living in Alcester, S.D. Florence took along with her family papers with information about all the descendants of Goro and Paul, and a new world opened for me, and not least for my father. He had great interest in family research and now he also had time to work with the family history. Fifty years after Rev. Kelmer Roe's visit to Gamme, the contact was now re-established.

In 1979 *Mannskoret K.K.* received an invitation from the Hadeland Lag to come to the Lag's 70th anniversary the next year. Many thought it was too early to travel to the U.S., it had only been three years since we had been there. First the finances would have to be in order. The choir received the use of some free land from some of the choir members, and potatoes and carrots were planted and harvested by the volunteer work of the choir members. Also a bank loan was taken out and if there would be enough people on the tour, it would not be so expensive. But everything turned out all right, and on July 8th the choir members and their spouses landed in Minneapolis. The Hadeland Lag with Morgan Olson in charge had again made up a fine program for the *K.K.* The entire next day was spent making a TV recording in Rochester, Minn. The *K.K.* sang many songs, and especially *Den store hvite flokk* with Ole O. Skiaker was recognized by many who saw the TV program. Our wives had a bunad style show, and the *K.K.*'s chairman, Ole P. Hvattum, was interviewed together with the tour committee chairman, Finn Holter.

There were many concerts lined up this time also. Minnesota, Wisconsin and South Dakota were the states we visited. July 10th was a special day. Morgen Olson had arranged a contact with Tuff Memorial Home in Hills, Minn. In 1872 Haagen O. Tuff and Anne Hvattum had emigrated to America. The next year they got married and had many children. Their son Gilbert in 1957 willed land and a large amount of money for a rest home for the district, and the *K.K.* visited that home. Fourteen of the choir's members were members of Haakon and Anne's extended families; it was a great experience for us to sing at the rest home and also to talk with many of the residents there.

American Schiagers and *Mannskoret K.K.* Skiakers - Sioux Falls SD

On July 11th the *K.K.* had a concert in Our Savior's Lutheran Church in Sioux Falls, S.D., and we were part of the *Nordland Fest* in the city. The next day we traveled to Marshall, Minn., where the 70th anniversary of the Hadeland Lag was celebrated. A dance group from the *Jevnaker Bygdeungdomslag* (Jevnaker Community Young People's Organization) also took part there. "500 Americans, most of them with Hadeland ancestry, met us with an applause we did not think would ever stop," reported Finn Holter on the telephone to the local newspaper, *Hadeland*.

During this *stevne* the *K.K.* also had another responsibility. On behalf of the newspaper *Hadeland* the choir's chairman Ole P. Hvattum had the responsibility to give the year's *Hadelandspris* to Norwegian-American Peder Nelson, author, long-time editor of *Brua* and perhaps the one who had gathered more emigrant history than anyone else with Norwegian blood in America.

After participating in Norway Day in Minneapolis and more concerts in Wisconsin, the last in Mt. Horeb, we had the last week free for private visits. Another wonderful America tour was over, we had met many new relatives, relatives who we in all the years afterward have had the pleasure to visit in the U.S. and to be visited by in Hadeland.

The America Tour in 1986

Sangerfest in Decorah

In the years following 1980 there was a great deal of contact between the Hadeland Lag and the *K.K.* We had again received an invitation to come to the Midwest, but there was not enough interest. The *K.K.* had taken many other trips in the years that followed, including to Finland, the Soviet Union and Denmark. In 1986 the 7-Lag *Stevne* was in Decorah, Iowa. At the same time the Luren Singers were hosting The Norwegian Singers Association of America who were having their *Sangerstevne* (meeting of singing groups) in the town. The Hadeland Lag's president, Morgan Olson, also was president of the Singers organization. The *K.K.*'s soloist, Ole O. Skiaker, was invited to the *Sangerstevne*, and the *K.K.* offered to pay part of his travel expenses. "Ole the Soloist," as he was called all over Hadeland, had been educated as a singer before the war in 1940. His father said then that if he wanted to take over the farm, he had to come home and become the farmer. Singing therefore became a hobby for him for the following 65 years. Ole and his wife, Eva, wanted to go to America, but they wanted Helga and me to come along. Helga is Ole and Eva's niece, and we right away agreed to accompany them on this new America trip. Since 1980 we had been visited by many of Goro Gamme and Paul

Skiaker's descendants from America. One of these was Lois Schiager Rand, married to Dr. Sidney A. Rand who had been America's ambassador to Norway when Jimmy Carter was president of the U.S. Lois Rand was a very good pianist, violin player and organist, and she and Ole O. Skiaker had played many concerts during family get-togethers in Norway.

During the Song Fest in Decorah Ole O. was soloist with the Luren Singers for *Den Store Hvite Flokk*. The high point for those of us from Norway was certainly the evening in the large concert hall at Luther College, there we could participate in a combined concert with 350 singers from 14 American men's choirs who presented Norwegian songs in a fantastic manner. The next day I was privileged to be able to sing duets with Ole O. Skiaker, with Lois Rand on the grand piano in the same large hall. Many certainly thought that was special, here came a Skiaker and a Gamme from Hadeland in Norway and sang with a descendant of a Skiaker and a Gamme, who had emigrated in 1866, who played a grand piano!

The next day we participated in a church service in the Glenwood Church outside of Decorah, in that district in which so many from Hadeland settled in the 1800s. A new wonderful America tour was over. There was a sad message which came to us later that year: Morgan Olson had died. There are many in Hadeland in Norway and among Hadelanders in America and Canada who can thank that man for all he did for the Hadeland Lag of America!

Hadeland Tour Group to the American Midwest
July 9 - 24, 2001
As recalled by Harald Hvattum

After Hadeland Lag members returned to their homeland in Norway in 2000, there was great interest among the Norwegians to visit the place where so many of their relatives had settled in the American Midwest. Fifty Norwegians made the trip to America in July, 2001.

Visitors from Hadeland - 2001

Sunday, 8 July: In Minneapolis we were welcomed by Dean Sorum, treasurer of the Hadeland Lag, and escorted to the Hampton Inn. We each received a folder with our name on it filled with information that included a map of Minnesota and the Dakotas, which we put to good use during the trip. Some of the participants spent their first evening with friends and relatives in the Twin Cities.

Monday, 9 July: Our first day in this new country. We visited two states. We traveled through southeastern Minnesota to Iowa. Dean Sorum was the tour guide and Hans M. Næss translated. We visited the Vesterheim Norwegian-American Museum. At Vesterheim we met the president of the Hadeland Lag, Robert Rosendahl. He speaks Norwegian and acted as a guide. The other guide was a young girl whose grandfather was from Frilling in Jaren. We were treated to an outdoor lunch and were seriously reminded that it can be hot in America at this time of year! We visited Luther College, which was founded by immigrants in 1861 and today has an enrollment of 250. After the tour we were invited into a large concert hall where Ole Skiaker had sung in 1986.

Tuesday, 10 July: After spending the night at the Country Inn in Decorah, we began our trip to Sioux Falls, South Dakota. Our first stop was at a fish farm. This was followed by a visit to the Budde Berg dairy farm. We were served milkshakes at the conclusion of our farm visit. Glenwood Lutheran Church was our last stop in Iowa. We enjoyed a tour of the church and lunch in the church basement. In the cemetery we were interested to find gravestones with Hadeland names like Rosendal, Hotvedt, Blegen, Onsager, Egge Braten and Brynsaas. The Rosendahl family belongs to this church, and here we took our leave of Robert Rosendahl. We headed back into Minnesota and drove along Interstate 90 for several hours. We paid a quick visit to Tuff Memorial Home in Hills, Minnesota. This is a nursing home founded as a bequest from a man with Hadeland ancestry, Gilbert Tuff. Back on the road, we crossed into South Dakota where we were required to make a routine stop at a weigh station. The bus was found to be overweight and it took a long time to resolve the problem. A guard handed out free bags as compensation for our long wait. We finally arrived in Sioux Falls where we had dinner and met Delores Cleveland and Manfred Hill from the Hadeland Lag. The long day ended with a tour of the white wooden church named Nidaros, the oldest Lutheran church in South Dakota, built in 1878. Our guide at the church spoke with a Trønderlag dialect. We spent the night at the Baymont Inn.

Wednesday, 11 July: Verlyn and Evonne Anderson joined us as guides for the rest of the trip. We began the day with a tour of the battleship "South Dakota." Then we traveled to Manfred Hill's farm. Next stop, Canton Lutheran Church, where we again found many Hadeland names in the graveyard including Hvattum, Skiaker, Lunder, Tingelstad and Moldstad. We had lunch at a local eatery in Canton, where Main Street had been decorated with Norwegian flags in our honor. We visited the public library where there is a room honoring Governor Archie Gubbrud. He was the grandson of Peder T. Gubbrud who emigrated from Gubbrud in Røykenvik in 1865. We met one of his sons and a daughter, Maxine. A retired teacher provided a guided tour of Canton Lutheran Church, which was founded in 1888 by 23 Norwegian families. Kåre Lyngstad translated. We visited North Trinity and South Trinity Cemeteries, where we again found many Hadeland names. At Land

Church we found a tombstone for a man named Sogn and were served "juice drinks," which tasted very good on a hot day. The day ended with a tour of the Kennedy Mansion and a large banquet.

Thursday, 12 July: This day was a long trip west along Interstate 90. The term "infinity" as it was in the itinerary fit very well. On the trip we visited the Mitchell Corn Palace and the Lakota Indian Museum in Mitchell, South Dakota. Upon reaching Rapid City we were accommodated on the campus of the South Dakota School of Mines and Technology. Here we stayed for the three days of the 7-Lag *Stevne*. The *stevne* opened in a large hall with no air conditioning. It was a warm experience.

Friday, 13 July: A day trip through the Black Hills began at Hot Springs, which has a museum that displays large mammoth fossils. It is also possible to watch an actual archeological dig going on at the site. We were told that people paid to participate in these excavations. This was followed by a visit to Custer State Park, which has about 1500 buffalo. We had lunch at Blue Bell Lodge, where they served buffalo stew in a bread bowl. From there we visited the Crazy Horse Memorial and Mount Rushmore. The evening program at Mount Rushmore was impressive, made even moreso because former ambassador to Norway Sidney Rand and his wife Lois were masters of ceremonies.

Saturday, 14 July: The day began with the Hadeland Lag annual meeting. Greetings and gifts were exchanged. Presentations at the Hadeland Lag annual meeting included:

- Ole P. Gamme presented beautiful Hadeland crystal covered goblets to all officers of the Hadeland Lag. The pattern is called Regent and the royal family had also recently purchased these goblets for Crown Prince Haakon's wedding in August.
- Tom Skattum and Denny Tunell received framed drawings which had been designed by Kari Ruud Flem.
- Jan Lian, president of the Årbok Publishing Company, presented Verlyn and Evonne Anderson with copies of the *Årbok for Hadeland*.
- All were given framed Hadeland art drawings certificates which had been made by Kari Ruud Flem, a Hadeland artist. These included drawings of the churches in Hadeland and the *Dynnastein*.

After lunch, we visited Deadwood. Although now full of casinos, Deadwood began as a mining town. We visited Mt. Moriah Cemetery where the earthly remains of "Wild Bill" Hickok and "Calamity Jane" are buried. We had heard their stories during the Hadeland Lag meeting earlier in the day. Saturday evening the 7-Lag *Stevne* banquet began with a bunad parade followed by an American-style banquet. After a break, there was traditional Scandinavian music and a local folk singer. It was a long program in the heat.

Sunday, 15 July: The 7-Lag *Stevne* was over, so we said good-bye to Robert Rosendahl and Tom Skattum. Some of the Hadeland Lag directors joined us as we set out from Rapid City. Just outside Rapid City we visited the replica Borgund Stave Church. We traveled north through depopulated areas of South Dakota. There were many abandoned farms. We left the main road and drove down a gravel road into what was once the village of

Sorum. Kristian Sørum settled on a farm around 1910, and the village grew up around it. The Sorums left in the 1930s, and the village is now abandoned

Our last stop in South Dakota was at the Slim Buttes Lutheran Church where we had lunch. When we reached North Dakota, we turned onto Interstate 94, which runs right through the state from west to east. After dinner at the Pitchfork Fondue we saw the outdoor production of the "Medora Musical."

Monday, 16 July: The Medora Motel had no dining room so we had to get up early and buy breakfast in the city. Our next stop was Theodore Roosevelt National Park. This was a side trip a Norwegian will never forget. Here everything was different than what we had seen before. The huge flat areas were replaced by steep sometimes dramatic ridges. During a stop we saw a buffalo at such close range that the bus driver was quick to urge us back onto the bus. There had recently been a man killed by a buffalo. Two more attractions were on the itinerary before we reached Bismarck. Fort Abraham Lincoln was a reconstructed fort that also included the On-A-Slant Indian Village. In Bismarck our hotel, the Expressway Suites, was located right next to a large shopping center.

Tuesday, 17 July: The day began with a visit to the North Dakota State Capitol. From there it was a long drive east. As we approached Fargo, we got a glimpse of the Red River Valley, which is one of the flattest and widest stretches of land in wide North Dakota, and that says a lot. In Fargo we visited Bonanzaville, a large open air museum. We were treated to dinner and a cultural program at the Kringen Lodge of the Sons of Norway in Fargo, an experience we shared with *Landings* who were also visiting from Norway. This was followed by dancing to the music of an electric organ. Some of us had chosen instead to meet with American relatives at our hotel, the Holiday Inn, and experienced a tornado warning. Norwegians and Americans alike were told to sit on the floor in a long corridor while security guards explained the possible dangers. Those of us at the Kringen Club knew nothing about it, and no tornado occurred.

Wednesday, 18 July: This was a big day for the historians among us, with three church and cemetery visits. The day began with a tour of Concordia College. Then we visited Jevnaker Lutheran Church in rural Borup, Minnesota. This white wooden church was built in 1883. The next stop was the Gran Lutheran Church in rural Hawley, Minnesota. It was founded in 1879. We found familiar names in the cemetery including Hammerstad, Egge, Bjertnæs, Elna, and Blegen. The final stop on this tour was South Immanuel Lutheran Church in rural Rothsay, Minnesota. In this cemetery we found Hadeland names Hovland, Ohe and Ellefsrud. There were also many Hedmark and Gudbrandsdal names. At each church we were met by many people from the community and there was a program and exchange of gifts. Following the church visits we made a stop on the farm of Larry Ohe. Among other things he enjoys restoring old farm implements. The day ended with a visit to Dean Sorum's lake home. It was quite a place with a fine beach and boat.

Thursday 19 July: We traveled north from Fargo and first visited Gran Lutheran Church in rural Mayville, North Dakota. It was founded in 1873, and the cemetery included Hadeland names Sorum and Molden (many of the Molden family in the area now use the name Hanson). We were again met by church members, there was a program, and gifts were exchanged. As we traveled on to Northwood, North Dakota, we passed Bruflat Lutheran Church which was named after Bruflat Church in Etnedal, Valdres. Harriet Foss welcomed us to Northwood and invited us into her home. It was filled with Norwegian memorabilia from floor to ceiling! Northwood was also the home of Peder Nelson, whose large collection of Norwegian-American books was given to the Gran *Historielag*. Flowers were laid on Nelson's grave in the Northwood Cemetery where we again found many Hadeland names, including Onsaker and Tingelstad. We returned to Fargo-Moorhead and ended the day with a tour of the Hjemkomst Center in Moorhead, Minnesota.

Friday, 20 July: We said good-bye to Fargo and North Dakota and traveled to Montevideo, which was not the shortest route to Minneapolis. Our first stop was at a small town called Milan. At the local museum Leslie Ruud, a farmer with ancestors from Jevnaker, was able to answer many questions. We also visited Kviteseid Church. The familiar name Struxnes was among candidates for confirmation in the 1940s. On our way out of town, we experienced how it can really rain in the Midwest. Our next stop was Jevnaker Lutheran Church in rural Montevideo, Minnesota. This church was first built in 1896, but had to be rebuilt in 1913 after a fire. The program there began with the singing of four young boys, followed by a good lunch and exchange of gifts. Before we left the church, a picture was taken of all the Hadeland travelers. We took leave of Dean and Carol Sorum, who had been with us since we had arrived. Our day ended at the Hampton Inn in Bloomington, Minnesota, which would be our base for the rest of our stay.

Saturday, 21 July: We were invited by Sidney and Lois Rand to visit Northfield and tour St. Olaf College. After the tour we had lunch with the Rands and former Hadeland Lag president Palmer Rockswold. Gifts were exchanged. From Northfield we made our way to the busy and crowded Mall of America. With 600 shops, we were able to buy all we needed and much, much more.

Sunday, 22 July: We were invited to worship at the *Mindekirken* in Minneapolis. After the service Hadeland Lag member Betty Volney was among the hosts for coffee in the church basement. We then visited the interesting museum at the Minnesota History Center and found a rich variety of Norwegian-American literature in its bookstore. Some of the group who were traveling home via Amsterdam left that evening.

Monday, 23 July: We visited downtown Minneapolis and its high rise buildings. As we drove to the Minnesota State Capitol, we were able to see the many mansions on Summit Avenue in St. Paul. Our last stop was at Fort Snelling, which won the hearts of the Norwegian tourists because the information brochure was in Norwegian! We said good-bye to Verlyn and Evonne Anderson at Charles Lindbergh Airport with great thanks for their hospitality and that of the entire Hadeland Lag.

Tuesday, 24 July: The last group of travelers landed at Gardermoen Airport. A wonderful trip had come to an end.

Chapter Eighteen
Hadeland Today

One of the most popular features in the *Brua* was introduced in February 2002. In his regular "Hadeland Today" column, Ole Gamme offers his perspective on events in Norway and the U.S. and shares a little of everyday life in Hadeland. Included here are representative musings in winter, spring, summer and fall.

Winter - February 2002

It is a sparkling winter day in Hadeland today – 5 degrees above Fahrenheit, 12 inches of snow on the ground, beautiful sunshine and completely wind-free. Hadeland, the district from which nearly 10,000 people immigrated to America between 1840 and 1910, today has about 27,500 residents and includes the three municipalities or communities of Gran, Jevnaker and Lunner. The land area of Hadeland is 1,375 square kilometers or slightly more than 500 square miles (about *one half the size of the state of Rhode Island*). Hadeland is located in the southern part of Oppland *fylke* (county), one of Norway's 19 counties. Oppland and Hedmark Counties are the only two counties that do not border the ocean. The distance to Oslo, Norway's capital city, is about a one-hour drive, and to drive to Gardermoen International Airport takes only about 45 minutes. Work has begun on a new road in Gardermoen Airport from Hadeland. It will go from Grua in Lunner and directly eastward to the airport. The first part of the new road will go through a three-mile tunnel through the mountain. When the new road is ready, it will take less than a half-hour to drive from Gardermoen to Hadeland.

The New Year is already nearly a month old and life in Hadeland continues very much as usual. But we are living in a world which is constantly changing. That which was usual or ordinary 50 years ago is historical today. A person can wonder what the emigrants of over 150 years ago would say if they could come back to Norway today. Nearly all families have computers and Internet where we can have contact with people all over the world in just a few seconds. On our TV's we can see and hear President Bush at the same time as he says something on American TV. On September 11 last year we here in Hadeland could see the tragedies in New York and Washington on our TV's at the same time as you did in America.

Christmas in Hadeland is celebrated in the traditional fashion. Before Christmas all of the choirs and instrumental groups present their concerts. In recent years many professional musicians have traveled around the country with Christmas concerts. This also happened in Hadeland. This occurred again this year, but the interest in attending these concerts has diminished somewhat. On the other hand, the churches are full to capacity when local choirs and other musical groups have concerts. The *Mannskoret K. K.* had its traditional Christmas concert on the third day of Christmas (27 December) and the Nikolai Church at Granavollen was completely filled.

That which more and more leaves its mark on the time before Christmas is the increasing expenditures of money on gifts, Christmas parties and the buying of many things that are perhaps not always essential. We have a population of only 4.5 million in Norway, but there are so many shopping centers and businesses here that there could easily be a population of 10 million and we would still have enough places to buy what we need. Christmas shopping increases every year. Now in January most of the stores have sales where a person can buy items at one-half of the price they cost before Christmas. All of the firms and other working places also arrange what we call *julebørd* (a Christmas party), a gathering of all who work together for an evening at a restaurant with lots of good food and drinks, or a week-end at a hotel, or a tour on a ship to, for example, Denmark.

During Christmas the churches in Hadeland are full of people for all the worship services. That is not so usual during the rest of the year. In Norway we have what we call a state church. The vast majority of the Norwegians are members of the state church. It is an Evangelical Lutheran Church. The state and the local municipalities pay for the cost of maintaining the churches, and the salaries of the ministers and the other people who work in the church. As a result, the interest and the involvement of the Norwegian people in the churches is not as great as, for example, in America. But when the churches need restoration, as a rule, the local municipalities do not have enough money, so they must collect or gather in additional money for that. One of the churches in Gran, the Grymyr Church, burned down three years ago and the plans for the new church are now ready. The construction of it will begin next summer. A fund drive to furnish this new church is now in progress.

This week the Gran congregations have had visits by Bishop Rosemarie Køhn. She is bishop of the Hamar Diocese; Hadeland is in that diocese. She is the first female bishop in Norway. She is here for five days visiting churches, schools and meetings with representatives from the local government and members of the congregations. Her visit will conclude on Sunday, January 27, with festival worship services in the Sister Churches.

Schools in Hadeland started up again on January 7 after the Christmas vacation. In Norway the children begin elementary school the year they are six years old. They go to elementary school for seven years followed by three years in junior high school. After that all have the chance to attend *videregående* (upper secondary school). We have three such schools in Hadeland – in Brandbu, Gran, and in Roa in Lunner. This school is also for three years and the students can choose from many different subject lines. Those that wish to study beyond this must travel from Hadeland to Oslo or other places where schools of higher education are located. Some also travel to other countries to study; this year, for example, there are three students from Hadeland enrolled in the South Dakota School of Mines and Technology in Rapid City. In addition, many others are studying in other places in America.

In families in Norway today it is usual that both parents work at jobs outside the home. Because of this, we have child daycare facilities throughout the land where children can be when their parents are working. The parents have to pay quite a bit for this, but the state pays subsidies to both public and private childcare centers. Schools for children, ages six and up, are free and paid for by the municipalities, counties and the federal government.

In January many retired people in Norway travel to places in southern Europe for a week or longer. In February the schools have a week of winter vacation and whole families go to the mountains, to hotels, to private cottages for a week-long vacation, or with skis on their feet travel to alpine ski centers and ski trails. Many families also go to the South (southern Europe) during this week. That is about the same as I guess it is for you in the Midwest. I know that as I sit and write this, both the president and the vice president of the Hadeland Lag are in Arizona, and the editor of the *Brua* is in Hawaii. I hope you all are doing well.

Spring - May 2005

Spring has come to Hadeland. After a mild winter with little snow, all of nature is awakening again into a renewed life after a long winter's sleep. We are fortunate that we live in a land where all of nature changes several times a year. Every season of the year has its charm, but spring is my favorite time of the year. When the earliest spring flowers begin to appear in the woods and when the new-born lambs on the neighboring farm hop, run around and bleat together with the singing of the migratory birds who have recently returned from their winter sojourn in Southern Europe, then the blood pulses faster in my 60-year-old body and makes me feel as though I am a youth again!

Spring's work has begun on the farms in Hadeland; the first barley fields have already been seeded. On our farm we raise mostly hay for the silo and hay that will be baled. It is on these fields that we apply the commercial fertilizers. Now is also the time of the year that we haul out the manure which is also spread out on the fields; the fences of the pastures must be repaired and the cattle are let out of the barn after spending the long winter indoors.

All of us see how our society is constantly changing. Many of these changes are for the better. We say that "the times are changing" or "it is a new time now; we must follow with the times." The Norwegian author, Arne Garborg, said it this way, "Time does not change, it is we, the people who change the times." I think he had a good point, this makes sense.

Agriculture in Hadeland, yes, in all Norway, has changed very much in the past few years. In 1979 there were 1,415 operating farms in Hadeland, now there are only 540 farms. The small farms are now becoming only places of residence for the owners; the land is rented out to others. There are 85 dairy farms in Hadeland today. That is a decrease of 40 (*32%*) in just the past five years. This is a politically driven development. Everyone who thinks they know something about economics think that we have an all-too expensive food production system in Norway. They do not see the values of having people residing throughout our land in vital living communities. Without farms and farmers, a large part of Norway will become vacant and that certainly will be less attractive for the tourists who visit our country.

In Norway there are about 430 municipalities (*kommuner*) and 19 counties (*fylker*). That is far too many, according to the thinking of our present government officials. Here in Hadeland we had four municipalities until 1962 – Brandbu, Gran, Jevnaker and Lunner. Brandbu and Gran were merged into one municipality in 1962 which today is called Gran. At that time there was a lot of controversy about this merger. Each of these communities had a business center, Brandbu *sentrum* in the northern part of the proposed municipality and Gran *sentrum* to the south. For this reason, they felt they needed to place the new governmental center building in Jaren, half-way between Brandbu and Gran. During this past winter the politicians have used a great deal of time discussing the geographic structure of municipalities and what would be the most appropriate for the future of the Hadeland municipalities. One alternative is to make Hadeland into one large municipality, made up of the now existing three municipalities. Another is to merge Gran and Lunner into one political unit. Many of the citizens of Jevnaker say that they would rather become a part of Ringerike, located to their south. The Lunner citizens who live in the farthest south area of that municipality say that they would rather become a part of the Nittedal municipality to their south. I have not yet seen anything about what advantages there would be in forming larger municipalities. What I am most certain of is that the larger the municipalities become, or for that matter as a company or an organization gets larger, the less interest there is among the people to do volunteer work. Now today, those on the advisory boards should be paid for their meeting time, including mileage for their transportation costs; yes, even for reimbursement for childcare so that they can participate in the meeting. When Brandbu and Gran became one municipality in 1962, it was said that we would save a considerable amount of money on administration costs because of this merger. Today there are many times as many employees in the Gran municipality as there were in both Brandbu and Gran in 1962!

Also in many other areas there are major changes occurring. Small schools are being closed and replaced by larger centralized facilities. The children must be transported to these schools in busses. Many of the small shops and grocery stores are gone – large supermarkets have taken over and replaced them. Today there are only four "chains" that control the sale of all foodstuffs in Norway. Now there is a big discussion about the structure or geographic distribution of hospitals in our country. Experts want to have large centralized hospitals. They say that this will improve their effectiveness. Museums are also merging into larger units. The museums in Hadeland and Land have now become *Randsfjordmuseene* (the Randfjord Museums). Prior to this development the museums were, in part, staffed by interested volunteers; now that has changed. Museums now should be managed by politically appointed or elected people who should be paid for being members of various advisory boards of the museum. More paid staff members are hired, exhibition areas are remodeled into offices for these additional staff members and interest for volunteers in these museums has lessened.

The present government in Norway has a strong belief that the market should determine the direction of the development of the society. Most of the former public utilities should now be privatized. The telephone and post office operations which earlier were publicly owned and managed have now been privatized. Competition and free choice are now primary. Nearly every day we have someone who telephones and tells us how much cheaper it would be for us if we changed to their telephone service. Packages mailed from America, with their postage paid to the addressee in Norway, used to be delivered directly to our home. Now, these packages go to a private company when they get to Norway. This company now charges us extra to get the package sent from Oslo to Hadeland – even though the postage has been paid in America for delivery to the individual residences in Hadeland. Radio and television stations were also publicly owned utilities. Now we are flooded with many radio and television channels that are paid by advertisements. On these radio and television programs there is no talk of putting one's money into a savings account or of any realistic rationale for buying their products. Soon in Norway we will only have jobs in the public sector or in the service industries. Manufacturing has left Norway and gone to lower cost countries. The food we need can be imported, just like we do for the majority of the goods that we need, say the officials.

We have politicians here in Hadeland who think that this is the correct development, but who protest loudly if they themselves lose a benefit in their own particular work situation or occupation. A committee has now come to the conclusion that the main public library of our municipality should be moved to Gran which is known by all as the regional business center of Hadeland. This main public library is now located in Brandbu, with a branch of the library in Gran. "No!" say the politicians from Brandbu, "The library must remain in Brandbu, everything shouldn't be moved to Gran!" I certainly wonder about what would happen if all three municipalities in Hadeland today would be merged into one large Hadeland municipality. The controversy after the merger of Brandbu and Gran in 1962 is still not over!

Summer - August 2003

It is a warm Sunday morning. For almost two weeks, we have experienced American temperatures here in Hadeland, in the high 80s for many days, so now growth has stopped for many of the crops on the farms which do not have irrigation. It is the potato acres which need the most water, but the majority of the farmers who raise potatoes have irrigation equipment. All of the farmers are waiting for rain so that the drought damage which has already begun will be limited.

The warm weather is something that most of the people in Norway are happy to have in July when so many of them are on vacation. The bathing beaches are full of people who are taking advantage of the beautiful weather. The summers are short in our country and the sun and the warm weather feel good for almost everyone after seven months of winter.

Spring came at its usual time this year and spring work began the last part of April on some of the earliest places this year. But then came the rain, and it rained nearly every day in May, so that many were not finished before June with seeding their small grains and planting the potatoes. On our farm we grow mostly hay for the silo and for the hayloft, so the rain was good for us. The first hay crop was exceptionally good and many of the Hadeland farmers filled their silos with the firs crop. More and more of the hay is processed into large round bales which are then packaged in airtight plastic so, if we get a second hay crop, there will be many big white round bales to be seen around Hadeland this year. We also try to dry some of our hay so that it can be put into the loft. This was not easily done at the beginning of July when we got rain showers almost every day.

May 17, Norway's National Day, the day when Norway got its own Constitution in 1814, was celebrated in a traditional manner all over Hadeland. For us, who live near *Søsterkirkene* (the Sister Churches at Granavolden), the celebration began at 8:30 a.m. with a program at the grave of Åsmund Olavson Vinje, the well-known Norwegian author who is buried here in Gran. *Mannskoret K.K.* (The men's choir) sang Vinje songs, and there were speeches and a wreath layed on Vinje grave. After breakfast at the Granavolden *Gjestgiveri* (inn) which is across the street from the churches, the K.K. gave a concert in the *Nikolaikirken* (Nikolai Church) with national songs. May 17 is a children's day, and all marched in a children's parade which started in the center of Gran and went to the Sister Churches at 12:00 noon, a trip of about four kilometers (about 2.5 miles). Here there was the speech for the day, entertainment and activities for the children, laying wreaths on the graves of those who were killed in World War II, choir and band music. Afterwards the celebrating continued at the various schools in Gran. The choirs and bands visited the rest homes and other institutions in Hadeland, and did their best so that all who lived in them could take part in the celebration of our National Day. Tom Skattum, 89-year-old Hadeland Lag member, celebrated the day with us this year.

From June 19-22 *Schola Sancti Petri*, the choir in which my wife and daughter sing, arranged Church Music Days in Gran. There were concerts and lectures each day with both local artists, and musicians from Norway and other countries. During the winter *Mariakirken* (the Maria Church) got a new organ. The new organist in Gran, Ivan Sarajishvili, was born in Georgia (in the former U.S.S.R.). He searched on the Internet and found a used organ which was for sale in Germany. The organ was 30 years old, and had been in a church which was being torn down. The organ was purchased and the German organ builder Jürgen Arend, who had built the organ, came to Gran and re-built it. All experts say that this is one of the best organs in all of Norway. *Søsterkirkene* have now become a center for church music in Norway. Many thanks have to be given to composer and professor of church music, Trond Kverno, who lives in Gran, and directs *Schola Sancti Petri*.

Summer is also the time when the historical societies arrange trips to other communities to learn about historical places in Norway. In June 50 members of the Stange Historical Society in Hedmark visited Hadeland. In addition to visiting the museum, churches and *Grinakervev* (the Grinaker weavery), they also visited our farm to see and hear about the old grave mounds which are on our property.

Here on the Gamme farms there are about 20 burial mounds in one area which were used from about 200 B.C. until 1,000 A.D. when Christianity came to Norway. Some of the mounds were excavated in 1923, and were determined to be from the period 500-800 A.D. With the excavation of a mound in 1976 it was determined that the mounds were used as graves even before the time of Christ. At the bottom of the excavated mound, under a large flagstone, there was the grave of a woman who, when it was carbon-dated, was found to be more than 2,000 years old. In the grave were found 90 artifacts. The woman had with her in the grave both jewelry and articles for everyday use.

In old historical literary works, there are written many legends about the old Norwegian kings. Many of these kings have connections to Hadeland. *Halvdan Svarte* (Halvdan the Black), who was king of part of Norway in the middle of the 800s, drowned in the Randsfjord. His body was divided into four parts, of which one part is buried on the grounds of the *Hadeland Folkemuseum*. His burial mound is called *Halvdanshaugen*

(Halvdan's mound). Halvdan's son, Harald *Hårfagre* (Harald the Fair-Haired), in 872 became the first king to unite Norway into one kingdom. He traveled much around the country and produced many children with different wives. One time when Harald was in Hadeland as a guest at the farm Tuv, Svåse, a man of Finnish heritage, came to the king and invited him home to his *gamme* (turf hut). Harald went along home with Svåse's daughter Snefrid, who was "the most beautiful woman that Harald had ever seen." Snefrid served the king a large bowl of ale. Harald wanted to go to bed with her immediately, but her father said that Harald had to first marry Snefrid. Harald and Snefrid were married and eventually had four sons. When Snefrid died, her face retained its natural color and beauty, and it is written that Harald sat at her bedside for three years because he thought that she would come back to life again. Then there was someone who persuaded Harald that they should change Snefrid's clothes. When they turned her over, they found maggots and worms, and her body was immediately burned. Harald understood that Svåse and Snefrid had used witchcraft on the king. After that the king came to his senses. Harald had put one of the sons that he had with Snefrid, Ragnvald *Rettilbeine*, in charge of governing Hadeland. When Harald realized that these people practiced witchcraft, he got another of his sons, Erik *Blodøks* (Erik Bloodaxe) to kill Ragnvald. Ragnvald and 80 of his followers were burned to death on the farm Kløvstad at Tingelstad.

This is not exactly "Hadeland Today," but the Historical Society from Hedmark also heard this old legend from the *King's Sagas* and in addition, was served coffee and cakes when they visited our farm.

Fall - November 2004

It is a quiet and peaceful Saturday morning here at our Gamme farm. This is not just because my wife and daughter have gone to a rehearsal of the *Schola Sancti Petri*, a choir that they are members of, but also because there is absolutely no wind blowing, no cows are out there mooing, anxious to get into the barn, and most of the birds have flown to more southern latitudes for their winter sojourn. The local farmers have finished with their fall harvesting; manure spreading and plowing is also done. The only sound to be heard is the crackling of the good dry wood as it burns in our faithful stove, keeping our home warm so that it is very comfortable and cozy for me to sit at the computer and write.

Tomorrow the *Schola Sancti Petri Choir*, whose conductor is the well-known church musician, Trond H. F. Kverno, is performing Mozart's Requiem in the Tingelstad Church, together with the Oslo Symphony Orchestra and solists from the Norwegian Opera. This is a beautiful work which I am looking forward to hearing.

It has been a good year for the farmers in Hadeland again this year. The harvesting was a little more difficult this year because of too much rain, but now all the crops are safely harvested except for some potatoes that drowned out in the low-lying areas of our district. The barley harvest was excellent; many farmers got nearly 600 kilos per dekar (*A dekar is about ¼ of an acre and a kilo weighs 2.2 pounds so 600 kilos per dekar equates to about 5,200 pounds of barley or a little over a hundred bushels per acre.*). The wheat harvest was average, as was also the potato yield, but the grass crop for haylege, loose hay or bailing was very good. Now the livestock have all been brought into the barns for the winter. I have just finished clipping and trimming them – that makes it easier to keep them clean; but it also makes it more comfortable for the animals in the warm barn.

The fall is also the time for the government in Norway to propose a State Budget for the coming year. As usual, there is a crisis atmosphere in the country because the federal politicians have not proposed to transfer enough federal money to the municipalities and the county governments. The municipalities in Hadeland have to reduce their budgets for 2005 and that is difficult when most of the municipalities' expenditures are tied up in salaries to employees and other fixed expenses. A protest by the local municipalities in Norway has been started against the Norwegian government's proposed State Budget and before that budget will be adopted in the *Storting* (Parliament), the budget for the municipalities and the counties will be adjusted in several sectors. In the meantime, it is a fact that we have an enormous expenditure in salaries in the public sector in Norway. Norway and Sweden have the same number of people employed by the municipalities, the counties and in the federal government; however, Sweden has twice as many inhabitants as Norway! It is surely not a question whether or not we in Norway could save a lot of money if the public sector would be made more efficient. We have the world's best sick-leave regulations. In it workers have full sick-leave protection from their first day on a job. A person can decide himself if he/she is sick during the first days without a doctor's statement. The hours worked during a year, in Norway is the shortest of all the countries that are similar to ours. For example, the work time of the average Norwegian is annually 300 hours fewer than the same worker in the United States (*A 40 hour week makes for 2,080 hours annually. Three hundred hours equates to about a 15% reduction.*). Steadily reorganized departments within the various sectors of the municipalities, creating new leader or head positions, does not reduce the expenditures for salaries in these municipalities. The municipality of Gran has 13,000 inhabitants. 1,100 people work for the municipality and get their salaries or livelihood from this public sector. For instance, at the Sanne School, where I was a student 50 years ago, there were at that time three teachers. Today there are more than 20 and the number of students enrolled today is the same as there was then. To be sure, there are now students with various handicaps that are integrated into the classrooms and these students certainly need more help and attention.

When you are reading this, the Presidential elections in the U. S. will be over. Also here in Norway our various media have been occupied with your election. The television debates between President Bush and Senator Kerry were sent directly into our television channels, our newspapers and the television channels all have their reporters on the spot in Washington and their reports are sent to Norway every day. Norwegian journalists have, in the most part, been critical of the war in Iraq and think that Kerry should become the new President, but in a debate program this week on Norwegian television, the viewers had a chance to telephone in and give their choice of which of the candidates they would choose for President for the next four years. Several thousand called in and what was strange or unexpected was that each candidate got exactly 50% of the call-in votes! The interest in what is happening in the USA is great here in Norway – some individuals think that we are USA's

51st state! Most of the families in Norway had emigrants in their families and, because of this there is a close relationship with the United States and Canada here.

2004 is soon history. As certainly most of the *Brua's* readers also notice, the time goes faster and faster the older we become. It is good to recall all of the pleasant visits and contracts we have had during this past year, all of the interested Americans that we have met who have visited Hadeland, and the e-mails and letters that we have received with information about the emigrants from Hadeland and questions seeking help about family information. I hope that some of you have gotten such help and that you are continuing the excellent and important work that you are doing to find your family "roots," to collect and write your families histories. The *Kontaktforum's* work continues to make progress each day, information about emigrants from Hadeland is steadily being sent in to us. Unfortunately, sometimes it takes too much time before you get an answer to your requests and maybe even some mail may be set aside and forgotten, but please write again, if you have not received an answer to your request.

We, *Kontaktforum* members, are looking forward to the visit of as many of you as can come to Hadeland in June 2005. The local planning for your visit is well under way and we hope that many of you will decide to accompany the Hadeland Lag's visit to Hadeland and also the planning Hadeland Lag tour of Norway next year. Norway is a very expensive country, but we shall do everything that we can to make your stay in Hadeland as reasonably priced as possible. We hope that those of you who have not yet sent in information about your ancestors who emigrated from Hadeland will do so soon. Then we can attempt to locate the places where your ancestors were born and lived while they were here in Hadeland. In addition, we will also try to find your distant relatives who are living in Norway today.

Appendix

Appendix I: 1910 Constitution for Hadelandslag

Appendix II: 1984 Constitution for Hadeland Lag of America

Appendix III: 2004 Corporate By-Laws

Appendix IV: 2007 Articles of Incorporation

Appendix V: 2010 Terms of Use (Internet Policy)

Appendix VI: 2007 Cooperative Agreement among Members of *Kontaktforum Hadeland-Amerika*

This is a translation of the original constitution for the Hadelandslaget, which was written in Norwegian. Harriet Foss made this translation from a copy preserved by E. Palmer Rockswold's father. P. E. Rockswold was a charter member of Hadelandslag.

1910 Constitution for Hadelandslaget

1. This association shall be called Hadelandslaget.

2. The purpose of this lag is to gather all Hadelendings for mutual friendliness and knowledge. And to preserve memories of the Hadelendings thus resulting in a thorough understanding of the activities and pursuits here and at home in Norway.

3. Every man and woman with Hadeland ancestry is entitled to become a member.

4. The board of directors of Hadelandslaget shall consist of a president, a vice-president, and a secretary who also will be treasurer. Besides, there shall be three others elected so there will be a six-man board.

5. Hadelandslaget shall hold a regular meeting every year with the time and place decided by the board of directors. The board shall be elected at that meeting for a one year term.

6. The main speaker at the meetings shall be a Hadelending.

7. Every member shall, as often as is called for, write down as much information about himself and his lineage as possible including that which he or she deems permissible to record and preserve. Everything shall be submitted to the board.

8. Membership dues shall be $1 per year for men and $.50 for women.

9. All biographies and reports which are donated to Hadelandslaget shall be preserved in a fireproof location and the board will be responsible for the manner by which these valuables will be kept.

10. The fiscal year begins on the 7th of September.

Original Hadelandslag Constitution
"Gruudlov for Hadelandslaget"

Grundlov for Hadelandslaget.

§ 1. Denne Forening skal hedde Hadelandslaget.

§ 2. Lagets Formaal er at samle alle Hadelændinger til indbyrdes Venskab og Kjendskab. Og til at bevare Hadelændingernes Minder og faa et mere indgaaende Kjendskab til deres Færd og Syssel her og hjemme i Norge.

§ 3. Enhver Mand og Kvinde af Hadelands-Herkomst er berettiget til Medlemsskab.

§ 4. Lagets Styre skal bestaa af en Formand, en Viceformand og en Sekretær, som tillige er Kasserer. Dertil tre andre valgte, saa det bliver et Seksmandsstyre.

§ 5. Laget skal afholde et regulært Møde hvert Aar, Tid og Sted, hvor Styret bestemmer. Paa dette Møde vælges Styresmænd der vælges for et Aar ad Gangen.

§ 6. Til at holde Hovedtalen paa Lagets Møder skal der tages en Hadelænding.

§ 7. Ethvert Medlem skal, saa ofte det kræves, nedskrive og give til Styret saamegen Oplysning om sig selv og sin Æt, som det er muligt og som han eller hun er villig til at lade nedtegne og opbevares.

§ 8. Medlemsafgift pr. Aar for Mænd $1.00, Kvinder 50c.

§ 9. Alle Biografier og andre Beretninger, som kommer ind til Laget, skal opbevares paa et ildfrit Sted, og Styret er ansvarlig for hvorledes disse Sager bliver bevaret.

§ 10. Foreningsaaret regnes fra 7de September.

1912 Membership Card – P. E. Rockswold
signed by T. A. Walby and Per Jacobson

1984 Constitution for Hadeland Lag of America

Adopted at the annual meeting in July, 1984

Article I – Name

The name shall be Hadeland Lag of America.

Article II – Purpose

The purpose of the Hadeland Lag of America shall be:
1. To further and maintain fellowship among descendants of people from the Hadeland district of Norway.
2. To maintain a bond between Hadelendings in America and Norway.
3. To aid in the preservation of the best in Norwegian culture.
4. To hold an annual meeting or other meetings as deemed advisable and necessary; to send delegates to meetings with other lags.
5. To maintain communications among US Hadelendings thru a membership publication named *BRUA* which can include family or personal histories and other pertinent information regarding Norwegians and American Norwegians.

Article III – Membership

Any person of Hadeland, Norway descent, their husbands or wives and families may become members of the Hadeland Lag when paying annual membership dues. Hadeland Lag membership shall be on an annual basis from January 1 to December 31 and the dues shall be $5.00 for an individual and $7.00 for husband and wife (family).

Article IV – Annual Meeting

A meeting of the Hadeland Lag membership shall be held annually at a time and place determined by the board of directors, or decided by the membership. The annual meeting shall:
1. Elect a board of directors consisting of 5 members of the Hadeland Lag of America.
2. Conduct business matters of the Hadeland Lag.
3. Provide fellowship for Hadelendings.
4. Preserve Norwegian culture and traditions for future generations.

Article V – Board of Directors

A board of directors consisting of 5 members of the Hadeland Lag shall be elected annually at the annual meeting of the Hadeland Lag. The board of directors shall conduct the business of the Hadeland Lag between annual meetings. The terms of the board of directors shall be staggered so that all director terms do not expire in the same year. Beginning in 1984 two directors shall be elected for three years; two directors for two years; one director for a one year term. Thereafter each director shall be elected for a term of three years.

Article VI – Officers

The officers of the Hadeland Lag shall be a president, vice president, secretary and treasurer and shall be elected annually from and by the board of directors.

The president shall conduct all meetings of the Hadeland Lag, prepare an agenda for board meetings and the annual meeting. He may represent the Hadeland Lag in other organizations where representation is agreed upon or required.

The vice president shall act in the absence of the president.

The secretary shall be responsible for keeping minutes of the Hadeland Lag annual meeting and of board meetings and maintaining an accurate membership record.

The treasurer shall be responsible for receiving and recording all income and expenditures of the Hadeland Lag and paying by check authorized expenditures as directed by the board of directors.

Committees may be created as deemed necessary.

Article VII – Roberts Rules

Roberts Rules of Order shall apply to all meetings of the Hadeland Lag of America.

Article VIII – Amendments

The Hadeland Lag constitution may be amended by a two-thirds vote of the members of the Hadeland Lag present and voting at any annual meeting of the Hadeland Lag.

Corporate By-Laws
of the Hadeland Lag of America, Inc.

As approved by the membership at the Fall Meeting of the Hadeland Lag on October 16, 2004 and amended by a vote of the membership at the Annual Meeting of the Hadeland Lag on July 17, 2010.

ARTICLE ONE: OFFICES

The legal office of the Hadeland Lag of America Corporation is as specified in the Articles of Incorporation. The location of any working office is determined by the Board of Directors. This may include a post office box for receiving all correspondence for any of the officers.

ARTICLE II: BOARD OF DIRECTORS

1. General Powers: The affairs of the Hadeland Lag of America, Inc., (hereafter referred to as 'HLA') are managed by its Board of Directors. The Board of Directors
    a) has the power to recommend amendment to the articles of incorporation, to recommend by-law adoption for the government of HLA, to recommend adoption of Corporate Website Terms of Use, to recommend alteration, amendment, repeal, or change to the same;
    b) considers the opinion and wishes of the membership on any matter expressed by majority vote at any Members Meeting;
    c) causes the books, accounts, and records of the Treasurer or any other HLA officer receiving or expending moneys in excess of $300 to be audited;
    d) has the authority to define and determine the meaning and interpretation of the terms, "improper conduct," and "conduct unbecoming a member"; and
    e) keeps accurate, complete, and permanent records of all its proceedings.

2. Number, Tenure and Qualifications
    a) The Board of Directors consists of
        1) Eight (8) elected members: President, Vice President, Secretary, Treasurer, together forming the HLA Executive Committee; and Four (4) elected Directors;
        2) Three (3) non-elected administrative members currently serving as Genealogist, Newsletter Editor, and Webmaster; and
        3) The Immediate Past President as an ex-officio member, with voice and vote.
    b) The HLA membership, at a regular Members Meeting, may create additional administrative positions, which may be given voice or vote or both on the Board of Directors.
    c) All Officers and Directors are members in good standing of HLA.
    d) All Officers and Directors with the exception of the President have one vote at any Meeting of the Board.
    e) The Emeritus Advisory Council shall be made up of members whose knowledge and service continue to be of value to HLA Board and Membership despite their absence from active participation in HLA's Boards and Committees.

Appendix III: Corporate By-Laws

      1) Membership on the Emeritus Advisory Council shall be granted to all Past Presidents not otherwise serving and other members as appointed by HLA's Board of Directors and confirmed by the Membership.
      2) The duties of the Emeritus Advisory Council shall be to offer advice and guidance to the HLA Board and/or Membership.

3. Election of Officers and Directors:
   a) Officers and Directors are elected by vote of the members at the Annual Meeting, from a slate of Officers presented by the Nominating Committee or as offered from the floor with the nominee's permission.
   b) Elected officers serve for three (3) year staggered terms or until their successor is elected. The four (4) directors serve three (3) year, staggered terms or until their successors are elected.
   c) The term of office begins with the close of the annual meeting.

4. Regular Board Meetings: The Board of Directors may provide by resolution for regular meetings of the Board to be held at a fixed time and place. No further notice of these scheduled meetings need be given.

5. Special Meetings: Special meetings of the Board for any purpose or purposes:
   a) may be held at any time on the call of the President or Secretary; or
   b) are called by the Secretary on the written request of any three Board members.

6. Notice: Notice of date, place and time of any special meeting not set by Board Resolution is delivered to each board member either in writing or by telephone at least 24 hours prior to the meeting.

7. Quorum: Five (5) members of the Board of Directors constitute a quorum for the transaction of business at any meeting of the Board.

8. Manner of Acting:
   a) The Board of Directors holds its meetings in open session, unless personal confidentiality must be protected. At that time a limited closed session may be held.
   b) The act of a majority of the Board of Directors present at a properly constituted meeting of the Board is an act of the Board.
   c) Any matter capable of satisfactory resolution by mail or email vote, may be presented to each member of the board by either the President or a member or members designated to do so.

9. Acting without a meeting:
   a) Where votes are cast by mail
      1) A separate ballot from each member of the Board is marked and returned to the secretary within 30 days of delivery of such notice, as defined in the bylaws; and
      2) The affirmative vote of a majority of the Board of Directors is required to pass any resolution or table any action.

b) Where votes are cast by email
      1) The Secretary shall email each member of the Board notice of the issue to be considered and a formatted ballot;
      2) Each member of the Board shall reply to the secretary within 7 days of delivery of such notice;
      3) The Secretary shall reply to the email to indicate its receipt and how the vote has been recorded; and
      4) The affirmative vote of a majority of the Board of Directors is required to passed any resolution or table any action.
   c) Where a decision is made by telephone conference
      1) Decisions made by telephone must be confirmed as required by a) or b) above for a mail or email vote; and
   d) A written record (minutes) is made of all such actions.

10. Vacancies:
    a) The Board of Directors may appoint any member of HLA to fill any vacancies that occur during a term of office;
    b) Appointees to unexpired terms of 1 year or less shall serve until the end of that term of office;
    c) Appointees to unexpired terms of more than one year shall be confirmed or replaced by election at the next annual meeting; and
    d) If a vacancy occurs 90 days or less before the Annual Meeting, the board of directors has the authority to delay election to that vacancy until the next regularly scheduled Members Meeting.

11. Compensation: All members of the Board of Directors serve without compensation.

12. Presumption of Assent: Any Board of Directors member who is present at a meeting of the Board, or a committee thereof, at which action on any corporate matter is taken, is presumed to have assented to the action taken unless that members' dissent is delivered in writing to the person acting as secretary of the meeting, and entered in the minutes of the meeting before the meeting is adjourned.

ARTICLE III: OFFICERS

1. President: The duties of the President include, but are not exclusively limited to:
   a) being the principle executive officer of HLA;
   b) convening and presiding over HLA Members Meetings and preparing the agenda with the assistance of the Secretary;
   c) convening and presiding over HLA Board Meetings;
   d) extending greetings to all 7-Lag *Stevne* attendees on behalf of HLA;
   e) representing HLA on the 7-Lag Council and as a Director of Norwegian *Stevne*r, Inc.
   f) consulting with other Officers and Board Members to assure the business of HLA is being conducted in a timely fashion;
   g) seeing that the mission of HLA is being accomplished; and
   h) serving as a non-voting member of the Board until the next president replaces him/her.

Appendix III: Corporate By-Laws

        1) When a vote of the board is a tie, the President shall cast the deciding vote.

2. Vice President: The duties of the Vice President include, but are not exclusively limited to:
    a) assisting the President whenever possible by maintaining close liaison with the President to the end that both officers will be equally familiar with the instructions of the Board of Directors and the President's plans;
    b) acting in the absence of the President or in the event of the President's death, impeachment, inability, or refusal to act, and when acting has all the powers of the President and is subject to all the restrictions upon the President;
    c) serving as chairman of the Audit committee; and
    d) serving as a consultant, contact, and liaison with all committees not served by another director.
    e) performing such other duties as may be assigned by the President or by the Board of Directors.

3. Secretary: The duties of the Secretary include, but are not exclusively limited to:
    a) assisting the President in the preparation of agendas for Members and Board Meetings;
    b) preparing minutes of all official Members and Board Meetings;
    c) assuring that a summary of all official business Meetings are submitted for publication in the HLA newsletter and the detailed minutes are published on the Corporate Website;
    d) making such corrections as are noted at subsequent Members or Board Meetings;
    e) maintaining official copies of all minutes and other reports;
    f) preparing and distributing notices of HLA Meetings, and of regular and special Board Meetings, as called for in these By-Laws;
    g) handling HLA correspondence, in cooperation with the President and other members of the Board of Directors; and
    h) serving as Chair of the Constitution and By-Laws committee.

4. Treasurer: The duties of the Treasurer include, but are not exclusively limited to:
    a) maintaining the financial affairs of HLA: to pay HLA's bills in a timely manner, while conserving HLA's resources. This includes collecting, managing, and depositing moneys collected and, where appropriate, paying all bills by check;
    b) preparing the annual report and making all financial records for a calendar year available to the Audit committee following the close of the calendar year;
    c) presenting the annual report of HLA financial activities for the previous calendar year at the Annual Meeting;
    d) submitting the annual financial report for publication in the HLA Newsletter;
    e) preparing and presenting interim financial reports at all Members and Directors Meetings, or as requested by the Board;
    f) using accepted accounting practices for non-profit organizations;
    g) assuring that membership status is properly maintained and reported to

individual members, the Board, and the membership;
h) receiving, recording, and reporting member registration for all HLA Meetings and activities;
i) preparing and filing any tax and informational returns as may be required by federal, state, or local laws; and
j) serving as Chair of the Membership committee.

5. Director: The duties of the Director include, but are not exclusively limited to:
   a) providing advice and assistance to HLA officers;
   b) attending Board and Annual Meetings; and
   c) serving as consultant, contact, and liaison with committees, as determined by the Board of Directors.

6. *Bygdelagenes Fellesraad* Delegates: The *Bygdelagenes Fellesraad* Delegates are appointed by the Board of Directors. Their duties include, but are not exclusively limited to:
   a) representing the Hadeland Lag at the *Bygdelagenes Fellesraad* annual meeting and participating in their activities on HLA's behalf; and
   b) reporting on Bygdelgenes Fellesraad activities to the Board of Directors.

ARTICLE IV: COMMITTEES

1. The Board of Directors is responsible for oversight and assignment of responsibilities and duties to all HLA committees.
   a) All committee chairs are responsible to the Board of Directors for:
      1) assuring that all committee assignments are completed in a timely manner; and
      2) recruiting and appointing committee members as the need arises.
         a) Committee appointments are subject to formal approval by the Board of Directors.
      3) keeping a written record of the committee's activities;
      4) reporting at each Board Meeting on all activities of his/her committee. This report should include personnel assignments and projects and tasks undertaken, and is given for the purposes of
         a) informing the Board of the committee's activities;
         b) receiving the Board's approval for committee projects and tasks; and
         c) recommending formal appointment of committee members by the Board.
      5) submitting a report at each Members Meeting on current activities of his/her committee.

2. HLA has the following standing committees, with the members, positions and responsibilities shown:

   A. Audit Committee:
      1) Audits HLA's financial records following the close of each calendar year and the preparation of the annual financial report;
      2) Consists of the vice president as Chair and other members as appointed by the Board of Directors; and

Appendix III: Corporate By-Laws

        3) Reports their findings to the Board of Directors.

B. Constitution and By-Laws Committee:
   1) maintains the Articles of Incorporation and By-Laws, as directed by the Board of Directors;
   2) Consists of the Secretary as Chair and other members as appointed by the Board of Directors;
   3) acts as authority on questions of procedure to assure actions taken by the Board of Directors and the membership are consistent with the Articles of Incorporation and By-Laws;
   4) investigates and recommends changes to the Articles of Incorporation to the Board of Directors; and
   5) presents the wording of proposed changes to the By-Laws at Board and Members Meetings.

C. Events Committee
   1) coordinates HLA sponsored events such as Board and Members Meetings. The responsibilities of the committee include, but are not exclusively limited to:
      a) recommending meeting locations, dates and times;
      b) arranging for meeting space and catering;
      c) planning programs for HLA Meetings;
      d) working with counterparts in other lags and organizations when joint meetings (including the 7-Lag *Stevne*) are held in order to assure the success of the larger meeting; and
      e) recruiting and scheduling staffing requirements for HLA Meetings, activities and events.
   2) consists of a Chair who is elected from and by the Board of Directors, and other members as appointed by the Board of Directors.

D. Genealogy Committee
   1) provides genealogical access and assistance to HLA members under conditions approved by the Board of Directors;
   2) cooperates with *Kontaktforum Hadeland-Amerika*, Hadeland Folk Museum, and genealogists from other lags and organizations;
   3) assesses the genealogical needs and interests of HLA members and reports these to the Board of Directors;
   4) collects and properly stores the HLA genealogical collection including use of archival quality storage materials in appropriate climatic storage areas; and
   5) Consists of the Genealogist as chair and other members as appointed by the Board of Directors.
   6) Genealogist: The Duties of the Genealogist include, but are not exclusively limited to:
      a) coordinating and providing genealogical assistance to HLA members, under conditions consented to by the Board of Directors

            b) advising the board regarding the conditions under which genealogical assistance is or should be provided to HLA members;
            c) assuring that the HLA genealogical collection is available at the 7-Lag *stevne* and other meetings as directed;
            d) assuring that Genealogy committee member/volunteer assistance is available to HLA members during all scheduled research hours at the 7-Lag *Stevne* and other meetings as directed;
            e) improving access to genealogical data for Hadeland through
                  1) additions to HLA's genealogical collection;
                  2) knowledge of additions to other collections; and
                  3) purchase of additional materials for HLA's genealogical collection with the consent of the Board of Directors;
                  4) appropriate use of the Lag website; and
                  5) other activities and actions deemed appropriate by the Board of Directors
            f) Attending Member Meetings and open Board Meetings; and
            g) Serving as Chair of the Genealogy committee.

    E. Heritage-Historical Committee
        1) Apprises members of the history of Hadeland and of the Hadeland Lag of America, Inc. through various means;
        2) Maintains the historical artifacts of HLA;
        3) Researches and recommends appropriate gifts for individuals or organizations to the Board of Directors; and
        4) Consists of a chair who acts as HLA historian and is appointed by the board of directors, and other members as appointed by the Board of Directors.
        5) Historian: The duties of the Historian include, but are not exclusively limited to:
            a) collecting and maintaining the collection of artifacts belonging to or donated to HLA (except genealogical);
            b) Maintaining records of artifacts, including such information as identification, donor(s), and location of each artifact. Records may be written, computerized, photographic or maintained by any other appropriate technologies;
            c) Properly storing of artifacts, including use of archival quality storage materials and appropriate climatic storage areas;
            d) Accounting to the Board of Directors for custodianship; and
            e) Maintaining a record of gifts given, including such information as the nature and cost of the gift, reason and occasion for the gift, the date and to whom the gift was given;

Appendix III: Corporate By-Laws

        f) Coordinating with the Secretary and Chair of the Publications Committee to assure that current records and publications are added to the archives; and

        g) Serving as chair of the History and Heritage Committee.

F. Membership Committee
1) maintains a current membership list and informs Board of Directors of membership status;
2) ensures that individual members are informed of potential dues lapses;
3) develops strategies and methods to promote membership and recruit new members; and
4) consists of a chair who is the Treasurer and other members as appointed by the Board of Directors.
5) Membership Secretary: The duties of the membership secretary include, but are not exclusively limited to
    a) maintaining the HLA membership records
    b) providing current and correct mailing information for each issue of the HLA Newsletter; and
    c) ensuring that individual HLA members are informed of potential dues lapses.

G. Nominating Committee:
1) Gathers a slate of officers and directors for elections held at Members Meetings;
2) Contacts potential nominees to assure they are willing to be nominated and to serve if elected;
3) Creates printed ballots for use in scheduled Members Meeting elections;
4) Supervises all election activities during Members Meetings; and
5) Consists of the immediate past president of HLA as Chair and at least two additional at large members as appointed by the Board of Directors subject to the following qualifications:
    a) At large nominating committee members may not be Lag Officers or Board Members;
    b) Nominating committee members are not permitted to nominate themselves; and
    c) If the Immediate Past President is unable to serve, the Chair of the committee shall be appointed by the Board of Directors. The Board may appoint a Chair who holds elected office, but the Chair may not stand for election during service on the Nominating Committee.

H. Publications Committee:
1) ensures that newsletters, special publications and webpages authorized by Members Meetings and the Board of Directors are published in a timely manner, with quality workmanship;

2) Receives and reviews all "Requests for Permission to Publish" applications and recommends action to the Board of Directors;
3) consists of the Newsletter Editor acting as Chair, Webmaster, and Special Publications Editor(s) when appointed. Other members may be appointed by the Board of Directors.
4) Newsletter Editor: The duties of the Newsletter Editor include, but are not exclusively limited to:
   a) preparing and publishing a minimum of four (4) issues of the HLA newsletter each year; and
   b) attending HLA open Board of Directors and Members Meetings.
5) Webmaster: The duties of the Webmaster include, but are not exclusively limited to:
   a) creating and maintaining the HLA website;
   b) ensuring that postings that require follow-up are routed to the appropriate individual or committee; and
   c) Attending HLA open Board of Directors and Members Meetings.
6) Special Publication(s) editor(s) are appointed as needed. The duties the Special Publications Editor(s) include, but are not exclusively limited to:
   a) preparing and publishing the special publications of HLA as directed by Members Meetings and the Board of Directors; and
   b) attending HLA open board of Directors and Members meetings.

ARTICLE V: MEETINGS OF THE HADELAND LAG OF AMERICA, INC.

1. Scheduling of Members Meetings
   a) Meetings of the HLA Membership may be scheduled for any reason by resolution of the Board of Directors or a majority vote of those present at any Members Meeting.
   b) Summer Meeting: An HLA Members Meeting is scheduled during the 7-Lag *Stevne*.
      1) The Board of Directors may schedule the Summer Members Meeting at another time and/or place, when HLA and/or activities of HLA justify the change.
   c) Fall Meeting: An HLA Members Meeting is held each fall.
      1) The Board of Directors schedules a Members Meeting during the fall of the year at a time and place of their choosing.

2. Annual Meeting: The HLA fall meeting is designated as the Annual Meeting.
   a) The public business of HLA is conducted at the Annual Meeting. Business includes the annual election of officers and directors.

ARTICLE VI: MEMBERSHIP

1. Membership in HLA is open to persons meeting one of the following criteria:

a) Norwegian-Americans able to trace descent from Hadeland in Oppland fylke, Norway.
b) Norwegians living in Hadeland or able to trace descent from Hadeland in Oppland *fylke*, Norway.
c) Any person who is interested in furthering the purpose of HLA.
2. Each HLA membership may include immediate family members who share a household and mailing address.
3. Members are encouraged to submit their Norwegian ancestry information to the Genealogy committee.
4. The membership application process is regulated by the Board of Directors.

ARTICLE VII: DUES

1. Dues are assessed based upon a yearly membership.
2. The Board of Directors determines the amount of the dues, to assure financial stability of HLA.

ARTICLE VIII: PROPERTY AND FINANCIAL ASSETS

Any property owned by the Corporation shall be controlled by the Board of Directors. Specific members of the Board of Directors may be designated as custodians by the Board of Directors.

ARTICLE IX: CAPITALIZATION

This corporation is non-profit, with no stock being issued.

ARTICLE X: AMENDMENTS

These Bylaws may be altered, amended or repealed and new Bylaws adopted by a simple majority vote of voting members at any regular members meeting.

ARTICLE XI: ROBERT'S RULES OF ORDER

While meetings shall generally be operated in an informal manner, should an issue arise as to procedures to follow, the latest edition of Robert's Rules of Order shall be used to resolve the issue.

The Articles of Incorporation were filed with the State of Minnesota on June 4, 2007 file number 2379909-2.

ARTICLES OF INCORPORATION
OF HADELAND LAG OF AMERICA, INC.

The undersigned, for purposes of forming a non-profit corporation pursuant to the provisions of Minnesota Statutes Chapter 317A, and all laws amendatory thereto, adopts the following Articles of Incorporation.

ARTICLE I.
Name
The name of the corporation shall be "Hadeland Lag of America, Inc."

ARTICLE II.
Purposes

This corporation is organized and shall be operated as contemplated and permitted by Sections 170(c) (2) and 501(c) (3) of the Internal Revenue Code of 1954, as amended (the "Code"), and the specifics and primary purpose of this corporation shall be:

1) To promote education in the cultural heritage and history of the descendants of immigrants in North America from the districts (*kommunes*) of Gran, Jevnaker and Lunner in Norway; to provide assistance in support for genealogical research by descendants of emigrants from that area; to collect and preserve historical and genealogical information about this area; and to promote contact and communication among those who share these interests.

2) No part of the net earnings of the corporation shall inure to the benefit of, or be distributed to, its members, board members, officers or other private persons, except that the corporation shall be authorized and empowered to pay reasonable compensation for services rendered.

3) No substantial part of the activities of the corporation shall involve the carrying on of propaganda or otherwise attempting to influence legislation and the corporation shall not participate in or intervene, including the publishing or distribution of statements, in any political campaign on behalf of any candidate for public office.

4) Notwithstanding any of the provisions of these articles, the corporation shall not carry on any other activities not permitted to be carried on:
    (a) by a corporation exempt from federal income tax under Section 501(c) (3) of the Code (or the corresponding provision of any future United States Internal Revenue law); or

    (b) by a corporation, contributions to which are deductible under Section 170(c) (2) of the Code (or the corresponding provision of any future United States Internal Revenue law).

Within the limitations of these purposes, this corporation shall have and exercise all rights and powers conferred on nonprofit corporations under the laws of the State of Minnesota, including the power to contract, rent, buy or sell personal or real property provided, however, that this corporation shall not engage in any activities or exercise any powers that are not consistent with and in furtherance of the primary purposes of this corporation, nor shall it engage in any activities or exercise any powers that are not within the contemplation of Section 501(c) (3) of the Code.

ARTICLE III.
Duration
The period of duration of this corporation shall be perpetual.

ARTICLE IV.
Registered Office
The registered office of this corporation shall be 3329 Seventh Street NW, Rochester, MN 55901.

ARTICLE V.
Incorporators
The name and address of the incorporator of this corporation, who is a natural person of legal age, is as follows:

Jan Heusinkveld
3329 Seventh Street NW
Rochester, MN 55901

ARTICLE VI.
Registered Agent
The name and address of the registered agent of this corporation is as follows:

Jan Heusinkveld
3329 Seventh Street NW
Rochester, MN 55907.

ARTICLE VII.
Membership
The authorized number and qualifications of the members of this corporation, the different classes of membership, if any, and the voting and other rights and privileges of members shall be as set forth in the by-laws of this corporation.

ARTICLE VIII.
No Personal Liability
The directors, officers and members of this corporation shall not be personally liable to any extent whatsoever for obligations of this corporation.

Appendix IV: Articles of Incorporation

ARTICLE IX.
No Capital Stock

This corporation shall have no capital stock.

ARTICLE X.
Effective Date of Incorporation

The effective date of incorporation is the date on which the certificate of incorporation is issued by the Minnesota Secretary of State.

ARTICLE XI.
Dissolution

Upon dissolution of the corporation, the Board of Directors shall, after paying or making provisions for the payment of all of the liabilities of the corporation, dispose of all of the assets of the corporation exclusively for the purposes of the corporation in such manner, or to such organizations organized and operated exclusively for charitable, educational, religious or scientific purposes as shall at the time qualify as an exempt organization or organizations under Section 501(c) (3) of the Code (or the corresponding provision of any future United States Internal Revenue Law) as the Board of Directors shall determine. Any such assets not so disposed of shall be disposed of by the District Court of the county in which the principal office of the corporation is then located, exclusively for such purposes, or to such organization or organizations as said court shall determine which are organized and operated exclusively for such purposes.

ARTICLE XII
Amendment

These Articles of Incorporation may be amended in the manner prescribed by the Minnesota Non-Profit Corporation Act.

The IRS approved tax exempt status under section 501c3 of the Internal Revenue Code in a letter dated January 29, 2008.

Appendix V: Terms of Use Agreement

TERMS OF USE AGREEMENT

In January, 2010 the Hadeland Lag's Board of Directors approved the following terms of use agreement as drafted by Laurie S. Young of the law firm Nikolai and Mersereau.

The Hadeland Lag of America, Inc. ("HLA") presents the Content contained on the HLA website www.hadelandlag.org ("HLA Website") for the purpose of educating members of the public who are interested in family history, genealogy and in the culture and heritage of Gran, Jevnaker and Lunner *kommuner* (municipalities) in Oppland *Fylke* (county), Norway.

The Users of the HLA Website are subject to the following Terms and Conditions. By using the HLA Website the Users agree to be bound by the Terms and Conditions set forth below.

I. DEFINITIONS

1. Content – refers to and means all words, images, video and other media which is displayed on the HLA Website.
2. Individual or Individuals – refers to and means any person or people who use the HLA Website for any purpose.
3. Not-for-Profit Entity – refers to and means any business, organization or employee of any business or organization which does not distribute any surplus funds or earnings to the owners, partners or shareholders, but only uses the surplus funds or earnings to advance the business' or organization's goals and purposes.
4. Users – refers to and means any person or people who access the HLA Website for any purpose.

II. CONTENT

The Content of the HLA website is the exclusive property of the HLA or has been licensed by the HLA.

1. The HLA will, at times, publish new Content on the HLA Website which is authored by a non-employee or volunteer of the HLA. The HLA shall credit the non-employee or volunteer author for the work in a manner that the HLA believes best achieves the goals and purposes of the HLA and maintaining the integrity of the HLA Website. The Content published on the HLA Website may include inaccuracies, typographical errors, or other misprints. The HLA does not warrant the accuracy of any of the Content, and provides all Content "AS IS."
2. All Content on the HLA Website is updated as Content is received.
3. The HLA reserves the right to modify the Content or provide the Content "AS IS".
4. The HLA reserves the right to remove any Content from the HLA Website for any purpose.
5. The HLA does not warrant that the Content of the HLA Website will be available at all times.

III. THE LIMITED ACCESS ARCHIVE

1. The HLA operates online-accessible Databases which contain genealogical information related to people from the Hadeland area of Norway and their descendants.
2. Access to the Limited Access Archive is granted by the HLA only to Members in good standing of the HLA.
3. A Member who wishes to access the Limited Access Archive will be granted a user-identification and a password which is unique to each Member. A Member's user-identification and password will remain valid so long as the Member remains in good standing with the HLA.
4. A Member shall not provide the Member's user-identification or password to any other person. A Member shall not allow another person access to the Limited Access Archive for any purpose.
5. A Member shall only use the Content contained in the Limited Access Archive, including the Kontaktforum Emigrant Database (ISSN 2151-223X) for the Member's own family history research.
6. A Member shall only download, save, store or print Content from the Limited Access Archive which is directly related to the Member's own family history research.
7. A Member shall not download, save, store or print the entire Kontaktforum Database (ISSN 2151-223X).

IV. LICENSE

1. Any Individual who provides Content to the HLA grants the HLA a non-exclusive, royalty-free license to use, publish, distribute in any manner and permit authorized Users or Members to use the Content.
2. The Individual grants to the HLA the right to modify the Content provided by the Individual to achieve the purposes and goals of the HLA.
3. The Individual warrants all Content provided to the HLA is not in violation of the United States Copyright laws as provided in 17 U.S.C. §101 et seq.
4. The Individual agrees to defend, indemnify and hold harmless the HLA, its employees, directors, officers, and agents against any claim which may be brought against any of them regarding the Content the Individual provided to the HLA. The Individual shall be responsible for his/her own legal fees related to any claim regarding the Content the Individual provided.

V. COPYRIGHTED CONTENT

1. The User agrees that he/she shall not publish any Content from the HLA Website without receiving prior written approval from the HLA Board of Directors. The HLA Board of Directors reserves the right to deny any request for publication for any purpose.
2. If such Content is to be published by a User, the User shall first submit a "Notification of Intent to Publish." The "Notification of Intent to Publish" must be approved in writing by the HLA prior to such time as a User publishes the Content.
3. Any Content published in any medium must provide a conspicuous notification adjacent to the Content crediting the HLA. Any Content published on a website must, in a conspicuous manner, credit the HLA for providing the Content and provide the HLA Website link adjacent to the Content.

4. If any Content from the HLA Website or Databases is intended for use from which a profit could be made by the User or a third-party, the Member or User shall first submit a "Notification of Intent to Publish" and a statement indicating why the User requires the Content for potential profit-making purposes to the HLA Board of Directors prior to publishing any Content from the HLA Website or Databases. The HLA Board of Directors reserves the right to request a draft of the work in which the Content will be incorporated, prior to the User receiving written approval. The HLA Board of Directors reserves the right to deny any request for publication for any purpose, or require a separate Use agreement that includes specific stipulations and may include a payment schedule for use of the HLA Content. If a User receives written approval from the HLA Board of Directors permitting the User the right to publish the Content on any medium, the User must provide a conspicuous notification adjacent to the Content crediting the HLA.
5. Users who seek approval to publish Content from the HLA Website should know that the HLA typically only authorizes Members or Users who are Individuals and Not-for-Profit Entities to use the Content in and on the HLA Website and Databases for re-publishing purposes. Such Individuals and Not-for-Profit Entities are typically only authorized to re-publish the Content from the HLA Website and Databases for uses which advance the goals and purposes of both the HLA and the Not-for-Profit Entity, or for the Individual's own non-profit making goals and purposes.

VI. BREACH OF CONTRACT

1. In the event a User fails to abide by the terms of this Agreement, or otherwise breaches this Agreement, the HLA shall have the right to terminate this Agreement.
2. In the event a Member fails to abide by the terms of this Agreement or otherwise breaches this Agreement, the HLA reserves the right to seek an injunction against the Member prohibiting the Member from accessing the HLA Website and Databases and from using any Content from the HLA Website and Databases. The HLA further reserves the right to deactivate the Member's username and password.
3. The HLA reserves the right to prohibit a Member from renewing membership should the Member fail to abide by the terms of this Agreement.
4. The HLA reserves the right to seek relief against a Member for violations of the United States Copyright laws according to 17 U.S.C. §101 et seq.
5. Termination of this Agreement pursuant to the terms and conditions contained herein shall be without prejudice to the HLA's other rights and remedies at law or in equity.
6. The rights stated above in the event of a breach of this Agreement are in addition to all other rights of the HLA in law and in equity, and are expressly reserved.

VII. CONSTRUCTION

1. This Agreement shall be interpreted and construed in accordance with the laws of the State of Minnesota.

VIII. JURISDICTION

1. Users and Members consent to the personal jurisdiction and venue of the courts of the state of Minnesota and of the United States Court for the District of Minnesota, and further consent to any

processes or notice of motion or other application to the Court or a Judge which may be served outside the state of Minnesota by registered certified mail or by personal service, provided a reasonable time for appearance is allowed.

IX. SEVERABILITY

1. If any provision or any portion of any provision of this Agreement shall be construed to be illegal, invalid or unenforceable, such provision or portion thereof shall be deemed stricken and deleted from this Agreement to the same extent and effect as if never incorporated herein, but all other provisions of this Agreement and the remaining portion of any provision which is construed to be illegal, invalid or unenforceable in part shall continue in full force and effect.
2. If any provision or any portion of any provision of this Agreement shall be construed to be contradictory to any portion or provision in a related agreement or a counterpart to this Agreement, this Agreement shall control.

X. ENTIRE AGREEMENT

1. This Agreement constitutes the entire agreement of the parties hereto with respect to the subject matter hereof. No prior oral or written understanding shall be of any force or effect with respect to those matters covered herein. This Agreement may not be amended or modified except in a writing signed by both parties.

XII. NON-WAIVER

1. A failure of either party to enforce at any time any term, provision or condition of this Agreement, or to exercise any right or option herein, shall in no way operate as a waiver thereof, nor shall any single or partial exercise preclude any other right or option herein; in no way shall a waiver of any term, provision or condition of this Agreement be valid unless in writing, signed by the waiving party, and only to the extent set forth in such writing.

Cooperative Agreement among Members of the *Kontaktforum Hadeland-Amerika*

1. The *Kontakforum Hadeland-Amerika* is a cooperative agreement among the Gran Historical Society, the Jevnaker historical Society, the Lunner historical Society and the Hadeland Lag of America.

2. The *Kontaktforum Hadeland-Amerika* is governed by an executive committee, consisting of one representative from each of the cooperating organizations. This committee selects its own chairman. The executive committee is also free to invite other resource persons to assist the *Kontaktforum* in its research or other needs. The executive committee is also empowered to select a person or persons who will be the secretary and / or treasurer of the *Kontaktforum Hadeland-Amerika*.

3. The annual meeting of the *Kontaktforum* is held each February. The chairmen of the respective historical societies are strongly encouraged to attend the annual meeting together with the executive committee of the *Kontaktforum*. Each annual meeting must consider the following matters:

    a. Review the annual reports of the chairperson, secretary and treasurer.
    b. Audit the financial records of the *Kontaktforum*.

4. Duties and responsibilities: The responsibilities of *Kontaktforum Hadeland-Amerika* shall include:

    a. Manage the membership records of the Norwegian members of the Hadeland Lag and process the renewal of their membership. In addition, the *Kontaktforum* is also responsible for the distribution of the newsletter, *BRUA*, in Norway.
    b. Distribute the *Hadeland Yearbook*, the *Hadeland Calendar*, as well as other publications of local historical interest, to the Hadeland Lag of America.
    c. Function as the central agency that accepts genealogy inquiries and requests for other information from Hadeland Lag members in America to Hadeland and vice versa.
    d. Responsible for the acquisitions of books, articles, genealogical studies and other records about Hadeland-related information that is published in the United States and Canada.
    e. Make certain that the above resources are housed in secure but accessible archives in Hadeland.

5. Practical Activity: The executive committee is responsible for conducting the current, day-to-day activities of the *Kontaktforum* as outlined in subsection 4) above. Furthermore, the historical societies and their members are obligated to assist in the guiding and transportation within the Hadeland area whenever members of the Hadeland Lag of America are visiting Hadeland. The boards of the historical societies are also requested to designate a group of volunteers who can be contacted when such assistance is needed. Likewise, the Hadeland Lag shall be of assistance in the planning of tours to the United States by the Hadeland historical societies and by Hadeland Lag members who reside in Norway.

6. Concerning Genealogical Research: The Hadeland Lag of America shall actively participate in the genealogical research about Hadeland emigrants and shall collect information regarding these emigrants and their immediate descendants in the United States and Canada. Likewise, the three historical societies in Hadeland shall also actively participate in researching and gathering information about these Hadeland emigrants.

7. Concerning Financial Matters: The executive committee is responsible for preparing an annual budget and raising the necessary capital to sustain the activities of the *Kontaktforum Hadeland-Amerika*.

8. Withdrawal from membership in the *Kontaktforum*: Through a written announcement made available prior to the 1st of July, any cooperating member may withdraw from this cooperation, beginning January 1st of the following year.

9. This document was signed by officers of the three Historical Societies of Hadeland at a meeting in Jevnaker on February 18th, 2007. It was read, discussed and approved by the Board of the Hadeland Lag of America at their meeting in St. Cloud, Minnesota on March 31, 2007 and signed by lag president Jan Heusinkveld.

Index

Chapter Ten's 'Membership List 1990-2010' (pages 134-145) and Chapter Thirteen's 'Farm Names in the 1801 Census' (pages 179-182) are *not* included in this index.

7 Lag *Stevner* 52-83
A Century of Norwegian Independence 73
Aabogen,Kongsvinger NO 1
Aamodt,Allison 51
Aamodt,Jason 51
Aamodt,Joanna 84
Aamodt,John 51,84
Abendroth,Mary 67
Adams ND 10
Afton House Inn 84
Afton WI 84
Agriculture Soil Conservation Office 112
Agriculture in Hadeland 232
Agriculture,US Dept of 112
Agrimsdtr,Kari 133
Aid Society Norden 4
Aker Church 196
Akershus Fortress 32,42
Akershus NO 149
Ål church 196
Albert Lea MN 1,43
Albuquerque NM 40,44
ALC Commission on Research and Social Action 122
Alcester SD 37,112,222
Alexander ND 116
Alexandria MN 155
All Saints Lutheran Church 117
Allegiance Software 108
Alm farm 149,177,188
Alm,Erick 106
Alm,Hans Olesen 106
Alm,Peter 123
Alta NO 40
Alturas CA 116
Amber Waves of Grain 72
American Legion 61,109,121
Amerika Feber 57
Amerikabesøk 40
Amundsen,Kjersti 151
An Illustrated History of the Counties of Rock and Pipestone,Minnesota 164
Andersdtr,Maren 22,111
Andersen,Karl Johan 109
Anderson,Albert 36

Anderson,Alma 36
Anderson,Arthur 20,36,111
Anderson,Betsy 67
Anderson,Cora Orvetta Hovland 20, 36,111,112
Anderson,David,M/M 36
Anderson,Don 67
Anderson,Evonne O Beastrom 20,27, 28,31,40,43,46,50,51,77,82,83,84, 111,113-114,229
Anderson,Harold 59
Anderson,James 20
Anderson,Jeanne 43
Anderson,Karen Linnae 111
Anderson,Kristi Luann 111
Anderson,Ole 5,112,129
Anderson,Randa Tessem 112
Anderson,Randi Jo 111
Anderson,Ron 55
Anderson,Verlyn,Dr 16,20,25,27-28, 31,36,38,40,43,46,49,50,51,56,59, 61,63,64,67,70,73,77,78,82,83,84, 104,111- 112,220,221,227,228,229
Anderson,Vonnie 59
Andreason,Karin 66
Anfinson,Matilda 116
Angelo 1
Antiques and Collectibles Club 119
Årbok for Hadeland 98,117
Årbok Publishing Company 227
Archaeology display,Hadeland *Folkemuseum* 202
Arend,Jürgen 235
Argonne FR 162
Argyle High School 122
Arizona State University 116
Arleta CA 116
Army Corps of Engineers-Sacramento 120
Army Signal Corps 8
Arnesen,Joen 173,174
Arneson,Olive 3
Arnson,Anton 2
Articles of Incorporation 73,77, 254-256
Arv Hus Museum 57
Arvada CA 46
Aschehoug,Marit 22

Aschim,Hans,Mrs 95
Ashland WI 106
Askim(eiet) farm 125,147,149
Askviken,Deanna 123
Aslak og Ingebret 78
Assisi Heights 72
Astrid,daughter of Gunnvor 26,170
Athens WI 51
Audobon MN 165
Aufi,brother named 185
Augedal farm 213
Augsburg College 110,122
Augustana Academy 112
Augustana College 75,112
Aurora SD 46
Aurskog NO 68
Austin High School 121
Austin MN 44
Austin State Junior College 121
Aws,Anna Graven 36
B&B Anderson Store 165
Babbit,Isaac 205
Babcock,Darrell 43
Babcock,Sharon 43
Bagg Farm 59
Bagley MN 7
Baird,Susan 75
Bakken,Harris 15,16,20
Balkan,Loren 51,84
Balkan,Marlene 51,84
Bamble NO 118
Bang,Anton Christian 178
Bank of America 115
Bårehus (mausoleum) 195
Battelle 115
Battle Horns 175
Battle of Liepzig 96
Battle of Stiklestad 197
Baxter,Carol 46,51
Baxter,Jenna 51
Baxter,Jonathan C 46
Bayfield WI 43
Baymont Inn 227
Beastrom,Barb 51
Beastrom,Eric 51,84
Beastrom,Gary 51
Becker County MN 154
Bekkum Homestead 61

Index

Belgum, Marilyn 53
Bellesen, Paul 125
Bellflower CA 116
Belmont WI 22,36
Bemidji MN 114
Benedict ND 130,131
Benson MN 68,163
Beresford SD 112,113
Berg, Budde farm 226
Berg, Christian 193
Berge, Etta 46
Bergen NO 40,112,170
Berger, Ingeborg Gudbrandsdtr 151
Bergeson, Eric 72
Bergmannsbefaring 211
Bergslia NO 22
Bergverksmuseum (Mining Museum) 42,210
Berquist, John 30
Bertha High School 107
Bertha MN 107
Bethania Lutheran Church 62,64,65
Bethel Lutheran Church 5,109
Bidne, Gertrude 115
Bid-Well Concrete Pavers 68
Big Lake MN 76
Bilden farm 42,149
Bilden, Jacob 158
Bilden, Josef 159
Bilden, Oliver 159
Bilden, Paul 158,159,160
Billings MT 37
Bily Clock Museum 65
Binford ND 37,106
Bishop of Oslo 192
Bishopric Council 197,198
Bislingen 45
Bislingen Fjellstue 36
Bismarck ND 7,228
Bjellum 173
Bjellum, Kjell G Gulbrandsen 147
Bjertnæs farm 122
Bjonelva 209
Bjoneroa 48,208
Bjoneroa *Kulturbygg* 48
Bjøralt farm 149
Bjørkvik, Randi 19,35
Bjorngjeld, Art 62
Bjørnson, Bjørnstjerne 178
Black Brook Wi 5
Black Death 170,171,187
Black Hills 68,227
Blaine MN 122
Blanchardville WI 10
Blegan, Louis 4,5,11

Bloomington MN 229
Blue Bell Lodge 227
Blue Earth MN 131
Bly, J 159
Bø, Telemark NO 70
bobbin lace 215
Bockoven, Arlene 40
Bodø NO 67
Bohemia 108
Bøhmer, Gudbrand 220
Bonanzaville 228
Bonder class 171
Bøndernes Hus 35
Borchgrevin, H K 211
Borgen, Agnes Skorud 119
Borgen, Carl E 119
Borgund Lodge 69
Borgund Stave Church 227
Børmarken, Egil 24,25
Borup MN 221,229
Botti, Elizabeth 46,51,213
Boy Scouts of America 8
Braastad, Aase 58
Braastad, Nels 58
Braastad, Vigdis 58
Braaten, Harold, M/M 36
Braaten, John 14
Brainerd MN 67,69
Brandbu *Almenning* 209
Brandbu NO 6,10,27,36,42,25,58, 117,128, 129,149,169,191,193, 213,233,234
Brandbu *sentrum* 233
Brandon MN 51
Bratvold, Amy 43
Bratvold, Bodil 43,46
Bratvold, Erik 51
Bratvold, Kelsey 46
Bratvold, Owen 43,46,51
Bratvold, Thomas 51
Bredeson, Robert 36
Brekke Travel 35
Brinchmann, H 205
brickworks 207,208
Bridging the Generations 79
Bristol County MA 4
British Isles 25
British Museum 202
Britton SD 37,67
Bronson, Ellen 60
Bronze Age 169
Bronze Bucks 41
Brookings SD 116
Brooklyn Center MN 43
Brørby, Agda Marie 117

Brørby, Berit 42
Brørby, Brynjulf 219
Brørby, Ingeborg 219
Brørby, Jacob 158
Brørby, Mari 112
Broshius, Jean 46
Brown, Harris 43
Brown, Jean 46
Brown, Lee 84
Brown, Marie 84
Brua 11,12,15,17,25,26,39,57,72, 96,97,100,103,104,111,113,114, 117,118,128,134,153,183,203,204, 223,203,204,223,230,232,238
Bruflat Lutheran Church 229
Brynsaas, Mae 40
Brynsaas, Norman 40,43,56,57
Brynsaas, Robert 43
Brynsås, Berthe Torstensdtr 123
Brynsås, Paul Gulbrandsen 123
Buche, Helen 81
budget, Norwegian state 237
Bugge, Soren 191
bunads 62,95,212-213, 221,227
bunad parade 53,55,58,59,62,63,64, 65,66,69,72,73,77,80,81,212,223
burial mounds 169,235
Burke, Karl 67
Burnett County WI 106,107
Burnsville MN 43,46,51
Bush, President 230,237
Buskerud NO 17,106,108,122
Buskerud Old Time Orchestra 59
busserull 49,216-217
Bustul, Bertha Stenbek 107
Bustul, Hans 107
Butterfly House 75
Buxrude, Rodney 43
Buxrude, Sara 43
Buxton ND 132
Bye, Erik 27,131
Bygdelagenes Fellesraad 2,56,66, 79,81,84,85,94,110,119
Bygdelags Forbundet 90
by-laws 82,103,244-253
cableway 210
Café Minnesota 73
Calamity Jane 69,227
California Polytechnic University 116
Call of the Lur 56,174-175
Calvin, Frank 5
Cambridge WI 74
Canfield farm 165
Canton Lutheran Church 68,112,227
Canton SD 44,46,68,95,112,127,227

Index

Carl Johan of Sweden,Prince 97
Carl of Denmark,Prince 73
Carlson,Allan 51
Carlson,Kathy 51
Carroll,James,Mrs 5
Cartwright Center 60
Cedar Falls IA 36
Central High School 119
Central Lutheran Church 8
Central Washington University 115
Chahinkapa Park 59,62,64
Challis National Forest 116
Chamberlain SD 46
Champion Harvester Company 1,3
Champlin MN 44
Chapel in the Hills SD 69
Charles Lindbergh Airport 229
    see also *Lindbergh, Charles*
Chicago IL 131,160
Chippewa City Pioneer Village 60
Chippewa County MN 106,108,
    116,122,124,161
Christensen,Brian 46,114-115,146
Christensen,Deanna 114
Christensen,G Wayne 114
Christensen,Lia Randi 114
Christensen,Randi Lee Hvattum 114
Christian Fredrik,Prince 96
Christian III,King 210
Christian IV,King 188
Christiania NO 34,164,176,177,178
Christianity 170
Christiansdtr,Anna 120
Christiansdtr,Caroline 120
Christiansdtr,Kjersti 119
Christiansdtr,Marie 120
Christiansdtr,Paula 119
Christiansen Ole 120
Christiansen,Hans 173
Christiansen,Peter 120
Church Music Days 235
Church of Norway 197-201
Cistersian Sisters 184
Civil War 67
Civil War Letters 6,61,62
Civil War Round Table,Rochester 109
Clackamas OR 75
Claremont IA 127
Clay County MN 165
Clayton County IA 132
Clemson SC 116
Clemson University 116
Cleveland OH 115
Cleveland,Annie 112

Cleveland,Delores Wevik 18,43,46,
    72,73,74,75,76,82,83,84,103,
    112-113,227
Cleveland,Harold 112
Cleveland,Ingvald 112
Cliffside Park NJ 40
Coeur d'Alene ID 43,46,51
Cokato MN 2
Colbjørnsdtr,Anne 176
Colgate ND 108
Colgate Presbyterian Church 129
Collegeville MN 53
Columbus ND 112
Communication Consultants Inc
    108,130
Como Park 10
Concordia College 6,7,16,21,35,111,
    113,122,220,221,229
Constitution,1910 240-241
Constitution,1984 242-243
Constitutional Assembly-Eidsvoll 96
Cool and Crazy 71
Coolidge,Calvin,President 11
Coon Valley WI 77
Cooper,Bruce 119
Cooper,Gloria Borgen 104,119-120
Cooper,Merton 119
Cooper,Paul 119
Cooper,Steven 119
Cooper,Susan 82,83,119
Corner of G & S,The 74
Cory CO 117
Cost comparisons to 2010 167
Cotter 171
Coughlin,Rev 5
Country Inn 226
Court House,Minneapolis MN 10
Covered Wagon 153-156
Cravath Park 74
Crazy Horse Memorial 227
Cross of Glory Lutheran Church 127
Cultural Center,NDSCS 55
Cunard Steamship Company 4
Custer State Park 227
Cylon Township WI 1
Dæhlen farm 149,177
Dahle,Alfield Norma 130
Dahle,Alfred 120
Dahle,Gardes 36
Dahle,Nora 36,120
Dahlen farm 133
Dahlen,Siri Hansdtr 129
Dalager,Elaine 82,83
Dalagutta 53
Dalton MN 105,121

Danielson,Janice 43
Danish nobility 171
Darlington High School 110
Darlington WI 110
daycare in Norway 230
Days Inn 77
Dayton OH 51,129
Deaconness School of Chicago 160
Deadwood SD 69,228
Dean,Darrold 51
Dean,Linda 51
Decatur IL 132
Decorah IA 7,11,18,40,43,44,62,
    64,66,95,219,222,224,226
Decorah Posten 26,186
Deer Park Wi 1,3
DeGraff Bank 163
Delavan MN 105
Delta CO 116
Delta Kappa Gamma 108
Den gamle Tingelstadkirke 188-189
Den store hvite flokk 223
Denmark 10,36,73,96,116,171,175,
    176,183,188,197,199,224,231
Detroit Lakes *Leikarring* 55
Detroit Lakes MN 109
Devils Lake ND 159
Digitalarkivet 18
Digitaltmuseum 202
Dillerud,Dhyre 155
Discher,Jack 64
Discover Norway Tour 43,67
*Discovering Norwegian Heritage in
    the Old West* 68
Dorph,Bailiff 173,174
Doseth,Else 220
Douglas ND 115
Draget NO 208
Drammen NO 66,218
Drengestua 102
Drew,Erin 124
Drew,Kelley 124
Drovdahl,Olaf 12
Dubuque IA 65
Duke University 122
Duluth MN 20
Durkee,Dorothy 67
Dvergsten farm 149,175-177,188
Dybdal,Phil 72
Dynna farm 25
Dynna,Ingvald 114
Dynna,Karen Ingebretsdtr 151
Dynnastein (Dynna Stone) 22,25,
    43,92,170
Eagan MN 40,43,109

Index

East Freeborn Lutheran Church 121
East Koshkonong Church 74
East Nidaros Church 75
Eastvold,John 14
Eau Claire WI 3
Ebenezer Lutheran Church 4
Edick,Ruth 40
Edina MN 39,40
Edwards,Alice 36
Egge farm 149
Egge,Gunnar 58
Egge,Iver Olsen 151
Egge,Mayor 34
Eglon Township 165
Eichen,Knud 173
Eide,Iver,M/M 36
Eidskogen NO 157
Eidsvoll NO 96,113
Eina NO 118
Elbow Lake MN 65
electrical works 207
Elken farm 117
Elken,B L 10
Ellensburg WA 116
Ellis Island 119
Ellsworth High School 113
Ellsworth WI 113,119
Elsace,France/Germany 116
Elstad MN 115
Elverum NO 118
Elvind Lundby Orchestra 58
Embrey,Esther 40
Embrey,Leland 40
Emeritus Advisory Council 82, 126-133
Emigrant Identification Project see *Kontaktforum Hadeland-Amerika*
Emigrant Protocol of Kristinia 57
Emigration 146-167
Enchanted April 81
Endresdtr,Else 125
Endresdtr,Marin 125
Endresen cabin 72,73
Enig og Tro til Dovre Faller! 96
Erhard MN 112
Erik *Blodøks (Blood axe)* 168,236
Erickson,Carl 40
Erickson,Wanda 40
Eriksdtr,Anne 123
Eriksdtr,Randi 151
Erlie,Alfield 36,40,59,103,120
Erlien,Darryl Alan 130
Erlien,Duane Lavern 131
Erlien,Ellef 14,36,40,54,55,57, 104,120,126,130-131

Erlien,Ole 131
Erlien,Sharon Elaine 131
Erlien,Sigurd Hanson 131
Erlien,Yvonne Norma 131
ermkjole 214
EROS Data Center 75
Etnedal NO 229
Europeana 202
Evansville MN 155
Ever the Land 61
Everson,Hans 111
Evjen,Thomas 158
Exploring Norway Tour 46
Expressway Suites 228
Fairview School of Nursing 119,126
Falls Park 76
Fargo Lions Club 130
Fargo ND 12,15,20,35,37,40,44,51, 55,66,70,74,77,108,129,130,132, 221,228
Fargo Public Library Bookmobile 132
Faribault MN 51
Farm Service Agency 112
Farmall F-12 tractor 163
Farmall F-20 tractor 163
Farwell MN 51
Fergus Falls MN 10,44,46,58,61,120,122,155
Fertile MN 3,4,130
Fiddlers Three 58
Fillmore County MN 70,115,153,154
Fine Arts Building,NDSCS 56
Finley-Sharon-Aneta ND Community Chorus 21
Fivelsdal,Hilde Brørby 48
Flem,Kari Ruud 41,43,172,227
Fløm NO 130
Floyds Knob IN 46,114
Fluberg NO 157
Fogdall,Judy 36
folk dress 212-217
Follmuth,Lorraine Marie 121
Folsom CA 46
Forest City IA 62,63,114
Forest Lake MN 51
Forsburg,Betty 43
Fort Abercrombie SD 58
Fort Abraham Lincoln ND 228
Fort Hood TX 121
Fort Leavenworth KS 109
Fort Lewis WA 162
Fort Renville MN 57
Fort Ridgely MN 105
Fort Sam Houston TX 109
Fort Snelling MN 229

Fort Toten ND 159
Foss,Harriet Thingelstad 15,16,20, 26,27,40,59,61,62,67,80,95, 102, 103,104,126,131-132,219,221,229
Foss,Percy 40,59,131,132
Fossum,Minnie 124
Fountain Hills AZ 44
Fragot,Kari Gudbrandsdtr 151
Framstad farm 149
Framstadgjerdingen,Sessilina Pedersdtr 1
Frankville IA 128
Frear,James A 3
Frederick III,King of Denmark 176
Freeborn County MN 122,158
Fridley MN 126
Frilling NO 226
Frogner Park,Oslo NO 45
From the Fjords to the Falls 75
Froslee,Mikal H 10
Froslie,Hans 37
Furua,Stephen Hanson,Mrs 115
Fylkesmannen 209
Fyresdal NO 106
gaard (farm) 171
Gabrielson,Stephen 'Gabe',Dr 65
Gade,F G 32
Gamalt fra Hadeland 14,26
Gamkinn farm 23
Gamme farm 22,23,117,221
Gamme Ole 231
Gamme,Birgitha 62
Gamme,Goro 218,222,224
Gamme,Helga 30,49,72,76, 117,219,22-,222,224
Gamme,Iver Paulsen 127
Gamme,Ole P 25,30,40,44,48,49,62, 64,69,72,74,76,77,97,98,100,117, 218,227,230
Gamme,Ole Iversen 218
Gamme,Paul 62
Gamme,Paul Iversen 218
Gamme,Paul O 117
Gamme,Rangdi Paulsdtr 127
Garborg,Arne 232
Garborg,Hulda 212
Gardermoen airport 35,42,48,220, 229
Garfield Township MN 120
Gautvedt farm 123
Gayville SD 113
George IA 127
Georgetown MN 160
Gerhard,Karen Andreasdtr 205
Germany 12,37,116,120,205,235

Index

Gilberton,Gerald Merlin 126
Gilbertson (Gulbrandson),Ole 22
Gilbertson,George 126
Gilbertson,John Phillip 127
Gilbertson,Karen Lyngstad Olson 126
Gilbertson,Mark David 126
Gilbertson,Norma Kyro 23,43, 62,69,82,83,84,126-127
Gilbertson,Paul Matthew 127
Gilbertson,Rebecca Susan 127
Gilbertson,Ruth Mary 127
Gilbertson,Stephen Luke 127
Gilbertson,Tilda Caroline 22
Gilsrud,Frances 60
Gjessing,Conservator 32
Glaser,Hans 210
Glassrud,P O 160
glassworks terminology 204
Glen Ullen ND 7
Glenwood Church 225
Decorah IA 225
Glenwood Church 62,226
Glenwood IA 116
Godli farm 122
Godli,Anne Larsdtr 122
Godli,Peder Olsen 122
Golden Valley MN 7
Goodman,Bill 61
Goodman,Susan 61
Goose River ND 131,158,160-161
Grace Lutheran Cemetery 112
Gran Church 21,33,221
Gran Church (Hawley MN) 43,228
Gran Church (Mayville ND) 43,160, 161,228
Gran coat-of-arms 96,172
Gran *Historielag* (Historical Society) 26,27,42,97,98,118,132,229
Gran Library 27
Gran NO 10,17,19,45,48,54,101,106, 113,114,115,117,118,122,123,124, 125,126,127,133,149,160,161,169, 173,177,178,179,207,209,216,219, 230,233,234
Gran parish 178,191
Gran Parsonage 33
Gran *sentrum* 42,196,233
Gran Sparebank 10,14,17,23,24,65
Granasen,Ragnar,Rev 28
Granavolden (Granavollen) NO 33,36, 46,49,169,196,173,174,177,230, 234
Granavolden *Gjæstgiveri* 28,46, 170,235
Granavolden,Gregers 34

Granavollen Pilgrim's Center 185
Granavollen Runestone 185
Grand Forks ND 35,108
Grand Mesa National Forest 116
Grandfather Ole 165
Granite quarry 171
Granrud,Ole 155
Grant County MN 155
Grantsburg WI 107
Grass Valley CA 116
Gratiot WI 37
Green Bay WI 40
Green County WI 6,123
Greenfield WI 46
Greenville SC 46
Grefsrud,Earl 40,53,54,56
Grefsrud,Priscilla 54
Greftegrev,Johanne Gulbrandsdtr 204
Gregersstuen 33
Grenora High School 130
Grenora ND 131
Grevstad,Mathilde Berg 154
Grieg,Edvard 72
Grieg Men's Choir of Madison 74
Grinager farm 117,120,149
Grinager Stave Church
  see *Grinaker Stave Church*
Grinager,Alta M Isaacson 120
Grinager,Eunice 40,120
Grinager,Haavel Knutson 120,121
Grinager,Isabel Martin 121
Grinager,Kathleen 120
Grinager,Kenneth 120
Grinager,Kjersti Pedersdtr 120
Grinager,Knud Hansen 120
Grinager,Lars 39
Grinager,Nettie 160
Grinager,Patricia 40
Grinager,Paul 40,54,61,62,66,120, 187
Grinager,Paul Augustine 120
Grinager,Paula 120
Grinaker Stave Church 42,54,92,120,170,187,189,190,191
Grinaker Weavery (*Grinakervev*) 42, 45,49,217,235
Grinaker,Carol 37
Grinaker,Vernon 37
Grinna,Grant M/M 37
Grover Club 130
Grover,Gerald 105
Grover,Ruby Alm 105
Grua Church 45
Grua NO 171,210,211,230

Grymyr church 45,194,231
Gubbrud,Archie 37-38, 60,68,222,227
Gubbrud,Florence 37-38,222,227
Gubbrud,Maxine 227
Gudbrandsdal Lag 17
Gudbrandsdal NO 10,178
Gudbrandsdalen NO 116,175
Gudbrandsdtr,Ingeborg 122
Gudbrandsen,Gudbrand 151
Gudbrandsen,Martin 151
Gudmundshagen farm 106
Gulbrandsdtr,Kari 123
Gulbrandsen,Anton Refonde 151
Gulbrandsen,Arnhold 205
Gulbrandsen,Gerhard 204
Gulbrandsen,Hjalmer Gerhard 205
Gulbrandsen,Lars 123
Gulden,Committee Chairman Attorney 33,34
Gully MN 37
Gundersen Glassworks 204,205
Gundersen,Robert 205
Gundersen-Pairpoint Glassworks 205
Gunderson,Alice 37
Gunderson,David 29,46,82,103,121
Gunderson,Elene Tokerud 121
Gunderson,Harlick 37
Gunderson,Norton Albert 121
Gunderson,Olaus 121
Gunnison National Forest 116
Gunstad farm 6
Gunter,Daniel 40
Guri,beautiful girl named 175
Gustafson,Bob 64
Guttormson,Susan 51,130
Haagenstad farm 105,149
Haakon VII,King 12,27,74
Haakon,Crown Prince 227
Habbestad,Kjell 65
Habert,Mary 84
Hackensack MN 51
Hackman,Jean 46
"Hade" 169
Hadeland Band 36
Hadeland Brewery 207
Hadeland Dancers 57
Hadeland Emigrant Database 99
Hadeland *Folkemuseum* 17,18,24, 25,36,39,43,46,49,50,65,67,69,70, 97,98,170,187,188,201-211,214, 217,235
Hadeland Glassworks 35,39,45, 48,157,171,203-205,206,208
Hadeland Glassworks Band 33,34

267

Index

Hadeland Hotel 42
Hadeland *Kalendar* 98
Hadeland Lag artifacts 85-96
Hadeland Lag Banner (*fane*) 95-96
Hadeland Lag Centennial 18,48-51, 81-84
Hadeland Lag Fall Meetings 52-84
Hadeland Lag website 18
Hadeland Manufacturing Co. 42
Hadeland Prize (*Hadelandspris*) 22, 59,118,223
Hadeland Tour 1921 32-34
Hadeland Tour 1978 35-39
Hadeland Tour 1990 39-40
Hadeland Tour 2000 40-44
Hadeland Tour 2005 45-47
Hadeland Tour 2010 48-51
Hadeland, a brief history 169-172
Hadeland's Bygdenes Historie,IV 173
Hadeland's Historical Societies 101-102
Hadelandsbusserull 217
Hadelandsdrakten (Hadeland folk costume) 214-215
Hadelandsgruben 211
Hadelandslag-Oslo 24,90
Hadland,Donna 43
Hadland,Robert 43
Haga,Carl 110
Haga,Ester 40,44,98,110
Haga,Gudmund 158
Haga,Gudmund Johnsen 110
Haga,Luella 110
Haga,Mathilde 37
Hagberg,Joyce 63
Hagen,Albert 160
Hagen,Ole 158
Hagen,Ole H M/M 160
Hakadal 211
Halbert,Mary 67,76,93
Halbert,Ralph 76,84,93
Hallingdal NO 10,158
Hallingen 26
Hallinglag 30
Hallock MN 43
Halvdan *Svarte* (the Black) King, 170,201,2365
Halvdanshaugen 34,36,201,235
Halvorsen,Anne 124
Halvorson,Jon 46
Halvorson,Kari 160
Hamar, diocese of 176,231
Hamar NO 28,57,61
Hamm,William,Dr 62
Hammer,Magne 15

Hammer,Marie (Mrs Lars) 14,15
Hammer,Ronald 43
Hammerstad,Gro E 24
Hampton Inn 226,229
Han Ola og Han Per 70
Handcraft association (*Husflidslag*) 212,214,215
Hanford WA 115
Hansdtr,Randi 106,123
Hansen,Niels 26
Hanson,Adeline 37
Hanson,Adolph 37
Hanson,Ansgar 37
Hanson,Karl 49,51
Hanson,Kelsey 51
Hanson,Larry M/M 161
Hanson,Mildred 37
Hanvold,Martin 157
Harald *Hårfagre* (Fair-hair) 168,170,236
Harald V,King 27,28,78, 200
Harald,King 170
Hardanger embroidery 72
Harding,President 4
Harleysville PA 51
Harmony MN 44
Harris,Sheriff Harold O 2,3
Hatterstad,Emma 129
Hatton ND 15,37,115
Haug,Pernille Hansdtr 6
Hauge Synod 105
Haugen,Ed 37
Haugland,Zacharias T 127
Haugtvedt farm 115
Haugtvedt,Erick Hanson 115
Haugtvedt,Jens Larson 115
Haward at Duærgæstæn 176
Hawley MN 44,46,51,123,221,229
Hayward MN 121
Hedberg,Blaine 77
Hedmark 170,230,235
Hedmark College 28
Hedmark,Historical Society of 236
Heen,H H 10
Heimskringla 170
Helgakereiet farm 123
Helgeson,Eunice 53
Hendrickson,Sandra 30,81
Henriksdtr,Guri 116
Heritage Collection 85-97
Heritage Education Commission 114
Heroes of Telemark 79
Hessler,Jean 44
Hessler,Josephine 46
Hessler,Steven 44,46

Hettinger ND 129
Heusinkveld,Dawn 105
Heusinkveld,Janice 18,29,30,44,48, 49,51,70,76,77,81,82,83,84,95,103
Heusinkveld,Laurie 105
Heusinkveld,Lisa 105
Heusinkveld,Sherry 105
Hiawatha Golf Club 68
Hickok,Wild Bill 69,227
Hickson ND 7
High River AB CAN 37
Highland Prairie Lutheran Church 70
Hilden farm 149
Hilden,Berthe Knotterud 159
Hilden,Ole 159
Hill,Carla 127
Hill,Charley 127
Hill,Leona 44,127
Hill,Manfred 44,46,68,82,83,103, 126,127-128,227
Hill,Nora Roe 127
Hill,Paulette 127
Hill,Randall 127
Hill,Renee 127
Hill,Richard 127
Hill,Verlyn 46
Hills MN 165,223,227
Hillsboro ND 37
Univ. of Oslo Historical Museum 32
History of Lake Park 166
History of the Hadeland Lag 1910-1990 52,54,131
Hitterdal MN 40
Hjemkomst Center 17,65,71,229
Hjemmefrontmuseet 42
Hjemsø,Teacher 33
Hobart WA 51
Hoeg,Laura Hjelle 95
Hoff Lutheran Church 105
Hoff,Harlan 68
Hoffsbro farm 216
Hoffsbro textile factory 216,217
Høghaug,Kari Lette Pollestad,Pastor 49,50,75,76
Hole farm (west) 6
Hole,Hans Larson 10
Hole-Kanten farm 106
holiday *busserull* 216
Holiday Inn Convention Center 75
Holland 108
Hollandale WI 37
Holm,John Ballangrud 10
Holman,Andrea 53
Holman,Bob 44,51,53
Holmenkollen 32,42

Index

Holmstykket,Anders 110
Holtan,Ruth 63
Holtan,Stanford 63
Holter,Finn 223
Holy Redeemer Lutheran Church 116
honnlue 215
Hope Lutheran Church 127
Hopperstad Stave Church 71
Hordaland County NO 115
Horgen farm 149
Hot Springs SD 227
Houston County MN 70
Hova NO 116
Høvik Glassworks 204,205
Hovland,Anne Teslo 108
Hovland,Carl 158
Hovland,Dale 82,83,84
Hovland,Halvor 158
Hovland,Hans 158
Hovland,Larry 51
Hovland,Myron 44
Hovland,Nils 112
Hovland,Ole 108,158
Hovseiet farm 111
Hudson Bay Company 155,160
Hudson Cemetery 2
Hudson SD 37
Hudson WI 1,10,18,51,84
Hull,Jack 51
Hull,John 51
Human Services,MN Dept of 106
Humphrey Theatre 53
Humphrey,Hubert H Senator 167
Hurdal NO 149
Husby,Even 113
Husby,Ida 113
Husby,Johanne Olson 113
Husflidslag 212,214,215
Husmann (*med jord*) 171
Hvaleby(eiet) farm 123,149
Hvalebyeiet,Dorthe Johansdtr 151
Hvalseiet farm 122
Hvamstad,Per 14,219
Hvamstad,Sheriff 33
Hvattum,Anne 223
Hvattum,Anne Klara Dynna 117
Hvattum,Harald 40,97,98,100,
 117-118
Hvattum,Hovel 115
Hvattum,Ole P 223
Hvattum,Randi Skjervum 115
Hvattum,Sigmund 117
Hvattum,Thorsten "Thomas"
 Hovelsen 114
Hvinden,Lars Jacobsen 191

Hytta farm 105
Immigrant monument IA 63
Independent Telephone Pioneers
 Association 130
India 127
Industrialization of Norway 206
Intercim 109
Internal Revenue Service 121
International Harvester Co. 2,3,4,9
Internet policy 18,257-260
Iowa County WI 6
Ireland 172
Irmo SC 46
iron mining 171,210,211
Isfjorden NO 175
Iverson,Hans 111
Ja Mom's restaurant 60
Jacobson,Anna Lynne 37
Jacobson,Don 61
Jacobson,Erling 10
Jacobson,Per 10
Jacobson,Phyllis 61
Jakobsen,Thorsten 124
Janda,Andrew 106
Janda,Anne 30,82,83,103,104,106
Janda,Elizabeth 106
Janda,Mark 106
Janesville WI 110
Jaren NO 226,233
Jefsen,Paul 62
Jelen,Annette 40
Jensdtr,Kjersti 110
Jensen,Nels 5
Jensen,Sonja 51,130
*Jevnaker Bondeungdomslag
 Dansegruppe* (Jevnaker Youth Folk
 Dance Group) 35
Jevnaker Bygdeungdomslag
 (Jevnaker Community Youth
 Organization) 98,223
*Jevnaker Bygdeungdomslag
 Leikarring* (the Jevnaker Youth
 Folk Dance Group) 39
Jevnaker Church 45,49,192
Jevnaker Church (Borup MN) 43,221,
 228
Jevnaker Church (Montevideo MN)
 43,161,229
Jevnaker Church parsonage 102
Jevnaker coat-of-arms 96,172
Jevnaker Historical Society
 (*Historielag*) 42,97, 98,102,192
Jevnaker NO 6,10,17,19,42,45, 48,
 109,110,111,112,113,122,124,
 149,157,169,171,194,218,230,233

Jevnaker parish 192
Johannesdtr,Anne Marie 151
Johansen,Gulbrand 205
John Marshall High School 109
Johnson,Andrew
Johnson,Fred 58
Johnson,Jadde 59
Johnson,Kevin 28
Johnson,Leonard 55
Johnson,Martha Amalia 6
Johnson,Willard C 55
Johnsrudsverksted building 217
Join Hands and Dance 70
Jones,J B 3
Jones,James 82,83
Jones,Richard 82
Jorstad,Anne Lise 27,46,49
Jotunheimen 177
Judicial system,Norwegian 173-174
Judisch,David,Dr 66
Juel,Joseph 46
Juel,Martha 46
Juel,Melvin 95
julebørd 231
Junior *Spelmannslag* 70
Jutullaget 64
Kalamazoo MI 37
Kalmoe,Lois 44
Kammerud,Hans 174
Kandi Entertainment Center 69
Kandiyohi County Hist'l Society 69
Kanten,Anne Gulbrandsdtr 106
Kanten,Anne Iversdtr 106
Kanten,Iver Halvorsen 106
Karlson,Karen 109
Karlsrud,Anne Nilsdtr 151
Kawatski,Sandra 60
Keeping the Old Traditions 64
Keith,Jeanne 46
Kelly Farm 76
Kennedy House 68,227
Kennedy,President 167
Kennedy,Robert 167
Kenner LA 51
Kent WA 44
Kerry,Senator 237
Keswick VA 46
Kilbourn WI 160
Kindred ND 40,44
King,Martin Luther 167
King's Guard 117
King's Highway 36,169,175
King's Island 36
King's Medal of Honor 118
Kingsbury County SD 116

269

Index

Kirkestue 195
Kistefos Museum 42,45,49
Kistefos Træsliberi 206
Kittelson,Anton 107
Kittelson,Sophie 107
Kjell Habbestad Family 65
Kjørven,Anders 158
Kjos farm 149
Kjos,Torsten 158
Kleboe,Ole 173
Kleiveland,Ingvald,112
Klokkerlaven 42
Kloten ND 37
Kløvstad farm 157,6 Hall 12
Knutson,Bertina 166
Køhn,Rosemarie,Bishop 231
Kolbu NO 118
Kollecas,Lauren 46
Kolstø,Pastor 32
Kongeveyen (Old King's Highway) 36,169,175
Kongsberg Silvermining Co 211
Kongsvinger,Olive Arnesdtr 1
Kontaktforum Hadeland-Amerika 18, 31,44,48,49,50,70,72,74,76, 97-100,110,112,115,117,118,121, 146,205,238
Kontaktforum Hadeland-Amerika, agreement with 261-262
Kon-Tiki Museum 42
Kornfeld,Doris 46
Kornfeld,Lacy 46
Korsvolden,Lars Olsen 174
Koshkonong WI 60,74
Kringen Klub Kor 55
Kringen,Battle of 175
Kristiania NO *see* Christiania NO
Kristiansen,Gunnar,Pastor 67
Kristin Lavansdatter 71
Krodsherad NO 106
Krohn,Julia 17
Kroshus,John Anderson 106
Kroshus,Kari Pedersdtr 106
Kroshus,Marie 106
Kroshus,Oleanna 106
Kroshus,Pauline 106
Kroshus,Tilford 67
Kruse,Karen 44,82,83
Kvelsrud farm 35
Kverno Trond 235,236
Kviteseid Church MN 63,229
Kyro,Maria Emelia Koskela 126
Kyro,Otto 126
Lac qui Parle State Park 57
Lacey WA 46

LaCrosse WI 37,60,77,160
Lærdal NO 130
Lafayette County WI 111
LaFollette,Robert M 2,3
Lake Mills IA 63
Lake of the Woods MN 131
Lake Oswego OR 44,46
Lake Park MN 123,154,165
Lake Region Hospital 120
Lake Region Pioneer Threshermen's Association 121
Lakeville MN 10
Lakota Indian Museum 227
Land Church 227
Land NO 10
Land of Milk and Honey 60
Land,Logging,Legends 78
Landingslag 15,18,30,52,62, 63,66,67,74,78,81,82,83,229
Landingsleiken 78
Lands Museum 206
Lanesboro MN 81
Lange,Ase A 24,40,217
Laporte MN 51
Larmerud,Anders 49
Larsdtr Kari 22
Larsdtr,Berthe 115
Larsen,Helen 37
Larsen,Lars 22
Larson,Clara 160
Larson,Eleanora 115
Larson,Erich 125
Larson,Gordon Howard 115
Larson,Ingebret 160,161
Larson,Iver 160
Larson,Jens 115
Larson,Lars 115
Larson,Leroy 60,79
Larson,Lewis 115
Larson,Linda Lee 46,115-116
Larson,Orice 37
Larson,Severt Haugtvedt 116
Larson,Vivian 37
LaRue,Pat 60
Las Vegas NV 46
Lead mines 211
Lee,Andrew 114
Lee,John 10
Leikarring Dancers 69
Leikarring Noreg 66
Lennox SD 112
Leonard,Odelle 46
Les mines du Hadeland 211
Let's Rally in the Valley 76
Lian,Jan 227

Lider,Barbara 51
Lider,Wilbur 51
Lie,Editor 33
Lillehammer NO 220
Lily of the Valley (*liljekonvall*) 173
Lilyen,Beata Melom 105
Limestone quarry 171
Limited Access Archive 18
Linbergh,Charles 167
Lincoln County SD 112
Lincoln NE 122
Lindstad farm 125
Lindstad,Carl 20,37
Lindstad,Maren Endresdtr 125
Lindstadeiet,Kjersti Paulsdtr 151
Liråk,Hilde 110
Littleton CO 51
Livdahl,Grace (Olson) 6
Livingston MT 51
Llmajoki FI
Løberg,Lars 56
Lofoten NO 40
Log driving 207-209
London UK 170
Long Beach CA 116
Long Lake MN 40,44,65
Los Angeles CA 132
Louisville KY 51,114
Louvre 202
Lovoll,Odd,Dr 30
Lumijoki FI 126
Lund Vernon,54,60,63
Lunden,Anders Guttormsen 124
Lunden,Inger D Johannesdtr 124
Lunder farm 149
Lunder,Hans Gudmund 49
Lunner Church 42,45,48,105,186
Lunner coat-of-arms 96,173
Lunner Dancers 36
Lunner Historical Society (*Historielag*) 25,42,97,98,101
Lunner Kommune 1898-1998 43
Lunner NO 10,17,19,42,45,48,58,109, 110,131,149,169,171,186,230,233
Lunner parish 192
Lunner *Radhus* (City Hall) 43
Lur,Call of the 174-175
Luren Singers 219,222,224
Luren Singing Society 66
Luther College 11,66,222,225, 226
Luther Seminary 80
Lutheran Church of Christ the King 108,130
Lutheran Council in the USA 122

Index

Lutheran Social Services 119
Lutheran Theological Seminary 122
Lyngstad farm 126
Lyngstad,Christopher 126
Lyngstad,Kåre 69,227
Lynne farm 149
Lynne,Anders 124
Lynne,Edvard 124
Lynne,Eline Andersdtr 124
Lynne,Ingel 124
Lynne,Nikolai Daniel 124
Lynne,Otto 124
Lynne,Palmer 37
Lynne,Thorvald 124
Lynne,Torsten 124
Lynnebakken farm 124
Lynner,Jens A 186
Lynnwood WA 115
Lyon County IA 127
Lysen farm 125
Lysenstøen,Halvor Larson 146
Mabel MN 95
Machinery Hill 9
Mack,Rose 44
Madison MN 36,128
Madison WI 29,46
Madsen,Ole 155
Madsen,Ole Jr 155
Magnor Glassworks 204
Mahle,Alphina 40
Maine 221
Majorstuen NO 32
Malacek,Judy 44
Mall of America 229
Malm Basselurskan Harmonica Orchestra 72
Mandan ND 69
Mandt Lutheran Church 122
Mandt Twp MN 122
Mannskor KK 16,21,27,28,34, 35,36,39,40,42,45,49,62,69,95,98, 117,165,196,218,219-225,230,235
Maple Plain MN 51,107
Marble quarry 171
Margaret I (Margrethe),Queen 188
Maria Church (*Mariakirken*) 184-185,235
Marion NC 44
Marriott Hotel 78
Marshall MN 16,36,40,223
Martha,Crown Princess 12
Martin Township 164
Martin,Janet 30,71
Martineau,Colleen 44
Martinsdtr,Eline 124

Mason,Tom,M/M 37
Mau,Janey 37
Mau,Kaari 37
Mau,Krista 37
Mau,Lt Donald 37
Mau,Melissa 37
Mau,Richard 37
Mau,Wesley 37
mausoleum (*bårehus*) 195
Maynard MN 116
Mayo Clinic 105
Mayvile ND 10,15,19,20,21, 22,36,37,160-161,221,229
Mayville State College 19,20
McCormick Harvester Company 2
McHenry ND 106
Means,Margaret 40
Means,Robert 39,40
Medora Motel 228
Medora Musical 228
Medtronic 114
Meier,Run 28
Melaas,Anne Olsdtr 151
Melaas,Joseph 12
Melaas,Ole Nerstua 159
Melbostadeiet,Anne Hansdtr 151
Mellum,Martin 155
Mellum,Mikkel 154,156
Melom,Anne Irene Erickson 105
Melom,Johan Fillip 105
Melom,Johanne Hansdtr 105
Melom,Johannes Halvorsen 105
Melom,Marie Iversdtr 105
Mentor MN 40
Meroa IA 115
Mesa AZ 43
Metis 156
Meyer,Kris 63
Mickelson,Christian 119
Middle Ages 170,192
Midelfort,Christine 71
Midland Cooperative 6,7
Midsteigen,Per 65
Midsummer Day 39
Midwest Norwegian-American Chamber of Commerce 79
Mikkelson Collection 70
Milan MN 36,57,229
Miller,Don 69
Miller,Laura Mae Tostenson 122
Miller,Lester Joseph 122
Miller,Michael 51,104,122
Miller,Susan 122
Mindegaven Memorial Fund 10,12, 14,15,17,23-26,43,65,67

Mindekirken 67,80,229
mining in Hadeland 210-211
Mining Museum (*Bergverksmuseum*) 42,210
Ministry of Church Affairs 199,200
Minneapolis MN 7,10,11,12,19,37, 40, 44,107,110,113,114,119,122, 126,155,219,222,226,229
Minnehaha *Mannskor* 76
Minnesota Historical Society 8
Minnesota History Center 73,229
Minnesota MENSA 108
Minnesota Petroleum Ass'n 124
Minnesota Scandinavian Ensemble Band 60,79
Minnesota Sesquicentennial 29-30
Minnesota State Fair 9,10,11
Minnesota State University-Mankato 121,132
Minnesota State University-Moorhead 108,114,122,129
Minnetonka MN 44,46
Minot ND 12.109
Minot State Teachers College 130
Miron,Charlotte 40
Mississippi River 155
Mitchell Corn Palace SD 227
Mitchell County IA 115
MN Army National Guard 109
Model T 162,166
Modoc National Forest 116
Moe,John 106
Moe,Mary Alm 106
Moen church 195
Moen farm 130,149
Moen *Musikforening* 49
Moeseiet farm 111
Molden farm 149
Molden,Andrew Hanson 160
Molden,Gulbrand Hanson 160
Molden,Hans Hanson 160
Moline,Thelma 40
Møllerstuen farm 129
Monroe WI 110
Monson,Albert 107
Monson,Andreas 107
Monson,Johan Martin 107
Monson,John 107
Monson,Karen 107
Monson,Kari 107
Monson,Ole 107
Monson,Paul,M/M 37
Monte Trio 57
Montevideo MN 37,40,54,57, 59,63,109,122,161,219,221,229

Index

Montevideo VFW 54
Montrose MN 51,122
Moody County SD 116
Moorhead MN 7,16,17,35,36,40,
 43,44,46,51,65,70,105,108,111,
 113,122,130,165,220,229
Moorhead State University
 See *Minnesota State U-Moorhead*
Møre 175
Morgan Ave Lutheran Church 126
Morris MN 67
Morstad farm 149
Morstad,Carl Max 51
Morstad,Mary 51
Morstad,Noel 51
Moses,Maureen 44
Mount Horeb WI 37,223
Mount Moriah Cemetery 69,227
Mount Rushmore 69,227
Mount Sinai Hospital 126
Mount Valley Twp 121
Mozart's Requiem 236
Mueller,Jeff 79
Muller,Chad 70
Muncie IN 46
Mutta NO 211
Myhre,Anne 174
Myhre,Erik Larsen 147
Myhre,Kjell Henrik 40,69,97,98,100
Myhrstuen,Geir Arne 44,97,100
Myhrstuen,Kåre 100
Myra,Lars Larson 115
Næs (Nes) Church 42,45,157,193
Næs Brewery 207
Næs(eiet) farm 107,116,149
Næs,Ragne Eriksdtr 151
Næss Hans M 40,44,69,77,97,98,
 99,100,118,226
Nanstad NO 109
Napoleon 96
Narro Leikarring (dance group) 56
Nat'l Ass'n of Norwegian Singers 7
National Assembly 197
National Church Council 198
National Council of Norwegian-
 American Bygdelags 6
Nat'l Society of Prof'l Engineers 130
National Theatre (Norwegian) 34
Navarre,Harry 40
Navarre,Irene 40,44,82,83
Nazi Germany 12
Nedre Gamme farm 218
Nelson,Abner 37
Nelson,Carol 55
Nelson,Dave 72

Nelson,Don 63
Nelson,Ernest,Rev 95
Nelson,Gene 53,83
Nelson,Hans 122
Nelson,Luella 37,40
Nelson,Olaf 16,20,37,40,54,55,56,
 57,58,59,60,103,104,122,219,221
Nelson,Peder H 15,17,20,26,
 131,219,221,223,229
Nelson,Peder H Book
 Collection,17,26-27,42,
 67,101,102,132
Nelson,Rhoda Moen 37,40,54,
 55,57,122,219,221
Nelson,Suzann 30
Nelson,Walter,M/M 37
Nelsonville Lutheran Church 78
Nelsonville Mill 78
Nernst,Bailiff 173
Nervig,Casper 36
Nervig,Casper M/M 37
Nervig,Louise 37
Nes Church 42,193
Nesbakken farm 42,157
New Auburn WI 37
New Bedford MA 204,205
New Hope MN 119
New Richmond Heritage Center 79
New York NY 11,204
Newburyport MA 51
Nidaros Cathedral 2,185,197
Nidaros Church SD 227
Nielsen,Emil 216
Nielsen,Kari 216
Nielsen,Nils 216,217
Nikolai and Merserau 107
Nikolai Church 10,28,36,39,
 42,43,45,49,184-185,230
Nikolaus of Bari,Archbishop 184
Niles IL 20,37
Nilsen,Johannes 157
Nilsen,Lars 122
Nittedal NO 118,233
Nøkleby,Helga Thørstensdatter 124
Nøkleby,Henry 158
Nøkleby,Jon 158
non-profit status 18
Norby,Lavonne 83
Nord Hedmark & Hedemarken 30
Nordan,Jacob Wilhelm 191
Nordengeneiet farm 122
Nordfjord NO 10
Nordfjordlaget 30
Nordic Festival 222
Nordkapp Mannskor 7,222

Nordland Fest 223
Nordland NO 10
Nordlandslaget 109
Nordre Land NO 106
Nordsmanns Forbundet 32,33
Norema Manufacturing Company 45
Normandale Community College 106
Normandy Park WA 46
Norse Centennial Celebration 11
Norse Glee Club of Sioux Falls 95
Norsk Fest 2
Norsk Sangere 56
Norskedalen 60,61,77
Norskedalen Trio 60
North American immigrant statistics
 146-152
North Dakota Engineers Council 130
North Dakota Society of Professional
 Engineers 130
North Dakota State College of
 Science 54,57,59,61,64,67,76
North Dakota State University 108,
 129
North Framstad farm 123
North High School 126
North Odal NO 113
North Preston SD 116
North St Paul High School 127
North Trinity Cemetery 227
Northfield Am Legion Ballroom 70
Northfield MN 40,70,99,229
Northwood ND 11,15,26,40,62,
 101,110,123,131,132,158-160,
 219,229
Norway Day 223
Norwegian Broadcasting Co 131
Norwegian Centennial 2,4
Norwegian coat-of-arms 188,189
Norwegian Constitution 96,197
Norwegian Council for National
 Costumes 212
Norwegian Grove MN 116,154
Norwegian Lutheran Church in
 America 12
Norwegian Memorial Church 222
Norwegian Ministry of Culture 210
Norwegian Museum of Cultural
 History 26
Norwegian Opera 236
Norwegian Peace Committee 2
Norwegian Royal Coat-of-Arms 93
Norwegian Statehood Pioneer
 Project 29-30
Norwegian Stevner Inc (NSI) 17,
 60,127,130

Index

Norwegian-American Bygdelag Centennial 66
Norwegian-American Genealogical Center-Naeseth Library 29,77,111
Norwegian-American Historical Association 69,99
Norwegian-Minnesotan Sesquicentennial Celebration 78
Norwegian Singers Ass'n of America 224
NorWin Singers 81
Novato CA 40
Nowland,Ron,Pastor 71
Numedal NO 10,58,108
Numedalslag 17,52,55
Nybo's Landing 58
Nyseter NO 211
Nyster 211
Nysveen,Duane,M/M 37
Oak Grove High School 66,130
Ocean View DE 46
Ohe,Harriet 44
Ohe,Jeanette 154
Ohe,Karen 112
Ohe,Larry 44,229
Ohe,Lars Larsen 112
Ohe,Martin 155
Ohe,Theodore 154
Oien,Janet Sue 116
Oien,Jenifer Bjelke 83,116
Oien,Jens Richard 116
Oien,John 83,116-117
Oien,Julie Kristine 116
Oien,Kathryn Lillian Hoffman 116
Oien,Paul Olaf 116
Olav Haraldson,King 197
Olav V,King 56
Olav,Crown Prince 12
Old King's Road 36,169,175
Old Muskego Church 80
Old Widow's Farm 178
Ole and Sven 72,73
Ole-Iver and Johanne Berg,Pioneers: Account of Covered Wagon Days 154
Olerud,Engebret Amundsen 133
Olerud,Kari Ingebretson 133
Oleson,Ole 6
Olimb farm 149
Olin,Agnes Louise 106,107
Olin,John Cheney 107
Olin,Josephine Harriet 107
Olsdatter,Anne 107
Olsdtr,Maren 157
Olsdtr,Randi 150

Olsen,Ole 174
Olseth,O H 95
Olson James 8
Olson,Alvin 109
Olson,Anne Roatterud 113
Olson,Borghild 37
Olson,Carrie Helene 128
Olson,DeLos 30,46,51,55,76, 83,84,104, 108-109
Olson,Donald 46,83
Olson,Francis Mary McCutcheon 109
Olson,Grace (Mrs Morgan) 6-7, 20,29,54
Olson,Ingeborg Raffelson 109
Olson,James 7
Olson,Jules 166
Olson,Lars 162
Olson,Martha 20
Olson,Morgan 6-8,15,16,17,19,20, 21,24,36,37,61,62,219,221,222, 223,224
Olson,Morgan Peter 6
Olson,Norman 51
Olson,Obed Henry 6
Olson,Oline Alm 106
Olson,Rollin 6,61
Olson,Steffen S 113
Olssen,Pastor 33,34
On-A-Slant Indian Village 228
Onsager,Anders 158
Onsager,Ole 158
Onsaker Brickworks 207
Opdahl,LaRee 83,84
Opdahl,Loren 83,84
Opdalslaget 30
Opheim NO 115
Oppland County Association 213
Oppland County Coat-of-Arms 93
Oppland NO 17,93,106,169,210,213, 230
Opsahl,Larry 55
Oregon State University 115
Osage IA 114,115
Oseberg Viking Burial Ship 32
Oslo NO 32,34,35,36,40,49, 61,107,117,149,164,170,196,230
Oslo Agricultural College 117
Oslo Cathedral 49
Oslo Opera House 49
Oslo Rift 210
Oslo Symphony Orchestra 236
Osseo WI 46
Osten,Simon Larsen 115
Osterøy NO 112
Østfold NO 121

Østre Bjoneelvens Fellesfløtningsforening 208
Østre Bjonevatnet 208
Otta NO 175
Otter Tail County MN 107,112, 116,154,155
Otter Tail County Museum 61,77
Ottesen,Bertha 111
Our Savior's Lutheran Church 105, 116,223
Our Vines Have Tender Grapes 78
Øvre Gamme farm 218
Øyer NO 51
Paalserud,Nils Torstensen 123
Pairpoint Manufacturing Co 205
Pairpoint,Thomas 205
Palo Alto CA 40
Paramount High School 116
Park Hotel 95
Passage to the Prairie 59
Pataskala OH 51
Paulsdtr Kari 123
Paulsdtr Ragnhild 123
Paulsdtr,Birthe 123
Paulsdtr,Marthe 123
Paulson,Gulbrand 123
Paulson,Johannes 123
Paulson,Martin 124
Paulson,Paul 40
Paulson,Peter 160
Paulson,Torsten 123
Paulsrud,Henry 106
Paulsrud,Johanna Alm 106
Peder H Nelson Book Collection see *Nelson,Peder H*
Pedersdtr Kari 107
Pedersdtr,Atlanta 151
Pedersdtr,Birthe 122
Pedersdtr,Gudbjør 122
Pedersdtr,Marte Helene 26
Pedersdtr,Pernilla 119
Pedersen,Christian 122
Pedersen,Gregers 193
Pedersen,Hans 106
Pedersen,Lars 122
Pederson,Johan 116
Pelican Rapids MN 12,44,51, 58,62,112
Pelican Valley Nursing Home 112
pension plan,Norwegian 204
Per,Immigrant and Pioneer 58, 59,62,128
Personalities of the West and Midwest 128
Peruvia 218

Index

Petaluma CA 43
Peterson,Anne Louise 106
Peterson,Emily 110
Peterson,James 40
Peterson,LeRoy 51,84
Peterson,Maurice Alton 106
Peterson,Myrna C 128
Peterson,Sharon Jorgenson 51,84, 104,110-111
Pettersdtr,Petrine Mathea 6
Pettersen,Halvard 63
Peyton CO 44
Pfeffer,Alma Kittelson 107
Pfeffer,Dan 107
Pfeffer,David 29,30,51,83,103, 107-108
Pfeffer,George 107
Pfeffer,Joe 107
Pfeffer,Nicole 107
Pfeffer,Rebecca 107
Pfeffer,Thresia 107
Phelps Mill 77
Phi Beta Kappa 108
Philadephia PA 122
Pickens SC 46
Pilgrim's Way 185
Pioneer Life `165-167
Pitchfork Fondue 228
Plain Hearts 77
Plaza ND 19,124
Pleasant Consolidated High School 132
Pleasant Valley WI 1,3
Plomasen,Bruce 46
Plomasen,Julia 46
Plummer MN 32
Polk County MN 5,120
Pomme de Terre MN 155
Porsgrund Porcelain 48
Portage County 78
Portland OR 40,115
Pramhus farm 157
Prefsrud,Priscilla 40
Prestholdt,Orville 7
Prestkvern,Kjersti 214
Preston MN 155
profanity 204
Progressive Party 2
Promise of America sculpture 63
public schools in Norway 198
Pullman WA 115
quarries 210
Raasiet farm 6
Raastad,Mary Andersdtr 120
Rabenberg,Glen,M/M 37

Radtke,Gloria 44
Radtke,Harvey 44
Raffelson,Anton Edvart 109
Ragnilrud,Berthe Torsgtensdtr 151
Ragnvald *Rettilbeine* 168, 236
Raknerud,Torstein 211
Ramada Stevens Point Hotel & Conference Center 78
Rand,Lois Schiager 40,53,54, 62,69,225,227,229
Rand,Sidney A 40,53,62,225,227,229
Randall MN 162
Randsfjord (Randsfjorden) 6,35,36, 48,169,170,191,193,194,206,207, 208,235
Randsfjord Creamery 157
Randsfjordmuseene (Randsfjord Museum) 205,210,233
Ransom County ND 130
Rapid City SD 68,98
Rasmus,son of Anne Colbjørnsdtr 176
Rasmussen,Don 53
Rasmusslette 176
Raukr Viking Museum 45
Red Hill PA 46
Red Lodge MT 44,51
Red River 160
Red River Valley 7,228
Red Wing Lion's Club 124
Red Wing MN 40,58,113,119
Rees,Dick 56,62
Reflections Antiques 78
Regimental Period 210
Reidem,Jan 220
Rekstad Family 161-163
Rekstad,Edwin 162,163
Rekstad,Erik 106,161,162
Rekstad,H P 10
Rekstad,Helga 163
Rekstad,Jens 163
Rekstad,Martia Alm 106,161,162
Rekstad,Mary Margaret 161
Rekstad,Ole 162,163
Rekstad,Rudolph 161,162,163
Renlie NO 127
Renner Lutheran Church 75
Reno NV 116
Renton WA 40
Renville County MN 105
Republican Party 2,3,4
Restauration 11
Richfield High School 124
Richfield MN 8
Richland County ND 132
Richland WA 51,115

Ringerike Drammen Districts Lag 17,52
Ringerike NO 170,233
River Falls WI 9,56
Rivers,Rails and Trails 71
Roa NO 231
Roa train station 36
Robbinsdale MN 6,122
Robin's Island 73
Robinson,Donna 46
Robinson,Edgar G 78
Rochester Accordion Band 30
Rochester City Library 78,79
Rochester Junior College 109
Rochester MN 44,46,51,55, 78,105,109,223
Rock County MN 164
Rock Creek Cemetery 115
Rock Springs WI 51,110
Rock Twp IA 115
Rockall Island 156
Rockdale WI 74
Rockswold,Betty Lou 40,128
Rockswold,E Palmer 17,40,53,54, 56,58,59,62,96,103,104,126,128, 165,229
Rockswold,Gary Kent 128
Rockswold,Gaylan Lee 128
Rockswold,Gordon Alvin 128
Rockswold,Grant Allen 128
Rockswold,Myrna C Peterson 128
Rockswold,Paul 56
Rockswold,Peder E 128
Rockswold,Serianna Bergethe Haarsager 128
Roder,Elaine 40
Roder,Elsie 40
Roe,Ingeborg Schiager 127
Roe,Kelmer N 218,222
Roe,Nels 127
Roen Bridge 102
Roen,Ole 40,98
Rogne farm 133
Rogne,Brynjulf Johannesen 133
Rogne,Duane 44
Rogne,Katherine Kazmark 132
Rogne,Leah 132
Rogne,Leslie 17,40,44,55,57, 62,63,69,72,80,103,126,132-133
Rogne,Seward 132
Rogne,Trana 132
Røken,Birgit 220
Rolf,James 51
Rolf,Mary 51
Rollo 32

Rolvaag, Ole 55
Rolvsen, Torsten 22
Roman Catholic Church 176,197
Romerike NO 170
Romerikslaget 30
Romsdal NO 175
Roosevelt, President 4
Roosevelt, Teddy 9
Rooted in Norway, Branches Grow 81
Rosendahl, Christian Olsen 129
Rosendahl, Georgia 30
Rosendahl, Hans Olsen 129
Rosendahl, Leona 40,44,129
Rosendahl, Oscar 129
Rosendahl, Oscar Nelius 128
Rosendahl, Robert 17,40,44,59,61,
    62,64,66,67,68,69,103,126,
    128-129,226,227
Rosendahlseiet farm 123,129
Roseni Cemetery 113
Roseni Lutheran Church 112
Ross, Ernest 4
Rothsay High School 111
Rothsay MN 12,36,43,44,
    46,51,111,229
Rowberg Biographical File 99,118
Rowberg, Andrew A 99
Rowe, Murray 68
Røykeneiet farm 107
Røykenvik Bay 36
Røykenvik farm 227
Røykenvika NO 207
Rud, Leslie 40
Rud, Ruth 40
Rudd IA 46
Rude, Niels 173
Ruden NO 115
Rudh, Adeline 37
Rupert, Jim 56
Rushford MN 154
Russian emigrants 156
Rusten, Kristen 84
Rusten, Øystein 84
Ruud, Leslie 229
Ruud, Thorvald 158
Ruudsbraaten farm 218
Rya Eli Halvorsdtr 110
Sacramento CA 40,46,51,120
Sacred Heart MN 10,44,105
Sagamore MA 205
Saint Catherine 176
Saint Cloud MN 155
Saint Croix County WI 2,3,4
Saint Croix River 18,84
Saint Hans Day 39

Saint Helen Island 156
Saint John's Abbey & University 53
Saint John's Hospital 119
Saint John's University 107
Saint Olaf 12
Saint Olaf College 70,99,110,127,229
Saint Olav's Medal 27,28,78,112
Saint Otto's Cemetery 120
Saint Paul MN 9,10,11,67,73,76,
    80,122,127,128,155,160,229
Saint Petri Church 170,187,
    188-189,190,201
    See also *Tingelstad Old Church*
Saint Stephen's Church 67
Salmon ID 116
Salmon National Forest 116
Sandven, Sherman, M/M 37
Sangerfest (Sangerstevne) 224
Sangnes apple farm 45
Sangslund, Andrew 5
Sanne School 237
Sanner Hotel 35,36,44,48,49,50
Santhansdagen 160
Sarajishvili, Ivan 235
Sarles, Marian 40
Saron Lutheran Church 76
Sayles, Marilyn 44
Sayles, Wilbur 44
Scandinavian Center 7
Scandinavian Melodies 65
Scandinavian Regiment 61
Scandium 81
Schiager, Guro Iversdtr 127
Schiager, Paul 222
Schiager, Paul Gundersen 127
Schiager, Simon 127
Schmid, Byron 104,122-123
Schmitt, Barb Helstedt 46,51,
    83,84,104,109-110
Schmitt, Pete 46,51,109
Schola Sancti Petri 235,236
Schou, Chef 33
Schulz, Karen 51
Schwanke Museum 70
Scobey MT 14
Sears-Roebuck 166
Seattle University 115
Seattle WA 36,44,115
Selmer-Anderssen, Johan 196
Senior Citizen Services, Rochester 109
Septon, Thorvall 37
seters (mountain pastures) 174
Setesdal NO 10
Sharples, Glenda 44,46
Sheldon Theater 58

Sherman, Theo 44
Sherva, Amanda 110
Sherva, Anders Andersen 110
Sherva, Christ 14
Sherva, Fredrik 158
Sherva, Ingeborg Christiansdtr 110
Sherva, Kristian 158
Shoemaker, Karen 51
Sigdalslag 17,52
Sigma Zi 108
silver mines 211
Simundson, Judith 65
Sinding-Larsen, Chief Architect 32
Sing for Joy 68
Sioux Falls SD 43,46,51,75,112,
    223,226,227
Sioux Uprising 58
Sister Churches 36,46,62,91,95,
    126,172,177,178,184-185,
    195,196,234
Sivesin, Alfred, Mrs 95
Sjo farm 178,179
Skafså NO 106
Skalmusikk Group 69
Skandinavian Hottshots 62,63
Skapalen, Anders Larson 1
Skattum, Anders 22,111
Skattum, Berte Marie 111
Skattum, Lars Larsen 111
Skattum, Thomas 16,20,22-23,37,40,
    59,61,62,63,64,67,221,227,235
Skiaker farm 127
Skiaker, Eva 224
Skiaker, Mathilde 218
Skiaker, Ole 223,224,226
Skiaker, Paul 218,219,224
Skiaker, Randi Maria 218
Skiaker, Simen 218
Skirstad farm 23
Skirstadeiet farm 111
Skjaker, Gudbrand 38,39
Skjerpemyr NO 211
Skjervold, Chris 66
Skjervum, Gunder Gundersen 127
Skogfjorden 114
Skogrand, Marvin 37,40
Skorud, Gina 119
Skorud, M (MIkel) Michelson 119
Skree, Jim 30
skru (needle made lace) 215
Sladky, Anne 29,30,70,83,
    104,105-106
Sladky, Steven 106
Sletta NO 28
Slim Buttes Lutheran Church 228

Index

Sløvika 102
Smerud farm, 6
Smithsonian Institution 111
Snefrid Svåsesdtr 236
Snelling Avenue 9
Snelling, Lynn 37
Social Security Administration 121
Social Welfare Board, Gran 24
Social Welfare Board, Jevnaker 24
Social Welfare Board, Lunner 24
Sogn farm 23
Sogn NO 10
Sogn, a man named 227
Sogn, Anders 23
Sognefjord NO 113
Sognelag 130
Solberg, Leif 220
Solem, Anders 113
Solem, Helen Jensen 113
Solem, Helena 113
Solend, Arne 37
Solien, Ruth 40
Solien, Vernon 40,66
solje 213
Sollum, Lenore 8
Solobservatoriet 45
Solør Lag 10
Solum, Peder Pedersen 151
Sølve the troll 176
Solvorn NO 113
Sølvsberget 176
Somdahl, Marilyn 81
Somdahl, Narv 81
Sommers, Marlene 46
Somsen Hall 71
Sondre Brørby 112
Søndre Land 78
Sonja, Queen 106
Sons of Norway (SON) 105
SON-District 6 125
SON Hall 55
SON-King Olav V Lodge 113
SON-Kringen Lodge 74,77,111,113, 130,221,228
SON-Kristiania Lodge 109
SON-Valkyrien Lodge 2
SON-Vestafjell Lodge 117
SON-Vinji Lodge 4
SON-Vnrekretsen Lodge 127
Sønsteby, Per 22
Sør Aurdal NO 106
Søråsen NO 48
Sorenson, Marilyn 53,66
Sørum church 48,187,191
Sørum farm 191

Sorum SD 129,228
Sørum, Anders Olsen 191
Sorum, Ann 44
Sørum, Anne Synove 57
Sorum, Carol 37,40,44,46,51, 65,66,83,84,104,108,129,229
Sorum, Charles 58
Sorum, Chris 129
Sorum, Christian Merle Lowe 129
Sorum, Christian Mickelson 12,130
Sorum, Dean see *Sorum, H Dean*
Sorum, Doris 37
Sorum, H Dean 37,40,44,46,51,55,59, 60,65,68,73,83,84,103,108,126, 129-130,226,229
Sorum, Ida 129,130
Sorum, Jon 44
Sorum, Jonathan Dean 130
Sørum, Kristian 228
Sorum, Paul 59,130
Sørum, Sverre 57
Sørumsengen farm 132
Sørumsiet Dorthe Johansdtr 151
Søsterkirkene see *Sister Churches*
Sound Traditions 72
South Dakota 37,38
South Dakota School of Mines 68,227
South High School 108
South Immanuel Lutheran Church 229
South Land NO 157
South New Hope Lutheran Church 78
South Trinity Cemetery 227
Spande, Beverly 83,84
Sparta Township 124
Spelmanslag (violin ensemble) 56
Spillville IA 65
Spring Grove MN 7,46
Spring Grove: Minnesota's First Norwegian Settlement 70
Spring Valley MN 105
SS Norge 156
Stabbur 63
Stadsbygd NO 128
Stadum, Beverly 51
Stange Historical Society 235
Stange NO 113,154
Star Prairie WI 126
State Archives, Hamar NO 19,114
State Capitol, Minnesota 229
State Capitol, North Dakota 228
State Church of Norway 197-201,232
State College PA 44
Stavanger NO 11,113

Staxrud, Gail 44
Staxrud, Inger 48
Staxrud, Kris 44
Steen, Bernt Martinsen 157
Steen, Borghild 157
Steen, Hedevig 157
Steen, Hjørdis 157
Steen, Johan Martinius 157
Steen, Konrad Marius 157
Steen, Mathilde Josefine Nilsen 157
Steen, O M 11
Steen, Osvald 157
Steffensen, Olaf 150
Steinhus (Stone House) 33,42,46,185
Stenersen, Berte 177
Stenersen, Christopher 177
Stenhus, Bertha 122
Stensrud, Karl B 14,19
Stensrud, Roy 25
Stetvold, 'Old Man' 155
Stevens Point WI 78
Stiklestad, Battle of 12,197
Stillwater MN 40,51
Stock, Bonita 44
Stockfleth, Hans Eggertsen 176
Stoltenberg, Veslemøy Nystedt 185
Stone Age 169
Stone Church 70
Stone Ring 42
Stord NO 127
Stormoe, Kristen 37
Stormoen, Harald 34
Storting 35,73,197,198,199,200,237
Stowman, Mary Pauline Sorum 129
Stowman, Pauline 46
Straand, Torgeir 79,80
Strande, Ingeborg 116
Strande, Lars Torstensen 116
Strande, Marie 116
Sturlason, Snorre 170
Suchy, Chuck 55,69
Summit Avenue 229
Sunnyside #27 school 112
Super 8 Motel 84
Surbeck Center 69
Surnadal NO 108
Svåse, a Finn 236
Svenrud, Even 106
Svenrud, Randi Alm 106
Swanson, Melvin 5
Sweden 36,96,124,167, 175,199,216,237
Sweet Adelines 108
Sweet Land 78
Swift County MN 108

Synod Conference Assembly 197
Syttende Mai 97
Tabbut,Judy 44
Tacoma WA 40
Taft,William H,President 9
Tahoe National Forest 116
Tandberg,Nils 159
Tandberg,S T 160
Tangen,S H 160
tax exempt status 64,73,76,78
Taylor,Arielle 106
Taylor,Graham 106
Taylor,William 106
Telelaget 17,30,52,121
Telemark NO 10,106,108,177,178
Tennessee Ernie Fjord & Company 77
terms of Use 18,257-260
Theodore Roosevelt Nat'l Park 228
Thingelstad,Bertina Asheim 131
Thingelstad,Eli Olsdtr Moger 132
Thingelstad,Hans 132
Thingelstad,Hassel T 131
Thingelstad,Ole Hansen 132
Thingelstad,Peder 132
Thoen,Anders T 204
Thoen,David C 204
Thoen,Engebret Paulsen 204
Thoen,Margaret 204
Thoen,Olaf 204
Thoen,Olga 204
Thoen,Signa 204
Thompson (Paalserud),Andrena 123
Thompson (Paalserud),Caroline 123
Thompson (Paalserud),Edward 123
Thompson (Paalserud),Erick 123
Thompson (Paalserud),Ingeborg 123
Thompson (Paalserud),Ned 123
Thompson (Paalserud),Ragnhild 123
Thompson (Paalserud),Torsten 123
Thompson,Carol 44
Thompson,Don 44,69
Thompson,Helen 83,84
Thomuson,Oscar,Rev 5
Three Voices Speaking from the Past 75
Tideman,Adolph 95
Timish,Father 53
Tina and Lena 64,72
Tingelstad *Almenning* 195,209
Tingelstad Brass Ensemble 34
Tingelstad New Church 48,187, 189,190
Tingelstad NO 6,10,106,111,117, 120,125,130,132,149,159,169, 195,236

Tingelstad Old Church 42,50,170, 175,187,188-189,190,201,236
Tingelstad,Bert 158
Tingelstad,Eli 159
Tingelstad,Hans 158,159,160
Tingelstad,Iver 159
Tingelstad,Kari 158
Tingelstad,Marit 42
Tingelstad,Peder 158
Tingvold Church 77
Toastmasters 105
Toelle,Beverly 44
Toiyabe National Forest 116
Tømte,Erik Johnsen 151
Tonka Toys 107
Torbeck,Jerie 51
Torbjørnsrud Seminar & Conference Center 42
Torersdtr,Marthe Karine 150
Torgerson,Henry 166
Torgersrud farm 123
Torleif Braaten,56
Torstensdtr,Anne 22
Torstensdtr,Mari 22
Torstensdtr,Randi 22
Toso school 102
Tosobråtan farm 102
Toten Lag 10,14,17,18,30, 52,81,82,83
Toten NO 58,111,195
Tourist Hotel 39
Toverud Power Station 207
Traill County ND 115
Trana,Emma 133
Treasures from the Trunk 62
Treaty of Kiel 96
Trempeleau County 81
Troll Boys 68
Trolls at Wahpeton 54
Tromsø NO 40
Trøndelag 30,72,227
Trondheim (Trondhjem) NO 2,10, 36,116,128
Trondhjem Twp MN 112,154
Trosvik,'Old Mrs' 155
Trosvik,Anders 155
Trosvik,John 155
Trosvik,Martin 155
Trulserud,Johan 195
Trulserud,Kjersti 195
Tuff Memorial Home 165,223,227
Tuff,Anne 164
Tuff,Gilbert 165,223,227
Tuff,Haagen O 223
Tuff,Håkon 164

Tunell,Denny 44,227
Tunell,Maxine 44
Tunsberg Township MN 106
turbines 206
Tursithotel 54
Tustin CA 51
Tuv farm 236
Tuv,Niels Bentsen 176
Tveito,Tone Jorunn 79,80
Tweito,Andy 46
Tweito,Daniel 46
Tweito,Ted 46
Twin Cities *Hardingfelalag* 78
Twin Valley MN 36,40,120,131
Tyriksdtr,Gunnvor 26,170
Uff Da Brudders 67
Ulven,Anders 123,124
Ulven,Anne Marie 123
Ulven,Bent 123
Ulven,Deanna 44,46,51
Ulven,Hans 123
Ulven,Ingeborg,123
Ulven,Jens Andersen 123
Ulven,Juul 123
Ulven,Ken 123,124
Ulven,Ron 44,46,51,103, 107,123-124
Ulven,Thelma Leverson 123
Ulvilden,Paul Decorah IA 66
Uncompahgre National Forest 116
Underdal,Mr 34
Underwood MN 77
Undlieseiet,Ole Carstensen 151
unemployment benefits 204
Union County SD 112
Unity Hospital 126
University Museum of Antiquities 170
University of Minnesota 107,111,113
University of North Dakota 108, 128,129
University of Oslo 117
University of Texas-El Paso 107
University of Wisconsin (UW)-Eau Claire 106
UW-LaCrosse 60
UW-River Falls 56,79
UW-Whitewater 73
Urdal NO Folk Dancers & Musicians 58
Urnes,Christoffer 211
US Air Force 129,132
US Army 107,121,129,130
US Army Air Force 127
US Forest Service 116

Index

US Navy 105,116
USS South Dakota 227
Vagama,Gudbrandsdal NO 64
Valdres NO 127,178,229
Valdres Samband 10
Valley City State College 128
Valley Grove Lutheran Church 70
Vane,Floie 40
Vang NO 118
Vaterud,Ingeborg Torgersdtr 112
Velva ND 7,37
verken (fabric) 214
Vesteralen NO 128
Vesterheim Museum 7,11,62,
  109,111,226
Vestfold NO 170
Vestlandslaget 130
Vestoppland bunad 86,212-213
Vestoppland Genealogical Society
  97,118
Vestre Brandbu 149
Vestre Gran 149
VFW Hall 59
Victory Restaurant 76
Videregående 231
Vigen,Karl 46
Vigen,Larry 46
Vigen,Mary Ann 46
Vik,Per Inge,Pastor 30
Viking Age 169
Viking Ship Museum 42
Vikings: Journeys to New Worlds 75
Village Shores Senior Campus 107
Vind,Carol 51,84
Vind,Tom 84
Vindorum,Egil 28
Vindorum,Nils H Guldeneiet 151
Vining MN 10,37
Vinje NO 106,177
Vinje,Aamund Olavsson 177-179,235
Vinje,Lyla 37
Vinstra NO 63
Volda NO 62
Volla,Teacher 34
Volney,Anne 124
Volney,Betty Lynne 40,44,65,
  67,84,104,124,229
Volney,Eric Scott 124
Volney,Kristin Noelle 124
Volney,Lisbeth 124
Volney,Michael 124
Volney,Vernon 124
Voss NO 10,133
Vossestrand NO 115
Wabasha MN 119

Waconia MN 113
Wagner,Diane 44
Wagstrom Funeral Home 131
Wahpeton ND 54,57,59,61,64,67,76
Walby,Arthur Sigvald 2,4
Walby,Christ Andersen 1,5
Walby,Ella Mathilde 2
Walby,Elmer Kenneth 2,4
Walby,Herbert Merian 2,4
Walby,Orville Perry 3,4
Walby,Pearl 2,4
Walby,Thomas A 1-5,9,10,11,
  12,18,32,33,84
Waldoch,Faith 51
Waldoch,Laura 51
Waldorf College 62
Walker MN 106
Wanderers,The 61
Wangen,Russell 56
War in Iraq 237
Ward County ND 115
Ward,Brian 57
Ward,Martha Wold 7,8,57
Washburn McReavy-Welander Quist
  DuSchane Chapel 8
Washington DC 105
Washington Pavilion Cinedome 75
Washington State University 115
Waterwheel 206
Watson MN 106,161
Watterud,P N 158
Waukon IA 37
We All Have A History 67
Weather vane 188
Webb,Ashley 46
Webb,Ellen Bratvold 46
Webb,Robb 46
Webb,Ryan 46
Weberg,Dag C 35
Webster,Beverly Lanning 44,46
Webster,Keith 44,46
Wergeland Dancers 60,71
West Koshkonong Church 74
West Marshland WI 107
West Prairie Lutheran Church 112
Westby,Martin 61
West Norway Emigration Center 28
Western,Iver,M/M 37
Western,Kirsten Heier 97,100
Westminster CO 44
Wevik,Alfred 112
Wevik,Delmar 46
Wevik,Ida Husby 112
Wevik,Joyce 46
Wevik,Lizzie Solem 113

Wevik,Ole Sr 113
Wheeler,Janice 44
Whitewater WI 73
Whitsuntide 176
Who's Who in the Midwest 128
Wiebe,Marie 127
Wiebe,William 127
Wien,Ole 211
Wieniet,Kirsti Gudbrandsdtr 151
Williams IA 46
Williams Wagon Shop 1
Williston ND 37
Willmar Convention Center 72
Willmar MN 44,46,67,69,72
Willow River Cemetery 5
Wilson,Carolyn 124
Wilson,George 124
Wilson,Margaret Paulson 17,40,
  59,104,124
Wilson,Martin 124
Wilson,Michael 124
Wilson,Paul 67
Wilson,Robert 124
Wilson,Wilfred 40,124
Winden,Anders 158
Winden,Peter 158
Winkelman,Frances Larson 125
Winkelman,Marlys Hanson 124
Winkelman,Paul 124
Winkelman,Wendy 73,103,124-125
Winnebago Church 63
Winnebago County IA 121
Winnipeg,MB 2
Winnishiek County IA 128
Winona Fiddlers 71
Winona MN 71,81
Winona State University 71,81
Wiota WI 110,111
Wisconsin 15th Regiment 61
Wisconsin Dells WI 160
Wisconsin Regiment 8
Witte,Ardis 72
Witte,Marvin 72
Wøien,Randi 58
Wøien,Sigmund 58
Wolf Point MT 124
Women's Rights 164-165
wood pulp factories 208
Woodcarvers Club,Rochester 109
Woodside Township 107
Woog,Jean 84
World Craft Show Gold Medal 39
World War I 10
World War II 23,120,127,193,235
World War II Resistance Museum 42

Index

World's Fair, 1940 204
Worsham College of Mortuary Science 131

Wright Patterson Air Force Base 129
Young, Cynthia 51
Youngstown OH 37

Zeisemer, Gerald 46, 76
zinc mines 211
Zion Lutheran Church 120, 121

www.ingramcontent.com/pod-product-compliance
Lightning Source LLC
Chambersburg PA
CBHW081218170426
43198CB00017B/2643